TAKING SIDES

Clashing Views on

Educational Issues

TAKING SIDES

Clashing Views on

Educational Issues

SEVENTEENTH EDITION

Selected, Edited, and with Introductions by

James Wm. Noll
University of Maryland

The McGraw·Hill Companies

Connect
Learn
Succeed™

TAKING SIDES: CLASHING VIEWS ON EDUCATIONAL ISSUES,
SEVENTEENTH EDITION

Published by McGraw-Hill, a business unit of The McGraw-Hill Companies, Inc., 1221 Avenue
of the Americas, New York, NY 10020. Copyright © 2013 by The McGraw-Hill Companies, Inc.
All rights reserved. Printed in the United States of America. Previous edition(s) © 2011, 2010,
and 2009. No part of this publication may be reproduced or distributed in any form or by any
means, or stored in a database or retrieval system, without the prior written consent of The
McGraw-Hill Companies, Inc., including, but not limited to, in any network or other electronic
storage or transmission, or broadcast for distance learning.

Some ancillaries, including electronic and print components, may not be available to customers
outside the United States.

This book is printed on acid-free paper.

Taking Sides® is a registered trademark of the McGraw-Hill Companies, Inc.
Taking Sides is published by the **Contemporary Learning Series** group within the McGraw-Hill
Higher Education division.

1 2 3 4 5 6 7 8 9 0 DOC/DOC 1 0 9 8 7 6 5 4 3 2

MHID: 0-07-805035-9
ISBN: 978-0-07-805035-0
ISSN: 1091-8817

Managing Editor: *Larry Loeppke*
Senior Developmental Editor: *Jade Benedict*
Permissions Coordinator: *DeAnna Dausener*
Marketing Specialist: *Alice Link*
Lead Project Manager: *Jane Mohr*
Design Coordinator: *Brenda A. Rolwes*
Cover Design: *Rick D. Noel*
Buyer: *Nicole Baumgartner*
Media Project Manager: *Sridevi Palani*

Compositor: MPS Limited, a Macmillan Company
Cover Image: © Blend Images LLC RF

www.mhhe.com

Editors/Academic Advisory Board

Members of the Academic Advisory Board are instrumental in the final selection of articles for each edition of TAKING SIDES. Their review of articles for content, level, and appropriateness provides critical direction to the editors and staff. We think that you will find their careful consideration well reflected in this volume.

TAKING SIDES: Clashing Views on EDUCATIONAL ISSUES

Seventeenth Edition

EDITOR

James Wm. Noll
University of Maryland

ACADEMIC ADVISORY BOARD MEMBERS

Joseph Akpan
Mount Vernon Nazarene University

Brenda Alward
Macomb Community College

Fred Bartelheim
University of Northern Colorado

Felicia Blacher-Wilson
Southeastern Louisiana University

Charles Blackledge
Bishop State Community College

Robert Blake
Towson University

Sally Blake
University of Memphis

Christopher Boe
Pfeiffer University

Brenda Light Bredemeier
University of Missouri, St. Louis

Elizabeth Y. Brinkerhoff
University of Massachusetts, Amherst

Kathleen Briseno
College of DuPage

Mary Ellen Burke
National Louis University

Darilyn Butler
Queens University Of Charlotte

James Calder
Middle Tennessee State University

Esther Chang
Soka University of America

Darryl Cherry
St. Louis Community College, Forest Park

Stephen Coffin
Montclair State University

Noble Corey
Indiana State University

Elaine Coughlin
Pacific University

David Cox
Arkansas State University

Patricia Cruzeiro
University of Nebraska, Kearney

Kimberly Dadisman
University of North Carolina, Chapel Hill

Robert Dahlgren
SUNY Fredonia

Ann V. Dean
SUNY New Paltz

Brian Dotts
The University of Georgia

Celina Echols
Southeastern Louisiana University

Dionne H. Edison
University Of West Alabama

William Edwards
Missouri Southern State University

Deborah Ellermeyer
Clarion University of Pennsylvania

JoAnne Ellsworth
Eastern Arizona College

R.L. Erion
South Dakota State University

Editors/Academic Advisory Board continued

Editors/Academic Advisory Board continued

Preface

Controversy is the basis of change and often of improvement. Its lack signifies the presence of complacency, the authoritarian limitation of viewpoint expression, or the absence of realistic alternatives to the existing circumstances. An articulate presentation of a point of view on a controversial matter breathes new life into abiding human and social concerns. Controversy prompts reexamination and perhaps renewal.

Education is controversial. Arguments over the most appropriate aims, the most propitious means, and the most effective control have raged over the centuries. Particularly in the United States, where the systematic effort to provide education has been more democratically dispersed and more varied than elsewhere, educational issues have been contentiously debated. Philosophers, psychologists, sociologists, professional educators, lobbyists, government officials, school boards, local pressure groups, taxpayers, parents, and students have all voiced their views.

This book presents opposing or sharply varying viewpoints on educational issues of current concern. Unit 1 offers consideration of five basic theoretical issues that have been discussed by scholars and practitioners in past decades and are still debated today: the purpose of education, curriculum content and its imposition upon the young, the motivational atmosphere of schools, the philosophical underpinning of the process of education, and the conception of public education. Unit 2 features five issues that are fundamental to understanding the present circumstances that shape American education: democratic classrooms for citizenship preparation, legitimization of school vouchers, federal initiatives in school improvement, improving schools for children of poverty, and the role of local school boards. Unit 3 examines more specific issues currently being discussed: undocumented immigrants, universal preschool, privatization, inclusive classrooms, single-sex instruction, zero-tolerance policies, computer usage, merit pay for teachers, teachers, unions, time allocation, and twenty-first century skills development.

I have made every effort to select views from a wide range of thinkers—philosophers, psychologists, sociologists, professional educators, political leaders, historians, researchers, and gadflies.

Each issue is accompanied by an *introduction,* which sets the stage for the debate, and each issue concludes with a *postscript* that considers other views on the issue and suggests additional readings. I have also provided relevant Internet site addresses (URLs) on the *Internet References* page that accompanies each part opener. By combining the material in this volume with the informational background provided by a good introductory textbook, students should be prepared to address the problems confronting schools today.

My hope is that students will find challenges in the material presented here—provocations that will inspire them to better understand the roots of educational controversy, to attain a greater awareness of possible alternatives in dealing with the various issues, and to stretch their personal powers of creative thinking in the search for more promising resolutions of the problems.

Changes to this edition   This seventeenth edition offers five new issues (two of which were included in the expanded version of the previous edition) and four new articles in repeat issues. These are the new issues: Can Failing Schools Be Turned Around? (Issue 9), Are Local School Boards Obsolete? (Issue 10), Do Teachers Unions Stymie School Reform? (Issue 15), Do American Students Need More Time in School? (Issue 19), and Is the "21st Century Skills" Movement Viable? (Issue 21). New articles have been added to the issues on the purpose of education (Issue 1), the psychological foundations of learning (Issue 3), federal education policy (Issue 8), and merit pay for teachers (Issue 16).

A word to the instructor   *An Instructor's Resource Guide with Test Questions* (multiple choice and essay) is available through the publisher for the instructor using *Taking Sides* in the classroom. A general guidebook, called *Using Taking Sides in the Classroom,* which discusses methods and techniques for integrating the pro/con approach into any classroom setting, is also available. An online version of *Using Taking Sides in the Classroom* and a correspondence service for *Taking Sides* adopters can be found at http://www.mhcls.com/usingts/.

   Taking Sides: Clashing Views on Educational Issues is only one title in the *Taking Sides* series. If you are interested in seeing the table of contents for any of the other titles, please visit the Taking Sides Web site at http://www.mhcls .com/takingsides/.

Acknowledgments   I am thankful for the kind and efficient assistance given to me by Jade Benedict, Larry Loeppke, and the other members of the production staff at McGraw-Hill Contemporary Learning Series.

James Wm. Noll
University of Maryland

Contents in Brief

Contents

Philosopher John Dewey suggests a reconsideration of traditional approaches to schooling, giving fuller attention to the social development of the learner and the quality of his or her total experience. British philosopher Roger Scruton expresses the traditionalist view that Dewey's progressive education, with its emphasis on "child-centeredness" and "relevance," has had a disastrous effect on quality education.

Philosopher Mortimer J. Adler contends that democracy is best served by a public school system that establishes uniform curricular objectives for all students. Educator John Holt argues that an imposed curriculum damages the individual and usurps a basic human right to select one's own path of development.

Professor of educational psychology Carson M. Bennett presents the case for adopting the radical behaviorism of B. F. Skinner to improve the power and efficiency of the process of learning. Professor of psychology and psychiatry Carl R. Rogers offers the "humanistic" alternative to behaviorism, insisting on the reality of subjective forces in human motivation.

Child development professor David Elkind contends that the philosophical positions found in constructivism, though often difficult to apply, are necessary elements in a meaningful reform of educational practices. Jamin Carson, an assistant professor of education and former high school teacher, offers a close critique of constructivism and argues that the philosophy of objectivism is a more realistic and usable basis for the process of education.

Frederick M. Hess, a resident scholar at the American Enterprise Institute, advocates a broadening of the definition of "public schooling" in light of recent developments such as vouchers, charter schools, and home schooling. Linda Nathan, Joe Nathan, Ray Bacchetti, and Evans Clinchy express a variety of concerns about the conceptual expansion that Hess proposes.

Associate professor of education Kristan A. Morrison explores historical and theoretical bases for implementing democratic practices in schools that would make student experience more appealing and productive. Professor of education Gary K. Clabaugh examines such factors as top-down management, compulsory attendance, business world influences, and federal mandates to declare Morrison's ideas to be "out of touch" with reality.

Issue 7. Has the Supreme Court Reconfigured American Education?   109

YES: Charles L. Glenn, from "Fanatical Secularism," *Education Next* (Winter 2003)   *111*

NO: Paul E. Peterson, from "Victory for Vouchers?" *Commentary* (September 2002)   *118*

Professor of education Charles L. Glenn argues that the Supreme Court's decision in *Zelman v. Simmons-Harris* is an immediate antidote to the public school's secularist philosophy. Professor of government Paul E. Peterson, while welcoming the decision, contends that the barricades against widespread use of vouchers in religious schools will postpone any lasting effects.

Issue 8. Is No Child Left Behind a Flawed Policy?   126

YES: Frederick M. Hess and Chester E. Finn, Jr., from "Crash Course: NCLB Is Driven by Education Politics," *Education Next* (Fall 2007)   *128*

NO: Dianne Piché, from "Basically a Good Model," *Education Next* (Fall 2007)   *134*

Frederick M. Hess and Chester E. Finn, Jr., review the development of the NCLB policy and conclude that political compromises have produced sputtering machinery and weak sanctions that require an extreme makeover. Dianne Piché, executive director of the Citizens' Commission on Civil Rights, supports the testing and accountability measures of the federal law as the best way to advance the interests of the poor and minorities.

Issue 9. Can Failing Schools Be Turned Around?   139

YES: Karin Chenoweth, from "It Can Be Done, It's Being Done, and Here's How," *Phi Delta Kappan* (September 2009)   *141*

NO: Andy Smarick, from "The Turnaround Fallacy," *Education Next* (Winter 2010)   *147*

Karin Chenoweth, a senior writer with the Education Trust and author of *How It's Being Done*, describes strategies employed to bring about dramatic improvements in low-performing schools. Andy Smarick, a visiting fellow at the Thomas B. Fordham Institute, advocates the closing of failing schools to make room for replacements through chartering.

Issue 10.   Are Local School Boards Obsolete?   156

YES: Marc Tucker, from "Changing the System Is the Only Solution," *Phi Delta Kappan* (March 2010)   *158*

NO: Diane Ravitch, from "Why Public Schools Need Democratic Governance," *Phi Delta Kappan* (March 2010)   *162*

Marc Tucker, president of the National Center on Education and the Economy, calls for shifting the running of public schools to the states, allowing local boards to focus solely on the improvement of learning. Education historian Diane Ravitch feels that a movement of control to the state level or to the mayor's office will undermine democratic deliberation and move toward a top-down business model.

UNIT 3   CURRENT SPECIFIC ISSUES   169

Justice William Brennan argues that the action of the Texas state legislature to authorize local school districts to deny enrollment in public schools to children not "legally admitted" to the country violates the Fourteenth Amendment. Chief Justice Warren Burger, in dissent, counters that the Court has no business assuming a policymaking role simply because the legislative branches of government fail to act appropriately.

David L. Kirp, a professor of public policy and author of *The Sandbox Investment*, calls for expansion of federal support for universal preschool and other child care services. Professor Douglas J. Besharov and research associate Douglas M. Call of the University of Maryland School of Public Policy examine the development of child care programs and conclude that the case for universal preschool is not as strong as it seems.

Chris Whittle, founder and CEO of Edison Schools, contends that public school systems still operate in an eighteenth-century mindset and offers an "independent learning" model as a replacement. Professor of economics and education Henry Levin criticizes the assumptions on which Whittle bases his prediction of successful operation of schools by for-profit management organizations such as Edison.

Professor of inclusive education Mara Sapon-Shevin presents a redefinition of the inclusive classroom and offers specific strategies for bringing it about in practice. Associate professor of education Wade A. Carpenter expresses concerns about the inclusive ideology's uncritical infatuation with socialization.

Andrew Coulson, director of the Center for Educational Freedom at the Cato Institute, contends that the NEA and AFT monopolize public school operations, resulting in a collapse of productivity. Louis Malfaro, an AFT vice president, sees the teachers unions as uniquely able to build productive relationships and exert positive influence on the improvement of teaching and learning.

Steven Malanga, a senior fellow of the Manhattan Institute, draws on examples from the corporate world and from public school systems in Cincinnati, Iowa, and Denver to make his case for performance-based merit pay for teachers. Professor of education reform Jay P. Greene and doctoral fellow Stuart Buck recognize the theoretical and empirical reasons for expecting merit pay to have a positive impact but contend that the prospects are not promising for a variety of reasons.

Journalist Peter Meyer examines the history of single-sex schools and recent concerns about "shortchanging" girls and the "crisis" in boys' education and lauds the current resurgence of single-sex schooling. Associate professor of education Vincent A. Anfara, Jr. and assistant professor of education Steven B. Mertens review research on student culture, academic climate, and attitudinal effects, concluding that the benefits of single-sex schooling remain unclear.

Supreme Court justice David Souter, delivering the opinion of the Court, hold that school officials, in carrying out a zero-tolerance policy on drug possession, violated a student's Fourth Amendment right against unreasonable search and seizure when they included a strip search of the girl. Justice Clarence Thomas, in dissent, states that the majority opinion imposes too vague a standard on school officials and that it grants judges sweeping authority to second-guess measures those officials take to maintain discipline and ensure safety.

National Center on Time and Learning chairman Chris Gabrieli claims that current school time schedules are outmoded and calls for expansion of the instructional day and year to close the achievement gap and provide enrichment opportunities. Stanford University professor emeritus Larry Cuban reviews the history of school time expansion and finds scant research to support such demands.

Lowell Monke, an assistant professor of education, expresses deep concerns that the uncritical faith in computer technology in schools has led to sacrifices in intellectual growth and creativity. Frederick M. Hess, while sharing some of Monke's observations, believes that the tools of technology, used appropriately, can support innovation and reinvention in education.

Education policy expert Rotherham and psychology professor Willingham
see great promise in the movement to bring needed skills to all students
if the delivery system works satisfactorily. Education writer and former
teacher Diana Senechal expresses deep concern about the movement's
focus on current societal needs to the detriment of core academic
studies.

Correlation Guide

The *Taking Sides* series presents current issues in a debate-style format designed to stimulate student interest and develop critical thinking skills. Each issue is thoughtfully framed with an issue summary, an issue introduction, and a postscript. The pro and con essays—selected for their liveliness and substance—represent the arguments of leading scholars and commentators in their fields.

Taking Sides: Clashing Views on Educational Issues, 17/e, is an easy-to-use reader that presents issues on important topics such as *democratic classrooms, universal preschool,* and *merit pay for teachers.* For more information on *Taking Sides* and other *McGraw-Hill Contemporary Learning Series* titles, visit http://www.mhhe.com/cls.

This convenient guide matches the issues in **Taking Sides: Educational Issues, 17/e,** with the corresponding chapters in three of our best-selling McGraw-Hill Education textbooks by Arends, Sadker/Zittleman and Spring.

Taking Sides: Educational Issues, 17/e	Learning to Teach, 9/e by Arends	Teachers, Schools, and Society: A Brief Introduction to Education, 3/e by Sadker/Zittleman	American Education, 15/e by Spring
Issue 1: Should Schooling Be Based on Social Experiences?	**Chapter 2:** Student Learning in Diverse Classrooms	**Chapter 2:** Different Ways of Learning	**Chapter 1:** The History and Goals of Public Schooling
Issue 2: Should the Curriculum Be Standardized for All?	**Chapter 6:** Assessment and Evaluation	**Chapter 6:** Philosophy of Education **Chapter 7:** Financing and Governing America's Schools **Chapter 10:** Curriculum, Standards, Testing	**Chapter 1:** The History and Goals of Public Schooling **Chapter 9:** Power and Control at State and National Levels
Issue 3: Should Behaviorism Shape Educational Practices?	**Chapter 11:** Problem-Based Learning	**Chapter 2:** Different Ways of Learning	**Chapter 1:** The History and Goals of Public Schooling
Issue 4: Is Constructivism the Best Philosophy of Education?	**Chapter 13:** Connecting the Models and Differentiating Instruction	**Chapter 6:** Philosophy of Education	**Chapter 1:** The History and Goals of Public Schooling
Issue 5: Should "Public Schooling" Be Redefined?	**Chapter 4:** Learning Communities and Student Motivation	**Chapter 7:** Financing and Governing America's Schools **Chapter 9:** Reforming America's Schools	**Chapter 1:** The History and Goals of Public Schooling **Chapter 11:** Globalization of Education

(Continued)

Taking Sides: Educational Issues, 17/e	Learning to Teach, 9/e by Arends	Teachers, Schools, and Society: A Brief Introduction to Education, 3/e by Sadker/Zittleman	American Education, 15/e by Spring
Issue 6: Are Truly Democratic Classrooms Possible?	**Chapter 4:** Learning Communities and Student Motivation	**Chapter 6:** Philosophy of Education	**Chapter 3:** Education and Equality of Opportunity
Issue 7: Has the Supreme Court Reconfigured American Education?	**Chapter 14:** School Leadership and Collaboration	**Chapter 9:** Reforming America's Schools	**Chapter 9:** Power and Control at State and National Levels
Issue 8: Is No Child Left Behind a Flawed Policy?	**Chapter 6:** Assessment and Evaluation	**Chapter 9:** Reforming America's Schools	**Chapter 9:** Power and Control at State and National Levels
Issue 9: Can Failing Schools Be Turned Around?	**Chapter 4:** Learning Communities and Student Motivation	**Chapter 3:** Teaching Your Diverse Students **Chapter 8:** School Law and Ethics	**Chapter 5:** Equality of Educational Opportunity: Race, Gender, and Special Needs
Issue 10: Are Local School Boards Obsolete?	**Chapter 4:** Learning Communities and Student Motivation	**Chapter 7:** Financing and Governing America's Schools	**Chapter 8:** Local Control, Choice, Charter Schools, and Home Schooling
Issue 11: Are Undocumented Immigrants Entitled to Public Education?	**Chapter 2:** Student Learning in Diverse Classrooms **Chapter 4:** Learning Communities and Student Motivation	**Chapter 3:** Teaching Your Diverse Students **Chapter 8:** School Law and Ethics	**Chapter 6:** Student Diversity
Issue 12: Has the Time Arrived for Universal Preschool?	**Chapter 14:** School Leadership and Collaboration	**Chapter 6:** Philosophy of Education **Chapter 7:** Financing and Governing America's Schools	**Chapter 4:** The Economic Goals of Schooling: Human Capital, Global Economy and Preschool
Issue 13: Is Privatization the Hope of the Future?	**Chapter 14:** School Leadership and Collaboration	**Chapter 7:** Financing and Governing America's Schools	**Chapter 8:** Local Control, Choice, Charter Schools, and Home Schooling
Issue 14: Is the Inclusive Classroom Model Workable?	**Chapter 13:** Connecting the Models and Differentiating Instruction	**Chapter 3:** Teaching Your Diverse Students	**Chapter 3:** Education and Equality of Opportunity

Taking Sides: Educational Issues, 17/e	Learning to Teach, 9/e by Arends	Teachers, Schools, and Society: A Brief Introduction to Education, 3/e by Sadker/Zittleman	American Education, 15/e by Spring
Issue 15: Do Teachers Unions Stymie School Reform?	**Chapter 4:** Learning Communities and Student Motivation	**Chapter 9:** Reforming America's Schools	**Chapter 4:** The Economic Goals of Schooling: Human Capital, Global Economy and Preschool
Issue 16: Can Merit Pay Accelerate School Improvement?	**Chapter 14:** School Leadership and Collaboration	**Chapter 9:** Reforming America's Schools	**Chapter 10:** The Profession of Teaching
Issue 17: Are Single-Sex Schools and Classes Effective?	**Chapter 2:** Student Learning in Diverse Classrooms	**Chapter 4:** Student Life in School and at Home **Chapter 9:** Reforming America's Schools	**Chapter 3:** Education and Equality of Opportunity **Chapter 7:** Multicultural and Multilingual Education
Issue 18: Can Zero Tolerance Violate Students Rights?	**Chapter 5:** Classroom Management	**Chapter 8:** School Law and Ethics	**Chapter 2:** The Social Goals of Schooling
Issue 19: Do American Students Need More Time in School?	**Chapter 4:** Learning Communities and Student Motivation	**Chapter 4:** Student Life in School and at Home	**Chapter 4:** The Economic Goals of Schooling: Human Capital, Global Economy and Preschool
Issue 20: Do Computers Negatively Affect Student Growth?	**Chapter 6:** Assessment and Evaluation **Chapter 8:** Direct Instruction	**Chapter 4:** Student Life in School and at Home	**Chapter 2:** The Social Goals of Schooling
Issue 21: Is the "21st Century Skills" Movement Viable?	**Chapter 1:** The Scientific Basis for the Art of Teaching **Chapter 13:** Connecting the Models and Differentiating Instruction	**Chapter 10:** Curriculum, Standards, Testing	**Chapter 4:** The Economic Goals of Schooling: Human Capital, Global Economy and Preschool

Topic Guide

T his topic guide suggests how the selections in this book relate to the subjects covered in your course. You may want to use the topics listed on these pages to search the Web more easily. On the following pages, a number of Web sites have been gathered specifically for this book. They are arranged to reflect the issues of this Taking Sides reader. You can link to these sites by going to http://www.mhhe.com/cls. All the articles that relate to each topic are listed below the bold-faced term.

Achievement Gaps

8. Is No Child Left Behind a Flawed Policy?

Behaviorism

3. Should Behaviorism Shape Educational Practices?

Curriculum

2. Should the Curriculum Be Standardized for All?
19. Do American Students Need More Time in School?
20. Do Computers Negatively Affect Student Growth?
21. Is the "21st Century Skills" Movement Viable?

Constructivism

4. Is Constructivism the Best Philosophy of Education?

Democratic Classrooms

6. Are Truly Democratic Classrooms Possible?

Diversity

11. Are Undocumented Immigrants Entitled to Public Education?
14. Is the Inclusive Classroom Model Workable?
17. Are Single-Sex Schools and Classes Effective?

Early Childhood Education

12. Has the Time Arrived for Universal Preschool?

Education Leadership

10. Are Local School Boards Obsolete?
15. Do Teachers Unions Stymie School Reform?

Education Philosophy

1. Should Schooling Be Based on Social Experiences?
3. Should Behaviorism Shape Educational Practices?

Education Policies

11. Are Undocumented Immigrants Entitled to Public Education?
16. Can Merit Pay Accelerate School Improvement?
18. Can Zero Tolerance Violate Students Rights?

Engaging Students

17. Are Single-Sex Schools and Classes Effective?
20. Do Computers Negatively Affect Student Growth?

Future of Education

13. Is Privatization the Hope of the Future?

Home Schooling

5. Should "Public Schooling" Be Redefined?
19. Do American Students Need More Time in School?

No Child Left Behind

8. Is No Child Left Behind a Flawed Policy?

Introduction

Ways of Thinking About Educational Issues

James Wm. Noll

Concern about the quality of education has been expressed by philosophers, politicians, and parents for centuries. There has been a perpetual and unresolved debate regarding the definition of education, the relationship between school and society, the distribution of decision-making power in educational matters, and the means for improving all aspects of the educational enterprise.

In recent decades the growing influence of thinking drawn from the humanities and the behavioral and social sciences has brought about the development of interpretive, normative, and critical perspectives, which have sharpened the focus on educational concerns. These perspectives have allowed scholars and researchers to closely examine the contextual variables, value orientations, and philosophical and political assumptions that shape both the status quo and reform efforts.

The study of education involves the application of many perspectives to the analysis of "what is and how it got that way" and "what can be and how we can get there." Central to such study are the prevailing philosophical assumptions, theories, and visions that find their way into real-life educational situations. The application situation, with its attendant political pressures, sociocultural differences, community expectations, parental influence, and professional problems, provides a testing ground for contending theories and ideals.

This "testing ground" image applies only insofar as the status quo is malleable enough to allow the examination and trial of alternative views. Historically, institutionalized education has been characteristically rigid. As a testing ground of ideas, it has often lacked an orientation encouraging innovation and futuristic thinking. Its political grounding has usually been conservative.

As social psychologist Allen Wheelis points out in *The Quest for Identity* (1958), social institutions by definition tend toward solidification and protectionism. His depiction of the dialectical development of civilizations centers on the tension between the security and authoritarianism of "institutional processes" and the dynamism and change-orientation of "instrumental processes."

The field of education seems to graphically illustrate this observation. Educational practices are primarily tradition bound. The twentieth-century reform movement, spurred by the ideas of John Dewey, A. S. Neill, and a host of critics who campaigned for change in the 1960s, challenged the structural rigidity of schooling. In more recent decades, reformers have either attempted to restore uniformity in the curriculum and in assessment of results or campaigned for the support of alternatives to the public school monopoly. The latter group comes from both the right and the left of the political spectrum.

We are left with the abiding questions: What is an "educated" person? What should be the primary purpose of organized education? Who should control the decisions influencing the educational process? Should the schools follow society or lead it toward change? Should schooling be compulsory?

Long-standing forces have molded a wide variety of responses to these fundamental questions. The religious impetus, nationalistic fervor, philosophical ideas, the march of science and technology, varied interpretations of "societal needs," and the desire to use the schools as a means for social reform have been historically influential. In recent times other factors have emerged to contribute to the complexity of the search for answers—social class differences, demographic shifts, increasing bureaucratization, the growth of the textbook industry, the changing financial base for schooling, teacher unionization, and strengthening of parental and community pressure groups.

The struggle to find the most appropriate answers to these questions now involves, as in the past, an interplay of societal aims, educational purposes, and individual intentions. Moral development, the quest for wisdom, citizenship training, socioeconomic improvement, mental discipline, the rational control of life, job preparation, liberation of the individual, freedom of inquiry—these and many others continue to be topics of discourse on education.

A detailed historical perspective on these questions and topics may be gained by reading the interpretations of noted scholars in the field. R. Freeman Butts has written a brief but effective summary portrayal in "Search for Freedom—The Story of American Education," *NEA Journal* (March 1960). A partial listing of other sources includes R. Freeman Butts and Lawrence Cremin, *A History of Education in American Culture;* S. E. Frost, Jr., *Historical and Philosophical Foundations of Western Education;* Harry Good and Edwin Teller, *A History of Education;* Adolphe Meyer, *An Educational History of the American People;* Robert L. Church and Michael W. Sedlak, *Education in the United States: An Interpretive History;* Merle Curti, *The Social Ideas of American Educators;* Henry J. Perkinson, *The Imperfect Panacea: American Faith in Education, 1865–1965;* Clarence Karier, *Man, Society, and Education;* V. T. Thayer, *Formative Ideas in American Education;* H. Warren Button and Eugene F. Provenzo, Jr., *History of Education and Culture in America;* David Tyack and Elisabeth Hansot, *Managers of Virtue: Public School Leadership in America, 1820–1980;* Joel Spring, *The American School, 1642–1990;* S. Alexander Rippa, *Education in a Free Society: An American History;* John D. Pulliam, *History of Education in America;* Edward Stevens and George H. Wood, *Justice, Ideology, and Education;* and Walter Feinberg and Jonas F. Soltis, *School and Society.*

These and other historical accounts of the development of schooling demonstrate the continuing need to address educational questions in terms of cultural and social dynamics. A careful analysis of contemporary education demands attention not only to the historical interpretation of developmental influences but also to the philosophical forces that define formal education and the social and cultural factors that form the basis of informal education.

Examining Viewpoints

In his book *A New Public Education* (1976), Seymour Itzkoff examines the interplay between informal and formal education, concluding that economic and technological expansion have pulled people away from the informal culture by placing a premium on success in formal education. This has brought about a reactive search for less artificial educational contexts within the informal cultural community, which recognizes the impact of individual personality in shaping educational experiences.

This search for a reconstructed philosophical base for education has produced a barrage of critical commentary. Those who seek radical change in education characterize the present schools as mindless, manipulative, factorylike, bureaucratic institutions that offer little sense of community, pay scant attention to personal meaning, fail to achieve curricular integration, and maintain a psychological atmosphere of competitiveness, tension, fear, and alienation. Others deplore the ideological movement away from the formal organization of education, fearing an abandonment of standards, a dilution of the curriculum, an erosion of intellectual and behavioral discipline, and a decline in adult and institutional authority.

Students of education (whether prospective teachers, practicing professionals, or interested laypeople) must examine closely the assumptions and values underlying alternative positions in order to clarify their own viewpoints. This tri-level task may best be organized around the basic themes of purpose, power, and reform. These themes offer access to the theoretical grounding of actions in the field of education, to the political grounding of such actions, and to the future orientation of action decisions.

A general model for the examination of positions on educational issues includes the following dimensions: identification of the viewpoint, recognition of the stated or implied assumptions underlying the viewpoint, analysis of the validity of the supporting argument, and evaluation of the conclusions and action-suggestions of the originator of the position. The stated or implied assumptions may be derived from a philosophical or religious orientation, from scientific theory, from social or personal values, or from accumulated experience. Acceptance by the reader of an author's assumptions opens the way for a receptive attitude regarding the specific viewpoint expressed and its implications for action. The argument offered in justification of the viewpoint may be based on logic, common experience, controlled experiments, information and data, legal precedents, emotional appeals, and a host of other persuasive devices.

Holding the basic model in mind, readers of the positions presented in this volume (or anywhere else, for that matter) can examine the constituent elements of arguments—basic assumptions, viewpoint statements, supporting evidence, conclusions, and suggestions for action. The careful reader will accept or reject the individual elements of the total position. One might see reasonableness in a viewpoint and its justification but be unable to accept the assumptions on which it is based. Or one might accept the flow of argument from assumptions to viewpoint to evidence but find illogic or impracticality in the stated conclusions and suggestions for action. In any event, the reader's personal view is tested and honed through the process of analyzing the views of others.

Philosophical Considerations

Historically, organized education has been initiated and instituted to serve many purposes—spiritual salvation, political socialization, moral uplift, societal stability, social mobility, mental discipline, vocational efficiency, and social reform, among others. The various purposes have usually reflected the dominant philosophical conception of human nature and the prevailing assumptions about the relationship between the individual and society. At any given time, competing conceptions may vie for dominance—social conceptions, economic conceptions, conceptions that emphasize spirituality, or conceptions that stress the uniqueness and dignity of the individual, for example.

These considerations of human nature and individual—society relationships are grounded in philosophical assumptions, and these assumptions find their way to such practical domains as schooling. In Western civilization there has been an identifiable (but far from consistent and clear-cut) historical trend in the basic assumptions about reality, knowledge, values, and the human condition. This trend, made manifest in the philosophical positions of idealism, realism, pragmatism, and existentialism, has involved a shift in emphasis from the spiritual world to nature to human behavior to the social individual to the free individual, and from eternal ideas to fixed natural laws to social interaction to the inner person.

The idealist tradition, which dominated much of philosophical and educational thought until the eighteenth and nineteenth centuries, separates the changing, imperfect, material world and the permanent, perfect, spiritual or mental world. As Plato saw it, for example, human beings and all other physical entities are particular manifestations of an ideal reality that in material existence humans can never fully know. The purpose of education is to bring us closer to the absolute ideals, pure forms, and universal standards that exist spiritually, by awakening and strengthening our rational powers. For Plato, a curriculum based on mathematics, logic, and music would serve this purpose, especially in the training of leaders whose rationality must exert control over emotionality and baser instincts.

Against this tradition, which shaped the liberal arts curriculum in schools for centuries, the realism of Aristotle, with its finding of the "forms" of things *within* the material world, brought an emphasis on scientific investigation and on environmental factors in the development of human potential. This fundamental view has influenced two philosophical movements in education: naturalism, based on following or gently assisting nature (as in the approaches of John Amos Comenius, Jean-Jacques Rousseau, and Johann Heinrich Pestalozzi), and scientific realism, based on uncovering the natural laws of human behavior and shaping the educational environment to maximize their effectiveness (as in the approaches of John Locke, Johann Friedrich Herbart, and Edward Thorndike).

In the twentieth century, two philosophical forces (pragmatism and existentialism) have challenged these traditions. Each has moved primary attention away from fixed spiritual or natural influences and toward the individual as shaper of knowledge and values. The pragmatic position, articulated in America by Charles Sanders Peirce, William James, and John Dewey, turns from metaphysical abstractions toward concrete results of action. In a world of change and relativity, human beings must forge their own truths and values as they interact with their environments and each other. The European-based philosophy of existentialism, emerging from such thinkers as Gabriel Marcel, Martin Buber, Martin Heidegger, and Jean-Paul Sartre, has more recently influenced education here. Existentialism places the burdens of freedom, choice, and responsibility squarely on the individual, viewing the current encroachment of external forces and the tendency of people to "escape from freedom" as a serious diminishment of our human possibilities.

These many theoretical slants contend for recognition and acceptance as we continue the search for broad purposes in education and as we attempt to create curricula, methodologies, and learning environments that fulfill our stated purposes. This is carried out, of course, in the real world of the public schools in which social, political, and economic forces often predominate.

Power and Control

Plato, in the fourth century B.C., found existing education manipulative and confining and, in the *Republic,* described a meritocratic approach designed to nurture intellectual powers so as to form and sustain a rational society. Reform-oriented as Plato's suggestions were, he nevertheless insisted on certain restrictions and controls so that his particular version of the ideal could be met.

The ways and means of education have been fertile grounds for power struggles throughout history. Many educational efforts have been initiated by religious bodies, often creating a conflict situation when secular authorities have moved into the field. Schools have usually been seen as repositories of culture and social values and, as such, have been overseen by the more conservative forces in society. To others, bent on social reform, the schools have been treated as a spawning ground for change. Given these basic political forces, conflict is inevitable.

When one speaks of the control of education, the range of influence is indeed wide. Political influences, governmental actions, court decisions, professional militancy, parental power, and student assertion all contribute to the phenomenon of control. And the domain of control is equally broad—school finances, curriculum, instructional means and objectives, teacher certification, accountability, student discipline, censorship of school materials, determination of access and opportunity, and determination of inclusion and exclusion.

The general topic of power and control leads to a multitude of questions: Who should make policy decisions? Must the schools be puppets of the government? Can the schools function in the vanguard of social change? Can cultural indoctrination be avoided? Can the schools lead the way to full social integration? Can the effects of social class be eradicated? Can and should the schools teach values? Dealing with such questions is complicated by the increasing power of the federal government in educational matters. Congressional legislation has broadened substantially from the early land grants and aid to agricultural and vocational programs to more recent laws covering aid to federally impacted areas, school construction aid, student loans and fellowships, support for several academic areas of the curriculum, work-study programs, compensatory education, employment opportunities for youth, adult education, aid to libraries, teacher preparation, educational research, career education, education of the handicapped, and equal opportunity for females. This proliferation of areas of influence has caused the federal administrative bureaucracy to blossom from its meager beginnings in 1867 into a cabinet-level Department of Education in 1979.

State legislatures and state departments of education have also grown in power, handling greater percentages of school appropriations and controlling basic curricular decisions, attendance laws, accreditation, research, and so on. Local school boards, once the sole authorities in policy making, now share the role with higher governmental echelons as the financial support sources shift away from the local scene. Simultaneously, strengthened teacher organizations and increasingly vocal pressure groups at the local, state, and national levels have forced a widening of the base for policy decisions.

Some Concluding Remarks

The schools often seem to be either facing backward or completely absorbed in the tribulations of the present, lacking a vision of possible futures that might guide current decisions. The present is inescapable, obviously, and certainly the historical and philosophical underpinnings of the present situation must be understood, but true improvement often requires a break with conventionality—a surge toward a desired future.

The radical reform critique of government-sponsored compulsory schooling has depicted organized education as a form of cultural or political imprisonment that traps young people in an artificial and mainly irrelevant environment and rewards conformity and docility while inhibiting curiosity and creativity. Constructive reform ideas that have come from this critique include the creation of open classrooms, the de-emphasis of external motivators, the diversification of educational experience, and the building of a true sense of community within the instructional environment.

Starting with Francis Wayland Parker's schools in Quincy, Massachusetts, and John Dewey's laboratory school at the University of Chicago around the turn of the twentieth century, the campaign to make schools into more productive and humane places has been relentless. The duplication of A. S. Neill's Summerhill model in the free school movement in the 1960s, the open classroom/open space experiments, the several curricular variations, and the emergence of schools without walls, charter schools, privatization of management, and home schooling across the country testify to the desire to reform the present system or to build alternatives to it.

The progressive education movement, the development of "life adjustment" goals and curricula, and the "whole person" theories of educational psychology moved the schools toward an expanded concept of schooling that embraced new subject matters and new approaches to discipline during the first half of this century. Since the 1950s, however, pressure for a return to a narrower concept of schooling as intellectual training has sparked new waves of debate. Out of this situation have come attempts by educators and academicians to design new curricular approaches in the basic subject matter areas, efforts by private foundations to stimulate organizational innovations and to improve the training of teachers, and federal government support of educational technology. Yet criticism of the schools abounds. The schools, according to many who use their services, remain too factorylike, too age-segregated, and too custodial. Alternative paths are still sought—paths that would allow action-learning, work-study, and a diversity of ways to achieve success.

H. G. Wells has told us that human history becomes more and more a race between education and catastrophe. What is needed in order to win this race is the generation of new ideas regarding cultural change, human relationships, ethical norms, the uses of technology, and the quality of life. These new ideas, of course, may be old ideas newly applied. One could do worse, in thinking through the problem of improving the quality of education, than to turn to the third-century philosopher Plotinus, who called for an education directed to "the outer, the inner, and the whole." For Plotinus, "the outer" represented the public person, or the socioeconomic dimension of the total human being; "the inner" reflected the subjective dimension, the uniquely experiencing individual, or the "I"; and "the whole" signified the universe of meaning and relatedness, or the realm of human, natural, and spiritual connectedness. It would seem that education must address all of these dimensions if it is to truly help people in the lifelong struggle to shape a meaningful existence. If educational experiences can be improved in these directions, the end result might be people who are not just filling space, filling time, or filling a social role, but who are capable of saying something worthwhile with their lives.

Internet References . . .

The Center for Dewey Studies

Southern Illinois University site offers a wealth of source materials on the ideas of philosopher-educator John Dewey and the progressive education movement.

http://www.siuc.edu/~deweyctr/about_links.html

The National Paideia Center

Promotes and supports efforts of educators who are implementing the long-term systemic school reform known as the Paideia Program based on the ideas of philosopher Mortimer J. Adler.

http://www.paideia.org

Learn in Freedom!

Provides ideas, resources, and encouragement for unschoolers, homeschoolers, and all learners within or without school.

http://www.learninfreedom.org

Behaviorism

Stanford Encyclopedia of Philosophy offers articles on B. F. Skinner and other behaviorists plus links to other sites.

http://plato.stanford.edu/entries/behaviorism

The Association for Humanistic Psychology

Features material on the theories of Carl Rogers, Abraham Maslow, Rollo May, and others, as well as links to Web resources.

http://ahpweb.org

Constructivism vs. Instructivism

Offers research on two dominant pedagogical approaches and the philosophical assumptions lying behind them.

http://roushan.myweb.uga.edu/EDIT6150/tech3.html

Basic Theoretical Issues

*W*hat is the basic purpose of education? How should the curriculum be organized and how much control should students have over their own development? What is the best way to teach and motivate students to learn? What philosophy of education should guide the process of education? These questions have been discussed throughout the history of American education and continue to be debated today. In this section, some major figures from the 20th century—John Dewey, Mortimer J. Adler, John Holt, and Carl R. Rogers—and a number of current scholars in the field of education address these basic questions.

- Should Schooling Be Based on Social Experiences?
- Should the Curriculum Be Standardized for All?
- Should Behaviorism Shape Educational Practices?
- Is Constructivism the Best Philosophy of Education?
- Should "Public Schooling" Be Redefined?

ISSUE 1

Should Schooling Be Based on Social Experiences?

YES: John Dewey, from *Experience and Education* (Macmillan, 1938)

NO: Roger Scruton, from "Schools and Schooling," *The American Spectator* (June 2006)

ISSUE SUMMARY

YES: Philosopher John Dewey suggests a reconsideration of traditional approaches to schooling, giving fuller attention to the social development of the learner and the quality of his or her total experience.

NO: British philosopher Roger Scruton expresses the traditionalist view that Dewey's progressive education, with its emphasis on "child-centeredness" and "relevance," has had a disastrous effect on quality education.

Throughout history, organized education has served many purposes—the transmission of tradition, knowledge, and skills; the acculturation and socialization of the young; the building and preserving of political-economic systems; the provision of opportunity for social mobility; the enhancement of the quality of life; and the cultivation of individual potential, among others. At any given time, schools pursue a number of such goals, but the elucidation of a primary or overriding goal, which gives focus to all others, has been a source of continuous contention.

Schooling in America has been extended in the last 100 years to vast numbers of young people, and during this time the argument over aims has gained momentum. At the turn of the century, John Dewey was raising serious questions about the efficacy of the prevailing approach to schooling. He believed that schooling was often arid, pedantic, and detached from the real lives of children and youths. In establishing his laboratory school at the University of Chicago, Dewey hoped to demonstrate that experiences provided by schools could be meaningful extensions of the normal social activities of learners, having as their primary aim the full experiential growth of the individual.

To accomplish this, Dewey sought to bring the learner into an active and intimate relationship with the subject matter. The problem-solving, or inquiry, approach that he and his colleagues at Columbia University in New York City devised became the cornerstone of the "new education"—the progressive education movement.

In 1938 Dewey himself (as expressed in the YES selection) sounded a note of caution to progressive educators who may have abandoned too completely the traditional disciplines in their attempt to link schooling with the needs and interests of the learners. Having spawned an educational revolution, Dewey, in his later years, emerges as more of a compromiser.

In that same year, William C. Bagley, in "An Essentialists' Platform for the Advancement of American Education," harshly criticized what he felt were anti-intellectual excesses promulgated by progressivism. In the 1950s and 1960s this theme was elaborated on by other academics, among them Robert M. Hutchins, Hyman Rickover, Arthur Bestor, and Max Rafferty, who demanded a return to intellectual discipline, higher standards, and moral guidance.

Hutchins' critique of Dewey's pragmatic philosophy was perhaps the best reasoned. He felt that the emphasis on immediate needs and desires of students and the focus on change and relativism detracted from the development of the intellectual skills needed for the realization of human potential.

A renewal of scholarly interest in the philosophical and educational ideas of both Dewey and Hutchins has resulted in a number of books, among which are *Hutchins' University: A Memoir of the University of Chicago* by William H. O'Neill (1991); *Robert M. Hutchins: Portrait of an Educator* by Mary Ann Dzuback (1991); *John Dewey and American Democracy* by Robert B. Westbrook (1991); *The End of Epistemology: Dewey and His Allies on the Spectator Theory of Knowledge* by Christopher B. Kulp (1992); and *The Promise of Pragmatism* by John Patrick Diggins (1994). Their continuing influence is charted by Rene Vincente Arcilla in "Metaphysics in Education After Hutchins and Dewey," *Teachers College Record* (Winter 1991).

More recent articles on the legacies of Dewey's progressivism and the traditionalism of Hutchins include "Why Traditional Education Is More Progressive," by E. D. Hirsch, Jr., *The American Enterprise* (March 1997); "The Plight of Children Is Our Plight," by William H. Schubert, *Educational Horizons* (Winter 1998); Diana Schaub's "Can Liberal Education Survive Liberal Democracy?" *The Public Interest* (Spring 2002); and Stanley Pogrow's "The Bermuda Triangle of American Education: Pure Traditionalism, Pure Progressivism, and Good Intentions," *Phi Delta Kappan* (October 2006).

In the YES selection, Dewey charts what he considers a necessary shift from the abstractness and isolation of traditional schooling to the concreteness and vitality of the newer concept. In the NO selection, Scruton reviews his personal schooling experience, which he judges to be far superior to the antiacademic approaches inspired by Dewey and his followers.

YES ← John Dewey

Experience and Education

Mankind likes to think in terms of extreme opposites. It is given to formulating its beliefs in terms of *Either-Ors*, between which it recognizes no intermediate possibilities. When forced to recognize that the extremes cannot be acted upon, it is still inclined to hold that they are all right in theory but that when it comes to practical matters circumstances compel us to compromise. Educational philosophy is no exception. The history of educational theory is marked by opposition between the idea that education is development from within and that it is formation from without; that it is based upon natural endowments and that education is a process of overcoming natural inclination and substituting in its place habits acquired under external pressure.

At present, the opposition, so far as practical affairs of the school are concerned, tends to take the form of contrast between traditional and progressive education. If the underlying ideas of the former are formulated broadly, without the qualifications required for accurate statement, they are found to be about as follows: The subject-matter of education consists of bodies of information and of skills that have been worked out in the past; therefore, the chief business of the school is to transmit them to the new generation. In the past, there have also been developed standards and rules of conduct; moral training consists of forming habits of action in conformity with these rules and standards. Finally, the general pattern of school organization (by which I mean the relations of pupils to one another and to the teachers) constitutes the school as a kind of institution sharply marked off from other social institutions. Call up in imagination the ordinary schoolroom, its time schedules, schemes of classification, of examination and promotion, of rules of order, and I think you will grasp what is meant by "pattern of organization." If then you contrast this scene with what goes on in the family, for example, you will appreciate what is meant by the school being a kind of institution sharply marked off from any other form of social organization.

The three characteristics just mentioned fix the aims and methods of instruction and discipline. The main purpose or objective is to prepare the young for future responsibilities and for success in life, by means of acquisition of the organized bodies of information and prepared forms of skill which comprehend the material of instruction. Since the subject-matter as well as standards of proper conduct are handed down from the past, the attitude of pupils must, upon the whole, be one of docility, receptivity, and obedience. Books,

From *Experience and Education,* 1938, excerpts from chapters 1, 7, 8. Copyright © 1938 by Kappa Delta Pi. Reprinted by permission.

especially textbooks, are the chief representatives of the lore and wisdom of the past, while teachers are the organs through which pupils are brought into effective connection with the material. Teachers are the agents through which knowledge and skills are communicated and rules of conduct enforced.

I have not made this brief summary for the purpose of criticizing the underlying philosophy. The rise of what is called new education and progressive schools is of itself a product of discontent with traditional education. In effect it is a criticism of the latter. When the implied criticism is made explicit it reads somewhat as follows: The traditional scheme is, in essence, one of imposition from above and from outside. It imposes adult standards, subject-matter, and methods upon those who are only growing slowly toward maturity. The gap is so great that the required subject-matter, the methods of learning and of behaving are foreign to the existing capacities of the young. They are beyond the reach of the experience the young learners already possess. Consequently, they must be imposed; even though good teachers will use devices of art to cover up the imposition so as to relieve it of obviously brutal features.

But the gulf between the mature or adult products and the experience and abilities of the young is so wide that the very situation forbids much active participation by pupils in the development of what is taught. Theirs is to do— and learn, as it was the part of the six hundred to do and die. Learning here means acquisition of what already is incorporated in books and in the heads of the elders. Moreover, that which is taught is thought of as essentially static. It is taught as a finished product, with little regard either to the ways in which it was originally built up or to changes that will surely occur in the future. It is to a large extent the cultural product of societies that assumed the future would be much like the past, and yet it is used as educational food in a society where change is the rule, not the exception.

If one attempts to formulate the philosophy of education implicit in the practices of the new education, we may, I think, discover certain common principles amid the variety of progressive schools now existing. To imposition from above is opposed expression and cultivation of individuality; to external discipline is opposed free activity; to learning from texts and teachers, learning through experience; to acquisition of isolated skills and techniques by drill, is opposed acquisition of them as means of attaining ends which make direct vital appeal; to preparation for a more or less remote future is opposed making the most of the opportunities of present life; to static aims and materials is opposed acquaintance with a changing world.

Now, all principles by themselves are abstract. They become concrete only in the consequences which result from their application. Just because the principles set forth are so fundamental and far-reaching, everything depends upon the interpretation given them as they are put into practice in the school and the home. It is at this point that the reference made earlier to *Either-Or* philosophies becomes peculiarly pertinent. The general philosophy of the new education may be sound, and yet the difference in abstract principles will not decide the way in which the moral and intellectual preference involved shall be worked out in practice. There is always the danger in a new movement that in rejecting the aims and methods of that which it would supplant, it may develop its principles negatively rather than positively and constructively. Then it takes its cue in practice from that which is rejected instead of from the constructive development its own philosophy.

I take it that the fundamental unity of the newer philosophy is found in the idea that there is an intimate and necessary relation between the processes of actual experience and education. If this be true, then a positive and constructive development of its own basic idea depends upon having a correct idea of experience. Take, for example, the question of organized subject-matter. . . . The problem for progressive education is: What is the place and meaning of subject-matter and of organization *within* experience? How does subject-matter function? Is there anything inherent in experience which tends towards progressive organization of its contents? What results follow when the materials of experience are not progressively organized? A philosophy which proceeds on the basis of rejection, of sheer opposition, will neglect these questions. It will tend to suppose that because the old education was based on ready-made organization, therefore it suffices to reject the principle of organization *in toto*, instead of striving to discover what it means and how it is to be attained on the basis of experience. We might go through all the points of difference between the new and the old education and reach similar conclusions. When external control is rejected, the problem becomes that of finding the factors of control that are inherent within experience. When external authority is rejected, it does not follow that all authority should be rejected, but rather that there is need to search for a more effective source of authority. Because the older education imposed the knowledge, methods, and the rules of conduct of the mature person upon the young, it does not follow, except upon the basis of the extreme *Either-Or* philosophy, that the knowledge and skill of the mature person has no directive value for the experience of the immature. On the contrary, basing education upon personal experience may mean more multiplied and more intimate contacts between the mature and the immature than ever existed in the traditional school, and consequently more, rather than less, guidance by others. The problem, then, is: how these contacts can be established without violating the principle of learning through personal experience. The solution of this problem requires a well thought-out philosophy of the social factors that operate in the constitution of individual experience.

What is indicated in the foregoing remarks is that the general principles of the new education do not of themselves solve any of the problems of the actual or practical conduct and management of progressive schools. Rather, they set new problems which have to be worked out on the basis of a new philosophy of experience. The problems are not even recognized, to say nothing of being solved, when it is assumed that it suffices to reject the ideas and practices of the old education and then go to the opposite extreme. Yet I am sure that you will appreciate what is meant when I say that many of the newer schools tend to make little or nothing of organized subject-matter of study; to proceed as if any form of direction and guidance by adults were an invasion of individual freedom, and as if the idea that education should be concerned with the present and future meant that acquaintance with the past has little or no role to play in education. Without pressing these defects to the point of exaggeration, they at least illustrate what is meant by a theory and practice of education which proceeds negatively or by reaction against what has been current in education rather than by a positive and constructive development of purposes, methods, and subject-matter on the foundation of a theory of experience and its educational potentialities.

It is not too much to say that an educational philosophy which professes to be based on the idea of freedom may become as dogmatic as ever was the traditional education which is reacted against. For any theory and set of practices is dogmatic which is not based upon critical examination of its own underlying principles. Let us say that the new education emphasizes the freedom of the learner. Very well. A problem is now set. What does freedom mean and what are the conditions under which it is capable of realization? Let us say that the kind of external imposition which was so common in the traditional school limited rather than promoted the intellectual and moral development of the young. Again, very well. Recognition of this serious defect sets a problem. Just what is the role of the teacher and of books in promoting the educational development of the immature? Admit that traditional education employed as the subject-matter for study facts and ideas so bound up with the past as to give little help in dealing with the issues of the present and future. Very well. Now we have the problem of discovering the connection which actually exists *within* experience between the achievements of the past and the issues of the present. We have the problem of ascertaining how acquaintance with the past may be translated into a potent instrumentality for dealing effectively with the future. We may reject knowledge of the past as the *end* of education and thereby only emphasize its importance as a *means*. When we do that we have a problem that is new in the story of education: How shall the young become acquainted with the past in such a way that the acquaintance is a potent agent in appreciation of the living present? . . .

In short, the point I am making is that rejection of the philosophy and practice of traditional education sets a new type of difficult educational problem for those who believe in the new type of education. We shall operate blindly and in confusion until we recognize this fact; until we thoroughly appreciate that departure from the old solves no problems. What is said in the following pages is, accordingly, intended to indicate some of the main problems with which the newer education is confronted and to suggest the main lines along which their solution is to be sought. I assume that amid all uncertainties there is one permanent frame of reference: namely, the organic connection between education and personal experience; or, that the new philosophy of education is committed to some kind of empirical and experimental philosophy. But experience and experiment are not self-explanatory ideas. Rather, their meaning is part of the problem to be explored. To know the meaning of empiricism we need to understand what experience is.

The belief that all genuine education comes about through experience does not mean that all experiences are genuinely or equally educative. Experience and education cannot be directly equated to each other. For some experiences are miseducative. Any experience is miseducative that has the effect of arresting or distorting the growth of further experience. An experience may be such as to engender callousness; it may produce lack of sensitivity and of responsiveness. Then the possibilities of having richer experience in the future are restricted. Again, a given experience may increase a person's automatic skill in a particular direction and yet tend to land him in a groove or rut; the effect again is to narrow the field of further experience. An experience may be immediately enjoyable and yet promote the formation of a slack and careless attitude; this attitude then operates to modify the quality of subsequent experiences so as to prevent a person from getting out of them what they have to give. Again, experiences may be so disconnected from one another that, while each is agreeable or even exciting in itself, they are not linked cumulatively to one another. Energy is then dissipated and a person becomes scatter-brained. Each experience may be lively, vivid, and "interesting," and yet their disconnectedness may artificially generate dispersive, disintegrated, centrifugal habits. The consequence of formation of such habits is inability to control future experiences. They are then taken, either by way of enjoyment or of discontent and revolt, just as they come. Under such circumstances, it is idle to talk of self-control.

Traditional education offers a plethora of examples of experiences of the kinds just mentioned. It is a great mistake to suppose, even tacitly, that the traditional schoolroom was not a place in which pupils had experiences. Yet this is tacitly assumed when progressive education as a plan of learning by experience is placed in sharp opposition to the old. The proper line of attack is that the experiences which were had, by pupils and teachers alike, were largely of a wrong kind. How many students, for example, were rendered callous to ideas, and how many lost the impetus to learn because of the way in which learning was experienced by them? How many acquired special skills by means of automatic drill so that their power of judgment and capacity to act intelligently in new situations was limited? How many came to associate the learning process with ennui and boredom? How many found what they did learn so foreign to the situations of life outside the school as to give them no power of control over the latter? How many came to associate books with dull drudgery, so that they were "conditioned" to all but flashy reading matter?

If I ask these questions, it is not for the sake of wholesale condemnation of the old education. It is for quite another purpose. It is to emphasize the fact, first, that young people in traditional schools do have experiences; and, secondly, that the trouble is not the absence of experiences, but their defective and wrong character—wrong and defective from the standpoint of connection with further experience. The positive side of this point is even more important in connection with progressive education. It is not enough to insist upon the necessity of experience, nor even of activity in experience. Everything depends upon the *quality* of the experience which is had. The quality of an experience has two aspects. There is an immediate aspect of agreeableness or disagreeableness, and there is its influence upon later experiences. The first is obvious and easy to judge. The *effect* of an experience is not borne on its face. It sets a problem to the educator. It is his business to arrange for the kind of experiences which, while they do not repel the student, but rather engage his activities are, nevertheless, more than immediately enjoyable since they promote having desirable future experiences. Just as no man lives or dies to himself, so no experience lives or dies to itself. Wholly independent of desire or intent, every experience lives on in further experiences. Hence the central problem of an education based upon experience is to select the kind of present experiences that live fruitfully and creatively in subsequent experiences.

. . . Here I wish simply to emphasize the importance of this principle [of the continuity of experience] for the philosophy of educative experience. A philosophy of education, like my theory, has to be stated in words, in symbols. But so far as it is more than verbal it is a plan for conducting education. Like any plan, it must be framed with reference to what is to be done and how it is to be done. The more definitely and sincerely it is held that education is a development within, by, and for experience, the more important it is that there shall be clear conceptions of what experience is. Unless experience is so conceived that the result is a plan for deciding upon subject-matter, upon methods of instruction and discipline, and upon material equipment and social organization of the school, it is wholly in the air. It is reduced to a form of words which may be emotionally stirring but for which any other set of words might equally well be substituted unless they indicate operations to be initiated and executed. Just because traditional education was a matter of routine in which the plans and programs were handed down from the past, it does not follow that progressive education is a matter of planless improvisation.

The traditional school could get along without any consistently developed philosophy of education. About all it required in that line was a set of abstract words like culture, discipline, our great cultural heritage, etc., actual guidance being derived not from them but from custom and established routines. Just because progressive schools cannot rely upon established traditions and institutional habits, they must either proceed more or less haphazardly or be directed by ideas which, when they are made articulate and coherent, form a philosophy of education. Revolt against the kind of organization characteristic of the traditional school constitutes a demand for a kind of organization based upon ideas. I think that only slight acquaintance with the history of education is needed to prove that educational reformers and innovators alone have felt the need for a philosophy of education. Those who adhered to the established system needed merely a few fine-sounding words to justify existing practices. The real work was done by habits which were so fixed as to be institutional. The lesson for progressive education is that it requires in an urgent degree, a degree more pressing than was incumbent upon former innovators, a philosophy of education based upon a philosophy of experience.

I remarked incidentally that the philosophy in question is, to paraphrase the saying of Lincoln about democracy, one of education of, by, and for experience. No one of these words, *of, by,* or *for,* names anything which is self-evident. Each of them is a challenge to discover and put into operation a principle of order and organization which follows from understanding what education experience signifies.

It is, accordingly, a much more difficult task to work out the kinds of materials, of methods, and of social relationships that are appropriate to the new education than is the case with traditional education. I think many of the difficulties experienced in the conduct of progressive schools and many of the criticisms leveled against them arise from this source. The difficulties are aggravated and the criticisms are increased when it is supposed that the new education is somehow easier than the old. This belief is, I imagine, more or less current. Perhaps it illustrates again the *Either-Or* philosophy, springing from the idea that about all which is required is not to do what is done in traditional schools.

I admit gladly that the new education is *simpler* in principle than the old. It is in harmony with principles of growth, while there is very much which is artificial in the old selection and arrangement of subjects and methods, and artificiality always leads to unnecessary complexity. But the easy and the simple are not identical. To discover what is really simple and to act upon the discovery is an exceedingly difficult task. After the artificial and complex is once institutionally established and ingrained in custom and routine, it is easier to walk in the paths that have been beaten than it is, after taking a new point of view, to work out what is practically involved in the new point of view. The old Ptolemaic astronomical system was more complicated with its cycles and epicycles than the Copernican system. But until organization of actual astronomical phenomena on the ground of the latter principle had been effected the easiest course was to follow the line of least resistance provided by the old intellectual habit. So we come back to the idea that a coherent *theory* of experience, affording positive direction to selection and organization of appropriate educational methods and materials, is required by the attempt to give new direction to the work of the schools. The process is a slow and arduous one. It is a matter of growth, and there are many obstacles which tend to obstruct growth and to deflect it into wrong lines.

 . . . [W]e must escape from the tendency to think of organization in terms of the *kind* of organization, whether of content (or subject-matter), or of methods and social relations, that mark traditional education. I think that a good deal of the current opposition to the idea of organization is due to the fact that it is so hard to get away from the picture of the studies of the old school. The moment "organization" is mentioned imagination goes almost automatically to the kind of organization that is familiar, and in revolting against that we are led to shrink from the very idea of any organization. On the other hand, educational reactionaries, who are now gathering force, use the absence of adequate intellectual and moral organization in the newer type of school as proof not only of the need of organization, but to identify any and every kind of organization with that instituted before the rise of experimental science. Failure to develop a conception of organization upon the empirical and experimental basis gives reactionaries a too easy victory. But the fact that the empirical sciences now offer the best type of intellectual organization which can be found in any field shows that there is no reason why we, who call ourselves empiricists, should be "pushovers" in the matter of order and organization.

Roger Scruton

NO

Schools and Schooling

The school where I was educated from my 11th to my 17th year was an English "grammar" school—one of those old Tudor foundations that had become incorporated into the state educational system but which still retained, in those post-war decades, the ethos of public service. The teachers were graduates of the old universities; some had returned from active service in the colonies; one or two had held fellowships in Oxbridge colleges; almost all had wished to pursue an academic career, reluctantly accepting the role of schoolmaster as an honorable second-best.

Those teachers were distinguished from their successors by two all-important characteristics. First, they knew nothing about "education." The idea that there was such a subject—that there could be experts in education, theories of education, and recipes for putting those theories into practice—such an idea had never crossed their minds. A "professor of education" would have been, in their eyes, a creature as risible as a professor of television, of hairdressing, or of underwater basketball.

Secondly, although they knew nothing about education, they knew an awful lot about something else: namely, the subject they had been appointed to teach. Our physics master had worked with Rutherford on the splitting of the atom; our chemistry master had published a textbook on hydrocarbons; and the music master was an amateur composer, friend of our local celebrity, the symphonist Edmund Rubbra. Sixth-form English was taught by a pupil of F.R. Leavis, and the school library contained all of English literature, organized according to the system of T.S. Eliot, who had taught in the school in his Prufrock days. Our Latin master, whose infectious love of Virgil made many converts among the boys, also wrote poetry in Latin and English, and was something of an expert on both Catullus and Yeats.

Sure, it was an exceptional school. But the principles on which it was run were not exceptional at all. Each school, whether in the private or the public sector, recruited teachers with knowledge, on the quite reasonable assumption that knowledge was its business. Of course, the school would do its best to ascertain that its recruits were competent in the classroom. But it would act on the assumption that, failing some accident like vampire teeth or a crippling stutter, knowledge would tend to pass of its own accord from the one who displayed it to the one who saw it on display. And that assumption was, by and large, correct.

That public-sector schools are not like that today, either in Europe or in America, goes without saying. But it is worth asking why. Every place has its own sorry story to tell, but in each country we can trace the decline to a few common factors. The most important has been the rise of "education" as an academic subject. The question what to teach the young occupies many pages of Plato, Aristotle, Cicero, and Quintilian. But the idea that you could be an expert in education, while knowing next to nothing about anything else, is a peculiarly modern fallacy, and one whose appeal rests entirely on its subversive effect. The graduate in education, competing with the pupil of Lord Rutherford for a job teaching physics, can say: sure *he* knows some physics; but *I* know how to *teach* it. The idea of education as a field of expertise thereby gives the ignorant an insuperable advantage over the learned, whom they outnumber in any case by ten to one.

But that is not all there is to it. Education, as an academic discipline, was itself shaped by subversives. It takes its inspiration from Rousseau, whose novel *Emile* outlines a new form of teaching, in which knowledge is not authoritatively displayed but gently *elicited,* in a mind already poised on the brink of it. Admirers of this preposterous book somehow fail to notice that education, as Rousseau conceives it, requires day-by-day one-to-one coaching from an expensive private tutor, whose devotion to the cause of knowledge has left him no time whatsoever to acquire it.

The other great influence on schools of education has been John Dewey, a figure with an equally preposterous and equally *a priori* approach. For Dewey education should be purged of all residues of authority, so as to proceed through the child's self-expression. People had made the mistake, he thought, of focusing on the teacher, when the true object of education is the child. Child-centered education proceeds by awakening, eliciting, encouraging: the child should be exploring the world, and the teacher must therefore present him with things that are relevant to his interests and stimulating to a mind like his.

Thus there entered into schooling the two ideas that have destroyed it: child-centered education, and relevance. Add them to the campaigning zeal of the egalitarians, who have always hated learning since real learning discriminates, and the result is a deadly weapon in the battle against knowledge. In Britain this battle took on a new form in the 1960s. My schoolmasters had never encountered "education," since the only qualification required of them was knowledge. Those who attended teacher-training colleges, however, who were by and large those who had failed to get to university, had encountered virtually nothing *except* "education." Competing for jobs with learned graduates they made it transparently obvious that they had nothing to offer save fashionable nonsense. The socialist government of Harold Wilson therefore devised a cunning strategy designed to give "education" an insuperable advantage over knowledge. A "postgraduate certificate of education" was invented, to provide a compulsory hurdle in the path of all who had made the mistake of learning something. Henceforth graduates with genuine competence in a subject could no longer teach in the public sector, unless they had undergone another year of study—which was not a year of study at all, but a period of mind-numbing indoctrination in official nonsense. The best of them shrugged their shoulders and went to work in the city.

Since then good teachers have been gradually driven from the system, often accused of "insensitivity" towards the needs of children, and castigated for the irrelevance of what they presume to know. Examinations have been reshaped to endorse the new "relevant" curriculum, and when it is pointed out that 30 percent of British children now leave school unable to read or write, the educationists cheerfully point to the "irrelevance" of reading and writing in the "information culture." And it is true that information, as currently conceived, is the enemy of knowledge—a mass of unsorted facts and factoids, pouring from the screen with the incoherence of a madman's monologue.

Not that the situation is better in France, Germany, or America. Everywhere we encounter the triumph of "education" over knowledge. And the mark of this triumph is the unchallenged belief that, if knowledge is to be permitted in school, it is in order to benefit the child. My teachers had the opposite belief. For them, if children are permitted in school it is in order to benefit knowledge. Children have their lives ahead of them; they can carry knowledge into the future and keep it from decay—they might even add to it. It is therefore right to allow them into the classroom, so long as nothing "relevant" occurs there, the mark of true knowledge being its total irrelevance to the world of a child. My teachers valued knowledge for its pristine uselessness. Like harmony and counterpoint, like Latin and poetry, like the laws of quantum mechanics or the theory of transfinite cardinals, knowledge, for them, was its own justification, and never needed to stoop to a use. Any other way of treating it, my teachers thought, would lead to its disappearance. And they were right, since it did.

All attempts by the state to rectify the disaster are doomed, since they will be administered by the educationists. That is why Americans are right to turn to the home schooling movement, the first ray of hope for education since the state got its hands on it. When a mother sits down to teach her child, she is instinctively aware that her role is not to flatter ignorance but to pass on knowledge. She doesn't ask about the relevance or use of what she is teaching. To a child few beliefs are more useful than that the earth is flat, that all children are victims, that mine and thine are indistinguishable, or that $2 + 2 = 5$; few things are more relevant than pop stars, sitcoms, and advertising jingles. None of those appear on the home schooling curriculum since it is devoted, by its very nature, to passing on the knowledge that the parent values, whether or not the child perceives its relevance. My hope is that, as more and more parents take up the challenge, they will gradually learn to pool their resources, to divide the labor, to share their expertise, and to produce that precious thing which has all but disappeared from the world of ordinary people—the school.

Just down the road from us in rural Virginia is an old deserted cabin with a classroom, a tiny kitchen, and a toilet. From the windows you see the Blue Ridge Mountains, surmounted by Old Rag, and in the foreground a horse or two. The classroom has a blackboard, a bookshelf, and a few battered desks. No educationist has ever set foot in it, and no bureaucrat knows of its existence. All that it needs is a child or two, an adult or two, and the thing that they spontaneously generate when brought together, which is the pursuit of knowledge. It is from such costless resources that civilizations begin.

POSTSCRIPT

Should Schooling Be Based on Social Experiences?

Intellectual training versus social-emotional-mental growth—the argument between Dewey and Hutchins reflects a historical debate that flows from the ideas of Plato and Aristotle and that continues today. Psychologists, sociologists, curriculum and instruction specialists, and popular critics have joined philosophers in commenting on this central concern.

Followers of Dewey contend that training the mental powers cannot be isolated from other factors of development and, indeed, can be enhanced by attention to the concrete social situations in which learning occurs. Critics of Dewey worry that the expansion of effort into the social and emotional realm only detracts from the intellectual mission that is schooling's unique province.

Was the progressive education movement ruinous, or did it lay the foundation for the education of the future? A reasonably even-handed appraisal can be found in Lawrence Cremin's *The Transformation of the School* (1961). The free school movement of the 1960s, at least partly derived from progressivism, is analyzed in Allen Graubard's *Free the Children* (1973) and Jonathan Kozol's *Free Schools* (1972). Diane Ravitch's *Troubled Crusade* (1983) and Mary Eberstadt's "The Schools They Deserve," *Policy Review* (October/November 1999) offer effective critiques of progressivism.

Among the best general explorations of philosophical alternatives are Gerald L. Gutek's *Philosophical and Ideological Perspectives on Education* (1988); Edward J. Power's *Philosophy of Education: Studies in Philosophies, Schooling, and Educational Policies* (1990); and *Philosophical Foundations of Education* by Howard Ozmon and Samuel Craver (1990).

Also worth perusing are Philip W. Jackson's "Dewey's *Experience and Education* Revisited," *The Educational Forum* (Summer 1996); Jerome Bruner's 1996 book *The Culture of Education* (particularly chapter 3, "The Complexity of Educational Aims"); Christine McCarthy's "Dewey's Ethics: Philosophy or Science?" *Education Theory* (Summer 1999); Debra J. Anderson and Robert L. Major, "Dewey, Democracy, and Citizenship," *The Clearing House* (November/December 2001); Julie Webber, "Why Can't We Be Deweyan Citizens?" *Educational Theory* (Spring 2001); David B. Ackerman, "Taproots for a New Century: Tapping the Best of Traditional and Progressive Education," *Phi Delta Kappan* (January 2003); and William Hayes, "The Future of Progressive Education," *Educational Horizons* (Spring 2008).

Questions that must be addressed include: Can the "either/or" polarities of this basic argument be overcome? Is the articulation of overarching general aims essential to the charting of a worthwhile educational experience? And how can the classroom teacher relate to general philosophical aims?

Should the Curriculum Be Standardized for All?

YES: Mortimer J. Adler, from "The Paideia Proposal: Rediscovering the Essence of Education," *American School Board Journal* (July 1982)

NO: John Holt, from *Escape from Childhood* (E. P. Dutton, 1974)

ISSUE SUMMARY

YES: Philosopher Mortimer J. Adler contends that democracy is best served by a public school system that establishes uniform curricular objectives for all students.

NO: Educator John Holt argues that an imposed curriculum damages the individual and usurps a basic human right to select one's own path of development.

Controversy over the content of education has been particularly keen since the 1950s. The pendulum has swung from learner-centered progressive education to an emphasis on structured intellectual discipline to calls for radical reform in the direction of "openness" to the recent rally to go "back to basics."

The conservative viewpoint, articulated by such writers as Robert M. Hutchins, Clifton Fadiman, Jacques Barzun, Arthur Bestor, and Mortimer J. Adler, arises from concerns about the drift toward informalism and the decline in academic achievement in recent decades. Taking philosophical cues from Plato's contention that certain subject matters have universal qualities that prompt mental and characterological development, the "basics" advocates argue against incidental learning, student choice, and diminution of structure and standards. Barzun summarizes the viewpoint succinctly: "Nonsense is at the heart of those proposals that would replace definable subject matters with vague activities copied from 'life' or with courses organized around 'problems' or 'attitudes.'"

The reform viewpoint, represented by John Holt, Paul Goodman, Ivan Illich, Charles Silberman, Edgar Friedenberg, and others, portrays the typical traditional school as a mindless, indifferent, social institution dedicated to producing fear, docility, and conformity. In such an atmosphere, the viewpoint holds, learners either become alienated from the established curriculum or learn to play the school "game" and thus achieve a hollow success. Taking cues from the ideas of John Dewey and A. S. Neill, the "radical reformers" have given rise to a flurry of alternatives to regular schooling during recent decades. Among these are free schools, which follow the Summerhill model; urban storefront schools, which attempt to develop a true sense of "community"; "schools without walls," which follow the Philadelphia Parkway Program model; "commonwealth" schools, in which students, parents, and teachers share responsibility; and various "humanistic education" projects within regular school systems, which emphasize students' self-concept development and choice-making ability.

The utilitarian tradition that has descended from Benjamin Franklin, Horace Mann, and Herbert Spencer, Dewey's theory of active experiencing, and Neill's insistence on free and natural development support the reform position. The ideology rejects the factory model of schooling with its rigidly set curriculum, its neglect of individual differences, its social engineering function, and its pervasive formalism. "Basics" advocates, on the other hand, express deep concern over the erosion of authority and the watering down of demands upon students that result from the reform ideology.

Arguments for a more standardized curriculum have been embodied most recently in Theodore R. Sizer's Coalition of Essential Schools and the Core Knowledge Schools of E. D. Hirsch, Jr., whose 1996 book *The Schools We Need and Why We Don't Have Them* summarizes the basic points of this view. An interview with Hirsch by Mark F. Goldberg titled "Doing What Works" appeared in the September 1997 issue of *Phi Delta Kappan*. A thorough critique of Hirsch's position is presented by Kristen L. Buras in "Questioning Core Assumptions," *Harvard Educational Review* (Spring 1999). In 1998 Terry Roberts and the staff of the National Paideia Center at the University of North Carolina released *The Power of Paideia Schools: Defining Lives Through Learning*.

A broad spectrum of ideas on the curriculum may be found in John I. Goodlad's *A Place Called School* (1984), Maxine Green's *The Dialectic of Freedom* (1987), Theodore R. Sizer's *Horace* trilogy, and Ernest L. Boyer's *The Basic School* (1995). Some provocative ideas on this and related issues may be found in "The Goals of Education" by Richard Rothstein and Rebecca Jacobsen in *Phi Delta Kappan* (December 2006).

In the following selections, Mortimer J. Adler outlines his "Paideia Proposal," which calls for a uniform and unified curriculum and methodological approach—a common schooling for the development of a truly democratic society. In opposition, John Holt goes beyond his earlier concerns about the oppressiveness of the school curriculum to propose complete freedom for the learner to determine all aspects of his or her educational development.

YES ↵

Mortimer J. Adler

The Paideia Proposal: Rediscovering the Essence of Education

In the first 80 years of this century, we have met the obligation imposed on us by the principle of equal educational opportunity, but only in a quantitative sense. Now as we approach the end of the century, we must achieve equality in qualitative terms.

This means a completely on-track system of schooling. It means, at the basic level, giving all the young the same kind of schooling, whether or not they are college bound.

We are aware that children, although equal in their common humanity and fundamental human rights, are unequal as individuals, differing in their capacity to learn. In addition, the homes and environments from which they come to school are unequal—either predisposing the child for schooling or doing the opposite.

Consequently, the Paideia Proposal, faithful to the principle of equal educational opportunity, includes the suggestion that inequalities due to environmental factors must be overcome by some form of preschool preparation at least one year for all and two or even three for some. We know that to make such preschool tutelage compulsory at the public expense would be tantamount to increasing the duration of compulsory schooling from 12 years to 13, 14, or 15 years. Nevertheless, we think that this preschool adjunct to the 12 years of compulsory basic schooling is so important that some way must be found to make it available for all and to see that all use it to advantage.

The Essentials of Basic Schooling

The objectives of basic schooling should be the same for the whole school population. In our current two-track or multitrack system, the learning objectives are not the same for all. And even when the objectives aimed at those on the upper track are correct, the course of study now provided does not adequately realize these correct objectives. On all tracks in our current system, we fail to cultivate proficiency in the common tasks of learning, and we especially fail to develop sufficiently the indispensable skills of learning.

The uniform objectives of basic schooling should be threefold. They should correspond to three aspects of the common future to which all the children are destined: (1) Our society provides all children ample opportunity for personal development. Given such opportunity, each individual is under a moral obligation to make the most of himself and his life. Basic schooling must facilitate this accomplishment. (2) All the children will become, when of age, full-fledged citizens with suffrage and other political responsibilities. Basic schooling must do everything it can to make them good citizens, able to perform the duties of citizenship with all the trained intelligence that each is able to achieve. (3) When they are grown, all (or certainly most) of the children will engage in some form of work to earn a living. Basic schooling must prepare them for earning a living, but not by training them for this or that specific job while they are still in school.

To achieve these three objectives, the character of basic schooling must be general and liberal. It should have a single, required, 12-year course of study for all, with no electives except one—an elective choice with regard to a second language, to be selected from such modern languages as French, German, Italian, Spanish, Russian, and Chinese. The elimination of all electives, with this one exception, excludes what *should* be excluded—all forms of specialization, including particularized job training.

In its final form, the Paideia Proposal will detail this required course of study, but I will summarize the curriculum here in its bare outline. It consists of three main columns of teaching and learning, running through the 12 years and progressing, of course, from the simple to the more complex, from the less difficult to the more difficult, as the students grow older. Understand: The three columns (see Table 1) represent three distinct modes of teaching and learning. They do not represent a series of courses. A specific course or class may employ more than one mode of teaching and learning, but all three modes are essential to the overall course of study.

Table 1

The Paideia Curriculum

	Column One	Column Two	Column Three
Goals	Acquisition of Organized Knowledge	Development of Intellectual Skills and Skills of Learning	Improved Understading of Ideas and Values
	by means of	*by means of*	*by means of*
Means	Didactic Instruction, Lecturing, and Textbooks	Coaching, Exercises, Supervised Practice	Maieutic or Socratic Questioning and Active Participation
	in these three subject areas	*in these operations*	*in these activities*
Subject Areas, Operations, and Activities	Language, Literature, and Fine Arts; Mathematics and Natural Science; History, Geography, and Social Studies	Reading, Writing, Speaking, Listening, Calculating, Problem Solving, Observing, Measuring, Estimating, Exercising Critical Judgment	Discussion of Books (Not Textbooks) and Other Works of Art; Involvement in Music, Drama, and Visual Arts

The three columns do not correspond to separate courses, nor is one kind of teaching and learning necessarily confined to any one class.

The first column is devoted to acquiring knowledge in three subject areas: (A) language, literature, and the fine arts; (B) mathematics and natural science; (C) history, geography, and social studies.

The second column is devoted to developing the intellectual skills of learning. These include all the language skills necessary for thought and communication—the skills of reading, writing, speaking, listening. They also include mathematical and scientific skills; the skills of observing, measuring, estimating, and calculating; and skills in the use of the computer and of other scientific instruments. Together, these skills make it possible to think clearly and critically. They once were called the liberal arts—the intellectual skills indispensable to being competent as a learner.

The third column is devoted to enlarging the understanding of ideas and values. The materials of the third column are books (*not* textbooks), and other products of human artistry. These materials include books of every variety—historical, scientific, and philosophical as well as poems, stories, and essays—and also individual pieces of music, visual art, dramatic productions, dance productions, film or television productions. Music and works of visual art can be used in seminars in which ideas are discussed; but as with poetry and fiction, they also are to be experienced aesthetically, to be enjoyed and admired for their excellence. In this connection, exercises in the composition of poetry, music, and visual works and in the production of dramatic works should be used to develop the appreciation of excellence.

The three columns represent three different kinds of learning on the part of the student and three different kinds of instruction on the part of teachers.

In the first column, the students are engaged in acquiring information and organized knowledge about nature, man, and human society. The method of instruction here, using textbooks and manuals, is didactic. The teacher lectures, invites responses from the students, monitors the acquisition of knowledge, and tests that acquisition in various ways.

In the second column, the students are engaged in developing habits of performance, which is all that is involved in the development of an art or skill. Art, skill, or technique is nothing more than a cultivated, habitual ability to do a certain kind of thing well, whether that is swimming and dancing, or reading and writing. Here, students are acquiring linguistic, mathematical, scientific, and historical *know-how* in contrast to what they acquire in the first column, which is *know-that* with respect to language, literature, and the fine arts, mathematics and science, history, geography, and social studies. Here, the method of instruction cannot be didactic or monitorial; it cannot be dependent on textbooks. It must be coaching, the same kind used in the gym to develop bodily skills; only here it is used by a different kind of coach in the classroom to develop intellectual skills.

In the third column, students are engaged in a process of enlightenment, the process whereby they develop their understanding of the basic and controlling ideas in all fields of subject matter and come to appreciate better all the human values embodied in works of art. Here, students move progressively from understanding less to understanding more—understanding better what they already know and appreciating more what they already have experienced. Here, the method of instruction cannot be either didactic or coaching. It must be the Socratic, or maieutic, method of questioning and discussing. It should not occur in any ordinary classroom with the students sitting in rows and the teacher in front of the class, but in a seminar room, with the students sitting around a table and the teacher sitting with them as an equal, even though a little older and wiser.

Of these three main elements in the required curriculum, the third column is completely innovative. Nothing like this is done in our schools, and because it is completely absent from the ordinary curriculum of basic schooling, the students never have the experience of having their minds addressed in a challenging way or of being asked to think about the important ideas, to express their thoughts, to defend their opinions in a reasonable fashion.

The only thing that is innovative about the second column is the insistence that the method of instruction here must be coaching carried on either with one student at a time or with very small groups of students. Nothing else can be effective in the development of a skill, be it bodily or intellectual. The absence of such individualized coaching in our schools explains why most of the students cannot read well, write well, speak well, listen well, or perform well any of the other basic intellectual operations.

The three columns are closely interconnected and integrated, but the middle column—the one concerned with linguistic, mathematical, and scientific skills—is central. It both supports and is supported by the other two columns. All the intellectual skills with which it is concerned must be exercised in the study of the three basic subject-matters and in acquiring knowledge about them, and these intellectual skills must be exercised in the seminars devoted to the discussion of books and other things.

In addition to the three main columns in the curriculum, ascending through the 12 years of basic schooling, there are three adjuncts: One is 12 years of physical training, accompanied by instruction in bodily care and hygiene. The second, running through something less than 12 years, is the development of basic manual skills, such as cooking, sewing, carpentry, and the operation of all kinds of machines. The third, reserved for the last year or two, is an introduction to the whole world of work—the range of occupations in which human beings earn their livings. This is not particularized job training. It is the very opposite. It aims at a broad understanding of what is involved in working for a living and of the various ways in which that can be done. If, at the end of 12 years, students wish training for specific jobs, they should get that in two-year community or junior colleges, or on the job itself, or in technical institutes of one sort or another.

Everything that has not been specifically mentioned as occupying the time of the school day should be reserved for after-hours and have the status of extracurricular activities.

Please, note: The required course of study just described is as important for what it *displaces* as for what it introduces. It displaces a multitude of elective courses, especially those offered in our secondary schools, most of which make little or no contribution to general, liberal education. It eliminates all narrowly specialized job training, which now abounds in our schools. It throws out of the curriculum and into the category of optional extracurricular activities a variety of things that have little or no educational value.

If it did not call for all these displacements, there would not be enough time in the school day or year to accomplish everything that is essential to the general, liberal learning that must be the content of basic schooling.

The Quintessential Element

So far, I have set forth the bare essentials of the Paideia Proposal with regard to basic schooling. I have not yet mentioned the quintessential element—the *sine qua non*—without which nothing else can possibly come to fruition, no matter how sound it might be in principle. The heart of the matter is the quality of learning and the quality of teaching that occupies the school day, not to mention the quality of the homework after school.

First, the learning must be active. It must use the whole mind, not just the memory. It must be learning by discovery, in which the student, never the teacher, is the primary agent. Learning by discovery, which is the only genuine learning, may be either unaided or aided. It is unaided only for geniuses. For most students, discovery must be aided.

Here is where teachers come in—as aids in the process of learning by discovery not as knowers who attempt to put the knowledge they have into the minds of their students. The quality of the teaching, in short, depends crucially upon how the teacher conceives his role in the process of learning, and that must be as an aid to the student's process of discovery.

I am prepared for the questions that must be agitating you by now: How and where will we get the teachers who can perform as teachers should? How will we be able to staff the program with teachers so trained that they will be competent to provide the quality of instruction required for the quality of learning desired?

The first part of our answer to these questions is negative: We *cannot* get the teachers we need for the Paideia program from schools of education as *they are now constituted*. As teachers are now trained for teaching, they simply will not do. The ideal—an impracticable ideal—would be to ask for teachers who are, themselves, truly educated human beings. But truly educated human beings are too rare. Even if we could draft all who are now alive, there still would be far too few to staff our schools.

Well, then, what can we look for? Look for teachers who are actively engaged in the process of *becoming* educated human beings, who are themselves deeply motivated to develop their own minds. Assuming this is not too much to ask for the present, how should teachers be schooled and trained in the future? First, they should have the same kind of basic schooling that is recommended in the Paideia Proposal. Second, they should have additional schooling, at the college and even the university level, in which the same kind of general, liberal learning is carried on at advanced levels—more deeply, broadly, and intensively than it can be done in the first 12 years of schooling. Third, they must be given something analogous to the clinical experience in the training of physicians. They must engage in practice-teaching under supervision, which is another way of saying that they must be *coached* in the arts of teaching, not just given didactic instruction in educational psychology and in pedagogy. Finally, and most important of all, they must learn how to teach well by being exposed to the performances of those who are masters of the arts involved in teaching.

It is by watching a good teacher at work that they will be able to perceive what is involved in the process of assisting others to learn by discovery. Perceiving it, they must then try to emulate what they observe, and through this process, they slowly will become good teachers themselves.

The Paideia Proposal recognizes the need for three different kinds of institutions at the collegiate level: The two-year community or junior college should offer a wide choice of electives that give students some training in one or another specialized field, mainly those fields of study that have something to do with earning a living. The four-year college also should offer a wide variety of electives, to be chosen by students who aim at the various professional or technical occupations that require advanced study. Those elective majors chosen by students should be accompanied, for all students, by one required minor, in which the kind of general and liberal learning that was begun at the level of basic schooling is continued at a higher level in the four years of college. And we should have still a third type of collegiate institution—a four-year college in which general, liberal learning at a higher level constitutes a required course of study that is to be taken by all students. *It is this third type of college, by the way, that should be attended by all who plan to become teachers in our basic schools.*

At the university level, there should be a continuation of general, liberal learning at a still higher level to accompany intensive specialization in this or that field of science or scholarship, this or that learned profession. Our insistence on the continuation of general, liberal learning at all the higher levels of schooling stems from our concern with the worst cultural disease that is rampant in our society—*the barbarism of specialization.*

There is no question that our technologically advanced industrial society needs specialists of all sorts. There is no question that the advancement of knowledge in all fields of science and scholarship, and in all the learned professions, needs intense specialization. But for the sake of preserving and enhancing our cultural traditions, as well as for the health of science and scholarship, we need specialists who also are generalists—generally cultivated human beings, not just good plumbers. We need truly educated human beings who can perform their special tasks better precisely because they have general cultivation as well as intensely specialized training.

Changes indeed are needed in higher education, but those improvements cannot reasonably be expected unless improvement in basic schooling makes that possible.

The Future of Our Free Institutions

I already have declared as emphatically as I know how that the quality of human life in our society depends on the quality of the schooling we give our young people, both basic and advanced. But a marked elevation in the quality of human life is not the only reason improving the quality of schooling is so necessary—not the only reason we must move heaven and earth to stop the deterioration of our schools and turn them in the opposite direction. The other reason is to safeguard the future of our free institutions.

They cannot prosper, they may not even survive, unless we do something to rescue our schools from their current deplorable deterioration. Democracy, in the full sense of that term, came into existence only in this century and only in a few countries on earth, among which the United States is an outstanding example. But democracy came into existence in this century, only in its initial conditions, all of which hold out promises for the future that remain to be fulfilled. Unless we do something about improving the quality of basic schooling for all and the quality of advanced schooling for some, there is little chance that those promises ever will be fulfilled. And if they are not, our free institutions are doomed to decay and wither away.

We face many insistently urgent problems. Our prosperity and even our survival depend on the solution of those problems—the threat of nuclear war, the exhaustion of essential resources and of supplies of energy, the pollution or spoilage of the environment, the spiraling of inflation accompanied by the spread of unemployment.

To solve these problems, we need resourceful and innovative leadership. For that to arise and be effective, an educated populace is needed. Trained intelligence—not only on the part of leaders, but also on the part of followers— holds the key to the solution of the problems our society faces. Achieving peace, prosperity, and plenty could put us on the threshold of an early paradise. But a much better educational system than now exists also is needed, for that alone can carry us across the threshold. Without it, a poorly schooled population will not be able to put to good use the opportunities afforded by the achievement of the general welfare. Those who are not schooled to enjoy society can only despoil its institutions and corrupt themselves.

John Holt ➡ **NO**

Escape from Childhood

Young people should have the right to control and direct their own learning, that is, to decide what they want to learn, and when, where, how, how much, how fast, and with what help they want to learn it. To be still more specific, I want them to have the right to decide if, when, how much, and by whom they want to be *taught* and the right to decide whether they want to learn in a school and if so which one and for how much of the time.

No human right, except the right to life itself, is more fundamental than this. A person's freedom of learning is part of his freedom of thought, even more basic than his freedom of speech. If we take from someone his right to decide what he will be curious about, we destroy his freedom of thought. We say, in effect, you must think not about what interests and concerns you, but about what interests and concerns *us*.

We might call this the right of curiosity, the right to ask whatever questions are most important to us. As adults, we assume that we have the right to decide what does or does not interest us, what we will look into and what we will leave alone. We take this right for granted, cannot imagine that it might be taken away from us. Indeed, as far as I know, it has never been written into any body of law. Even the writers of our Constitution did not mention it. They thought it was enough to guarantee citizens the freedom of speech and the freedom to spread their ideas as widely as they wished and could. It did not occur to them that even the most tyrannical government would try to control people's minds, what they thought and knew. That idea was to come later, under the benevolent guise of compulsory universal education.

This right to each of us to control our own learning is now in danger. When we put into our laws the highly authoritarian notion that someone should and could decide what all young people were to learn and, beyond that, could do whatever might seem necessary (which now includes dosing them with drugs) to compel them to learn it, we took a long step down a very steep and dangerous path. The requirement that a child go to school, for about six hours a day, 180 days a year, for about ten years, whether or not he learns anything there, whether or not he already knows it or could learn it faster or better somewhere else, is such gross violation of civil liberties that few adults would stand for it. But the child who resists is treated as a criminal. With this requirement we created an industry, an army of people whose whole work was to tell young people what they had to learn and to try to make them learn it.

Some of these people, wanting to exercise even more power over others, to be even more "helpful," or simply because the industry is not growing fast enough to hold all the people who want to get into it, are now beginning to say, "If it is good for children for us to decide what they shall learn and to make them learn it, why wouldn't it be good for everyone? If compulsory education is a good thing, how can there be too much of it? Why should we allow anyone, of any age, to decide that he has had enough of it? Why should we allow older people, any more than young, not to know what we know when their ignorance may have bad consequences for all of us? Why should we not *make* them know what they *ought* to know?"

They are beginning to talk, as one man did on a nationwide TV show, about "womb-to-tomb" schooling. If hours of homework every night are good for the young, why wouldn't they be good for us all—they would keep us away from the TV set and other frivolous pursuits. Some group of experts, somewhere, would be glad to decide what we all ought to know and then every so often check up on us to make sure we knew it—with, of course, appropriate penalties if we did not.

I am very serious in saying that I think this is coming unless we prepare against it and take steps to prevent it. The right I ask for the young is a right that I want to preserve for the rest of us, the right *to decide what goes into our minds*. This is much more than the right to decide whether or when or how much to go to school or what school you want to go to. That right is important, but it is only part of a much larger and more fundamental right, which I might call the right to Learn, as opposed to being Educated, *i.e.*, made to learn what someone else thinks would be good for you. It is not just compulsory schooling but compulsory Education that I oppose and want to do away with.

That children might have the control of their own learning, including the right to decide if, when, how much, and where they wanted to go to school, frightens and angers many people. They ask me, "Are you saying that if the parents wanted the child to go to school, and the child didn't want to go, that he wouldn't have to go? Are you saying that if the parents wanted the child to go to one school, and the child wanted to go to another, that the child would have the right to decide?" Yes, that is what I say. Some people ask, "If school wasn't compulsory, wouldn't many parents take their children out of school to exploit their labors in one way or another?" Such questions are often both snobbish and hypocritical. The questioner assumes and implies (though rarely says) that these bad parents are people poorer and less schooled than he. Also, though he appears to be defending the right of children to go to school, what he really is defending is the right of the state to compel them to go whether they want to or not. What he wants, in short, is that children should be in school, not that they should have any choice about going.

But saying that children should have the right to choose to go or not to go to school does not mean that the ideas and wishes of the parents would have no weight. Unless he is estranged from his parents and rebelling against them, a child cares very much about what they think and want. Most of the time, he doesn't want to anger or worry or disappoint them. Right now, in families where the parents feel that they have some choice about their children's schooling, there is much bargaining about schools. Such parents, when their children are little, often ask them whether they want to go to nursery school or kindergarten. Or they may take them to school for a while to try it out. Or, if they have a choice of schools, they may take them to several to see which they think they will like the best. Later, they care whether the child likes his school. If he does not, they try to do something about it, get him out of it, find a school he will like.

I know some parents who for years had a running bargain with their children. "If on a given day you just can't stand the thought of school, you don't feel well, you are afraid of something that may happen, you have something of your own that you very much want to do—well, you can stay home." Needless to say, the schools, with their supporting experts, fight it with all their might— Don't Give in to Your Child, Make Him Go to School, He's Got to Learn. Some parents, when their own plans make it possible for them to take an interesting trip, take their children with them. They don't ask the schools' permission, they just go. If the child doesn't want to make the trip and would rather stay in school, they work out a way for him to do that. Some parents, when their child is frightened, unhappy, and suffering in school, as many children are, just take him out. Hal Bennett, in his excellent book *No More Public School,* talks about ways to do this.

A friend of mine told me that when her boy was in third grade, he had a bad teacher, bullying, contemptuous, sarcastic, cruel. Many of the class switched to another section, but this eight-year-old, being tough, defiant, and stubborn, hung on. One day—his parents did not learn this until about two years later— having had enough of the teacher's meanness, he just got up from his desk and without saying a word, walked out of the room and went home. But for all his toughness and resiliency of spirit, the experience was hard on him. He grew more timid and quarrelsome, less outgoing and confident. He lost his ordinary good humor. Even his handwriting began to go to pieces—it was much worse in the spring of the school year than in the previous fall. One spring day he sat at breakfast, eating his cereal. After a while he stopped eating and sat silently thinking about the day ahead. His eyes filled up with tears, and two big ones slowly rolled down his cheeks. His mother, who ordinarily stays out of the school life of her children, saw this and knew what it was about. "Listen," she said to him, "we don't have to go on with this. If you've had enough of that teacher, if she's making school so bad for you that you don't want to go any more, I'll be perfectly happy just to pull you right out. We can manage it. Just say the word." He was horrified and indignant. "No!" he said, "I couldn't do that." "Okay," she said, "whatever you want is fine. Just let me know." And so they left it. He had decided that he was going to tough it out, and he did. But I am sure knowing that he had the support of his mother and the chance to give it up if it got too much for him gave him the strength he needed to go on.

To say that children should have the right to control and direct their own learning, to go to school or not as they choose, does not mean that the law would forbid the parents to express an opinion or wish or strong desire on the matter. It only means that if their natural authority is not strong enough the parents can't call in the cops to make the child do what they are not able to persuade him to do. And the law may say that there is no limit to the amount of pressure or coercion the parents can apply to the child to deny him a choice that he has a legal right to make.

When I urge that children should control their learning, there is one argument that people bring up so often that I feel I must anticipate and meet it here. It says that schools are a place where children can for a while be protected against the bad influences of the world outside, particularly from its greed, dishonesty, and commercialism. It says that in school children may have a glimpse of a higher way of life, of people acting from other and better motives than greed and fear. People say, "We know that society is bad enough as it is and that if children go out into the larger world as soon as they wanted, they would be tempted and corrupted just that much sooner."

They seem to believe that schools are better, more honorable places than the world outside—what a friend of mine at Harvard once called "museums of virtue." Or that people in school, both children and adults, act from higher and better motives than people outside. In this they are mistaken. There are, of course, some good schools. But on the whole, far from being the opposite of, or an antidote to, the world outside, with all its envy, fear, greed, and obsessive competitiveness, the schools are very much like it. If anything, they are worse, a terrible, abstract, simplified caricature of it. In the world outside the school, some work, at least, is done honestly and well, for its own sake, not just to get ahead of others; people are not everywhere and always being set in competition against each other; people are not (or not yet) in every minute of their lives subject to the arbitrary, irrevocable orders and judgement of others. But in most schools, a student is every minute doing what others tell him, subject to their judgement, in situations in which he can only win at the expense of other students.

This is a harsh judgement. Let me say again, as I have before, that schools are worse than most of the people in them and that many of these people do many harmful things they would rather not do, and a great many other harmful things that they do not even see as harmful. The whole of school is much worse than the sum of its parts. There are very few people in the U.S. today (or perhaps anywhere, any time) in *any* occupation, who could be trusted with the kind of power that schools give most teachers over their students. Schools seem to me among the most anti-democratic, most authoritarian, most destructive, and most dangerous institutions of modern society. No other institution does more harm or more lasting harm to more people or destroys so much of their curiosity, independence, trust, dignity, and sense of identity and worth. Even quite kindly schools are inhibited and corrupted by the knowledge of children and teachers alike that they are *performing* for the judgement and approval of others—the children for the teachers; the teachers for the parents, supervisors, school board, or the state. No one is ever free from feeling that he is being judged all the time, or soon may be. Even after the best class experiences teachers must ask themselves, "Were we right to do that? Can we prove we were right? Will it get us in trouble?"

What corrupts the school, and makes it so much worse than most of the people in it, or than they would like it to be, is its power—just as their powerlessness corrupts the students. The school is corrupted by the endless anxious demand of the parents to know how their child is doing—meaning is he ahead of the other kids—and their demand that he be kept ahead. Schools do not protect children from the badness of the world outside. They are at least as bad as the world outside, and the harm they do to the children in their power creates much of the badness of the world outside. The sickness of the modern world is in many ways a school-induced sickness. It is in school that most people learn to expect and accept that some expert can always place them in some sort of rank or hierarchy. It is in school that we meet, become used to, and learn to believe in the totally controlled society. We do not learn much science, but we learn to worship "scientists" and to believe that anything we might conceivably need or want can only come, and someday will come, from them. The school is the closest we have yet been able to come to Huxley's *Brave New World*, with its alphas and betas, deltas and epsilons—and now it even has its soma. Everyone, including children, should have the right to say "No!" to it.

POSTSCRIPT

Should the Curriculum Be Standardized for All?

The free/open school movement values small, personalized educational settings in which students engage in activities that have personal meaning. One of the movement's ideological assumptions, emanating from the philosophy of Jean-Jacques Rousseau, is that given a reasonably unrestrictive atmosphere, the learner will pursue avenues of creative and intellectual self-development. This confidence in self-motivation is the cornerstone of Holt's advocacy of freedom for the learner, a position he elaborates upon in his books *Instead of Education* (1988) and *Teach Your Own* (1982). The argument has gained some potency with recent developments in home-based computer-assisted instruction.

Adler's proposal for a unified curricular and methodological approach, released in 1982 by the Institute for Philosophical Research, was fashioned by a group of distinguished scholars and practitioners and has its roots in such earlier works as Arthur Bestor's *Educational Wastelands* (1953), Mortimer Smith's *The Diminished Mind* (1954), and Paul Copperman's *The Literacy Hoax* (1978). The proposal has been widely discussed since its release, and it has been implemented in a number of school systems. See, for example, "Launching Paideia in Chattanooga," by Cynthia M. Gettys and Anne Wheelock, *Educational Leadership* (September 1994) and Terry Roberts and Audrey Trainor, "Performing for Yourself and Others: The Paideia Coached Project," *Phi Delta Kappan* (March 2004).

Holt's plea for freedom from an imposed curriculum has a champion in John Taylor Gatto, New York City and New York State Teacher of the Year. Gatto has produced two provocative books, *Dumbing Us Down: The Hidden Curriculum of Compulsory Schooling* (1992) and *Confederacy of Dunces: The Tyranny of Compulsory Schooling* (1992). Two other works that build upon Holt's basic views are Lewis J. Perelman's *School's Out: The New Technology and the End of Education* (1992) and George Leonard's "Notes: The End of School," *The Atlantic Monthly* (May 1992).

Among recent provocative books and articles dealing with the topic are Susan Ohanian, *Caught in the Middle: Nonstandard Kids and a Killing Curriculum* (2001); John Berlau, "What Happened to the Great Ideas?" *Insight on the News* (August 27, 2001); and Elliott W. Eisner, "The Kind of Schools We Need," *Phi Delta Kappan* (April 2002), which is a balanced and thoughtful presentation of needed alterations. Excellent articles by E. D. Hirsch, Jr., and Alfie Kohn may be found in *Principal Leadership* (March 2003). Also see Terry Roberts and Laura Billings, "Thinking Is Literacy, Literacy Thinking," *Educational Leadership* (February 2008).

ISSUE 3

Should Behaviorism Shape
Educational Practices?

YES: Carson M. Bennett, from "A Skinnerian View of Human Freedom," *The Humanist* (July/August 1990)

NO: Carl R. Rogers, from *Freedom to Learn for the Eighties* (Merrill, 1983)

ISSUE SUMMARY

YES: Professor of educational psychology Carson M. Bennett presents the case for adopting the radical behaviorism of B. F. Skinner to improve the power and efficiency of the process of learning.

NO: Professor of psychology and psychiatry Carl R. Rogers offers the "humanistic" alternative to behaviorism, insisting on the reality of subjective forces in human motivation.

Intimately enmeshed with considerations of aims and purposes and determination of curricular elements are the psychological base that affects the total setting in which learning takes place and the basic means of motivating learners. Historically, the atmosphere of schooling has often been characterized by harsh discipline, regimentation, and restriction. The prison metaphor often used by critics in describing school conditions rings true all too often.

Although calls to make schools pleasant have been sounded frequently, they have seldomly been heeded. Roman rhetorician Marcus Fabius Quintilian (ca. A.D. 35–100) advocated a constructive and enjoyable learning atmosphere. John Amos Comenius in the seventeenth century suggested a gardening metaphor in which learners were given kindly nurturance. Johann Heinrich Pestalozzi established a model school in the nineteenth century that replaced authoritarianism with love and respect.

Yet school as an institution retains the stigma of authoritarian control—attendance is compelled, social and psychological punishment is meted out, and the decision-making freedom of students is limited and often curtailed. These practices lead to rather obvious conclusions: the prevailing belief is either that young people are naturally evil and wild and therefore must be tamed in a restricting environment or that schooling as such is so unpalatable that people must be forced and cajoled to reap its benefits—or both.

Certainly, philosopher John Dewey (1895–1952) was concerned about this circumstance, citing at one time the superintendent of his native Burlington, Vermont, school district as admitting that the schools were a source of "grief and mortification" and were "unworthy of patronage." Dewey rejected both the need for "taming" and the defeatist attitude that the school environment must remain unappealing. He hoped to create a motivational atmosphere that would engage learners in real problem-solving activities, thereby sustaining curiosity, creativity, and attachment. The rewards were to flow from the sense of accomplishment and freedom, which was to be achieved through the disciplined actions necessary to solve the problem at hand.

More recent treatment of the allied issues of freedom, control, and motivation has come from the two major camps in the field of educational psychology: the behaviorists (rooted in the early-twentieth-century theories of Ivan Pavlov, Edward L. Thorndike, and John B. Watson) and the humanists (emanating from the Gestalt and field theory psychologies developed in Europe and America earlier in the twentieth century).

B. F. Skinner has been the dominant force in translating behaviorism into recommendations for school practices. He and his disciples, often referred to as "neobehaviorists," have contributed to widely used innovations such as behavioral objectives in instruction and testing, competency-based education, mastery learning, assertive discipline, and outcome-based education. The humanistic viewpoint has been championed by Carl R. Rogers, Abraham Maslow, Fritz Perls, Rollo May, and Erich Fromm, most of whom ground their psychological theories in the philosophical assumptions of existentialism and phenomenology.

Skinner believes that "inner" states are merely convenient myths, that motives and behaviors are shaped by environmental factors. These shaping forces, however, need not be negative, nor must they operate in an uncontrolled manner. Our present understanding of human behavior allows us the freedom to shape the environmental forces, which in turn shape us. With this power, Skinner contends, we can replace aversive controls in schooling with positive reinforcements that heighten the students' motivation level and make learning more efficient.

Recent manifestations of the continuing interest in Skinner's behaviorism and the humanistic psychology of Rogers include Virginia Richardson's "From Behaviorism to Constructivism in Teacher Education," *Teacher Education and Special Education* (Summer 1996) and Tobin Hart's "From Category to Contact: Epistemology and the Enlivening and Deadening of Spirit in Education," *Journal of Humanistic Education and Development* (September 1997).

In the YES selection, Carson M. Bennett renews Skinner's call for greater attention to the external forces that shape all behavior. In the NO selection, Carl R. Rogers critiques Skinner's behaviorist approach and sets forth his argument supporting the reality of freedom as an inner human state that is the wellspring of responsibility, will, and commitment.

YES ↵

Carson M. Bennett

A Skinnerian View of Human Freedom

Without question, human freedom must be preserved and extended. The question is: what is the nature of this freedom? In his highly controversial (and misunderstood) book, *Beyond Freedom and Dignity,* B.F. Skinner criticized the traditional view of freedom as the ability to make choices which are not controlled by highly aversive stimuli. In his view, the "literature of freedom" has not dealt effectively with techniques that "do not breed escape or revolt but nevertheless have aversive consequences." These "positive" control techniques have traditionally been overlooked because they are less conspicuous. Skinner's discussion of government control provides a good example. We are keenly aware of negative government controls; as Skinner observes, the state "is frequently defined in terms of its power to punish." However, when a positive control technique is used by the state—such as paying farmers to reduce production—it is viewed as an *invitation,* not a *compulsion.* Positive controls are difficult to resist because they frequently masquerade as something else—for example, benefits. But they influence behavior just as effectively (sometimes much more so) as compulsory, negative controls.

Skinner also points out that freedom has mistakenly been defined "in terms of states of mind or feelings." This directs our attention away from the *actions* necessary to counteract subtle positive controls on our behavior. In the behavioral view, freedom is maintained or lost as the result of environmental changes which enlarge or limit the arena of possible actions, not as a result of changes in the hearts and minds of humans.

The traditional view of human freedom is grounded in custom and in the experience of choice. The powerful awareness of our thoughts and feelings at the moment of choice leads us to assume that those thoughts and feelings—rather than environmental influences—are the generators of our actions. Many of these experiences are highly rewarding and give us a feeling of mastery, an integral part of the experience of freedom. Our language is replete with words that describe the mental and emotional states which we are taught to believe generate our actions. Religions which posit a soul as an internal governing agent support this interpretation; psychology substitutes the "ego" or the "self" for the soul. But what we really experience as freedom is the opportunity and ability to behave in ways that produce rewards and avoid punishments, *not* the absence of environmental controls on our behavior.

The traditional view of freedom is hard to defend on logical and empirical grounds. It also decreases our ability to respond effectively to serious social problems because it causes us to look in the wrong place for the causes of behavior—at psychological factors rather than at observable and measurable environmental and genetic influences. This has prevented the development of a science of behavior providing the basis for a set of effective personal and social changes. We have also confused the issue of responsibility by crediting or blaming individuals for behaviors which are the result of past and present environmental influences. The radical behavioral viewpoint developed by B.F. Skinner presents a different view of the control of behavior. It is an effective framework for personal and social change and is compatible with the protection of individual freedoms.

In Skinner's radical behavioral view of freedom, *all* behavior is determined by the interaction of past and present environmental influences. As philosopher Brand Blanshard observes in his essay "The Case for Determinism," we cannot "choose our choice" even though we can choose one *behavior* over another. *Choices* are determined by the interaction of environmental and genetic influences. When we choose a specific behavior over a number of possible alternatives, it is likely that the chosen behavior has been rewarded more often in the past than any of the alternatives. In "avoidance" situations, the chosen behavior has most likely resulted in negative consequences less often than any of the available alternatives.

For example, picture a man walking through a supposedly empty cemetery at midnight. A prankster hiding behind a large headstone lets out an unexpected and unnerving moan. The man bursts into a run, and does not stop until he has sprinted out of the cemetery. An *ABC* behavioral analysis of this situation provides an interesting contrast with an analysis based on the traditional view of human freedom. *A* is the *Antecedent event:* the unexpected and unnerving groan in a supposedly empty cemetery. *B* is the *Behavior:* the man runs away. *C* is the *Consequence:* the man has escaped from a frightening situation. In this *ABC* analysis, thoughts and feelings *accompany* rather than *generate* behavior. They are as much shaped by the environment as the observable behavior is. In reality, the man does not run from the cemetery because he is scared; properly understood, the groan triggers his behavior—the action to avoid an aversive situation by running. (In our terms, escaping the aversive situation is the "reward.") The feelings of panicked fright result from the same environmental influence—the groan—as did the observable behavior (his hasty departure from the cemetery). An important advantage of looking in the environment for the causes of behavior is that unprofitable circular reasoning is avoided. (Why did the man run? Because he was scared. How do we know he was scared? Because he ran.) Of course, internal neurological and psychological factors influence behavior as well and should be taken into account when they are able to be observed and measured.

We feel free in situations in which our behavior is controlled by positive events (rewards) because this gives us a feeling of mastery. We are not as likely to feel free when our behavior is controlled by aversive stimuli. For example, we feel free when we are on vacation, engaging in highly rewarding activities.

We may not feel free when meeting an unpleasant responsibility at work which we regard as an imposition. Our behavior, however, is *equally* under environmental control whether that control is positive or negative. This constant environmental control raises an important question, namely how can behavior be controlled in ethical ways? Control is ethical if it is agreed to by the individual or his or her parent or guardian *and* if it is in the best interest of the individual, *not* just in the interest or convenience of the controlling individual or institution. All relationships involve control and counter-control. "Powerless" groups such as children, the poor, the elderly, minority groups, and mental patients need to be helped to achieve more counter-control.

Why has the traditional view of human freedom persisted? There are many reasons. Most of the words we use in thinking describe the traditional view. The behavioral view seems both to threaten freedom and to contradict common sense. We appear to feel and think first and act second.

A number of factors contribute to this misunderstanding of freedom. It is rewarding to believe that our behavior can be free of any control except our thoughts and feelings. We think we are, as A.E. Henley's poem *Invictus* has it, the masters of our fate and captains of our soul. This is heady stuff! Moreover, when we make a choice, our attention is often directed toward the immediate (short-term) consequences of the act, not toward the past where the choice was shaped or the long-term consequences. For example, when a person buys an expensive sports car that is much more lavish than they really need or can afford, they are usually thinking about the immediate pleasures of owning such a fancy car, not reflecting on the past where their self-indulgent behavior was shaped or the long-term demands of making hefty car payments.

Finally, environmental influences are usually complex and subtle and thus difficult to detect. When we act, we are strongly aware of our thoughts and feelings and thus attribute our behavior to these things.

Skinner's radical behavioral view of freedom has frequently been misinterpreted. It is often confused with John Watson's earlier version of behaviorism, in which the role of consciousness was neglected, genetic influences were minimized, and learning occurred through Pavlovian conditioning. It is also often misunderstood as being inimical to freedom. Many people wonder if Skinner's approach would make a hash of the concept of personal responsibility. It would not. Society could continue to assign personal responsibility when needed. A distinction needs to be made between *personal* and *legal* responsibility. Individuals should be held responsible for illegal activities and accept the consequences. However, the assignment of *legal* responsibility should be tempered by a recognition of the need to help individuals change their environment. Responsibility—defined as the ability to and habit of considering the short- and long-term consequences of one's actions for oneself and others—should be taught both at home and at school.

What kind of social and personal gains would result if we adopted the radical behavioral viewpoint? For one thing, by looking for the determinants of behavior in the environment—where they are amenable to observation and change—we can control behavior more effectively. It seems clear, in retrospect, that many effective programs for social change have unknowingly used a radical behavioral approach. For example, attempts to reduce discriminatory behavior against minority groups by changing people's attitudes have been largely unsuccessful. Significant change occurred with the passage of civil rights legislation on education, housing, and employment. These provided a legislative and judicial system of rewards and punishments with which to control discriminatory behavior. This allowed individuals who *behaved* in nondiscriminatory ways to develop matching attitudes over time. For example, prejudiced students in desegregated schools frequently develop friendships with blacks. As behavior changes, so do the attitudes which *accompany* it.

Efforts to address the substantial underachievement of children in the lower socioeconomic class have been hampered by our tendency to look for the causes of underachievement in some personality defect of the children or their parents. In contrast, successful early childhood compensatory programs such as Head Start focused on specific environmental changes for children (for example, in learning materials and teaching methods), as well as on training parents how to change their home environment to increase achievement.

Many problems of the elderly could be addressed by designing environments which would compensate for their declining physical or intellectual resources. For example, approaches to adult education could be designed to compensate for the decline in old age of the ability to remember recently learned material.

By adopting the radical behavioral viewpoint, we would also avoid the pitfalls attendant upon our unwarranted and unproductive assignments of blame or credit. According to Skinner, "Any evidence that a person's behavior may be attributed to external circumstances seems to threaten his dignity or worth." He notes that the amount of credit a person receives is inversely related to the conspicuousness of the controlling factors. A speaker who is skilled in using a teleprompter may be given credit for extemporizing rather than reading well.

In *What Is B.F. Skinner Really Saying?*, behaviorist Robert D. Nye argues that even if we assume that "individuals are responsible for their behaviors" and thus "assigning blame for objectionable actions is justified, it doesn't consistently work well and it causes ill feelings." He suggests that when someone does something wrong, we should look at what is wrong with the environment, not what is wrong with the person.

The pitfalls of assigning unwarranted blame or credit have been addressed by writers as disparate as George Will and Nicholas von Hoffman. Will, in arguing for taxes as "a social obligation of the honorable," states, "Generally, people prosper, and pay more taxes, because of reasons for which they cannot claim responsibility." Von Hoffman characterizes "will power" as a "hard doctrine" because it leads to such "barbarously harsh" outcomes as sick people blaming themselves for their failure to get better.

Our society is fond of blaming the victim, such as the homeless or the welfare recipient. Society can help such victims by providing supportive environmental changes rather than by exhorting them to display more character or backbone. The assignment of exclusive personal credit or blame is both inappropriate and unproductive. This does not diminish the importance of frequently and consistently rewarding desirable behavior, but rewards should focus on the worth and skill of the *performance* to avoid the credit/blame pitfall.

Finally, by adopting the radical behavioral viewpoint, we would increase the effectiveness of behavioral controls by taking long-term consequences into consideration. Skinner has criticized our society for failing to teach its citizens to respond to the long-term as well as the short-term consequences of their actions. This limits our ability to respond adequately to many personal and social problems, such as poor health practices, environmental pollution, and the overconsumption of nonrenewable energy resources. On a personal level, overeating provides a good example of the failure to consider long-term consequences. The attractions of overeating—the pleasures of taste and the feelings of satiety and relaxation that accompany digestion—are short-term and immediately apparent; the negative consequences—increased potential for high blood pressure and heart attacks, decreased mobility, social and personal disapproval stemming from a less desirable appearance, and so on—are long-term and frequently ignored. There are also examples where the short-term consequences are negative and the long-term consequences are positive. A student will reluctantly forego the pleasures of an active social life and attend to the short-term unpleasant requirements of study in order to achieve the long-term benefits of better grades, a more rewarding education, and a better start on his or her career.

Consider as well the impact of this view on the intimate relationships we have with our close friends and lovers. At the beginning of a romance, we shower the other person with strong rewards for almost every action. Subsequently, we reward less and less often. The other person frequently interprets this as rejection and responds negatively. The honeymoon is over! It should have been recognized from the start that one person cannot provide all the necessary social rewards for another and that individuals will want to maintain more than one relationship. Some people are offended by the notion that friendship can be reduced to the mutual exchange of positive rewards. Many readers reacted negatively to the comment made by behavioral engineer T.E. Frazier in *Walden Two*, Skinner's description of a behavioral utopia: "What is love except another name for the use of positive reinforcement?" But, as Nye has pointed out, relationships can be explained in large part in this manner.

Implementation of the radical behavioral viewpoint could increase our personal and social power and deepen our experience of freedom. It is difficult for many individuals to accept that behavioral determinism and human freedom are not contradictory or mutually exclusive concepts. But, as Nye observes (and as Skinner himself has suggested), Skinner's assumptions do not change what actually exists: "Either we live in a wholly determined system or we do not." If we do, we are still capable of believing that we are free and that our behavior is meaningful. However, we are also capable of changing our environments to improve our behavior and increase our feeling of freedom. Consider the experience of the English scientist Sir Francis Galton, who kept track for some time of the occasions when he felt a sense of personal freedom while making important choices. Shortly afterward, he would look back on each episode to try to find constraints on his behavior which he had not noted at the time. Brand Blanshard reports in "The Case for Determinism" that Galton "found it so easy to bring such constraining factors to light that he surrendered to the determinist view."

Unfortunately, we continue to interpret behavior in terms of internal psychological causation and to be ineffective in personal and social change. As Nye has pointed out, newspaper and magazine editorials and articles are still full of comments such as "the darkness in man's soul that corrupts his best intentions," "the destructive tendencies hidden deep within the human psyche," "the failing American character that is bringing us to the edge of national disaster," "the lack of morality and will power among our citizens," and so on. Analyzing and changing our environments so that positive controls can be maximized and punitive and aversive controls minimized is hard, time-consuming work. It is quicker and easier to blame our behavioral problems on such ineffable or intangible factors as "moral deficiency" and "the darkness in man's soul." Indeed, most people—psychologists, priests, and the general public alike—continue to believe in some inner spark which guides our destiny, whether it is called the "ego," and "soul," or the "self."

Let us celebrate and preserve our freedom! But let us do so by analyzing and changing our environments to produce the kinds of behavior and the kind of society we want, instead of continuing to substitute empty rhetoric about "internal failings" for action.

Carl R. Rogers

NO

Freedom to Learn for the Eighties

One of the deepest issues in modern life, in modern man, is the question as to whether the concept of personal freedom has any meaning whatsoever in our present-day scientific world. The growing ability of the behavioral scientist to predict and to control behavior has brought the issue sharply to the fore. If we accept the logical positivism and strictly behavioristic emphases which are predominant in the American psychological scene, there is not even room for discussion. . . .

But if we step outside the narrowness of the behavioral sciences, this question is not only *an* issue, it is one of the primary issues which define modern man. Friedman in his book (1963, p. 251) makes his topic "the problematic of modern man—the alienation, the divided nature, the unresolved tension between personal freedom and psychological compulsion which follows on 'the death of God'." The issues of personal freedom and personal commitment have become very sharp indeed in a world in which man feels unsupported by a supernatural religion, and experiences keenly the division between his awareness and those elements of his dynamic functioning of which he is unaware. If he is to wrest any meaning from a universe which for all he knows may be indifferent, he must arrive at some stance which he can hold in regard to these timeless uncertainties.

So, writing as both a behavioral scientist and as one profoundly concerned with the human, the personal, the phenomenological and the intangible, I should like to contribute what I can to this continuing dialogue regarding the meaning of and the possibility of freedom.

Man Is Unfree

. . . In the minds of most behavioral scientists, man is not free, nor can he as a free man commit himself to some purpose, since he is controlled by factors outside of himself. Therefore, neither freedom nor commitment is even a possible concept to modern behavioral science as it is usually understood.

To show that I am not exaggerating, let me quote a statement from Dr. B. F. Skinner of Harvard, who is one of the most consistent advocates of a strictly behavioristic psychology. He says,

> The hypothesis that man is not free is essential to the application of scientific method to the study of human behavior. The free inner man

who is held responsible for his behavior is only a prescientific substitute for the kinds of causes which are discovered in the course of scientific analysis. All these alternative causes lie *outside* the individual (1953, p. 477).

This view is shared by many psychologists and others who feel, as does Dr. Skinner, that all the effective causes of behavior lie outside of the individual and that it is only through the external stimulus that behavior takes place. The scientific description of behavior avoids anything that partakes in any way of freedom. For example, Dr. Skinner (1964, pp. 90–91) describes an experiment in which a pigeon was conditioned to turn in a clockwise direction. The behavior of the pigeon was "shaped up" by rewarding any movement that approximated a clockwise turn until, increasingly, the bird was turning round and round in a steady movement. This is what is known as operant conditioning. Students who had watched the demonstration were asked to write an account of what they had seen. Their responses included the following ideas: that the pigeon was conditioned to *expect* reinforcement for the right kind of behavior; that the pigeon *hoped* that something would bring the food back again; that the pigeon *observed* that a certain behavior seemed to produce a particular result; that the pigeon *felt* that food would be given it because of its action; that the bird came to *associate* his action with the clock of the food dispenser. Skinner ridicules these statements because they all go beyond the observed behavior in using such words as *expect, hope, observe, felt,* and *associate.* The whole explanation from his point of view is that the bird was reinforced when it emitted a given kind of behavior; the pigeon walked around until the food container again appeared; a certain behavior produced a given result; food was given to the pigeon when it acted in a given way; the click of the food dispenser was related in time to the bird's action. These statements describe the pigeon's behavior from a scientific point of view.

Skinner goes on to point out that the students were undoubtedly reporting what they would have expected, felt and hoped under similar circumstances. But he then makes the case that there is no more reality to such ideas in the human being than there is in the pigeon, that it is only because such words have been reinforced by the verbal community in which the individual has developed, that such terms are used. He discusses the fact that the verbal community which conditioned them to use such terms saw no more of their behavior than they had seen of the pigeon's. In other words the internal events, if they indeed exist, have no scientific significance.

As to the methods used for changing the behavior of the pigeon, many people besides Dr. Skinner feel that through such positive reinforcement human behavior as well as animal behavior can be "shaped up" and controlled. In his book *Walden Two,* Skinner says,

> Now that we know how positive reinforcement works and how negative doesn't, we can be more deliberate and hence more successful in our cultural design. We can achieve a sort of control under which the controlled, though they are following a code much more scrupulously than was ever the case under the old system, nevertheless *feel free.* They are

doing what they want to do, not what they are forced to do. That's the source of the tremendous power of positive reinforcement—there is no restraint and no revolt. By a careful cultural design we control not the final behavior but the *inclination* to behave—the motives, the desires, the wishes. The curious thing is that in that case *the question of freedom never arises* (1948, p. 218).

. . . I think it is clear from all of this that man is a machine—a complex machine, to be sure, but one which is increasingly subject to scientific control. Whether behavior will be managed through operant conditioning as in *Walden Two* or whether we will be "shaped up" by the unplanned forms of conditioning implied in social pressure, or whether we will be controlled by electrodes in the brain, it seems quite clear that science is making out of man an object and that the purpose of such science is not only understanding and prediction but control. Thus it would seem to be quite clear that there could be no concept so foreign to the facts as that man is free. Man is a machine, man is unfree, man cannot commit himself in any meaningful sense; he is simply controlled by planned or unplanned forces outside of himself.

Man Is Free

I am impressed by the scientific advances illustrated in the examples I have given. I regard them as a great tribute to the ingenuity, insight, and persistence of the individuals making the investigations. They have added enormously to our knowledge. Yet for me they leave something very important unsaid. Let me try to illustrate this, first from my experience in therapy.

I think of a young man classed as schizophrenic with whom I had been working for a long time in a state hospital. He was a very inarticulate man, and during one hour he made a few remarks about individuals who had recently left the hospital; then he remained silent for almost forty minutes. When he got up to go, he mumbled almost under his breath, "If some of *them* can do it, maybe I can too." That was all—not a dramatic statement, not uttered with force and vigor, yet a statement of choice by this young man to work toward his own improvement and eventual release from the hospital. It is not too surprising that about eight months after that statement he was out of the hospital. I believe this experience of responsible choice is one of the deepest aspects of psychotherapy and one of the elements which most solidly underlies personality change.

I think of another young person, this time a young woman graduate student, who was deeply disturbed and on the borderline of a psychotic break. Yet after a number of interviews in which she talked very critically about all of the people who had failed to give her what she needed, she finally concluded: "Well, with that sort of a foundation, it's really up to *me*. I mean it seems to be really apparent to me that I can't depend on someone else to *give* me an education." And then she added very softly: "I'll really have to get it myself." She goes on to explore this experience of important and responsible choice. She finds it a frightening experience, and yet one which gives her a feeling of strength. A force seems to surge up within her which is big and strong, and yet she also feels very much alone and sort of cut off from support. She adds: "I am going to begin to do more things that I know I should do." And she did.

I could add many other examples. One young fellow talking about the way in which his whole life had been distorted and spoiled by his parents finally comes to the conclusion that, "Maybe now that I *see* that, it's up to *me*." . . .

For those of you [who] have seen the film *David and Lisa*—and I hope that you have had that rich experience—I can illustrate exactly what I have been discussing. David, the adolescent schizophrenic, goes into a panic if he is touched by anyone. He feels that "touching kills," and he is deathly afraid of it, and afraid of the closeness in human relationships which touching implies. Yet toward the close of the film he makes a bold and positive choice of the kind I have been describing. He has been trying to be of help to Lisa, the girl who is out of touch with reality. He tries to help at first in an intellectually contemptuous way, then increasingly in a warmer and more personal way. Finally, in a highly dramatic movement, he says to her, "Lisa, take my hand." He *chooses*, with obvious conflict and fear, to leave behind the safety of his untouchableness, and to venture into the world of real human relationships where he is literally and figuratively in *touch* with another. You are an unusual person if the film does not grow a bit misty at this point.

Perhaps a behaviorist could try to account for the reaching out of his hand by saying that it was the result of intermittent reinforcement of partial movements. I find such an explanation both inaccurate and inadequate. It is the *meaning* of the *decision* which is essential to understanding the act.

What I am trying to suggest in all of this is that I would be at a loss to explain the positive change which can occur in psychotherapy if I had to omit the importance of the sense of free and responsible choice on the part of my clients. I believe that this experience of freedom to choose is one of the deepest elements underlying change.

The Meaning of Freedom

Considering the scientific advances which I have mentioned, how can we even speak of freedom? In what sense is a client free? In what sense are any of us free? What possible definition of freedom can there be in the modern world? Let me attempt such a definition.

In the first place, the freedom that I am talking about is essentially an inner thing, something which exists in the living person quite aside from any of the outward choices of alternatives which we so often think of as constituting freedom. I am speaking of the kind of freedom which Viktor Frankl vividly describes in his experience of the concentration camp, when everything—possessions, status, identity—was taken from the prisoners. But even months and years in such an environment showed only "that everything can be taken from a man but one thing: the last of the human freedoms—to choose one's own attitude in any given set of circumstances, to choose one's own way" (1959, p. 65). It is this inner, subjective, existential freedom which

I have observed. It is the realization that "I can live myself, here and now, by my own choice." It is the quality of courage which enables a person to step into the uncertainty of the unknown as he chooses himself. It is the discovery of meaning from within oneself, meaning which comes from listening, sensitively and openly to the complexities of what one is experiencing. It is the burden of being responsible for the self one chooses to be. It is the recognition of a person that he is an emerging process, not a static end product. The individual who is thus deeply and courageously thinking his own thoughts, becoming his own uniqueness, responsibly choosing himself, may be fortunate in having hundreds of objective outer alternatives from which to choose, or he may be unfortunate in having none. But his freedom exists regardless. So we are first of all speaking of something which exists within the individual, something phenomenological rather than external, but nonetheless to be prized.

The second point in defining this experience of freedom is that it exists not as a contradiction of the picture of the psychological universe as a sequence of cause and effect, but as a complement to such a universe. Freedom rightly understood is a fulfillment by the person of the ordered sequence of his life. The free man moves out voluntarily, freely, responsibly, to play his significant part in a world whose determined events move through him and through his spontaneous choice and will.

I see this freedom of which I am speaking, then, as existing in a different *dimension* than the determined sequence of cause and effect. I regard it as a freedom which exists in the subjective person, a freedom which he courageously uses to live his potentialities. The fact that this type of freedom seems completely irreconcilable with the behaviorist's picture of man is something which I will discuss a bit later. . . .

The Emergence of Commitment

I have spoken thus far primarily about freedom. What about commitment? Certainly the disease of our age is lack of purpose, lack of meaning, lack of commitment on the part of individuals. Is there anything which I can say in regard to this?

It is clear to me that in therapy, as indicated in the examples that I have given, commitment to purpose and to meaning in life is one of the significant elements of change. It is only when the person decides, "I am someone; I am someone worth being: I am committed to being myself," that change becomes possible.

At a very interesting symposium at Rice University recently, Dr. Sigmund Koch sketched the revolution which is taking place in science, literature and the arts, in which a sense of commitment is again becoming evident after a long period in which that emphasis has been absent.

Part of what he meant by that may be illustrated by talking about Dr. Michael Polanyi, the philosopher of science, formerly a physicist, who has been presenting his notions about what science basically is. In his book, *Personal Knowledge*, Polanyi makes it clear that even scientific knowledge is personal knowledge, committed knowledge. We cannot rest comfortably on the belief that scientific knowledge is impersonal and "out there," that it has nothing to do with the individual who has discovered it. Instead, every aspect of science is pervaded by disciplined personal commitment, and Polanyi makes the case very persuasively that the whole attempt to divorce science from the person is a completely unrealistic one. I think I am stating his belief correctly when I say that in his judgment logical positivism and all the current structure of science cannot save us from the fact that all knowing is uncertain, involves risk, and is grasped and comprehended only through the deep, personal commitment of a disciplined search.

Perhaps a brief quotation will give something of the flavor of his thinking. Speaking of great scientists, he says:

> So we see that both Kepler and Einstein approached nature with intellectual passions and with beliefs inherent in these passions, which led them to their triumphs and misguided them to their errors. These passions and beliefs were theirs, personally, even universally. I believe that they were competent to follow these impulses, even though they risked being misled by them. And again, what I accept of their work today, I accept personally, guided by passions and beliefs similar to theirs, holding in my turn that my impulses are valid, universally, even though I must admit the possibility that they may be mistaken (1959, p. 145).

Thus we see that a modern philosopher of science believes that deep personal commitment is the only possible basis on which science can firmly stand. This is a far cry indeed from the logical positivism of twenty or thirty years ago, which placed knowledge far out in impersonal space.

Let me say a bit more about what I mean by commitment in the psychological sense. I think it is easy to give this word a much too shallow meaning, indicating that the individual has, simply by conscious choice, committed himself to one course of action or another. I think the meaning goes far deeper than that. Commitment is a total organismic direction involving not only the conscious mind but the whole direction of the organism as well.

In my judgment, commitment is something that one *discovers* within oneself. It is a trust of one's total reaction rather than of one's mind only. It has much to do with creativity. Einstein's explanation of how he moved toward his formulation of relativity without any clear knowledge of his goal is an excellent example of what I mean by the sense of commitment based on a total organismic reaction. He says:

> During all those years there was a feeling of direction, of going straight toward something concrete. It is, of course, very hard to express that feeling in words but it was decidedly the case and clearly to be distinguished from later considerations about the rational form of the solution (quoted in Wertheimer, 1945, pp. 183–184).

Thus commitment is more than a decision. It is the functioning of an individual who is searching for the directions which are emerging within himself. Kierkegaard has said, "The truth exists only in the process of becoming, in the process of appropriation" (1941, p. 72). It is this individual creation of a tentative personal truth through action which is the essence of commitment.

Man is most successful in such a commitment when he is functioning as an integrated, whole, unified individual. The more that he is functioning in this total manner the more confidence he has in the directions which he unconsciously chooses. He feels a trust in his experiencing, of which, even if he is fortunate, he has only partial glimpses in his awareness.

Thought of in the sense in which I am describing it, it is clear that commitment is an achievement. It is the kind of purposeful and meaningful direction which is only gradually achieved by the individual who has come increasingly to live closely in relationship with his own experiencing—a relationship in which his unconscious tendencies are as much respected as are his conscious choices. This is the kind of commitment toward which I believe individuals can move. It is an important aspect of living in a fully functioning way.

The Irreconcilable Contradiction

I trust it will be very clear that I have given two sharply divergent and irreconcilably contradictory points of view. On the one hand, modern psychological science and many other forces in modern life as well, hold the view that man is unfree, that he is controlled, that words such as purpose, choice, commitment have no significant meaning, that man is nothing but an object which we can more fully understand and more fully control. Enormous strides have been and are being made in implementing this perspective. It would seem heretical indeed to question this view.

Yet, as Polanyi has pointed out in another of his writings (1957), the dogmas of science can be in error. He says:

> In the days when an idea could be silenced by showing that it was contrary to religion, theology was the greatest single source of fallacies. Today, when any human thought can be discredited by branding it as unscientific, the power previously exercised by theology has passed over to science; hence science has become in its turn the greatest single source of error.

So I am emboldened to say that over against this view of man as unfree, as an object, is the evidence from therapy, from subjective living, and from objective research as well, that personal freedom and responsibility have a crucial significance, that one cannot live a complete life without such personal freedom and responsibility, and that self-understanding and responsible choice make a sharp and measurable difference in the behavior of the individual. In this context, commitment does have meaning. Commitment is the emerging and changing total direction of the individual, based on a close and acceptant relationship between the person and all of the trends in his life, conscious and unconscious. Unless, as individuals and as a society, we can make constructive use of this capacity for freedom and commitment, mankind, it seems to me, is set on a collision course with fate. . . .

A part of modern living is to face the paradox that, viewed from one perspective, man is a complex machine. We are every day moving toward a more precise understanding and a more precise control of this objective mechanism which we call man. On the other hand, in another significant dimension of his existence, man is subjectively free; his personal choice and responsibility account for the shape of his life; he is in fact the architect of himself. A truly crucial part of his existence is the discovery of his own meaningful commitment to life with all of his being.

POSTSCRIPT

Should Behaviorism Shape Educational Practices?

The freedom-determinism or freedom-control argument has raged in philosophical, political, and psychological circles down through the ages. Is freedom of choice and action a central, perhaps *the* central, characteristic of being human? Or is freedom only an illusion, a refusal to acknowledge the external shaping of all human actions?

Moving the debate into the field of education, John Dewey depicted a developmental freedom that is acquired through improving one's ability to cope with problems. A. S. Neill (*Summerhill: A Radical Approach to Child Rearing*, 1984), who advanced the ideas of early-twentieth-century progressive educators and the establishment of free schools, sees a more natural inborn freedom in human beings, which must be protected and allowed to flourish. Skinner refuses to recognize this "inner autonomous man" but sees freedom resulting from the scientific reshaping of the environment that influences us.

Just as Skinner has struggled to remove the stigma from the word *control*, arguing that it is the true gateway to freedom, John Holt, in *Freedom and Beyond* (1972), contends that freedom and free activities are not "unstructured"—indeed, that the structure of an open classroom is vastly more complicated than the structure of a traditional classroom.

If both of these views have validity, then we are in a position, as Dewey counselled, to go beyond either-or polemics on these matters and build a more constructive educational atmosphere. Jerome S. Bruner has consistently suggested ways in which free inquiry and subject matter structure can be effectively blended. Arthur W. Combs, in a report titled *Humanistic Education: Objectives and Assessment* (1978), helped to bridge the ideological gap between humanists and behaviorists by demonstrating that subjective outcomes can be assessed by direct or modified behavioral techniques.

Skinner's death in 1990 prompted a number of evaluations, among them "Skinner's Stimulus: The Legacy of Behaviorism's Grand Designer," by Jeff Meade, *Teacher* (November/December 1990); and "The Life and Contributions of Burrhus Frederic Skinner," by Robert P. Hawkins, *Education and Treatment of Children* (August 1990). Recently, neuroscience has come forward. See, for instance, "Brain-Compatible Learning: Fad or Foundation?" *The School Administrator* (December 2006) by Patricia Wolfe; "Which Brain Research Can Educators Trust?" *Phi Delta Kappan* (May 2007) by Judy Willis, M.D., and "A Fresh Look at Brain-Based Education," *Phi Delta Kappan* (February 2008), by Eric P. Jensen.

ISSUE 4

Is Constructivism the Best Philosophy of Education?

YES: David Elkind, from "The Problem with Constructivism," *The Educational Forum* (Summer 2004)

NO: Jamin Carson, from "Objectivism and Education: A Response to David Elkind's 'The Problem with Constructivism'," *The Educational Forum* (Spring 2005)

ISSUE SUMMARY

YES: Child development professor David Elkind contends that the philosophical positions found in constructivism, though often difficult to apply, are necessary elements in a meaningful reform of educational practices.

NO: Jamin Carson, an assistant professor of education and former high school teacher, offers a close critique of constructivism and argues that the philosophy of objectivism is a more realistic and usable basis for the process of education.

For years the term *constructivism* appeared only in journals read primarily by philosophers, epistemologists, and psychologists. Nowadays, *constructivism* regularly appears in the teacher's manuals of textbook series, state education department curriculum frameworks, education reform literature, and education journals. Constructivism now has a face and a name in education. So say educators Martin G. Brooks and Jacqueline Grennon Brooks in "The Courage to Be Constructivist," *Educational Leadership* (November 1999). According to them, the heart of the constructivist approach to education is that learners control their learning. This being the case, the philosophical orientation provided by John Dewey, John Holt, and Carl R. Rogers here in Part 1 would seem to feed into the development of David Elkind's ideas on this educational theory. The contrary positions taken by Hutchins, Adler, and Skinner would seem to contribute to the objectivist philosophy espoused by Jamin Carson.

Constructivism, which is additionally influenced by the theories of Jean Piaget, Lev Vygotsky, and Jerome Bruner, is an approach to learning in which students construct new understandings through active engagement with their past and present experiences. Constructivists contend that traditional instructional models emphasize knowledge transmission without producing deeper levels of understanding and internalization.

Objectivists and other critics of constructivism say that this approach to learning is imprecise, overly permissive, and lacking in rigor. This argument is quite well illustrated in a *Phi Delta Kappan* exchange between Lawrence A. Baines and Gregory Stanley on one hand and Lynn Chrenka on the other (Baines and Stanley, "We Want to See the Teacher: Constructivism and the Rage Against Expertise," in the December 2000 issue and Chrenka, "Misconstructing Constructivism," in the May 2001 issue). Baines and Stanley condemn the constructivists' adamant stand against direct instruction by lecturing and the sin of memorization. Chrenka replies that expertise is central in a constructivist classroom in which the teacher must develop "scaffolding strategies" needed for the learners to begin to construct their own meanings.

David N. Perkins of the Harvard Graduate School of Education, in "The Many Faces of Constructivism," *Educational Leadership* (November 1999), describes a tension between ideological constructivism and pragmatic constructionism, the former being seen as a rather rigid cure-all for traditional school ills and the latter as a flexible, circumstance-driven means of school improvement. While the constructivists' goal of producing active, collaborative, creative learners is certainly an antidote to the often prevalent emphasis on knowledge absorption by passive learners, the techniques for moving toward that goal are often difficult to implement and most always require more time than traditional methods.

These "theory-into-practice" difficulties have been elaborated upon by Mark Windschitl in "The Challenges of Sustaining a Constructivist Classroom Culture," *Phi Delta Kappan* (June 1999), and by Peter W. Airasian and Mary E. Walsh in "Constructivist Cautions," *Phi Delta Kappan* (February 1997). Windschitl sees constructivism as a culture, not a mere collection of practices, so its effectiveness as a guiding philosophy is realized only through major changes in curriculum, scheduling, and assessment. Airasian and Walsh insist that the "catch phrases" that flow from theorists to teachers are inadequate for dealing with implementation complexities.

These and similar concerns are addressed in the first of the following articles, in which constructivism advocate David Elkind examines three major barriers—societal, curricular, and pedagogical—that must be removed if the philosophy is to flourish in school settings. In the second article, Jamin Carson, an objectivist, attacks not only the practical aspects of constructivism's implementation but the very basic principles on which it is based.

YES ↵

David Elkind

The Problem with Constructivism

Constructivism, in all of its various incarnations, is now a major educational philosophy and pedagogy. What the various interpretations of constructivism have in common is the proposition that the child is an active participant in constructing reality and not just a passive recorder of it. Constructivism thus echoes the philosophy implicit in Rousseau's *Emile* (1962) in which he argued that children have their own ways of knowing and that these have to be valued and respected. It also reflects the Kantian (Kant 2002) resolution of the nature/nurture controversy. Kant argued that the mind provides the categories of knowing, while experience provides the content. Piaget (1950) created the contemporary version of constructivism by demonstrating that the categories of knowing, no less than the contents of knowledge, are constructed in the course of development. Vygotsky (1978) added the importance of social context to the constructivist epistemology—a theory of knowledge and knowledge acquisition.

Constructivism in education has been approached at many different levels and from a variety of perspectives (e.g., Larochelle, Bednarz, and Garrison 1998). In this essay, I will limit the discussion to those writers who have attempted to translate constructivism into a practical pedagogy (e.g., Brooks and Brooks 1993; Fosnot 1996; Gagnon and Collay 2001; Lambert et al. 1997). Though many different models have been created and put to test, none have been satisfactorily implemented. The failure of the constructivist reform movement is yet another in the long list of ill-fated educational reform movements (Gibboney 1994).

The inability to implement constructivist reforms is particularly instructive with regard to the failures of educational reforms in general. Constructivist reforms start from an epistemology. This sets constructivism apart from those educational reforms inspired by political events (such as the curriculum reform movement spurred by the Russian launching of the Sputnik) or by social events (such as the school reforms initiated by the Civil Rights Movement) or by a political agenda (e.g., *A Nation at Risk* [National Commission on Excellence in Education 1983]; the No Child Left Behind initiative). That is to say, the constructivist movement is generated by genuine pedagogical concerns and motivations.

The lack of success in implementing this widely accepted educational epistemology into the schools can be attributed to what might be called *failures of readiness*. Consider three types of readiness: teacher readiness, curricular

From *The Educational Forum*, vol. 68, Summer 2004, pp. 306–312. Copyright © 2004 by Kappa Delta Pi. Reprinted by permission.

readiness, and societal readiness. Teacher readiness requires teachers who are child development specialists with curricular and instructional expertise. Curriculum readiness requires courses of study that have been researched as to what, when, and how the subject matter should be taught. Societal readiness requires a nation that is willing—indeed eager—to accept educational change. For a reform movement to succeed, all three forms of readiness must be in alignment.

Teacher Readiness

Those who have tried to implement a constructivist pedagogy often argue that their efforts are blocked by unsupportive teachers. They claim that some teachers are wedded to an objectivist view that knowledge has an independent existence and needs only to be transmitted. Others have difficulty understanding how to integrate the learner's intuitive conceptions into the learning process. Still others are good at getting children actively involved in projects but are not able to translate them effectively into learning objectives. These problems are aggravated by an increasingly test-driven curriculum with little opportunity for creativity and innovation.

The problem, however, is not primarily with teachers but with teacher training. In the United States, many universities and colleges have done away with the undergraduate major in education. In Massachusetts, for example, a student with a bachelor's degree in any field can get a provisional certification after a year of supervised internship. After five years and the attainment of a master's degree, the candidate is eligible for permanent certification.

The demise of the undergraduate major in education can be attributed to a number of different factors that were enunciated in *Tomorrow's Schools of Education* (Holmes Group 1995) written by the deans of 80 of some of the nation's most prestigious schools of education. The report (1995, 45–46) targeted the education faculty who "ignore public schools to concentrate on theoretical research or to work with graduate students who do not intend careers as classroom teachers." In effect, the education faculty has failed to provide the kind of research that would be useful to teachers. As the report (1995, 45–46) argued, "Traditional forms of academic scholarship have a place in professional schools, but such institutions are obliged as well to learn from practice and to concern themselves with questions of applying knowledge." These observations are supported by the facts. Few teachers read the educational research journals, and few educational researchers read the journals directed at teachers such as *Educational Leadership* and *Young Children*. This also is true for researchers in the field of child development. Much of the research on children's cognitive, social, and emotional development is directly relevant to teaching. Yet, the educational implications of these studies are rarely, if ever, discussed in the literature.

The end result is that much of teaching as a profession has to be learned in the field. While this is true for all professions to a certain extent, it is particularly true of education. Indeed, one could make the case that teaching is, as yet, more art than profession. Professional training implies a body of knowledge and skills that are unique and that can be acquired only through a prescribed course of study. It is not clear that such a body of knowledge and skills exists for education. In fact, each educational reform movement challenges the practices currently in play. Perhaps it is because there is no agreed upon body of knowledge and skills that reform in education is so frequent and so unsuccessful. To be sure, all professions have disagreements but they all share some fundamental common ground, whether it is anatomy in medicine or legal precedence in the field of law. There is, however, no such common base in education.

Teaching will become a true profession only when we have a genuine science of education. Such a science will have to be multidisciplinary and include workers from traditional educational psychology, developmental psychology, sociology, and various subject matter disciplines. Researchers would investigate individual and group differences in learning styles in relation to the acquisition of the various tool subjects (i.e., reading, writing, arithmetic, science, and social studies) at different age levels. Teacher training would provide not only a solid grounding in child development but also would require domain specific knowledge as it applies to young people at different age levels. Teachers also would be knowledgeable about research and would have access to journals that serve both teachers and investigators.

The failure to treat education as a profession has a long history but was made patent by Flexner's (1910) report *Medical Education in the United States and Canada.* That report was critical of medical education in the United States and suggested that training in medicine should be a graduate program with an undergraduate major. It also argued for the establishment of teaching hospitals as a means of practical training under supervision. Though the report was mandated by the Carnegie Foundation for the Advancement of Teaching, no comparable critique and suggestions were made for teachers and teacher training. The only innovation taken from this report was the founding of lab schools which would serve the same function as teaching hospitals at various universities. These schools, however, were more often used for research than for training. Today, only a few lab schools remain in operation.

Before any serious, effective reform in education can be introduced, we must first reinvent teacher training. At the very least, teachers should be trained as child development specialists. But teachers need much more. Particularly today, with the technological revolution in our schools, teacher training should be a graduate program. Even with that, teaching will not become a true profession unless and until we have a true science of education (Elkind 1999).

Curricular Readiness

A constructivist approach to education presupposes a thorough understanding of the curriculum to be taught. Piaget understood this very well. Much of his research was aimed at shedding light on what might be called the *logical substructure* of the discipline. That is to say, to match the subject matter to the child's level of developing mental abilities, you have to understand the logical demands it makes upon the child's reasoning powers. In his research with

Inhelder (1964), Piaget demonstrated that for a child to engage in the addition and multiplication of classes, relations, and numbers, children first need to attain concrete operations. Similarly, Inhelder and Piaget (1958) showed that true experimental thinking and dealing with multiple variables require the formal mental operations not attained until adolescence. Task analysis of this sort is required in all curricular domains. Only when we successfully match children's ability levels with the demands of the task can we expect them to reconstruct the knowledge we would like them to acquire.

In addition to knowing the logical substructure of the task, we also need research regarding the timing of the introduction of various subject matters. For example, the planets often are taught at second grade. We know that children of seven or eight do not yet have a firm grasp of celestial space and time. Does teaching the planets at grade two give the child an advantage when studying astronomy at the college level? Similar questions might be asked about introducing the explorers as a social study topic in the early elementary grades. I am not arguing against the teaching of such material; I am contending that we need to know whether this is time well spent. We have little or no research on these issues.

Another type of curriculum information has to do with the sequence of topics within any particular course of study. In elementary math, is it more effective to teach coins before or after we teach units of distance and weight? Some sequences of concepts are more effective for learning than others. In most cases, we don't have data upon which to make that kind of decision. In most public school textbooks, the order of topical instruction is determined more by tradition, or by the competition, than by research. We find this practice even at the college level. Most introductory courses begin with a chapter on the history of the discipline. Yet many students might become more engaged in the subject if the first topic was one to which they could immediately relate. Again, we have little or no research on such matters. This is true for teaching in an integrated or linear curriculum format.

The argument that there is little connection between academic research and practical applications has many exceptions. Nonetheless, as long as these remain exceptions rather than the rule, we will not move toward a true science of education.

Societal Readiness

If the majority of teachers are not ready to adopt a constructivist pedagogy, neither are educational policy makers and the larger society. To be successfully implemented, any reform pedagogy must reflect a broad and energized social consensus. John Dewey was able to get broad backing for his Progressive Education Reform thanks to World War I and the negative reaction to all things European. Up until the First World War, our educational system followed the European classical model. It was based on the doctrine of formal discipline whereby training in Greek and Latin, as well as the classics, rigorously trained the mind. In contrast, Dewey (1899) offered a uniquely American functional pedagogy. He wanted to prepare students for the demands and occupations of everyday life. There was general consensus that this was the way to go.

The launching of the Russian Sputnik in 1957 was another event that energized the nation to demand curriculum reform. Russia, it seemed, had outstripped us scientifically, and this reflected badly on our math and science education. The National Science Foundation embarked on a program of science and math curriculum reform. To this end, the foundation recruited leading figures in the fields of science and math to construct new, up-to-date curricula in these fields. These scholars knew their discipline but, for the most part, they did not know children. The new curricula, which included variable-base arithmetic and teaching the principles of the discipline, were inappropriate for children. When these curricula failed, a new consensus emerged to advocate the need to go "back to basics." The resulting teacher-made curricula dominated education prior to the entrance of the academicians. While "back to basics" was touted as a "get tough" movement, it was actually a "get easier" movement because it reintroduced more age-appropriate material.

Many of the educational reforms of any category have not had much success since that time. Though *A Nation at Risk* (NCEE 1983) created a number of reforms, the report itself did not energize the nation, and there was not sufficient motivation to bring about real change. In large part, I believe that this was because there was no national consciousness of a felt need for change. The current educational movement, No Child Left Behind, was introduced for political rather than pedagogical reasons. This legislation was avowedly for the purpose of improving student achievement and changing the culture of American schools. These aims are to be achieved by requiring the states to test all children every year from grades three through eight. Schools that do not meet statewide or national standards may be closed or parents given an opportunity to send their children to other schools.

This is an ill-conceived program based on a business model that regards education as akin to a factory turning out products. Obviously, children are not containers to be filled up to a certain amount at each grade level. The program forces schools to focus on tests to the exclusion of what is really important in the educational process. Testing is expensive and depletes already scarce educational resources. Students are being coached to do well on the tests without regard to their true knowledge and understanding. The policy is corrupt in that it encourages schools to cheat. The negative results of this policy already are being felt. A number of states are choosing to opt out of the program. The No Child Left Behind legislation is a good example of bad policy promoted for political gain that is not in the best interests of children.

Other than a national crisis, there is another way for social consensus to bring about educational reform. In Kuhn's (1996) innovative book on scientific revolutions, he made the point that such revolutions do not come about by the gradual accretion of knowledge. Rather they come about as a result of conflicts between opposing points of view with one eventually winning out over the other. Evolution, for example, is still fighting a rearguard action against those who believe in the biblical account of the origin of man. In education, the long-running battle between nature and nurture (read development and learning) is not likely to be resolved soon by a higher order synthesis.

An alternative view was offered by Galison (1997), who argued that the history of science is one of tools rather than ideas. He used the history of particle physics as an example. The tools of particle physics are optical-like cloud chambers and electronic-like photographic emulsions that display particle interactions by way of images. One could make equal claims for the history of biology and astronomy. As both Kuhn and Galison acknowledged, scientific progress can come about by conflict or the introduction of new technologies.

Education seems likely to be changed by new tools rather than conflicting ideas. Computers are changing education's successive phases. In the first phase, computers simply replaced typewriters and calculators. In the second phase, computers began to change the ways in which we teach. The widespread use of e-mail, Blackboard, PowerPoint, and simulations are examples. And there is an active and growing field of computer education with its own journals and conferences (e.g., Advancement of Computer Education and Association for the Advancement of Computing in Education). The third phase already has begun, and we are now seeing changes in math and science curricula as a direct result of the availability of technology. Education is one of the last social institutions to be changed by technology, but its time has come.

Conclusion

In this paper, I have used the failure of the constructivist reform movement to illustrate what I believe is necessary for any true educational innovation to succeed. There must be teacher, curricular, and societal readiness for any educational innovation to be accepted and put into practice. In the past, reforms were generated by one or the other form of readiness, but without the support of the others. I believe that technology will change this. It is my sense that it will move us toward making teaching a true profession, the establishment of a multidisciplinary science of education, and a society ready and eager to embrace a technologically based education.

Education is, however, more than technology. It is, at its heart, people dealing with people. That is why any successful educational reform must build upon a human philosophy that makes clear its aims and objectives. Technology without a philosophy of education is mechanical, and a philosophy without an appropriate technology will be ineffective. Technology is forcing educational reform, but we need to harness it to the best philosophy of education we have available. I believe this to be constructivism. The current failure to implement constructivism is not because of its merits but because of a lack of readiness for it. We need to make every effort to ensure that the technological revolution in education creates the kinds of teachers, curricula, and social climate that will make constructivism a reality in our classrooms.

References

Brooks, J. G., and M. G. Brooks. 1993. *In search of understanding: The case for constructivist classrooms.* Alexandria, Va.: Association for Supervision and Curriculum Development.

Dewey, J. 1899. *The school and society.* Chicago: University of Chicago Press.

Elkind, D. 1999. Educational research and the science of education. *Educational Psychology* 11(3): 171–87.

Flexner, A. 1910. *Medical education in the United States and Canada.* New York: Carnegie Foundation for the Advancement of Teaching.

Fosnot, C. T. 1996. *Constructivism: Theory, perspectives, and practice.* New York: Teachers College Press.

Gagnon, G. W. J., and M. Collay. 2001. *Designing for learning: Six elements in constructivist classrooms.* Thousand Oaks, Calif.: Corwin Press.

Galison, P. L. 1997. *Image and logic: A material culture of microphysics.* Chicago: University of Chicago Press.

Gibboney, R. A. 1994. *The stone trumpet: A story of practical school reform.* Albany, N.Y.: State University of New York Press.

Holmes Group. 1995. *Tomorrow's schools of education.* Ann Arbor: University of Michigan.

Inhelder, B., and J. Piaget. 1958. *The growth of logical thinking from childhood to adolescence: An essay on the construction of formal operational structures,* trans. A. Parsons and S. Milgram. New York: Basic Books.

Inhelder, B., and J. Piaget. 1964. *The early growth of logic in the child, classification and seriation,* trans. E. A. Lunzer and D. Papert. New York: Harper and Row.

Kant, I. 2002. *Immanuel Kant: Theoretical philosophy after 1781,* trans. G. Hatfield and M. Friedman. New York: Cambridge University Press.

Kuhn, T. S. 1996. *The structure of scientific revolutions,* 3rd ed. Chicago: University of Chicago Press.

Lambert, L., M. Collay, M. Dietz, K. Kent, and A. E. Richert. 1997. *Who will save our schools? Teachers as constructivist leaders.* Thousand Oaks, Calif.: Corwin Press.

Larochelle, M., N. Bednarz, and J. Garrison. 1998. *Constructivism and education.* Cambridge, England: Cambridge University Press.

National Commission on Excellence in Education. 1983. *A nation at risk: The imperative for educational reform.* Washington, D.C.: U.S. Government Printing Office.

Piaget, J. 1950. *The psychology of intelligence,* trans. M. Piercy and D. E. Berlyne. London: Routledge and Paul.

Rousseau, J. J. 1962. *Emile,* trans. W. Boyd. New York: Teachers College Press.

Vygotsky, L. S. 1978. *Mind in society: The development of higher psychological processes,* ed. M. Cole. Cambridge, Mass.: Harvard University Press.

Objectivism and Education: A Response to David Elkind's 'The Problem with Constructivism'

In "The Problem with Constructivism," David Elkind (2004) made several claims about why constructivism has not been implemented in schools. He argued that constructivism will be implemented only when we have *teacher, curricular*, and *societal readiness*; that teaching needs to become a science before it can be a true profession; and that constructivism is the only philosophy that will reform education. In this essay, I present counterarguments for each of these claims.

Constructivism is the theory that students learn by individually or socially transforming information (Slavin 1997). This theory necessarily entails certain metaphysical and epistemological assumptions. To accept constructivism, one must believe that:

- reality is dependent upon the perceiver, and thus constructed;
- reason or logic is not the only means of understanding reality, but one of many; and
- knowledge or truth is subjective and relative to the individual or community.

One philosophy of education that challenges this theory is objectivism, which asserts that students must be engaged actively in the subject matter to learn. This theory does not advocate, however, that students "transform" or "construct" reality, reason, knowledge, or truth. Objectivism holds that one reality exists independent of anyone perceiving it, humankind is capable of knowing this reality only by the faculty of reason, and objective knowledge and truth is possible (Peikoff 1993). I argue against Elkind's claims primarily from an objectivist viewpoint.

Failures of Readiness

Elkind's main thesis was that constructivism has not been implemented in schools because of failures of teacher, curricular, and societal readiness. Teacher readiness requires that a teacher be educated in a science of education such as child development. Curricular readiness involves knowing exactly when and

From *The Educational Forum*, vol. 69, Spring 2005, pp. 232–238. Copyright © 2005 by Kappa Delta Pi. Reprinted by permission.

how students are developmentally ready to learn specific information. Societal readiness is when society is eager for educational reform or change.

Elkind did not explain the causal relationship between these states of readiness and the implementation of constructivism. He only implied that a causal relationship exists. There is no reason to believe that a relationship exists or that any state of readiness would lead to a specific philosophy of education. A teacher must accept the metaphysical and epistemological assumptions of a pedagogic practice before he or she can implement it.

Elkind's definitions of readiness also were problematic. When defining teacher readiness as having good teacher "training"—which comes only from scientific knowledge (e.g., child development)—he stated (2004, 308), "Teaching will become a true profession only when we have a genuine science of education." Though education is not a true science, teachers generally are taught one unique body of knowledge. Most college and university teacher preparation programs, alternative certification programs, and professional development seminars teach the same information, and a great deal of it is constructivist in nature or a variant of it.

Elkind's definition of curricular readiness also has problems. He (2004, 307–08) defined curricular readiness as knowledge of "what, when, and how the subject matter should be taught" and then claimed that "only when we successfully match children's ability levels with the demands of the task can we expect them to reconstruct the knowledge we would like them to acquire." The phrase "we would like them to acquire" contradicts constructivist metaphysics and epistemology. If constructivism assumes that students construct their own knowledge, then how can a constructivist teacher choose the knowledge they would like students to acquire? The phrase "we would like them to acquire" presupposes an objective philosophy which holds that given a specific context, some knowledge is objectively superior to other knowledge. For a constructivist, this is a contradiction, if one views reality, reason, knowledge, and truth as subjective and relative to the perceiver, then what is the basis for arguing for any knowledge at all, let alone one over another? Any curricular choice, according to constructivist philosophy, should be as valid as any other. When constructivists make absolute claims about what, when, and how something should be taught, they are either objectivists or making arbitrary claims.

Finally, there are problems with societal readiness. Elkind (2004, 310) suggested that "to be successfully implemented, any reform pedagogy must reflect a broad and energized social consensus," which the United States currently does not have. Yet, a broad and energized social consensus in the United States does exist. The concencus is that public education has not adequately educated its students, particularly those of lower socioeconomic status. This societal readiness has paved the way for programs like No Child Left Behind. Progressive reform pedagogies like constructivism are usually prescribed by administrators to improve education or raise test scores. Despite the social consensus that education needs reform pedagogy and constructivism has been one of those pedagogies, education still has not closed the gap between rich and poor—assuming that is education's aim in the first place.

Science of Education

Most teachers receive the same education, but not all teachers readily accept what they are taught, whether it be constructivism or some other philosophy of education. Unlike medical practitioners, for example, educators disagree about nearly all issues within their field. Medical practitioners simply observe whether or not the treatment cured the patient. They may disagree about why or how a treatment worked, but at least they have objective and verifiable evidence of whether or not the treatment worked. Education, on the other hand, possesses many more points of disagreement. How do people learn? What should people learn? How do we measure learning? The complexity of these questions results in virtually no consensus about what works among all educators. Though education draws from a unique body of knowledge to prepare its teachers, it is not scientific and probably never will be because there is so much disagreement about the definition of education.

Assuming that Elkind is correct in believing that education must become a science, his argument is still flawed. It is contradictory for a constructivist to advocate a science of education. The philosophical foundation of constructivism rejects an objectively knowable reality. The philosophical foundation of science claims that one reality is objectively knowable through the senses and reason. Science, therefore, undermines constructivism rather than serves as a prerequisite to it.

If Elkind used Kuhn's (1996) definition of science—reality is observed by a perceiver who sees it through the lens of socially constructed paradigms that are periodically overthrown by new paradigms that are incommensurate with past paradigms—then any science of education still has no claim of truth over any other method of inquiry within education. Claims like "teaching will become a true profession only when we have a genuine science of education" are equivalent to saying that teaching will be a profession only when it becomes an art. If we construct our own reality, what is the difference?

If Elkind believes that most of what educators consider science comes from constructivists like Rousseau, Kant, Piaget, and Vygotsky, his argument is flawed. It is circular logic for a constructivist to claim that a science of education is needed and then to select only constructivists as the founders of that science. Though some beliefs are obtained in experiments, most are not— especially philosophical views about *literally* constructing reality, which are not testable or falsifiable and thus should not be accepted as scientific.

Philosophy of Education

Elkind seems to have overlooked the role of the educator's metaphysical and epistemological assumptions in accepting constructivism or any philosophy of education. He admitted that educators who "are wedded to an objectivist view that knowledge has an independent existence" have resisted constructivism, but he quickly dismissed this cause in favor of teacher readiness. Ironically, teacher readiness is more likely the cause of resistance to constructivism. For an educator to implement a pedagogical practice, he or she must consciously or unconsciously accept its metaphysical and epistemological assumptions. Constructivists possess certain metaphysical and epistemological assumptions that lead to constructivist practices, while objectivists possess other metaphysical and epistemological assumptions that lead to objectivist practices. Elkind overlooked the possibility that not everyone holds the same assumptions about reality, reason, knowledge, and truth that lead to constructivist practices. Some have other worldviews and, therefore, reject constructivism as a theory of learning because it contradicts their philosophical assumptions.

Elkind said that constructivism is the "best philosophy of education we have available," and that it has been "widely accepted." This is true only at the university level, where the majority of professors possess the metaphysical and epistemological assumptions that lead to constructivism. It is not true at other levels of education, where one is likely to encounter different metaphysical and epistemological assumptions that lead to other pedagogical practices.

Constructivism is not the best philosophy of education. Objectivism is more reasonable from a theoretical and practical perspective than constructivism. Objectivism holds that there is one reality independent of anyone perceiving it. This means that regardless of whether or not someone perceives something, it still exists. For example, I can leave the room with a table in it and be convinced that the table still exists. Most people probably would agree with this statement. Constructivism, on the other hand, holds that reality is dependent upon the perceiver. This means that something exists only if someone perceives it. From a constructivist perspective, if I leave a room with a table in it, the table ceases to exist. Most people would disagree with such a statement or at least have difficulty accepting it.

Objectivism also holds that humankind takes in data through the senses and uses reason to obtain knowledge. Constructivism does not deny the efficacy of reason completely, but does consider it as only one of many ways of knowing. This belief is another theory that does not stand up in practice. The theory of multiple intelligences, for example, proposes at least ten "intelligences" or ways of knowing: verbal, logical, musical, physical, spatial, inter- and intra-personal, natural, existential, and spiritual. When analyzed or reduced to their epistemological foundation, these intelligences seem more like specialized bodies of acquired knowledge than actual processors of information. Reason exists in all of them, which suggests that each is the *primary* way of knowing.

Objectivism also holds that we have objective knowledge and truth. A person observes reality via his or her senses, forms concepts through the use of noncontradictory (i.e., Aristotelian) logic, and thus acquires knowledge and truth. Constructivism posits that only subjective knowledge and relative truth are possible. If knowledge is subjective or relative to an individual or a group, then *any* knowledge could be true. Sacrificing virgins to appease the gods or believing that the universe revolves around the earth would count as knowledge and truth. Notable constructivists (Lawson 1989; Noddings 1998; Rorty 2003) have raised these criticisms about constructivist metaphysics and epistemology and have admitted that they have no answer to them.

Constructivism in Practice

Practically, objectivism is more reasonable than constructivism. As a high school English teacher, I implemented constructivism in my classes by allowing the students to construct what an English class is—choosing its purpose, curriculum, and instruction. Most of the students did not understand how they could "construct" an English class. They expected me to define the English class for them—a very reasonable assumption considering how young they were and how limited their experience. After a fair amount of prompting, a few bold students thought English should be spelling and grammar. Some might argue that the students' answer proves only that they had been prevented from constructing previous curriculums, and thus had not learned to think for themselves or to question the curriculum. I concede that the students' previous conception of what constitutes schooling was part of their inability to construct the course. However, perhaps children naturally look to adults to share with them their learned and acquired knowledge. They expect teachers to pass on to them a body of knowledge, imperfect though it may be, that they can update according to their discoveries. Many practicing constructivists refuse to do this, believing instead that a child's knowledge is equal to that of an adult's and a student is no less an authority on a subject than a teacher. This assumption is untrue and dangerous. It assumes that children are better off entering a world with no knowledge and creating their own rather than entering a world full of knowledge, learning it, and then updating it if it does not stand the test of their scrutiny.

The students in my English class could not be pure constructivists in the context of day-to-day assignments either. For example, when we read *Romeo and Juliet* by William Shakespeare, the reality of the story presented obstacles. If the students would have said that the story was about an aging salesman who imagines he is a success when he is not, a constructivist teacher would have to accept their response—right or wrong—because reality is constructed. For an objectivist English teacher, however, every claim must be supported by textual evidence and logic—by reality. *Romeo and Juliet*, therefore, must be about what the text supports and what logic dictates, not about the subjective feelings of the reader, which may not be in accordance with reality. Constructivist English teachers who tell students that there are no right-or-wrong answers or that their interpretation is as correct as anyone else's only encourage students to be careless and uncritical readers, writers, and thinkers.

I shifted to giving students a choice supported by evidence and logic because of the flaws in the practical application of constructivism. Students could choose the purpose, curriculum, and assignments of the course, but ultimately their choices had to conform to reality, not to their subjective whims. In other words, their choices had to have a compelling connection to their literacy development.

Conclusion

Constructivists must ask themselves whether they want to cling to the literal interpretation of constructivism that sees reality as constructed or simply believe that students learn best when they are actively engaged in the learning process. The two definitions are not the same metaphysically or epistemologically. The former entails an untenable theory and practice and should be modified or rejected.

Noddings (1998, 117–18) addressed the distinction between moderate and radical constructivism in this way:

> [I]f radical constructivists are just saying that our perception and cognition are theory-laden, that all knowledge is mediated by our cognitive structures and theories, then they have lots of company among contemporary theorists. However, if they are saying that there is no mind-independent reality, then they seem to be arguing a line long ago rejected.

Though Noddings seemed to advocate a moderate constructivist view that denies a mind-dependent reality, I maintain that constructivists cannot be moderates. All constructivists necessarily must believe that reality is dependent upon the perceiver. It is logically impossible to believe that a person's perception and cognitive structures are theory-laden, while simultaneously believing that reality is independent of the perceiver. If reality is perceived by a theory-laden perceiver, then the reality is theory-laden too. The moment that one becomes theory-laden, one is prevented from knowing an objective reality.

Objectivists believe humans are not theory-laden in the pejorative sense of that word. Objectivists do not consider prior knowledge or cognitive structures as a subjective lens through which one views reality. Rather, one possesses prior knowledge that informs new knowledge and, consequently, makes the new knowledge meaningful. If the prior knowledge or cognitive structure is incorrect, eventually the new correct knowledge will conflict with it and a person will be forced to update his or her old knowledge. If constructivists believe in an independent reality, then they not only must believe in it, but also must possess an objective method of perceiving it and, therefore, have objective knowledge and truth. There is no middle ground.

References

Elkind, D. 2004. The problem with constructivism. *The Educational Forum* 68(4): 306–12.

Kuhn, T. S. 1996. *The structure of scientific revolutions*, 3rd ed. Chicago: The University of Chicago Press.

Lawson, H. 1989. Stories about stories. In *Dismantling truth: Reality in the post-modern world*, ed. H. Lawson and L. Appignanesi, xi–xxviii. London: Weidenfeld and Nicolson.

Noddings, N. 1998. *Philosophy of education*. Boulder, CO: Westview Press.

Piekoff, L. 1993. *Objectivism: The philosophy of Ayn Rand*. New York: Penguin Books.

Rorty, R. 2003. Dismantling truth: Solidarity versus objectivity. In *The theory of knowledge: Classical and contemporary readings*, 3rd ed., ed. L. P. Pojman, 324–30. Belmont, CA: Wadsworth/Thomson Learning.

Slavin, R. E. 1997. *Educational psychology: Theory and practice*, 5th ed. Boston: Allyn & Bacon.

POSTSCRIPT

Is Constructivism the Best Philosophy of Education?

So it can be seen that present-day constructivists like David Elkind draw a lot of inspiration from Dewey's portrayal of the active, probing learner immersed in social experience, Holt's learners who steer their own personal development unfettered by imposed curricula, and Rogers' self-exploring students whose subjective knowledge takes precedence. In contrast, objectivists like Carson most likely find comfort in Scruton's timeless rationality, Adler's concept of a single best curriculum for all, and Skinner's use of scientific principles and quantitative methods to create effective learners.

Elkind responded to Carson's critique in the Summer 2005 issue of *Educational Forum*, primarily refuting the accusation that constructivists deny that a physical world exists outside our sensory experiences. He states that "it is not that an external reality does not exist, only that we have to reconstruct it to know it . . . it is because humans share a common sensory apparatus that we can agree upon an external reality existing outside our experience." Our senses can be mistaken but "objective" reasoning is fallible as well, he concludes.

In the past decade, the philosophy of constructivism has been widely treated by those who praise it and those who deplore it. A sampling of sources includes Jacqueline Grennon Brooks and Martin G. Brooks, *In Search of Understanding: The Case for Constructivist Classrooms* (1993); Susan Ohanian, *One Size Fits Few* (1999); Karen R. Harris and Steve S. Graham, "Memo to Constructivists: Skills Count, Too," *Educational Leadership* (February 1996); Tony Wagner, "Change as Collaborative Inquiry: A 'Constructivist' Methodology for Reinventing Schools," *Phi Delta Kappan* (March 1998); Heinrich Mintrop, "Educating Students to Teach in a Constructivist Way—Can It All Be Done?" *Teachers College Record* (April 2001); and Rhoda Cummings and Steve Harlow, "The Constructivist Roots of Moral Education," *The Educational Forum* (Summer 2000).

Additional commentary may be found in Michael Glassman, "Running in Circles: Chasing Dewey," *Educational Theory* (August 2004); Donald G. Hackmann, "Constructivism and Block Scheduling: Making the Connection," *Phi Delta Kappan* (May 2004); Ian Moll, "Towards a Constructivist Montessori Education," *Perspectives in Education* (June 2004); and David Chicoine, "Ignoring the Obvious: A Constructivist Critique of a Traditional Teacher Education Program," *Educational Studies* (December 2004).

The discussion launched by Elkind and Carson has been continued in the Spring 2006, Fall 2006, and Summer 2007 issues of *Educational Forum*. See especially the Henry Pegues article, "Of Paradigm Wars: Constructivism, Objectivism, and Postmodern Stratagems," in the Summer 2007 issue.

ISSUE 5

Should "Public Schooling" Be Redefined?

YES: Frederick M. Hess, from "What Is a 'Public School?' Principles for a New Century," *Phi Delta Kappan* (February 2004)

NO: Linda Nathan et al., from "A Response to Frederick Hess," *Phi Delta Kappan* (February 2004)

ISSUE SUMMARY

YES: Frederick M. Hess, a resident scholar at the American Enterprise Institute, advocates a broadening of the definition of "public schooling" in light of recent developments such as vouchers, charter schools, and home schooling.

NO: Linda Nathan, Joe Nathan, Ray Bacchetti, and Evans Clinchy express a variety of concerns about the conceptual expansion that Hess proposes.

T he original public school crusade, led by Massachusetts education official Horace Mann (1796–1859) and other activists, built on the growing sentiment among citizens, politicians, and business leaders that public schools were needed to deal with the increase in immigration, urbanization, and industrialism, as well as to bind together the American population and to prepare everyone for participatory democracy. For the most part, the right of the government to compel school attendance, dating from Massachusetts legislation in 1852, went unchallenged, although Catholics formed their own private school system in reaction to the predominant Protestantism of public schools in certain areas. In the 1920s there were efforts to eliminate all alternatives to government-run public schools to ensure attendance compliance and curricular standardization. Such an effort in Oregon was challenged in court, and the U.S. Supreme Court ultimately ruled, in *Pierce v. Society of Sisters* (1925), that such legislation unreasonably interferes with parental rights. While this ruling preserved the private school option, it did not alter the governmental prerogative to compel school attendance.

This governmental authority met with sharp criticism from liberal writers in the 1950s and beyond, in works such as Paul Goodman's *Compulsory Mis-education* (1964), Ivan Illich's *Deschooling Society* (1971), John Holt's *Instead of Education* (1976), and John Taylor Gatto's *Dumbing Us Down: The Hidden Curriculum of Compulsory Schooling* (1992). Gatto condemned the public school system for its emphasis on obedience and subordination rather than the unleashing of the intellectual and creative powers of the individual. Since the 1980s, a parallel attack has come from conservatives, such as William J. Bennett, E. D. Hirsch, Jr., Chester E. Finn, Jr., Charles J. Sykes, Grover Norquist, and Cal Thomas, and conservative groups, such as Parents for School Choice, the Cato Institute, and the Alliance for Separation of School and State. Building on the findings of the 1983 *A Nation at Risk* report, a significant segment of the American population continues to express disdain for the public education "establishment" (the U. S. Department of Education, the National Education Association, and teacher-training institutions) for its inability or unwillingness to improve public school performance. Their basic contention is that only choice-driven competition will bring about lasting improvement. William J. Bennett, in "A Nation Still at Risk," *Policy Review* (July/August 1998), has stated that although choices are spreading, charter schools are proliferating, privately managed public schools have long waiting lists, and home schooling is expanding, "the elephant still has most of the power." He concludes that "we must never again assume that the education system will respond to good advice. It will change only when power relationships change, particularly when all parents gain the power to decide where their children go to school."

Educator-reformer Deborah Meier, in "The Road to Trust," *American School Board Journal* (September 2003), argues that we must make public education feel like a public enterprise again. Hers is a call for the rebuilding of trust between public schools and the communities they directly serve. "Our school boards need to turn their eyes to their constituencies—not just to following the dictates of state and federal government micromanagers."

In the following articles, Frederick M. Hess makes the case that the time has come for a reconception of "public schooling" while four prominent educators challenge what they perceive to be an unproductive assault on public schooling.

YES ⤶

What Is a 'Public School?'
Principles for a New Century

The phrase "public schooling" has become more a rhetorical device than
a useful guide to policy. As our world evolves, so too must our conception
of what "public" means. James Coleman eloquently made this point more
than two decades ago, implying a responsibility to periodically reappraise our
assumptions as to what constitutes "public schooling."[1] In a world where charter schooling, distance education, tuition tax credits, and other recent developments no longer fit neatly into our conventional mental boxes, it is clearly
time for such an effort. Nonetheless, rather than receiving the requisite consideration, "public schooling" has served as a flag around which critics of these
various reforms can rally. It is because the phrase resonates so powerfully that
critics of proposals like charter schooling, voucher programs, and rethinking teacher licensure have at times abandoned substantive debate in order to
attack such measures as "anti-public schooling."[2]

Those of us committed to the promise of public education are obliged to
see that the ideal does not become a tool of vested interests. The perception
that public schooling has strayed from its purpose and been captured by self-
interested parties has fueled lacerating critiques in recent years. Such critics
as Andrew Coulson and Douglas Dewey find a growing audience when they
suggest that the ideal of public schooling itself is nothing more than a call to
publicly subsidize the private agendas of bureaucrats, education school professors,
union officials, and leftist activists.[3] While I believe such attacks are misguided,
answering them effectively demands that we discern what it is that makes
schooling public and accept diverse arrangements that are consistent with
those tenets. Otherwise, growing numbers of reformers may come to regard
public schooling as a politicized obstacle rather than a shared ideal.

While I do not aim to provide a precise answer as to what public schooling should mean in the early 21st century, I will argue that public schools are
broadly defined by their commitment to preparing students to be productive
members of a social order, aware of their societal responsibilities, and respectful of constitutional strictures; that such schools cannot deny access to students
for reasons unrelated to their educational focus; and that the system of public
schools available in any community must provide an appropriate placement
for each student. In short, I suggest that it is appropriate to adopt a much more

From *Phi Delta Kappan*, February 2004, pp. 584–590. Copyright © 2004 by Phi Delta Kappan.
Reprinted by permission of Phi Delta Kappan and Frederick M. Hess.

expansive notion of public schooling than the one the education community holds today.

What Isn't Public?

Traditionally, "public schools" are deemed to be those directly accountable to elected officials or funded by tax dollars.[4] As a practical matter, such definitions are not very useful, largely because there are conventional "public" schools that do not fit within these definitions, while there are "private" providers that do.

We generally regard as "public schools" those in which policy making and oversight are the responsibility of governmental bodies, such as a local school board. Nongovernmental providers of educational services, such as independent schools or educational management organizations (EMOs), are labeled "nonpublic." The distinction is whether a formal political body is in charge, since these officials are accountable by election or appointment to the larger voting "public."

There are two particular problems here. First, how "hands on" must the government be for us to regard a service as publicly provided? The National Aeronautics and Space Administration, the Environmental Protection Agency, the U.S. Department of Education, and most other state, federal, and local government agencies contract with for-profit firms for support, to provide services, and to evaluate service delivery. Yet we tend to regard the services as "public" because they were initiated in response to a public directive and are monitored by public officials. It is not clear when government-directed activity ceases to be public. For instance, if a for-profit company manages a district school, is the school less public than it was when it purchased its texts from a for-profit textbook publisher and its professional development from a private consultant?

A second approach to defining "public" focuses on inputs. By this metric, any activity that involves government funds is public because it involves the expenditure of tax dollars. However, this distinction is more nebulous than we sometimes suppose. For instance, schools in the Milwaukee voucher program receive Wisconsin tax dollars. Does this mean that voucher schools ought to be regarded as de facto public schools? Similarly, Wisconsin dairy farmers receive federal subsidies. Does this make their farms public enterprises?

A particular complication is that many traditional public schools charge families money. For instance, during 2002–03, the families of more than 2,300 Indiana students were paying tuition of as much as $6,000 to enroll their children in a public school in another district. Public schools routinely charge fees to families that participate in interdistrict public choice plans, and they frequently charge families fees if a child participates in extra-curricular activities. Would proponents of a revenue-based definition suggest that such practices mean that these schools are no longer "public"?

A third approach, famously advanced by John Dewey, the esteemed champion of "public" education, recognizes that private institutions may serve public ends and that public institutions may fail to do so.[5] Such a recognition suggests that public schools are those that serve public ends, regardless of the monitoring arrangements or revenue sources. This approach is ultimately problematic, however, because we do *not* have clear agreement on appropriate public purposes. I'll have more to say on this point shortly.

What Is Public Schooling?

Previously, I have posed five questions to guide our efforts to bring more precision to our understanding of "public schooling."[6] Here, I offer these questions as a way to sketch principles that may help shape a contemporary conception of "public schooling."

What are the purposes of public schooling? Schooling entails both public and private purposes, though we often fail to note the degree to which the private benefits may serve the public interest. In particular, academic learning serves the individual and also the needs of the state. Successful democratic communities require a high level of literacy and numeracy and are anchored by the knowledge and the good sense of the population. Citizens who lack these skills are less likely to contribute effectively to the well-being of their communities and more likely to be a drain on public resources. Therefore, in a real sense, any school that helps children master reading, writing, mathematics, and other essential content is already advancing some significant public purposes.[7] It is troubling that prominent educational thinkers, including Frank Smith, Susan Ohanian, Deborah Meier, and Alfie Kohn, have rejected this fundamental premise and encouraged "public schools" to promote preferred social values even at the expense of basic academic mastery.[8]

More fundamentally, there are two distinct ways to comprehend the larger public purposes of education. One suggests that schools serve a public interest that transcends the needs of individuals. This line of thought, understood by Rousseau as the "general will," can be traced to Plato's conviction that nations need a far-sighted leader to determine their true interests, despite the shortsighted preferences of the mob. A second way of thinking about the public purposes of education accepts the classically "liberal" understanding of the public interest as the sum of the interests of individual citizens and rejects the idea of a transcendent general will. This pragmatic stance helped shape American public institutions that protect citizens from tyrannical majorities and overreaching public officials.

While neither perspective is necessarily "correct," our government of limited powers and separate branches leans heavily toward the more modest dictates of liberalism. Despite our tendency to suffuse education with the sweeping rhetoric of a disembodied national interest, our freedoms are secured by a system designed to resist such imperial visions.

The "public" components of schooling include the responsibility for teaching the principles, habits, and obligations of citizenship. While schools of education typically interpret this to mean that educators should preach "tolerance" or affirm "diversity," a firmer foundation for citizenship education would focus on respect for law, process, and individual rights. The problem with phrases like "tolerance" and "diversity" is that they are umbrella terms with multiple interpretations. When we try to define them more precisely—in policy or practice—it becomes clear that we must privilege some values at the expense of others. For instance, one can plausibly argue that tolerant citizens should respectfully hear out a radical Muslim calling for jihad against the U.S. or that tolerance extends only to legalistic protection and leaves one free to express social opprobrium. If educators promote the former, as their professional community generally advises, they have adopted a particular normative view that is at odds with that held by a large segment of the public.

Promoting any one particular conception of tolerance does not make schools more "public." In a liberal society, uniformly teaching students to accept teen pregnancy or homosexuality as normal and morally unobjectionable represents a jarring absolutism amidst profound moral disagreement.

Nonetheless, many traditional "public" schools (such as members of the Coalition of Essential Schools) today explicitly promote a particular world view and endorse a particular social ethos. In advancing "meaningful questions," for instance, faculty members at these schools often promote partisan attitudes toward American foreign policy, the propriety of affirmative action, or the morality of redistributive social policies. Faculty members in these schools can protest that they have no agenda other than cultivating critical inquiry, but observation of classrooms or perusal of curricular materials makes clear that most of these schools are not neutral on the larger substantive questions. This poses an ethical problem in a pluralist society where the parents of many students may reject the public educators' beliefs and where the educators have never been clearly empowered to stamp out "improper" thoughts.

Public schools should teach children the essential skills and knowledge that make for productive citizens, teach them to respect our constitutional order, and instruct them in the framework of rights and obligations that secure our democracy and protect our liberty. Any school that does so should be regarded as serving public purposes.

How should we apportion responsibility between families and public schools? The notion that schools can or should serve as a "corrective" against the family was first promulgated in the early 19th century by reformers who viewed the influx of immigrants as a threat to democratic processes and American norms. In the years since, encouraged by such thinkers as George Counts, Paulo Freire, Michael Apple, Peter McLaren, and Amy Gutmann, educational thinkers have unapologetically called for schooling to free students from the yoke of their family's provincial understandings.

The problem is that this conception of the "public interest" rests uneasily alongside America's pluralist traditions. American political thought, dating back to Madison's pragmatic embrace of "faction," has presumed that our various prejudices and biases can constructively counter one another, so long as the larger constitutional order and its attendant protections check our worst impulses.

The notion that schools are more "public" when they work harder to stamp out familial views and impress children with socially approved beliefs is one that ought to give pause to any civil libertarian or pluralist. Such schools are more attuned to the public purposes of a totalitarian regime than those of a democratic one. While a democratic nation can reasonably settle upon a range of state/family relationships, there is no reason to imagine that a regime that more heavily privileges the state is more "public." The relative "publicness" of education is not enhanced by having schools intrude more forcefully into the familial sphere.

Who should be permitted to provide public schooling? Given publicly determined purposes, it is not clear that public schooling needs to impose restrictions on who may provide services. There is no reason why for-profit or religious providers, in particular, ought to be regarded as suspect.

While traditional public schools have always dealt with for-profit providers of textbooks, teaching supplies, professional development, and so on, profit-seeking ventures have recently emerged as increasingly significant players in reform efforts. For instance, the for-profit, publicly held company Edison Schools is today managing scores of traditional district schools across the nation. Yet these are still regarded as "public" schools. In fact, Edison is managing the summer school programs, including curricula and personnel, for more than 70 public school *districts*. Yet those communities continue to regard summer school as public schooling.

Such arrangements seem to run afoul of our conventional use of the term "public," but the conflict is readily resolved when we recognize that all public agencies, including public hospitals and public transit systems, routinely harness the services of for-profit firms. Just as a public university is not thought to lose its public status merely because portions of it enter into for-profit ventures with regard to patents or athletics, so the entry of for-profit providers into a K–12 public school does not necessarily change the institution's fundamental nature. What matters in public higher education is whether the for-profit unit is controlled and overseen by those entrusted with the university's larger public mission. What matters in public schooling is whether profit seekers are hired to serve public ends and are monitored by public officials.

The status of religious providers has raised great concern among such groups as People for the American Way and the Center on Education Policy. However, the nation's early efforts to provide public education relied heavily upon local church officials to manage public funds, to provide a school facility, and to arrange the logistics of local schooling. It was not until the anti-Catholic fervor of the mid- and late-19th century that states distanced themselves from religious schooling. It was not until the mid-20th century that advocacy groups such as the American Civil Liberties Union pushed the remnants of religion out of state-run schools.

In recent decades, the U.S. Supreme Court has made clear that the push for a "wall of separation" had overreached and run afoul of First Amendment language protecting the "free exercise" of religion. Moreover, contemporary America has continued to evolve since the anti-Catholic zeal of the 19th century and the anti-religious intellectualism of the mid-20th century. Those conflicts were of a particular time and place. Today, church officials have less local sway and lack the unquestioned authority they once held, while they are more integrated into secular society. Just as some onetime opponents of single-sex schools can now, because of changes in the larger social order, imagine such schools serving the public interest, so too we should not reflexively shrink from viewing religious schools in a similar light. In most industrial democracies, including such nations as Canada, France, and the Netherlands, religious schools operate as part of the public system and are funded and regulated accordingly.

What obligations should public schools have to ensure opportunity for all students? We have never imagined that providing opportunity to all students means treating all students identically. The existence of magnet schools, special education, gifted classes, and exam schools makes it clear that we deem it appropriate for schools to select some children and exclude others in order to provide desirable academic environments. Our traditional school districts have never sought to ensure that every school or classroom should serve a random cross-section of children, only that systems as a whole should appropriately serve all children.

Given the tension between families who want their child schooled in an optimal environment and public officials who must construct systems that address competing needs, the principle that individual schools can exclude children but that systems cannot is both sensible and morally sound. That said, this principle does mean that some children will not attend school with the peers their parents might prefer.

The dilemma this presents is that no solitary good school can serve all the children who might wish to attend and that randomly admitting students may impede a school's effectiveness. Demanding that a science magnet school accept students with minimal science accomplishments or that any traditional school accept a habitually violent student threatens the ability of each school to accomplish its basic purposes. This is clearly not in the public interest. The same is true when a constructivist school is required to admit students from families who staunchly prefer back-to-basics instruction and will agitate for the curricula and pedagogy they prefer. In such cases, allowing schools to selectively admit students is consistent with the public interest—so long as the process furthers a legitimate educational purpose and the student has access to an appropriate alternative setting. Such publicly acceptable exclusion must be pursued for some reasonable educational purpose, and this creates a gray area that must be monitored. However, the need to patrol this area does not require that the practice be preemptively prohibited.

Moreover, self-selected or homogeneous communities are not necessarily less public than others. For instance, no one suggests that the University of Wyoming is less public than the University of Texas, though it is less geographically and ethnically representative of the nation. It has never been suggested that elections in San Francisco or Gopher Springs, West Virginia, would be more public if the communities included more residents who had not chosen to live there or whose views better reflected national norms. Nor has it been suggested that selective public institutions, such as the University of Michigan, are less public than are community colleges, even though they are selective about whom they admit. Moreover, there is always greater homogeneity in self-selected communities, such as magnet schools, as they attract educators and families who share certain views. None of this has been thought to undermine their essential "publicness."

Even champions of "public education," such as Deborah Meier and Ted Sizer, argue that this shared sense of commitment helps cultivate a participatory

and democratic ethos in self-selected schools. In other words, heightened familial involvement tends to make self-selected schools more participatory and
democratic. Kneeling before the false gods of heterogeneity or nonselectivity
undermines our ability to forge participatory or effective schools without making schools commensurately more "public."

Nowhere, after all, does the availability of a "public service" imply that
we get to choose our fellow users. In every field—whether public medicine,
public transportation, or public higher education—the term "public" implies
our right to a service, not our right to have buses serve a particular route or
to have a university cohort configured to our preferences. Even though such
considerations influence the quality of the service, the need for public providers to juggle the requirements of all the individuals they must serve necessarily
means that each member of the public cannot necessarily receive the service in
the manner he or she would ultimately prefer. "Public schooling" implies an
obligation to ensure that all students are appropriately served, not that every
school is open to all comers.

What parts of public schooling are public? Debates about publicness focus
on the classroom teaching and learning that is central to all schools. Maintenance, accounting, payroll, and food services are quite removed from the
public purposes of education discussed above. Even though these peripheral
services may take place in the same facility as teaching and learning, their
execution does not meaningfully affect the "publicness" of schooling. Rather,
we understand that it is sufficient to have ancillary services provided in a manner that is consistent with the wishes of a public education provider. For example, federal courts and state legislatures are indisputably public institutions, yet
they frequently procure supplies, services, and personnel from privately run,
for-profit enterprises. We properly regard these institutions as public because
of their core purposes, not because of the manner in which they arrange their
logistics.

Today's 'Public' Schools Often Aren't

Given the haphazard notion of public schooling that predominates today, it
comes as little surprise that we offer contemporary educators little guidance in
serving the public interest. This poses obvious problems, given that employment as an educator doesn't necessarily grant enhanced moral wisdom or personal virtue. If schools are to serve as places where educators advance purposes
and cultivate virtues that they happen to prefer, it is not clear in what sense
schools are serving "public purposes."

Blindly hoping that educators have internalized shared public purposes,
we empower individuals to proselytize under the banner of "public schooling." This state of affairs has long been endorsed by influential educational
theorists like George Counts, Paulo Freire, Henry Giroux, and Nel Noddings,
who argue that teachers have a charge to use their classrooms to promote
personal visions of social change, regardless of the broader public's beliefs.
For these thinkers, "public schooling" ironically implies a community obligation to support schools for the private purposes of educators. The problem is

that public institutions are not personal playthings. Just as it is unethical for a judge to disregard the law and instead rule on the basis of personal whimsy, so it is inappropriate for public school teachers to use their office to impose personal views upon a captive audience.

One appropriate public response is to specify public purposes and to demand that teachers reflect them, though we are reasonably cautious about adopting such an intrusive course. To the extent that explicit direction is absent, however, educators are left to their own devices. In such a case, our liberal tradition would recommend that we not subject children to the views of educators at an assigned school but allow families to avail themselves of a range of schools with diverse perspectives, so long as each teaches respect for our democratic and liberal tradition.

Conclusion

Today, our system of "public schooling" does little to ensure that our schools serve public purposes, while permitting some educators to use a publicly provided forum to promote their personal beliefs. Meanwhile, hiding behind the phrase's hallowed skirts are partisans who furiously attack any innovation that threatens their interests or beliefs.

There are many ways to provide legitimate public education. A restrictive state might tightly regulate school assignment, operations, and content, while another state might impose little regulation. However, there is no reason to regard the schools in the one state as more "public" than those in the other. The "publicness" of a school does not depend on class size, the use of certified teachers, rules governing employee termination, or the rest of the procedural apparatus that ensnares traditional district schools. The fact that public officials have the right to require public schools to comply with certain standards does not mean that schools subjected to more intrusive standards are somehow more public. The inclusion of religious schools in European systems, for instance, has been accompanied by intensive regulation of curricula and policy. Regulation on that order is not desirable, nor is it necessary for schools to operate as part of a public system; it is merely an operational choice made by officials in these relatively bureaucratic nations.

As opportunities to deliver, structure, and practice education evolve, it is periodically necessary to revisit assumptions about what constitutes public schooling. The ideology and institutional self-interest that infuse the dominant current conception have fueled withering attacks on the very legitimacy of public schooling itself. Failure to address this impoverished status quo will increasingly offer critics cause to challenge the purpose and justification of public education. Maintaining and strengthening our commitment to public schooling requires that we rededicate ourselves to essential principles of opportunity, liberal democracy, and public benefit, while freeing ourselves from political demands and historic happenstance.

In an age when social and technological change have made possible new approaches to teaching and learning, pinched renderings of "public schooling" have grown untenable and counterproductive. They stifle creative efforts, confuse debates, and divert attention from more useful questions. A more expansive conception is truer to our traditions, more likely to foster shared values, and better suited to the challenges of the new century.

Notes

1. James Coleman, "Public Schools, Private Schools, and the Public Interest," *Public Interest,* Summer 1981, pp. 19–30. See also idem, "Quality and Equality in American Education," *Phi Delta Kappan,* November 1981, pp. 159–64.

2. For the best empirical examination of the scope and nature of the "public school ideology," see Terry Moe, *Schools, Vouchers, and the American Public* (Washington, D.C.: Brookings, 2001).

3. See Andrew Coulson, *Market Education: The Unknown History* (New Brunswick, N.J.: Transaction Publishers, 1999); and Douglas Dewey, "An Echo, Not a Choice: School Vouchers Repeat the Error of Public Education," *Policy Review,* November/December 1996. . . .

4. See Frederick M. Hess, "Making Sense of the 'Public' in Public Education," unpublished paper, Progressive Policy Institute, Washington, D.C., 2002.

5. John Dewey, *The Public and Its Problems* (1927; reprint, Athens: Ohio University Press, 1954).

6. See Frederick M. Hess, "What Is 'Public' About Public Education?," *Education Week,* 8 January 2003, p. 56.

7. An extended discussion of this point can be found in Paul T. Hill, "What Is Public About Public Education?," in Terry Moe, ed., *A Primer on America's Schools* (Stanford, Calif.: Hoover Institution, 2001), pp. 285–316.

8. Frank Smith, "Overselling Literacy," *Phi Delta Kappan,* January 1989, pp. 353–59; Alfie Kohn, *No Contest: The Case Against Competition* (Boston: Houghton Mifflin, 1986); Susan Ohanian, "Capitalism, Calculus, and Conscience," *Phi Delta Kappan,* June 2003, pp. 736–47; and Deborah Meier, "Educating a Democracy," in idem, ed., *Will Standards Save Public Education?* (Boston: Beacon Press, 2000).

A Response to Frederick Hess

Linda Nathan, The Larger Purpose of Public Schools

At times I want to cheer for Frederick Hess's words in "What Is a 'Public School'? Principles for a New Century." How true it is that many reformers "regard public schooling as a politicized obstacle rather than a shared ideal." How true that "those of us committed to the promise of public education are obliged to see that the idea does not become a tool of vested interests."

Yet there is also something chilling about his article that stops the cheer in my throat. His use of innuendo in place of evidence, his sloppy logic, and his attacks on some of the most effective public school reformers—painting them as the enemy—suggest that his real agenda is not strengthening public education but privatizing it through vouchers and for-profit takeover schemes.

Hess's labored analysis obscures a simple fact: public schools have a larger and more democratic purpose than private and parochial schools (although this is not to say that these schools contribute nothing to public life). Public school systems are open to everyone regardless of disability, wealth, status, race, or religion. Private and parochial schools are not. While some are more open than others, they can have entrance exams and can explicitly exclude students with disabilities or those who otherwise don't fit a preferred profile. And of course they can also exclude those who can't pay. They can expel students who cause trouble, at their sole discretion, without recourse.

Hess himself acknowledges this core principle of universal access, conceding that public schooling "implies an obligation to ensure that all students are appropriately served." But he seems indifferent to the inequities inherent in his "more expansive" notion of what makes a school public.

Hess makes a false analogy when he equates schools that buy textbooks from for-profit companies with schools that are managed by for-profit firms. Basic educational decisions should be made by citizens of the local school community—not by distant shareholders looking only at a corporate balance sheet. (It's ironic that Hess picks as his exemplar Edison Schools, Inc., which sold off the textbooks, computers, lab supplies, and musical instruments of the Philadelphia public schools it had been hired to manage just days before school was to open in 2002 in order to pay down the company's mounting debt.)

Hess objects to teaching "tolerance" and affirming "diversity" because, he says, these words are open to multiple interpretations. Then he states that "public schools should teach children the essential skills and knowledge that make for productive citizens" and "teach them to respect our constitutional order," as if these were absolute truths *not* open to interpretation. The example of tolerance he cites, wherein a radical Muslim is calling for jihad, slyly exploits a hot-button issue to imply that the "professional community" of educators condones terrorism. Similarly, he smears the notion of defending tolerance as "uniformly teaching students to accept teen pregnancy as normal" and implies that liberals equate these activities with their definition of "public schooling." Nonsense.

His attack on Deborah Meier, Alfie Kohn, and others is equally baseless. It's the classic straw man fallacy: he attributes a position to them—that they oppose the teaching of basic academic mastery in favor of promoting "preferred social values"—that they have in fact never espoused. Meier's argument, with which Hess is surely familiar, is that such a tradeoff is unnecessary and that strong academic habits and mastery of literacy are essential and are furthered by an intellectually open and challenging spirit of inquiry.

The Coalition of Essential Schools, another of Hess's targets, gets similar treatment. Without offering a single example or other evidence of any kind, he asserts that faculty members at Coalition schools routinely promote partisan political views and are determined to "stamp out 'improper' thoughts." Of course, he's right that some teachers and schools—including many private and religious schools—do have a "party line," whether they're conscious of it or not. But he wants to have it both ways. While he attacks Coalition teachers for promoting values he dislikes, he argues at the same time that there should be choice in education so that parents can select schools that reflect their values.

Hess's argument with regard to the personal views and political leanings of educators is simply a red herring. The underlying issue is his fear that his own preferred values are being "stamped out." He uses that phrase again in making the absurd claim that the goal of liberal educators is to subvert the influence of families on their children. If he were serious about the rights of parents, Hess would be attacking the idea of a federalized education system—with or without vouchers—in which the *state* defines which values, priorities, intellectual habits, and performance standards will dominate and in which schools must accept intrusive guidelines to receive a stamp of approval and public funding. It seems to me that his scorn should fall not on Deborah Meier and Ted Sizer but on George W. Bush and the other proponents of top-down standardization.

Hess wants teachers to promote respect for the law—unless the laws in question are those that guarantee equal rights to people regardless of sexual orientation. When I began teaching in the late 1970s, it was dangerous for a teacher to be homosexual, not because of students' or parents' reactions but because of administrative reprisals. And it was dangerous in those days to talk about the threat of nuclear war or to suggest that the U.S.-sponsored war in El Salvador was unjust or even to imply that there was another view of these issues than the government's. My colleagues daily taught their students that might was right and homosexuality was a sin. I had my tires slashed by colleagues who felt that desegregation had ruined the Boston Public Schools. That we have created schools in which more open dialogue is possible indeed represents progress.

In calling for more innovation and choice in public education, Hess is absolutely right. In diversity, after all, there is strength. The U.S. has tried many experiments in public schooling over the past two centuries. We are in the midst of yet another experiment with our charter schools. In many ways, this kind of exploration is healthy. It allows us to look at different models and seek out best practices. Yet the charter school experiment has largely ignored issues of equity. In Boston and many other districts, charter schools often make no provision for accepting students who require special educational services or facilities, while traditional public schools are required to do so. This is one reason that some see charter schools as less "public" than other public schools. The same inequities exist in many parochial schools.

We need schools that help young people and adults learn and practice the skills necessary to be participants in a vibrant democracy. Such schools will be messy places that must balance the public interest with America's pluralist tradition. In their classrooms everyone learns to ask probing questions, to use evidence well, to make legitimate arguments, and to recognize fallacies and lies. I invite Frederick Hess to come to the Boston Arts Academy, where we will be happy to give him the opportunity to practice these skills with our students.

Joe Nathan, Some Questions for Advocates of Public Education

Three very specific questions for advocates of public education came to my mind as I read Frederick Hess's argument that we need to "reappraise our assumptions as to what constitutes 'public schooling.'" Let me pose them to *Kappan* readers, who no doubt are advocates for public education.

What is public about a suburban district in which the price of admission to the local public schools is the ability to purchase a home for more than one million dollars (and to pay tax-deductible property taxes on that home)?

What is public about an inner-city school with an admissions test that screens out all students with mental disabilities and more than 95% of the students in the surrounding district and so proclaims that it serves only the "cream of the crop"?

What is public about preventing some inner-city students from attending a magnet school just a few blocks from their homes that receives $1,500 per pupil more than the neighborhood school they attend? At the same time, in the name of integration, white students from wealthy suburbs are transported to this school—some via taxi.

These three questions form the basis for two larger questions that continue to trouble me even after being involved with public education for 33 years. I don't have definitive answers to these larger questions. But I share them with readers in the hope that they, too, will find them worth pondering. . . .

⋅◈⋅

. . . 1. *Since all public schools are not open to all kinds of students, what admissions standards should be acceptable for schools supported by public funds?* When my teachers in the Wichita public schools talked about public education, they stressed that a key difference between public and private schools was that public schools were open to all. Many of the authorities I read while I was at Carleton College, preparing to become a teacher, said the same thing.

This idea of "open to all" makes great sense to me. It seems like the right and just way to operate. Hess writes that he thinks it "appropriate" for some public schools to select some children and exclude others. I've disagreed with this position for more than 30 years. But lately, I'm not so sure.

When I began teaching I learned that many public schools were *not* open to all students. As I traveled the country, I learned that there were more than a thousand magnet schools and programs that have admissions tests. A study some years ago found that more than half of the nation's secondary magnet schools have admissions tests, as do about a quarter of the elementary magnets.[1]

Wisconsin Rep. Polly Williams, a Democrat and an African American state legislator, was enraged because most of the youngsters in her inner-city Milwaukee district were not able to get into exclusive magnet schools in the neighborhood, which brought in affluent, white, suburban students. Her frustration led her to fight successfully for the nation's first formal voucher plan.

Some opponents of vouchers insist that a level playing field isn't available when private schools can cherry-pick their students. I agree. But many educators, including me, have the same frustration about elite magnet schools: they have an unfair advantage over neighborhood public schools that are open to all in that they can screen out students with whom they don't wish to work.

I also learned that the country's single biggest choice system is called the suburbs. Millions of youngsters attend schools in the suburbs, and these schools clearly are *not* open to all students. They are open only to those whose families can afford to live in suburban communities.

A few years ago, I visited a school district on the northern coast of Long Island. Administrators there told me that the least expensive home in the district sold for $1,000,000. None of the district's teachers could afford to live there.

Today, some people argue that there should be publicly funded schools that are open only to young women. Two such schools have opened—one in New York, the other in Chicago. Even though I was not fond of this type of school, I visited the New York City district school, Young Women's Leadership Academy. I was impressed. The young women reported that, without boys around, they felt much more comfortable raising their hands in class and much more comfortable doing well on tests.

Should public funds go to some schools of choice that are only open to women? Or only to men? Five years ago, I would have said emphatically not. Today, I don't know.

2. *Shouldn't schools we describe as public accept and use some of the country's basic ideas to help improve education?* Americans generally endorse a number of ideas:

- choice of religion, job, neighborhood, places to obtain services, and so on;
- the provision of opportunities to try new ideas and approaches;
- the shared belief that this is a country not just of rights, but of responsibilities; and
- the notions that our cherished freedoms are not unlimited.

However, for three decades I've watched major public education groups vigorously oppose school choice programs, including public school choice programs, that are built on these principles. For example, there was intense opposition from educators in 1970 to the creation of the St. Paul Open School.

These organized groups ignore the professional and pedagogical rationales for public school choice, expressed best by veteran educator Deborah Meier:

> Choice is an essential tool in the effort to create . . . good public education. . . . We'll have to allow those most involved (teachers, administrators, parents) to exercise greater on-site power to put their collective wisdom into practice. Once we do all this, however, school X and school Y are going to start doing things differently. . . . Creating a school different from what any of those who work in the system are familiar with, one that runs counter to the experiences of most families, is possible only if teachers, parents, and students have time to agree on changes and a choice on whether or not they want to go along with them.[2]

Colleagues involved in other efforts to create new options over the last three decades have had similar experiences. During his tenure as president of the American Federation of Teachers, Al Shanker described what happened to teachers who proposed schools-within-schools:

> Many schools-within-schools were or are treated like traitors or outlaws for daring to move out of the lockstep and do something different. Their initiators had to move Heaven and Earth to get school officials to authorize them, and if they managed that, often they could look forward to insecurity, obscurity, or outright hostility.[3]

Over the past decade, with help from the Gates, Blandin, and Annenberg Foundations, the Center for School Change at the University of Minnesota has tried to help educators create new schools-within-schools in a number of communities. Shanker's words have often proved to be very accurate. The most intense, vigorous critics of offering a different kind of school—whether in a single building or in a district—have often been other educators.

Many educators have argued over the past 30 years that public, district schools serving racial minorities and students from low-income families are doing the best job they can with existing funds. According to the most recent

Phi Delta Kappa/Gallup poll, 80% of the public thinks the achievement gap between white children and minority children is mostly related to factors other than the quality of schooling.[4]

Perhaps in part because some educators have helped to convince the public that inner-city schools are mostly not responsible for the achievement gap, 58% of the nation and 62% of public school parents think it is possible to narrow the achievement gap *without* spending more money than is currently being spent on these students.[5] Unfortunately, many state legislators are opting not to raise taxes and not to give more to schools serving low-income, limited-English-speaking students.

Some of us vigorously disagree with these legislative actions and think that both more public school choice and more funding would help reduce the achievement gap. We have seen—and in some cases have worked in—schools that have served the public interest by helping all youngsters achieve their potential and have done much to close the gap between students of different races.

Despite encouragement from such strong public school supporters as former President Bill Clinton, former Secretary of Education Richard Riley, and the late Sen. Paul Wellstone (D-Minn.), efforts to create independent charter public schools still face huge opposition from state teacher, school board, and superintendent groups. The opposition uses the same arguments used in 1970 against the St. Paul Open School: new options take away our money.

But it isn't their money. Legislatures allocate money for the education of children, not for the preservation of a system. If 50 students move from a city to a suburb or from a suburb to a city, the dollars follow them. The money doesn't belong to "the system."

Thousands of parents and educators are voting with their feet. The number of states with a charter law has gone from one in 1991 to 40 in 2003. The number of charter schools has gone from one school in 1991 to more than 3,000 in 2003. Federal statistics show that low-income students and racial minorities are overrepresented in charter schools. While the evidence is mixed—and almost certainly will be so when charter and district schools are compared—some charters are clearly producing major achievement gains. Shouldn't we learn from and replicate their best practices?

Starting new schools is extremely difficult work. But whether it's a Pilot School in the Boston Public Schools or a New Visions option in New York City or a charter school in any of 40 states, the opportunity to try new approaches is as vital for education as it is for medicine, business, or technology.

Some Tentative Conclusions

So Frederick Hess wants to "discern what . . . makes schooling public and accept diverse arrangements that are consistent with those tenets." I'm not sure what standards all publicly supported schools should meet. But after 33 years, I offer these as minimum requirements for schools that serve the public interest and are thus eligible to receive public funds. Public schools should:

- be open to all kinds of students and not use admissions tests;
- follow due process procedures with regard to students and educators;

- use state-approved, standardized, and other measures to help monitor student progress or lack thereof;
- have closing the achievement gap between white students and racial minority and low-income students as an explicit, measurable goal;[6] and
- be actively chosen by faculty, families, and students.

Thanks to Hess and to the *Kappan* for urging a timely reconsideration of the basic principles of public education. As social justice activist Leonard Fein states it:

> The future is not something we discover around the next corner. It is something we shape, we create, we invent. To hold otherwise would be to view ourselves as an audience to history, and not its authors. History, and even our own lives, cannot always be turned and twisted to make them go exactly where we should like. But there is, for people of energy and purpose, more freedom of movement than most ever exercise.[7]

Notes

1. Lauri Steel and Roger Levine, *Educational Innovation in Multiracial Contexts: The Growth of Magnet Schools in American Education* (Palo Alto, Calif.: American Institutes for Research, 1994). This study was prepared for the U.S. Department of Education under Contract No. LC 90043001.
2. Deborah Meier, "Choice Can Save Public Education," *The Nation,* 4 March 1991.
3. Al Shanker, "Where We Stand: Convention Plots New Course—A Charter for Change," *New York Times* (paid advertisement), 10 July 1988, p. E-7.
4. Lowell C. Rose and Alec M. Gallup, "The 35th Annual Phi Delta Kappa/ Gallup Poll of the Public's Attitudes Toward the Public Schools," *Phi Delta Kappan,* September 2003, p. 48.
5. Ibid.
6. Student progress should be monitored using various measures, not just standardized tests. If there is not major improvement in narrowing the achievement gap in most areas over a five-year period, the school should be "reconstituted."
7. Leonard Fein et al., *Reform Is a Verb: Notes on Reform and Reforming Jews* (New York: Union of American Hebrew Congregations, 1972), p. 152.

Ray Bacchetti, An Ongoing Conversation

We don't look at the big issues of the principles and purposes of public schools often or carefully enough. Sadly, the political and philosophical conversation seems increasingly polarized. In Venn diagram terms, the two circles—labeled right/left, basics/constructivist, academic/child-centered, etc.—reveal at best a vanishingly thin region of overlap. When the true believers on either side look in the mirror, they see Dumbledore. Over their shoulders and gaining, they see Voldemort.

Frederick Hess's beefy rhetoric stakes out a position that reflects a more conservative world view than my own. In essence, he argues that the purposes of public education will be better served if we narrow the number of principles that define its publicness and expand the number of ways those principles can be implemented. In that expanded universe, religious schools, vouchers, for-profit ventures, and other alternatives would be welcome.

The principles advertised in Hess's title are woven through his essay, making it difficult to distinguish his main point from his subsidiary concerns. Here is what I take to be the core of his definition of what makes a school public. In addition to teaching skills and content, public schools should:

- prepare students to be "productive members of the social order";
- enable students to "become aware of their societal responsibilities," including the "principles, habits, and obligations of citizenship"; and
- educate students to be "respectful of constitutional strictures," including laws, process, and individual rights.

In carrying out these functions, public school systems should also:

- not "deny access to students for reasons unrelated to [a school's] educational focus"; and
- "provide an appropriate placement for each student" in every community.

Asserting by implication that the meanings of his key terms are inherently obvious, Hess goes on to argue that the terms others might use to set forth other principles are not. For example, he observes that "diversity" and "tolerance" are "umbrella terms with multiple interpretations." Therefore, they lie outside his cluster of principles because, when we try to define them more precisely, "it becomes clear that we must privilege some values at the expense of others." If he believes that a similar privileging of certain values might color his own key terms, such as "obligations of citizenship," "productive members of the social order," "societal responsibilities," "individual rights," and the like, he gives no indication.

Hess seems to arrive at his position partly for affirmative reasons (e.g., an emphasis on academic learning) and partly because of a surprisingly bitter view of educators (some of whom he names, but most of whom he only characterizes). In his view, these educators:

- "explicitly promote a particular world view and endorse a particular social ethos";
- "promote partisan attitudes toward American foreign policy, the propriety of affirmative action, or the morality of redistributive social policies";
- teach students to "accept teen pregnancy or homosexuality as normal and morally unobjectionable";

- attempt to "stamp out familial views and impress children with socially approved beliefs"; and
- treat public institutions as their personal playthings.

To illustrate his more general points, Hess portrays the "meaningful questions" asked in the classrooms of the Coalition of Essential Schools as a herd of Trojan ponies surreptitiously unloading the teachers' agendas. It's not clear what "meaningful questions" might be in the classrooms he approves of, though readers might infer that they would be limited to the rational analysis of topics that arise from well-developed and authoritatively taught subject matter. There is nothing wrong with such questions, of course. But anyone who thinks that they—or the answers to them—would be value-free is likely to have slept through his or her undergraduate philosophy classes.

More to the point, however, a narrow and academic definition of such questions would exclude from the public school universe those who think students should also wrestle with forming habits of the heart as well as the mind, should learn to use critical inquiry to amend and expand values and understandings as well as to confirm them, and should go beyond "my country, right or wrong" to embrace the rest of Carl Schurz's famous phrase, "if right, to be kept right; and if wrong, to be set right."

I have spent a fair amount of time in schools of late, witnessing heroic efforts of underfinanced and overregulated teachers to enact both the academic preparation *and* the democracy-building ethos that our schools were meant to embody. If Hess is suggesting that generally left-leaning personal agendas have dominated public school instruction for a generation or more, then we should be able to see around us a widely shared value system that reflects those views. However, when I survey newspapers, polls, elections, and even school reform debates at national and local levels, I see instead an enormous variety of values and priorities. Some may find that diversity of views troubling. What troubles me is not that people disagree but that we seem increasingly incapable of working through our differences to embed public school policies and practices in a conception of the common good that can transcend political perspectives without disrespecting them.

The sort of public conversations about public education that would open minds to a critical look at new ideas would be, as I'm sure Hess would agree, tough to structure and to conduct. Where he and I are likely to disagree is on whether the topic of those conversations will ever be settled and, more important, whether it ever should be. Teaching skills and developing in each generation the social cohesion on which so much else depends will be easier (though never easy) to approach than will matters of values, educational philosophies, social goals, and civic priorities. Moreover, balancing the relative claims of the student, family, community, nation, and the wider world on how and what schools teach is a democratic journey, not a settled destination.

From the start, Hess acknowledges the powerful resonance of the concept of public education. What seems to make him impatient, even exasperated, is that the people who lead what he and some others pejoratively call "government-run schools" aren't listening to him. Not listening can be a stance or a reaction. Seeing it as a *stance,* I join him in his exasperation. The habit of "reflexively shrinking" from a consideration of alternatives hardens the democratic arteries. Seeing it as a *reaction,* I worry that world views (a term I prefer to "ideology") too often appear as righteous opposites, leaving all but the most robust listeners wondering what's the point.

Finding areas of overlap in our views under such conditions isn't easy. Developing the skills of measured and thoughtful dialogue needed to create such overlap is even harder. The challenge of doing so, however, demonstrates why a free nation needs public schools that are set up to make public decision making meaningful at the daily, close-to-home levels, as well as at higher levels. Such deliberative procedures force us to ask not only what we want our own children to learn but also what we want all children to learn. Children are, after all, collectively as well as individually the next generation, and the education we bequeath to them is communal as well as personal.

We need to talk and listen our way into more overlap in our political/philosophical Venn diagrams. Having that running conversation looms large in my definition of what makes the public schools public. Hess seems to argue that, through a few principles and a multitude of entities all claiming the mantle of public education, we can make the need for that conversation go away. I would argue instead that getting better at it should be our number-one priority.

Evans Clinchy, Reimagining Public Education

I heartily agree with Frederick Hess that we need to rethink and reimagine our antiquated American system of public education. But not for the reasons he sets forth.

I also agree with his broad definition of the purposes of public schooling: "that public schools are . . . defined by their commitment to preparing students to be productive members of the social order" (and therefore active citizens of a democratic society) who are able to think and use their minds well and are "aware of their societal responsibilities and respectful of constitutional strictures" (including an understanding of the Constitution and especially the Bill of Rights); "that such schools cannot deny access to students for reasons unrelated to their educational focus" (i.e., no racially, ethnically, or economically segregated schools); "and that the system of public schools available in any community must provide an appropriate placement for each student" (all students and their parents must be offered the kind of schooling they believe is most suitable). But I do not agree that we should seek to create the kind of reimagined system Hess appears to be proposing.

Questions of Definition, Control, and Funding

Throughout most of the history of the U.S., a public school has been defined as a school created, operated, and largely paid for by the citizens of each community through a locally elected board of education. While the Constitution leaves the basic authority for education in the hands of the individual states, and even though such locally controlled schools have, over the past century, received increased funding from both state and federal sources, this tradition of local control has managed to endure more or less intact—at least until the past 25 or so years.

The continued importance of this tradition was underscored in 1973 by the U.S. Supreme Court in its *Rodriguez* decision. The majority opinion put the matter this way:

> In an era that has witnessed a consistent trend toward centralization of the functions of government, local sharing of responsibility for public education has survived. The merit of local control was recognized in both the majority and dissenting opinions in *Wright v. Council of the City of Emporia*. Mr. Justice Stewart stated there that "direct control over decisions vitally affecting the education of one's children is a need that is strongly felt in our society." The Chief Justice in his dissent agreed that local control is not only vital to continued public support of the schools, but it is of overriding importance from an educational standpoint as well.
>
> The persistence of attachment to government at its lowest level where education is concerned reflects the depth of commitment of its supporters. In part local control means . . . the freedom to devote more money to the education of one's children. Equally important, however, is the opportunity it offers for participation in the decision-making process that determines how those local dollars will be spent. Each locality is free to tailor local programs to local needs. Pluralism also affords some opportunity for experimentation, innovation, and a healthy competition for educational excellence. An analogy to the Nation-State relationship in our federal system seems uniquely appropriate. Mr. Justice Brandeis identified as one of the peculiar strengths of our form of government each state's freedom to "serve as a laboratory; to try novel social and economic experiments." No area of social concern stands to profit more from a multiplicity of viewpoints and from a diversity of approaches than does public education.
>
> Further, Justice William Brennan found in his dissent that "Here, there can be no doubt that education is inextricably linked to the right to participate in the electoral process and to the rights of free speech and association guaranteed by the First Amendment."[1]

During the past quarter century, however, the "consistent trend toward centralization of the functions of government" has run rampant in the field of public schooling. In the name of public school "reform," the states have usurped local control by imposing uniform, authoritarian, "high," "rigorous," one-size-fits-all academic standards and punitive high-stakes standardized testing on all students, all schools, and all school systems.

The federal education establishment, through its No Child Left Behind Act, has carried this intrusive, antidemocratic curricular control and standardized testing program to ludicrous extremes, requiring the testing of all students in grades 3 through 8 and insisting on annual progress in test scores with severe sanctions for schools that fail to show such progress. However, neither the federal government nor the states have provided the financial resources to pay for all this "reform" or to remedy the gross inequities that exist between those school systems that serve the wealthy and those that serve our poor and minority students and parents. I find these events distressing, but none of them appear to worry Hess very much.

If the powerful democratic tradition of local control is to be maintained and if we are to genuinely reimagine our public education system, we will need to do several things. First, we will have to abandon the authoritarian standards and high-stakes testing agenda that currently afflict our public schools and return to the citizens of our local communities the control over what is taught, how it will be taught, and who will teach it. State and federal interference should be limited to ensuring minimum competency in the basic skills of reading, writing, and mathematics.

Second, we will simultaneously need both state and federal governments to guarantee that all of the nation's public schools are fully and equitably funded and that the civil rights of all students and parents—but especially our poor and minority students and parents—are fully protected. Hess does not appear to recommend any of these policies.

The Threat of Vouchers and Privatization

We will also have to erect strong safeguards against the threat of vouchers and any further encroachment of the private corporate sector into the field of public schooling. Now that the Supreme Court has permitted the use of public funds to finance vouchers that can be used to pay tuition at nonpublic, including religious, schools, Hess appears to be saying that we should aim to create a system of public education similar to that of many European countries, where public funding is given directly to all nonpublic schools. Such a proposal would still violate both the First Amendment's separation of church and state and the democratic commitment to local public citizen control.

In addition, Hess proposes that we permit the private, for-profit sector to run both schools and school systems so long as those schools are monitored by some public body—despite the fact that the track record of Edison and other corporate EMOs (education management organizations) is educationally and economically dismal. Hess appears to believe that it is morally legitimate for private corporations to profit from the education of children, rather than being required to plow "profits" back into our chronically underfunded public schools. This thinking parallels the already-established view that it is somehow morally legitimate for corporate HMOs to make a profit out of caring for the sick, rather than being required to plow that money back into the health-care system. Neither of these policies is morally acceptable in any fair, just, and equitable system of democratic government.

A Truly Reimagined, Genuinely Democratic Public System of Diversity and Choice

Hess does raise an issue of fundamental importance when he points out that "there are many ways to provide legitimate public education." I assume that he means that there is no single kind of school—be it rigidly "traditional," wildly "progressive," or something in between—that could possibly serve the diverse educational beliefs of this nation's parents, the equally diverse professional philosophies of our public school educators, and most especially the enormously varied educational needs of our children and young people.

Strangely, however, Hess believes that many "prominent educational thinkers" (among others, he names Frank Smith, Susan Ohanian, Deborah Meier, and Alfie Kohn) have encouraged the public schools to promote "preferred social values" to the American public rather than advocating that all public schools limit themselves to teaching children "the essential skills and knowledge that make for productive citizens." He asserts that the "public schools should teach children . . . to respect our constitutional order and instruct them in the framework of rights and obligations that secure our democracy and protect our liberty." He argues this point as if this educational prescription were not itself an ideology—even if it is one that may be widely shared and one that in its main outlines is most certainly shared by his list of misguided thinkers.

Hess then goes on to advocate not just his own ideological prescription but the basic rule of what I would see as that truly reimagined public system we should be attempting to create. In order to encompass those diverse educational beliefs of parents and professional educators and to meet the varied educational needs of our children and young people, he says that we should "allow families to avail themselves of a range of schools with diverse perspectives, so long as each teaches respect for our democratic and liberal tradition." Thus we need that wide diversity of public schools—ranging from traditional to progressive—from which parents, teachers, administrators, and older students can choose the type of schooling they believe will most benefit each child and young person. As Hess puts it, such strictly public school choice would create "heightened family involvement" and produce "a shared sense of commitment" that would tend to make such "self-selected schools more participatory and democratic."

It is, I believe, the job of our local public school systems, assisted and encouraged by state and federal governments, to provide that diversity of options. But the basic control of what goes on in all of our public schools must always remain solely in the public domain and solidly anchored in the will of the citizens of our local communities.

Note

1. *San Antonio Independent School District* v. *Rodriguez*, U.S. Supreme Court, 411 U.S. 1 (1973).

POSTSCRIPT

Should "Public Schooling" Be Redefined?

In the February 2004 issue of *Phi Delta Kappan,* Frederick M. Hess put forth a rejoinder to his four critics in an article titled "Debating Principles for Public Schooling in a New Century." He lists some significant points of agreement, including that it is necessary and useful to reconsider the essence of "public schooling" in an age marked by radical changes in how education is being provided. However, these critics, Hess contends, attack reforms as "anti-public education" for permitting the same practices that some "public schools" already engage in—for example, schools that are not open to all students when located in an affluent community. He feels that some critics allow the notion of public schooling to become a rhetorical banner for bolstering partisan positions and delegitimatizing opposing ideas. Hess further states that "there is a real danger to the rhetorical strategy of branding objectionable reforms as de facto 'assaults on public schooling.' This device is fruitless and divisive. Perhaps more forebodingly, it excommunicates many who honor public education because they fail to endorse the 'right kind' of public schooling."

John C. Lundt, a professor of educational leadership, says that education is leaving the schoolhouse as technology increasingly makes it an anytime-anywhere activity. In a provocative article in the December 2004 issue of *The Futurist* titled "Learning for Ourselves: A New Paradigm for Education," Lundt concludes that the antiquated structure of today's school was designed to meet the needs of a world that no longer exists, that public schools will not change as long as they monopolize educational funding, and that growing numbers of parents find the activities and values of public schools inappropriate for their children. This basic concern about funding is echoed by reporter Joe Williams in his book *Cheating Our Kids: How Politics and Greed Ruin Education* (2005). Williams examines the impact of special-interest groups on local public school systems (specifically in New York and Milwaukee), finding that most "reform" money only expands already bloated district bureaucracies. He calls for a concerted effort by concerned parents to reclaim power.

Additional challenging ideas may be found in Paul A. Zoch's *Doomed to Fail: The Built-in Defects of American Education* (2004); Susan Ohanian's "Refrains of the School Critics," *The School Administrator* (August 2005); Hannah Lobel's "Putting the Public Back in Public Education," *Utne* (January–February 2009); and Ross Hubbard's "Tinkering Change vs. System Change," *Phi Delta Kappan* (June 2009).

Internet References . . .

National Alliance for Civic Education

Dedicated to ensuring that the next generation understands and values democracy and participates in its processes.

http://www.civnet.net

Center for Education Reform

Pro-voucher organization that features a reform update, reports, and a weekly newswire.

http://www.edreform.com

Rethinking Schools

Site features special reports on voucher failures across the nation as well as other attacks on privatization.

http://www.rethinkingschools.org

No Child Left Behind

U.S. Department of Education site examines implementation of NCLB and provides links for parents and teachers.

http://www.ed.gov./nclb

No Child Left

Site offering multiple reasons why NCLB must go.

http://nochildleft.com

Inner City Education Foundation

California-based organization sponsoring charter schools in poverty areas featuring a college-prep curriculum.

http://www.icefla.org

Turnaround for Children

Site offering guidance to school staff wishing to dramatically improve the quality of instruction.

http://turnaroundusa.org

Current Fundamental Issues

*T*he issues discussed in this unit cover a number of fundamental social, cultural, and political problems currently under consideration by education experts, social scientists, and politicians, as well as by parents, teachers, and the media. Positions on these issues are expressed by Kristan A. Morrison, Gary K. Clabaugh, Charles L. Glenn, Paul E. Peterson, Frederick M. Hess, Chester F. Finn, Jr., Dianne Piche, Karin Chenoweth, Andy Smarick, Marc Tucker, and Diane Ravitch.

- Are Truly Democratic Classrooms Possible?
- Has the Supreme Court Reconfigured American Education?
- Is No Child Left Behind a Flawed Policy?
- Can Failing Schools Be Turned Around?
- Are Local School Boards Obsolete?

ISSUE 6

Are Truly Democratic Classrooms Possible?

YES: Kristan A. Morrison, from "Democratic Classrooms: Promises and Challenges of Student Voice and Choice, Part One," *Educational Horizons* (Fall 2008)

NO: Gary K. Clabaugh, from "Second Thoughts About Democratic Classrooms," *Educational Horizons* (Fall 2008)

ISSUE SUMMARY

YES: Associate professor of education Kristan A. Morrison explores historical and theoretical bases for implementing democratic practices in schools that would make student experience more appealing and productive.

NO: Professor of education Gary K. Clabaugh examines such factors as top-down management, compulsory attendance, business world influences, and federal mandates to declare Morrison's ideas to be "out of touch" with reality.

Certainly everyone would agree that one of the primary aims of education is to produce citizens capable of effectively participating in their society. The controversial aspect of this aim resides in determining the best way of carrying it out. In recent years educators and theorists have renewed a basic question that has been discussed for over a hundred years, namely "Is it possible to produce democratic citizens if the schooling the young are subjected to is clearly undemocratic?"

As Charles C. Haynes, in "Schools of Conscience," *Educational Leadership* (May 2009), states, "We need schools that actually practice what their civics classes are supposed to teach. . . . At a time when the United States faces unprecedented challenges at home and abroad, public schools must do far more to prepare young people to be engaged, ethical advocates of 'liberty and justice for all.'" Haynes contends that education's highest aim is to create moral and civic habits of the heart. This central purpose was articulated by the early leaders of American education. Thomas Jefferson made the principles of democratic government an essential element in the free public education of the general citizenry. Horace Mann's common school was dedicated to producing people able to critically judge the political and social needs of the nation. Waves of European immigrants in the nineteenth century prompted a new emphasis on socialization strategies and the development of patriotism. As Joel Spring has pointed out in his book *Conflict of Interests,* "In a totalitarian society it is possible to teach a single interpretation of the laws and government in the public schools, but in a society such as that of the United States, which fosters a variety of political beliefs . . . , attempts to teach principles of government can result in major political battles."

In "Civic Education and Political Participation," *Phi Delta Kappan* (September 2003), William A. Galston declares that school-based civic education has been in decline over recent decades. He claims that every significant indicator of political engagement among the young has fallen. Community service programs in high schools are on the increase, but there is no evidence that such "mandatory volunteerism" leads to wider civic participation. He states that "the surge of patriotic sentiment among young people in the immediate wake of September 11th has not yielded a comparable surge in engaged, active citizenship."

If the school atmosphere is by design, by tradition, or by habit undemocratic can truly democratic citizens emerge? Haynes states that "to prepare students to be ethical, engaged citizens we must give them . . . meaningful opportunities to practice freedom responsibly in a school culture that encourages shared decision-making. . . . In short we need schools that actually practice . . . freedom and democracy, not censorship and repression."

Similarly, Marion Brady, in "Cover the Material—Or Teach Students to Think?" *Educational Leadership* (February 2008), claims that students need to tackle issues straight out of the complex world in which they live. "A focus on real-world issues . . . enables students and teachers to experience the 'meatiness' of the direct study of reality. . . . It shows respect for students, who become more than mere candidates for the next higher grade. . . . It disregards the arbitrary, artificial boundaries of the academic disciplines."

In "Democracy and Education: Empowering Students to Make Sense of Their World," *Phi Delta Kappan* (January 2008), William H. Garrison contends that the best learning happens under a truly democratic system in which students assume the freedom and responsibility to make choices and direct their learning experiences. His ideas certainly reflect the basic philosophy of John Dewey and the sentiments of John Holt.

In the articles presented here Kristan A. Morrison aligns herself with critical theorists in the field of education who feel that the public schools have been used by societal and political forces to curtail rather than release student freedom. Gary K. Clabaugh thinks that while some of Morrison's points are well-taken she naively ignores the shaping power of numerous internal and external factors.

Democratic Classrooms: Promises and Challenges of Student Voice and Choice

Abstract

If we ever hope to have schools that are engaging and that truly embody democracy, then the classes within them must provide opportunities for students to experience autonomy, freedom, and choice in what is studied, when, and how. This article explores both the historical and theoretical framework of democratic freedom-based education and the promises and challenges of implementing democratic practices in schools.

. . .

Introduction

Schools and society are reflections of one another. Certain values and beliefs are dominant in our society and inculcated in school. They include

- a competitive ethos and firm conviction that a meritocracy exists in our society
- a view that instrumental and extrinsic motivations are more important than intrinsic motivations
- an excessive valuing of academics
- a belief in the atomization and fragmentation of subjects of study, people, and nature
- the conviction that the characteristic of obedience (doing as one is told or believing as one is told) is of more value in our society than that of criticality
- the belief that one's worth can be defined by others (as good student or bad student)

Once students become adults, they perpetuate those same dominant values in both society and school.

This cycle is complicated, however, because beyond those dominant values, schools are "terrains of struggle" (Giroux 1988), places where contradictory values and ideals compete for prominence.

Reprinted with permission of *Educational Horizons*, quarterly journal of Pi Lambda Theta Inc., International Honor Society and Professional Association in Education, P O Box 6626, Bloomington, IN 47401, Fall 2008, pp. 50–59.

Critical educational theorists, who include John Dewey and more-contemporary authors such as Henry Giroux, Paulo Freire, Peter McLaren, bell hooks, David Purpel, and Maxine Greene, argue that certain moral, political, and intellectual ideals should take precedence over others in schools. They assert that our schools should emphasize commitment to a democratic system in which each citizen's autonomy and dignity are honored in an open, just, respectful, and pluralistic community, a community that values and encourages a critical approach in the intellectual search for truth and meaning in each individual's life (Purpel 1989).

The community these theorists seek is a delicately balanced synthesis between the individual (thesis) and a collection of individuals (antithesis). In other words, an individual's autonomy is delimited by others' rights to dignity, respect, safety, and the search for truth and meaning to everyone's lives; if person A decides to do something that somehow infringes on person B's rights, then person A is prohibited from taking that action and encouraged to find actions that can both express his or her autonomy and honor the rights of others.

Many of us know from experience that our society's schools often fall far short of fostering the development of people who value diversity, who are both autonomous yet cognizant of others' needs and rights, and who are open-minded yet equipped with critical-thinking skills to analyze contradictory ideas. Instead, many of our schools foster the development of very different sorts of individuals.

Does that indicate that the critical educational theorists are wrong? No, it just means that they and like-minded educators must struggle to actualize their ideals in schools. One way to do that, I would argue, is to institute more democratic and freedom-based practices within our educational system. This article explores the historical and theoretical framework of such practices, and then goes on to detail their promises and challenges.

Definitions and Historical/Theoretical Framework

The term "democratic education" as used in this article is linked with and synonymous with the term "freedom-based education," for just as democracy as a political system is grounded in individual freedoms, democracy as an educational system is also grounded in freedoms. The linkage between the two terms is supported by the self-descriptions of most freedom-based schools in the United States (e.g., "free schools," Sudbury Valley-modeled schools, "unschooling" families, etc.), which also identify themselves as sites of democratic education.

In democratic and freedom-based education, students are free to decide what they study, and how, and when they study it. This form of schooling has a number of historical antecedents, outlined by Bennis (2006). He argues that one genesis of this model of education is the form of learning found in most pre-industrial societies. In these societies (past and present), children are actively engaged in the life of a given society; they learn skills and knowledge by means of imitation, apprenticeship, modeling, and conversation rather than in any formal school setting. Freedom-based education is also rooted in the Western philosophical tradition of the ancient Greeks, in the Romantic thinkers (e.g., Rousseau and Froebel), in the libertarian-anarchist tradition, in the transcendentalist movement of nineteenth-century America, and in the twentieth-century free-school movement (e.g., Summerhill School, led by A. S. Neill, and the many U.S. free schools that cropped up during the countercultural revolution of the 1960s and 1970s) (pp. 23–32).

Democratic and freedom-based education is grounded in the premise that people are naturally curious and have an innate desire to learn and grow. If left un-fettered, un-coerced, and un-manipulated (e.g., by conventional educational practices that often diminish those innate characteristics), people will pursue their interests vigorously and with gusto, and thus learn and make meaning on their own and in concert with others. Individuals honored and respected in this process become socialized to honor and respect the dignity and autonomy of others (Dennison 1969; Hern 1996; Holt 1972, 1989; Illich 1971; Llewellyn 1997; Mercogliano 1998; Neill and Lamb 1992).

Although most contemporary freedom-based education is found in the form of private schools or the home-schooling version, "unschooling" (Morrison 2007b), American public schools could shift more closely to this model by adopting more-democratic practices and organizational structures (Reitzug 2003). Thus, enacting democratic practices within conventional, more-authoritarian and -bureaucratic schools could serve as a steppingstone toward adopting the model of democratic and freedom-based education more fully.

Democratic education can take multiple forms, ranging from the micro level of within-class democracy to the more-ideal macro level of whole-school democracy, and within each level, a number of different democratic practices can be enacted. For example, at the micro level, a teacher can utilize discussion; offer students test and assignment choices that attend to their unique learning preferences; allow students "protest rights" (Shor 1996); practice contract grading (Shor 1996) or self-grading; allow students to call the teacher by first name; and ask students to co-construct the course (have a voice in course content, grading, rubric creation, etc.). At the macro, whole-school level, schools can allow students to construct their entire curricula. (See Morrison 2007a, which examines the Albany Free School, a school where pre-K through eighth-grade students choose what, how, and when they study subjects, or see Goddard College for university-level self-development of curricula.)

Promises of Democratic Education

Proponents of democratic and freedom-based education argue that with autonomy and choice, people experience a much-different, much-better form of education than that offered by the conventional, hierarchical, more-coercive education system present in most public schools.

First, they argue that a democratic education promises much more meaningful learning. If people have choice and freedom to study what interests them, then they become more deeply engaged in, and thus less alienated from, their learning. More engagement leads to better retention and better critical reflection and analysis. For example, Watson wrote in *Summerhill: For and Against* (1970) that "pupils given freedom to decide what they will do, when, and how develop increasing independence, stronger interests, and better quality of work" (p. 177).

Gatto, in *Dumbing Us Down: The Hidden Curriculum of Compulsory Schools* (1992), echoes that argument, stating that our conventional education system infantilizes students by constantly compelling them and that this compulsion "guarantees that they will do [work] poorly, with a bad will, or indifferently" (p. 93). Democratic education, conversely, has no infantilizing effect; instead, it places great trust in the students, and they, more often than not, rise to the challenge. In the process, students become more mature, self-disciplined, and intrinsically motivated, seeing the value of learning above and beyond its usefulness to getting a "good job" (Bhave 1996; Labaree 1997).

Proponents of democratic education further argue that people who are given freedom and choice will ultimately become better democratic citizens because they have learned how to negotiate with others, to name obstacles, and to know themselves (Bhave 1996; Dewey 1916; Gatto 1992; Goodman 1962; Holt 1972; Holzman 1997; Illich 1971; Morrison 2007a; Shor 1996). That ultimately benefits all of society by developing people who are open to change and to listening to others so that all consider themselves vital to society. As Shor argued in *When Students Have Power* (1996): "Power-sharing . . . creates the desire and imagination of change while also creating the experience and skills for it. The critical-democratic class, then, is a context for change that develops the desire and imagination to make change" (p. 176).

Challenges of Democratic Education

Democratic education is, in many ways, antithetical to conventional school practices in our society. Student voice and choice don't fit particularly well into a system characterized by bureaucracy and hierarchical structure (Reitzug 2003). There are three main areas of challenge to instituting democratic practices in classrooms and schools—students, teachers, and the institution as a whole.

Student Challenges

Students educated in conventional schools for the majority of their lives represent one of the biggest challenges to democratic education. Because soliciting student voice and choice in the classroom lies so far outside the educational norm in our society, democratic education practices may be met, initially, by considerable student resistance. Most students are accustomed to being told what to do and to acting passively in the classroom; they are viewed, and may view themselves, as safe-deposit boxes waiting for deposits of knowledge to fill them (Freire 1970). The hidden curriculum trains students to be quiet and docile, to be indifferent to and bored with course content (because they have no say in what it is), and to accept being told what they and their work are worth (Gatto 1992; Giroux 1978; Illich 1971; Vallance 2003).

It should come as no surprise that students who have experienced this training, especially those students who have succeeded in the "game" of schooling, might resist changed rules that ask them to go against all they have been taught. Students who come from conventional education into classrooms or schools employing democratic practices will often feel uncomfortable with or even fearful of jeopardizing the only pattern of life they know (Goodman 1964). They may become "Siberians" (Shor 1996) who gravitate to the periphery of the class, where they sit silent and disconnected from democratic processes. Asked to play a role in content construction (e.g., explain what they are generally interested in studying, or a particular topic), they may be at a loss, for many have never even considered what their own interests might be. Spontaneous initiative, curiosity, and trust in themselves, by and large, may have been drummed out of them; they may have learned to view education as purely instrumental—a means to an end rather than an end in itself (Bhave 1996; Holt 1972; Labaree 1997). Students thus may resent anyone trying to show them differently. This resentment will be connected to a lack of trust and the antagonistic teacher-student relationships that are the norm. Students have been trained to start out viewing most teachers as "the enemy"—people who infringe on their will and their freedoms. To be asked suddenly to change this view is more than many students can handle.

Besides student resistance to democratic education, another challenge that arises is students mistaking positive freedom for negative freedom. Maxine Greene, in *The Dialectic of Freedom* (1988), has defined negative freedom as freedom from constraints. That is the starting point for positive freedom, but positive freedom also encompasses the freedom to work in concert with others to overcome limits. Democratic education is not negative freedom alone; it does not only mean freeing students to do whatever they want. As Dewey wrote in *Experience and Education* (1938): "For freedom from restriction, the negative side, is to be prized only as a means to a freedom which is power: power to frame purposes, to judge wisely;. . . power to select and order means to carry chosen ends into operation" (pp. 63–64). Because conventionally educated students have so little experience of any freedom in school, so little practice with democratic discussion or with assuming authority on their own, they will often mistake democratic, positive freedom practices for negative freedom only. Students may thus see the teacher who asks for democratic input as weak or unprepared, and they may attempt to evade, rather than make, their opportunities (e.g., push for lowered workloads, etc.) (Shor 1996).

Teacher Challenges

Students will not be the only ones who resist changes; teachers will balk as well. Very few teachers have experienced democratic education themselves, so to attempt to institute democratic practices in their classrooms represents a sizable leap into the unknown. Teachers may be fearful of this unknown, fearful that involving students' voices and choices in running a course will produce chaos and an overall lack of learning. Part of this fear stems from lack of trust in students. Teachers have become accustomed to viewing most students as lazy and uninterested, people who must be pushed, prodded, cajoled, and threatened into doing "what's best for them," and thus they fear that students will try to minimize challenges and take the easy way out (Goodman 1962; Gross 1973; Holt 1970, 1972; Rogers 1969; Sheffer 1996; Watson 1970). Another part of this fear of chaos and lack of learning lies in conventional ideas about what learning is. Many teachers, themselves schooled in conventional educational institutions, believe that their role is to fill students with curricular information. They might argue that students, who don't know what they don't know, cannot possibly exercise choice and freedom in curricular content to create real learning.

The idea that knowledge can be stuffed into the individual, as opposed to being constructed and mediated through the individual (Lamm 1972), has led to the conventional educational practices of mandated courses and pre-established syllabi. Teachers are used to coming, and in fact are expected by both students and their administrators to come, to the first class with content ready for delivery to interchangeable students. Teachers may feel that if they arrive without a pre-set syllabus and lesson plans, students and administrators will view them as weak, unprepared, or lacking in authority. The class's disrespect could lead to poor course and teacher evaluations as well as jeopardize their jobs. Besides losing control, teachers might also fear silence and an emptiness if they attempt democratic practices. They might also fear that some students will take over and silence others. Last, inviting student voice and choice might ill prepare students for the "real world," where they will have to learn to bow their wills to others and see their needs go unmet (Guterson 1996).

Conventionally schooled teachers who dare to implement democratic practices must grapple with all these fears. They must be willing to abandon plans and adjust to the process of dialogue; they must learn to listen more than talk, not apply one lesson plan to all sections of the same class, and surrender their authoritarian supports (Shor 1996). They must learn to trust students' innate curiosity, and if this curiosity has been crushed in the past, they must work to bring it back to life. Teachers must take to heart what Rogers wrote in *Freedom to Learn* (1969):

> If I distrust the human being, then I must cram him with information of my own choosing, lest he go his own mistaken way. But if I trust the capacity of the human individual for developing his own potentiality, then I can provide him with many opportunities and permit him to choose his own way and his own direction in his learning. (p. 114)

And teachers need to recognize that democratic educational practices may well lead students to reject the "real world" of hierarchical authority and to work for more true democracy in the larger economic, political, and social systems. Teachers who attempt more-democratic educational practices thus embrace education for the world that might be rather than for the world that is.

Institutional Challenges

The institutional structures of conventional education also represent significant stumbling blocks to enacting more-democratic practices. Unless the entire institution is itself fully democratic, teachers who attempt to bring democracy into heretofore undemocratic spaces will encounter challenges.

The "deep structures" of schools compose one such challenge: those "widely shared assumptions about what schools are for and how they should function" (Tye 1998, paragraph 5). One example of such deep structures is the conventional schools' view that knowledge exists outside and separate from human mediation and construction and that learning equals the transmission of this information from holders of this knowledge (teachers) to empty vessels (students).

This view of knowledge leads to conventional school practices: mandating that all students learn certain subjects; insisting that subjects be fragmented one from the other; and enforcing a certain progression of information that follows an external, discipline-specific logic (e.g., take algebra before geometry). Educational managers who hold this view of knowledge might argue, as mentioned in "Teacher Challenges," above, that students don't know what they don't know, so how could they possibly decide what should be included in a class? The managers also might worry that students who have voice and choice on subject inclusion might choose not to learn what the institution considers vital information.

That concern, a valid one, can be dealt with by establishing institutional structures and practices that allow time to explore the ideas of negative and positive freedom described earlier. Students' resistance to learning certain ideas often stems from feelings of powerlessness rather than from willed ignorance; if educational institutions can set forth rational and personalized arguments for the worth of some topic (beyond stating in a course catalog that the subject will make one liberally educated), students will willingly include that topic in their studies. Certainly this process can become time-consuming, but that is intrinsic to learning democratic habits of mind.

The view of knowledge and learning described above also impacts assumptions about class sizes. If the subject knowledge is simply to be transmitted to students, a high teacher-student ratio is logically efficient. Institutional structures of large classes and mandated, pre-arranged content render attempts to institute democratic practices uncertain. How can a teacher truly get a large number of students' voices and choices heard? Can a teacher stray too far from the mandated content if the teachers around her are working to perpetuate the curricular status quo? Won't a democratic teacher in a required class have a more difficult time breaking through and connecting with the students who resent this limitation of their freedom of choice?

An additional institutional constraint is the conventional system of grading. I have written elsewhere (Morrison 2003a, 2003b) about how grades can deflect students from creating personal meaning and toward simply performing for sought-for ends (e.g., diploma, college acceptance, scholarships, praise, lack of punishment, etc.). This performance orientation complicates the teacher-student relationship: students come to feel less powerful vis-à-vis the teacher and thus act subserviently to earn good grades. Student subservience manifests itself in not questioning or challenging the teacher in any really meaningful way; in essence, students have learned that classroom success often requires that they check their democratic rights at the door. Grading has, perhaps unintentionally, rendered many students voiceless and dependent. (Admittedly, students participate in their own oppression in this regard, but that makes it no less a form of oppression.)

A last major institutional constraint on introducing democratic educational practices to conventional school settings is the use of space and time. The conventional school day is broken into a series of relatively short periods (forty-five to ninety minutes each); school plants are typically divorced from the wider community (separate, often closed, campuses); and there is an extremely high population density. Such use of space and time is inimical to democracy, in which decisions, discussions, and building trust take time (longer than a semester or academic year, or longer than a single class period); connections to and involvement in community activities and spaces are highly valued; and the ability and space necessary to move about freely, and group and regroup, are needed.

Conclusion

Critical educational theorists believe that democratic values—the search for truth and personal meaning, justice, equality, and respect for the thoughts and humanity of others—will rarely result from schools in which students never have an opportunity to practice democratic habits of mind. Thus, these theorists support including democratic practices in school wherever possible. Clearly, though, there are significant roadblocks to instituting such practices, especially the more deeply these practices infiltrate the organizational structures of schools.

Some might argue that our schools were never meant to create democratic citizens because our society is not now and never truly will be a democracy; the undemocratic characteristics of our conventional schools exist by design. Although such cynicism may be warranted, given what we know about how power is used and abused in our society, critical educational theorists would counter that it is our "ontological vocation" (Freire 1970) to struggle for seemingly far-off ideals. Although we might lack a true democracy now, one will never be attained unless people work for it both inside and outside our educational institutions.

References

Bennis, D. M. 2006. "De-Mystifying Freedom-based Education." Master's thesis, Vermont College of Union Institute & University.

Bhave, V. 1996. "The Intimate and the Ultimate." In *Deschooling Our Lives*, ed. M. Hern, 16–22. Gabriola Island, B.C.: New Society Publishers.

Dennison, G. 1969. *The Lives of Children: The Story of the First Street School.* New York: Random House.

Dewey, J. 1916. *Democracy and Education.* New York: Macmillan Company.

————. 1938. *Experience and Education.* New York: Collier Macmillan Publishers.

Freire, P. 1970. *The Pedagogy of the Oppressed.* New York: Herder and Herder.

Gatto, J. T. 1992. *Dumbing Us Down: The Hidden Curriculum of Compulsory Schooling.* Gabriola Island, B.C.: New Society Publishers.

Giroux, H. 1978. "Developing Educational Programs and Overcoming the Hidden Curriculum." Clearing House 52(4): 148–151.

————. 1988. *Teachers as Intellectuals: Toward a Critical Pedagogy of Learning.* Westport, Conn.: Bergin and Garvey.

Goodman, P. 1962. *The Community of Scholars.* New York: Vintage Books.

————. 1964. *Compulsory Miseducation.* New York: Vintage Books.

Greene, M. 1988. *The Dialectic of Freedom.* New York: Teachers College Press.

Gross, R. 1973. "After Deschooling, Free Learning." In *After Deschooling, What?* ed. I. Illich, 148–160. New York: Harper and Row.

Guterson, D. 1996. "Family Matters: Why Home Schooling Makes Sense." In *Deschooling Our Lives,* ed. M. Hern, 16–22.

Hern, M., ed. 1996. *Deschooling Our Lives.* Gabriola Island, B.C.: New Society Publishers.

Holt, J. 1970. In *Summerhill: For and Against,* ed. H. Hart. New York: Hart Publishing Co.

————. 1972. *Freedom and Beyond.* New York: E.P. Dutton and Co.

————. 1989. *Learning All the Time.* New York: Addison-Wesley Publishing.

Holzman, L. 1997. *Schools for Growth.* Mahwah, N.J.: Lawrence Erlbaum Associates.

Illich, I. 1971. *Deschooling Society.* New York: Harper and Row.

Labaree, David E 1997. *How to Succeed in School without Really Learning: The Credentials Race in American Education.* New Haven: Yale University Press.

Lamm, Z. 1972. "The Status of Knowledge in the Radical Concept of Education." In *Curriculum and the Cultural Revolution,* ed. D. Purpel and M. Belanger, 149–168. Berkeley, Calif.: McCutchan.

Llewellyn, G. 1997. *The Teenage Liberation Handbook: How to Quit School and Get a Real Life and Education.* Shaftsbury, Dorset, U.K.: Element Books Limited.

Mercogliano, C. 1998. *Making It Up as We Go Along: The Story of the Albany Free School.* Portsmouth, N.H.: Heinemann.

Morrison, K. 2003a. "Is Grading Doing What We Want It to Do?" *Paths of Learning* 15 (Winter): 20–23.

————. 2003b. "What Else Besides Grading? Looking for Alternatives in All the Right Places." *Paths of Learning* 16 (Spring): 22–28.

————. 2007a. *Free School Teaching: A Journey into Radical Progressive Education.* Albany, N.Y.: SUNY Press.

————. 2007b. "Unschooling: Homeschools Can Provide the Freedom to Learn." *Encounter: Education for Meaning and Social Justice* 20(2): 42–49.

Neill, A. S., and A. Lamb, eds. 1992. *Summerhill School: A New View of Childhood.* New York: St. Martin's Press.

Purpel, D. 1989. *The Moral and Spiritual Crisis in Education.* New York: Bergin and Garvey.

Reitzug, U. 2003. "Bureaucratic and Democratic Ways of Organizing Schools: Implications for Teachers, Principals, Students, Parents, and Community." In *The Institution of Education,* ed. H. S. Shapiro, S. Harden, and A. Pennell, 4th ed., 85–98. Boston: Pearson Custom Publishing.

Rogers, C. 1969. *Freedom to Learn.* Columbus, Ohio: Charles E. Merrill Publishing.

Sheffer, S. 1996. "Doing Something Very Different: Growing without Schooling." In *Deschooling Our Lives,* ed. M. Hern, 16–22.

Shor, Ira. 1996. *When Students Have Power: Negotiating Authority in a Critical Pedagogy.* Chicago: The University of Chicago Press.

Tye, B. B. 1998. "The Deep Structure of Schooling: What It Is and How It Works." *The Clearing House* 71(6): 332–335. Retrieved February 1, 2006, from Info Trac One File database.

Vallance, E. 2003. "Hiding the Hidden Curriculum." In *The Institution of Education,* ed. Shapiro, Harden, and Pennell, 85–98. (Originally published in 1974. *Curriculum Theory Network* 4[1], 5–21.)

Watson, G. 1970. In *Summerhill,* ed. H. Hart. New York: Hart Publishing.

. . . .

Gary K. Clabaugh

→ **NO**

Second Thoughts about Democratic Classrooms

. . . Kristan A. Morrison's "Democratic Classrooms: Promises and Challenges of Student Voice and Choice" argues that students must experience autonomy, freedom, and choice if schools will ever be appealing and truly embody democracy. Those who found or find school tedious, oppressive, and uninteresting may be quick to agree, but how realistic is this proposal?

Cutting Costs with Mass Production

It has been well over one hundred years since America embarked on the ambitious venture of universal public schooling. The costs of this endeavor quickly became burdensome, and it was decided to model schools on factories and emphasize mass production and cost-effectiveness, rather than democracy or individuality.

For the most part, today's public schools still are factories. Management is top-down all the way. The federal government sets basic rules. State authorities implement the rules while adding many more. School boards make decisions based on federal and state rules plus fiscal and political realities. The superintendent executes the will of the board through his or her principals. They, in turn, tell teachers what to do and when to do it, and the teachers direct the youngsters in similar manner. Knowledge is fragmented and atomized. Children are compared to one another. Social and emotional development is neglected for more measurable outcomes. Economies of scale are sought at the expense of individuality. Teachers and students are managed.

Sometimes this industrial approach produces not only undemocratic, but peculiarly inefficient, results. One superintendent of the School District of Philadelphia, for example, boasted to the press that she could tell them what was happening in any classroom in the city at any given moment. What was actually happening was administratively induced chaos, because her standardized, teacher-proof curriculum was incapable of accommodating individual differences. Second-grade teachers were forbidden to use anything other than second-grade readers and the canned lesson of the day, even if some of the kids still couldn't read. Similarly, seventh-grade math teachers were forced to "teach" algebra to kids who couldn't even do fractions or long division.

Reprinted with permission of *Educational Horizons,* quarterly journal of Pi Lambda Theta Inc., International Honor Society and Professional Association in Education, P O Box 6626, Bloomington, IN 47401, Fall 2008.

In this kind of school system, autonomy, freedom, and choice are anathema. The focus is on standardization, teacher proofing, measured outcomes, and the prison shuffle.

Compulsory Freedom?

We should also consider that democratic, freedom-based schooling would be introduced into an institution in which attendance is compulsory. True, if one can afford an alternative, there is no requirement that kids attend public school. But in every state in the union school attendance of some kind, even if it is only home schooling, is required.

"Democratic Classrooms" indicates that democratic and freedom-based education is *grounded in the premise that people are naturally curious and have an innate desire to learn and grow. If left un-fettered, un-coerced and un-manipulated . . . people will pursue their interests vigorously and with gusto. . . .* Trouble is, when people are compelled to go to school they already are fettered, coerced, and manipulated. That's what we mean by compulsion. Wouldn't compulsory education have to be abolished before freedom-based education could be meaningfully initiated?

And why imagine that youngsters' natural curiosity will be directed at constructive things? One can imagine six-year-olds happily burning insects to death with sunlight and a magnifying glass, or sixteen-year-old inner-city gang members fulfilling their urgent desire to learn small-unit military tactics. Besides which, why assume that everyone is naturally curious? I've taught seventh-graders whose curiosity seemed decidedly undersized.

Of course kids of that age are terribly concerned about peer acceptance, and that places a profound limit on their freedom. Do advocates of freedom-based education adequately consider the tyranny of peers?

The Feds Weigh In

Remember too that there is a powerful new restriction on autonomy, freedom, choice, and democracy in schooling. Emphasizing measurable results, quality control, instrumental and extrinsic motivations, and atomization and fragmentation of knowledge, No Child Left Behind represents the near-total triumph of factory-model schooling in contemporary America. The whole weight of the federal government welds the public school as factory in place as never before.

"Democratic Classrooms" offers the happy prospect of dismantling factory schools and refocusing on student voice and choice. But it's not as if the article advocates moving from A to B. Given the present environment, it advocates moving from A to Z. What are the chances?

"The Business of America Is Business"[1]

Another factor militating against the success of the "Democratic Classrooms" prescription is that most Americans spend far more time in the business world than they do where they have a voice and a choice.

What are the work world's characteristics? It's competitive; instrumental and extrinsic motivations dominate, tasks are atomized and fragmented, obedience is required, believing what one is told is valued over criticality, and a person's worth is defined by comparison to others. In short, work-world values are virtually identical to the present school values decried in "Democratic Classsrooms." Surely that is not an accident.

What would happen if business leaders suddenly found themselves confronted with employees who expected a voice and a choice? Would the CEO of General Electric or Macy's, for example, be grateful? And could our lawmakers sleep if the nation's corporate moguls were dissatisfied?

The claim here isn't that the business of America *should* be business. It is that the business of America *is* business, and this reality has to be taken into account in any prescription written for the public schools.

Freedom: A Modern Luxury?

The article comments: *In democratic and freedom-based education, students are free to decide what they study, and how, and when they study it.* The article links that to *the form of learning found in most pre-industrial societies* [in which] *the children are actively engaged in the lives of a given society; they learn skills and knowledge by means of imitation, apprenticeship, modeling and conversation rather than in any formal school setting.*

Pre-industrial education, though, was not all that free and spontaneous. In my youth, for example, I learned barbering by means of an apprenticeship that closely resembled the apprentice system of the pre-industrial guilds; I was most emphatically *not* free to decide what to learn, or how and when to learn it. The master barber decided.

Remember too that in the pre-industrial era most children grew up on farms. And while those youngsters did learn to farm by imitation, modeling, and conversation, they did *not* have the luxury of freely choosing what they wanted to do and how and when they were going to do it. That's not farm life. If you are haying and it looks like rain, you have to work like hell to get the hay in the barn before it gets wet and spoils; otherwise the livestock starves that winter. Similarly, a kid might prefer not to spend hour after hour in the broiling sun picking potato bugs, but he or she still has to do it for the family to eat potatoes.

Perhaps freedom-based education is a luxury reserved for well-fixed modern kids whom harsh reality doesn't require to do tasks of immediate and urgent importance.

The True Secret of Education

John Locke, a philosopher who inspired the nation's founders, observes in *On Education*: "[I]f the mind be curb'd, and humbled too much in children; if their spirits be abas'd and broken much, by too strict an hand over them, they lose all their vigour and industry."

But Locke also cautions that

He that has not a mastery over his inclinations, he that knows not how to resist the importunity of present pleasure or pain, for the sake of what reason tells him is fit to be done, wants the true principle of virtue and industry, and is in danger never to be good for anything.

Locke, however, does not stop there. He immediately adds:

To avoid the danger that is on either hand, is the great art; and he that has found a way how to *keep up a child's spirit easy, active, and free, and yet at the same time to restrain him from many things he has a mind to, and to draw him to things that are uneasy to him* [emphasis added]; he, I say, that knows how to reconcile these seeming contradictions, has, in my opinion, got the true secret of education.[2]

The advocates of freedom-based education, then, may have avoided the first error Locke cautions against, only to stumble into the second. They seem to be overlooking the fact that some measure of mastery over one's inclinations is necessary to ever be good at anything. How can anyone learn to accomplish a truly skilled enterprise such as ballet, glass blowing, or engineering in a reasonable time if the initiate, not the expert, decides what to learn and when to learn it?

To be sure, present-day schooling hasn't got the balance right either. Here, in Locke's words, the mind is "curb'd and humbled too much" and the youngsters too frequently "lose all their vigour and industry." That is what "Democratic Classrooms" quite rightly condemns.

The Principle of Correspondence

Historically there has always been a close correspondence between any society's social structure, values, and norms and its schooling practices. In fact, a case can be made that such correspondence is a universal feature of schooling. And "Democratic Classrooms" gets it wrong when it says, "Schools and society are reflections of one another." No, the history of education demonstrates that schooling practices reflect the values and structures of the host society.

That is not to say that alternative schools of a freer, more-democratic nature can't exist in less-free societies. Various forms of them can be found in nations as different as Israel, Japan, New Zealand, Thailand, and the United States; A. S. Neill's Summerhill, perhaps the best-known, is located in Suffolk, England.[3] But these schools owe their uniqueness to the fact that they do not serve the broad masses at public expense. They have a self-selecting clientele and do not depend on public consensus or public funding.

Still, it's instructive to know that in 1999 Summerhill ran into difficulties with the U.K.'s educational bureaucracy. Despite the school's higher-than-national-average exam pass rates and extraordinary parental and pupil satisfaction, the U.K.'s education bureaucracy inspected the school and found it wanting. It called Summerhill's pupils "foul-mouthed" and accused them of "mistaking idleness for personal liberty." In effect, the report called for Summerhill's closure if the school failed to abandon the key freedoms it afforded its pupils.

Summerhill took the government to court and won the right to continue its practices. The school survived, and in 2007 another government inspection produced entirely different results. *The Guardian* quotes the new report as saying, "Pupils' personal development, including their spiritual, moral, social and cultural development, is outstanding." Students are "courteous, polite and considerate," make "good progress," and are "well-rounded, confident, and mature" when they leave.

Zoe Readhead, the head teacher and daughter of founder A. S. Neill, said: "The government has persistently refused to acknowledge the individual philosophy of the school, such as that children can learn just as well out of the classroom. We feel vindicated." She also added, "It is not the school that changed."[4] Her point, of course, was that it was the U.K. that had changed.[5]

Undemocratic Americans

"Democratic Classrooms" seems at least as out of step with American values in 2008 as Summerhill was to the U.K.'s in 1999. Certainly the values that "Democratic Classrooms" hopes to promote are anything but widespread. Only some Americans "truly value diversity" and are "truly autonomous yet cognizant of others' needs and rights." And only some Americans "are open-minded yet equipped with critical thinking skills to analyze contradictory ideas." Other Americans angrily deny marriage to gay couples; salivate whenever Rush Limbaugh and his ilk ring a bell; and don't have the vaguest understanding of either freedom or democracy. (They eagerly deny the former to anyone who's different and think of American democracy merely as majority rule.)

Individuals of this persuasion pack a political punch. And they will undoubtedly regard as un-American the values "Democratic Classrooms" prescribes for U.S. public schools. Its new freedoms for students would be understood as self-indulgence and an attack on traditional values such as hard work, discipline, and self-denial—none of which are they particularly keen on practicing themselves.

Remember too that day-to-day U.S. public school policy is set locally by some fifteen thousand elected school boards and, except for large urban districts, broadly representative of village values. So America's public schools have achieved their undemocratic condition in a decidedly democratic manner.

Conclusion

History suggests that public schools rarely, if ever, get out ahead of society. Indeed, they generally lag behind. That is why student voice and choice and all that goes with it will have to await a freer, more-democratic America. If and when that societal change happens, the public schools will follow. Until then, support will be lacking. That's not to say that what "Democratic Classrooms" champions is undesirable. But it may be unattainable, and it is certainly unlikely in the near or intermediate future.

Happily, reform need not be all or nothing. One can, with a little luck, quietly introduce more student voice and choice into one's own classroom. And we should all congratulate any teacher who can elevate the importance of intrinsic motivation; emphasize social and emotional development as well as academics; de-emphasize mere obedience; and get kids to define their own worth rather than let others do it for them. But it had better be done without fanfare and well out of sight of the philistines.

Notes

1. A statement made by Calvin Coolidge in the 1920s.
2. John Locke, "Some Thoughts Concerning Education" (sections 41–50), in *The Harvard Classics,* available at <http://www.bartleby.com/37/1/5.html>.
3. See Summerhill School's Web site: <http://www.summerhillschool.co.uk/pages/index.html>.
4. Jessica Shepherd, *Guardian* (Manchester), December 1, 2007, available at <http://www.guardian.co.uk/uk/2007/dec/01/ofsted.schools>.
5. Summerhill School, available at <http://www.summerhillschool.co.uk/bbc-drama.html>.

. . . .

POSTSCRIPT

Are Truly Democratic Classrooms Possible?

E. D. Hirsch, Jr., the well-known core knowledge advocate, in his latest book. *The Making of Americans: Democracy and Our Schools* (2009), is clearly at odds with the "truly democratic classrooms produce engaged citizens" ideology. As he has in his past works, Hirsch has no kind words for the followers of John Dewey whose progressive ideas, he claims, led to an abandonment of definite academic studies resulting in the diminishment of Americans' intellectual standing in the world. He sees hope in recent trends toward higher standards and the rise of Advanced Placement and International Baccalaureate programs in high schools. In a review of *The Making of Americans*, titled "I Pledge Allegiance to Core Knowledge" in *The Washington Post* (August 30, 2009), Jay Mathews states that Hirsch will settle for nothing less than "a coherent, content-based, multi-year curriculum right now to save our democracy from factionalism, inequality, and incompetence."

Another group of theorists settle in a middle-ground position between subject matter centeredness and an emphasis on student voice and choice. See, for example, "Disciplining the Mind" by Veronica Boix Mansilla and Howard Gardner in *Educational Leadership* (February 2008). They recommend the teaching of disciplinary thinking so as to prepare students to understand the real world in which they live and equip them for the future.

The following writers are supportive of Kristan A. Morrison's point of view: Dana L. Mitra, "Amplifying Student Voice," *Educational Leadership* (November 2008), who reviews research into student voice initiatives, including student involvement in reform and the professional development of teachers, and Eric B. Freedman, "Is Teaching for Social Justice Undemocratic?" *Harvard Educational Review* (Winter 2007), who examines the "critical consciousness" approaches of Ira Shor and Paulo Freire, addressing the question "When is education democratic?"

Additional interesting sources are Thomas R. Guskey and Eric M. Anderman, "Students at Bat," *Educational Leadership* (November 2008); Deborah Meier, "Democracy at Risk," *Educational Leadership* (May 2009); Chris W. Gallagher, "Democratic Policy Making and the Arts of Engagement," *Phi Delta Kappan* (January 2008); Stephen Macedo, "Crafting Good Citizens," *Education Next* (Spring 2004); Patrick J. Wolfe, "Civics Exam: Schools of Choice Boost Civic Values," *Education Next* (Summer 2007); Peter Levine, "The Civic Opportunity Gap," *Educational Leadership* (May 2009); Joetta Sack-Min, "A Valued Democracy," *American School Board Journal* (January 2009); Richard Neumann, "American Democracy at Risk," *Phi Delta Kappan* (January 2008); and James A. Banks, "Human Rights, Diversity, and Citizenship Education," *The Educational Forum* (April 2009). Exploration of some of these articles will open doors to a number of important related issues.

ISSUE 7

Has the Supreme Court Reconfigured American Education?

YES: Charles L. Glenn, from "Fanatical Secularism," *Education Next* (Winter 2003)

NO: Paul E. Peterson, from "Victory for Vouchers?" *Commentary* (September 2002)

ISSUE SUMMARY

YES: Professor of education Charles L. Glenn argues that the Supreme Court's decision in *Zelman v. Simmons-Harris* is an immediate antidote to the public school's secularist philosophy.

NO: Professor of government Paul E. Peterson, while welcoming the decision, contends that the barricades against widespread use of vouchers in religious schools will postpone any lasting effects.

In June 2002 the U.S. Supreme Court released its decision of *Zelman v. Simmons-Harris,* which dealt with Ohio's Pilot Project Scholarship Program. This program provides tuition vouchers to certain students in the Cleveland Public School District who wish to transfer from their assigned public school to a participating school of their choosing. The available choices include public schools in adjacent school districts, nonreligious private schools, and religious private schools. Controversy over this program stemmed from the fact that in the 1999–2000 school year, 96 percent of the Cleveland students who were receiving vouchers were enrolled in schools with religious affiliations. Ohio taxpayers (Doris Simmons-Harris et al.) sued state school officials (Superintendent Susan Tave Zelman et al.) to enjoin the program on the grounds that it violated the establishment clause of the U.S. Constitution, which mandates separation of church and state.

The Supreme Court found (by a 5–4 vote) that Ohio's voucher program does not offend the establishment clause, thereby reversing lower courts' judgments that the program is unconstitutional. The majority opinion—delivered by Chief Justice William H. Rehnquist—stated that the program was enacted for the valid secular purpose of providing educational assistance to poor children in a demonstrably failing public school system; that government aid reaches religious institutions only by way of the deliberate choices of individual recipients; and that the only preference in the program is for low-income families, who receive greater assistance and have priority for admission. In dissent, Justice John Paul Stevens queried, "Is a law that authorizes the use of public funds to pay for the indoctrination of thousands of children in particular religious faiths a 'law respecting an establishment of religion' within the meaning of the First Amendment?" He stated, "The voluntary character of the private choice to prefer a parochial education over an education in the public school system seems to me quite irrelevant to the question whether the government's choice to pay for religious indoctrination is Constitutionally permissible. Whenever we remove a brick from the wall that we designed to separate religion and government, we increase the risk of religious strife and weaken the foundation of our democracy."

The history of the Cleveland voucher program and the litigation surrounding it is summarized by Joseph P. Viteritti in "Vouchers on Trial," *Education Next* (Summer 2002). Begun in 1995, the program allows about 4,000 low-income students to attend private schools with up to $2,250 in public support. Since parochial schools were the only nonpublic schools with tuition rates low enough to accommodate voucher students, opponents maintained that the program was indeed an incentive to attend these schools.

Dan D. Goldhaber and Eric R. Eide, in "What Do We Know (and Need to Know) About the Impact of School Choice Reforms on Disadvantaged Students?" *Harvard Educational Review* (Summer 2002), examine empirical evidence and find that school choice programs have little clear-cut impact on either students in the programs or those who remain in their assigned public schools. They do cite evidence that there is greater support for vouchers among African Americans, however. Frederick M. Hess and Patrick J. McGuinn, in "Muffled by the Din: Competitive Noneffects of the Cleveland Voucher Program," *Teachers College Record* (June 2002), contend that the political and legal ambiguity about Cleveland's voucher program dampened the willingness of parochial and independent schools to expand their capacity to receive voucher students. These schools saw voucher programs as a minor threat as far as competitive pressure for reform is concerned. Perhaps the *Zelman* decision will convert this symbolic threat into a true reform movement.

In the following selections, Charles L. Glenn portrays the *Zelman* decision as a harbinger of the emergence of faith-based alternatives to the public school establishment's rampant secularism. Paul E. Peterson admits that *Zelman* is a welcome addition to the pro-voucher arsenal, but he expresses concern about establishment backlash and, even more so, governmental encroachment on religious schools' independence.

YES ↵

Charles L. Glenn

Fanatical Secularism

The Supreme Court's majority opinion in the Cleveland voucher case, *Zelman v. Simmons-Harris*, was of course the most newsworthy aspect of the decision, but the dissents were no less revealing. In about 500 words, Justice Stevens managed to use the word "indoctrination" four times and "religious strife" twice. Likewise, Justice Breyer's dissent begins and ends with warnings of "religiously based social conflict" resulting from allowing parents to use public funding to send their children to sectarian schools. Today it is a little startling to encounter these echoes of Justice Black's 1968 dissent in *Board of Education v. Allen*, in which he warned:

> The same powerful sectarian religious propagandists who have suc-
> ceeded in securing passage of the present law to help religious schools
> carry on their sectarian religious purposes can and doubtless will con-
> tinue their propaganda, looking toward complete domination and
> supremacy of their particular brand of religion. . . . The First Amend-
> ment's prohibition against governmental establishment of religion
> was written on the assumption that state aid to religion and religious
> schools generates discord, disharmony, hatred, and strife among our
> people, and that any government that supplies such aids is to that
> extent a tyranny. . . . The Court's affirmance here bodes nothing but
> evil to religious peace in this country.

Although the Supreme Court's decision in *Allen* has left no detectable sign of "disharmony, hatred, and strife among our people," the dissenting justices in the Cleveland case seem to believe that the only way to avoid "indoctrination" and religious warfare is to educate children in government-run schools (even though most industrialized countries provide support to religious schools). Concerns over deep entanglements between government and religion have of course haunted the nation from its very beginning. But in the education realm, the sheer hostility toward religious schools is not just a matter of separating church from state. It in part reflects and derives from the self-image of many educators, who like to think of themselves as having been specially anointed to decide what is in the best interest of children. Faith-based schools, they assume, are in the business of "indoctrinating" their pupils, while public schools are by definition committed to critical thinking and to the emancipation of their pupils' minds from the darkness of received opinions, even those of their own parents.

From *Education Next*, vol. 3, no. 1, Winter 2003, pp. 61–65. Copyright © 2003 by Education Next. Reprinted by permission of Hoover Institution, Stanford University.

What I have elsewhere called "the myth of the common school" is a deeply held view with tremendous political resonance, first articulated in the 1830s by Horace Mann and his allies. This myth insists that enlightenment is the exclusive province of public schools, which are thus the crucible of American life and character in a way that schools independent of government could never be.

The actual working out of this powerful idea in the 19th and early 20th centuries was not altogether benign. It included, for example, systematically denying that there were a number of ways to be a good American. Nor was the common school ideal ever fully realized, even in its New England home. Segregation by social class persisted, and black pupils were unofficially segregated in much of the North and West and officially segregated in all of the South. Even the famed "steamer classes" that served immigrant children in the cities of the East and Midwest often did not keep them in school beyond the first year or two.

Nonetheless, the myth of the "common school" deserves credit for many of the accomplishments of public education in this country. It articulated a coherent vision of the American character and of an America-in-process, and it made both convincingly attractive. In recent decades, however, this hopeful myth has been transmuted into an establishment ideology that borrows much of the language and the positive associations of the common school to serve a bureaucratized, monopolistic system that is increasingly unresponsive to what parents want for their children.

The Enlightenment Mission

In *The Myth of the Common School* (1988), a historical account of how the ideology of state schooling emerged, I traced the myth's development in 19th century France, the Netherlands, and the United States. To a great extent the myth was informed by a bias against orthodox religion, often in the name of what was considered a "higher and purer" form of Christianity stripped of "superstitious" elements such as an emphasis on sin and salvation, in favor of a purified morality and faith in progress. State-sponsored schooling was intended to replace religious particularism (whether Catholic or Calvinist) as well as local loyalties and norms with an emerging national identity and culture.

Enlightenment in this form was experienced by many as oppressive rather than liberating. In place of the convictions that had given meaning and direction, and often color and excitement, to their lives, people were offered a diffuse array of platitudes, a bloodless "secular faith" without power to shape moral obligation or to give direction to a life. The effect was to set people free for a new and more oppressive bondage, unrestrained by the custom and ceremony from which, as the Irish poet William Butler Yeats reminded us, innocence and beauty come to enrich our lives.

This political account of the development of public education continues to be helpful in understanding present-day conflicts in Western democracies. If we recognize that the attempt to achieve a government monopoly on schooling was intended to serve political purposes during a period of nation-building, we can see that this monopoly is no longer appropriate—if it ever was.

The case for charter schools, vouchers, and other forms of "marketized" education rests not only on educational performance but also on the claims of freedom of conscience. Parents have a fundamental right—written into the various international covenants protecting human rights—to choose the schooling that will shape their children's understanding of the world. But a right isn't really a right if it can't be exercised. Families who can't afford tuition at a private school or a move to the suburbs should still be able to make choices regarding their children's education.

There is, in other words, a strong argument against attempts by government to use schooling to achieve political or cultural change—or stability, for that matter. John Stuart Mill gave this argument definitive form in 1859, writing:

> All that has been said of the importance of individuality of character, and diversity in opinions and modes of conduct, involves, as of the same unspeakable importance, diversity of education. A general State education is a mere contrivance for moulding people to be exactly like one another; and as the mould in which it casts them is that which pleases the predominant power in the government . . . in proportion as it is efficient and successful, it establishes a despotism over the mind, leading by natural tendency to one over the body.

The same point was made in a lapidary phrase by the U.S. Supreme Court in its 1925 *Pierce v. Society of Sisters* decision: "the child is not the mere creature of the State."

But does this leave nothing to be said for the role of schools in fostering the qualities of civic virtue on which, all moralists agree, the meaningful exercise of freedom depends? Put another way, does a commitment to limiting government's role in the education realm also require that schools refrain from seeking to form the character and worldview of their pupils? This is one of the central dilemmas of a republican form of government, at least in its contemporary form of limited state power. While republics pledge to respect the freedom of their citizens, they also depend on the voluntary adherence of those citizens to often complex norms of civic life. As a result, as Montesquieu pointed out, "It is in republican government that the full power of education is needed." The citizens of a republic must be virtuous since they govern themselves.

Jean-Jacques Rousseau wrote that the teacher must choose whether he will make a man or a citizen. The choice is not so stark, but it is nevertheless real. The state may seek to mold citizens on a particular pattern, but citizens in a free society surely have a right not to be molded, in their opinions and character, by the state. The child is not the mere creature of the state.

Emancipating the Mind

Any account of the tensions between the educational goals of government and of families must consider the third side of the triangle: how teachers and other educators have understood their mission. It is easy to assume that public school teachers line up on the side of the "state project" in education, while teachers in faith-based and other nonstate schools line up on the side of parents.

But the reality is much more complex. Indeed, the simple state-versus-parents dichotomy fails to do justice to many educators' perception of themselves as emancipators of the minds of their students.

As noted, education theorists have long contrasted the emancipatory role of the public school with the "indoctrination" they attribute to religious schools. This strikes a note with tremendous cultural resonance. "Emancipation," Jacques Barzun tells us, is "the modern theme par excellence." The most influential of contemporary educators like to think of themselves as liberators of the minds of their pupils rather than as conveyors of "dead" information, such as the traditions of Western culture.

As a result, those who set the pace in the world of American education, and those who follow their lead, look down on the teachers, parents, and policymakers who do not share this understanding of the teacher's mission. Leadership for American education has increasingly been provided by big-city and state superintendents, professors of education, and officials of the education associations and teacher unions who see little need to respond to the uninformed views of the general public and of parents. This was illustrated by a 1997 Public Agenda survey of "teachers of teachers," professors in teacher-training institutions. Of the 900 professors surveyed, 79 percent agreed that "the general public has outmoded and mistaken beliefs about what good teaching means." They considered communication with parents important, but not in order to learn what education parents wanted for their children. Parents were to be "educated or reeducated about how learning ought to happen in today's classroom."

The professors of education surveyed were convinced, for example, that "the intellectual process of searching and struggling to learn is far more important . . . than whether or not students ultimately master a particular set of facts." Sixty percent of them called for less memorization in classrooms, with one professor in Boston insisting that it was "politically dangerous . . . when students have to memorize and spout back." By contrast, according to another Public Agenda study, 86 percent of the public and 73 percent of teachers want students to memorize the multiplication tables and to learn to do math by hand before using calculators.

These are not purely technical questions; they reflect assumptions about the very nature of education. The professors are expressing one form of the "cosmopolitan" values that have been promoted by American schooling over the past century. This perspective has made the exclusion of religion from the public schools seem not a matter of political convenience or respect for societal diversity, but essential to the mission of education. It is also a sign of intellectual laziness. Teaching facts requires knowledge, which is acquired through rigorous study and research. All it takes to teach values is the ability to spout your own beliefs and prejudices.

Platonic Education

The marks of this condescension can be found in the various controversies that swirl around public schooling. State-imposed curriculum frameworks and standardized tests are condemned as distractions from the teaching of "critical thinking." Lecturing is rejected as an unsound practice because it wrongly assumes that the teacher holds some authority. Nor should the teacher stress right and wrong solutions to the problems that she poses; what is important is the pupil's engagement with the search for an answer. This self-censorship on the part of teachers is even more important when it comes to sex education, where talk of "character" and "virtue" is deeply suspect.

So much is this set of attitudes—the priority of "liberation" or "emancipation" as the central metaphor for the teacher's work—taken for granted among American educators that the higher performance of pupils in other countries on international tests in math and science is often dismissed as reflecting other countries' inappropriate stress on drill and memorization. The possibility that a stress on rich curriculum content can result in lively, engaged classrooms is seldom credited. American pupils may not know as much, we are told, but they know how to think and to solve problems creatively.

This complacent assumption rests on a fundamental misunderstanding. Mental "emancipation" can be a very good thing, of course, when it removes the chains of misinformation and when it arouses a thirst for the truth that can be satisfied only by hard, honest mental effort. This is the traditional justification for a "liberal" education.

The classic description of such an emancipation is Plato's parable of prisoners in an underground cavern, convinced that the shadows on the wall are the only reality. One of the prisoners, in a process that Plato explicitly calls an analogy for education, is freed from his chains and brought to a state, literally, of enlightenment.

Plato makes it clear, though, that it is not enough to loosen the chains; the prisoner must be forced to turn toward the light and compelled to venture out of the cavern. Only gradually can he bear the light of day, and only after much experience can he look directly at the source of light and truth. Even the gifted youth who are being groomed for leadership, we are told elsewhere in *The Republic*, should not be exposed to the pleasures and rigors of the search for truth through argument until they have mastered the disciplines of music and gymnastics and have matured through responsibility. Otherwise, Plato warns, they will just play with ideas, without any solid foundation or useful result.

While Plato stressed the laborious acquisition of knowledge and understanding as the means to enlightenment, our impatient age has preferred to think of the emancipation to be achieved through education as simply the removal of the chains of illusion (conventional morality and traditional religious worldviews) without the discipline of seeking truth or the confidence that there is truth to be found.

Critical thinking and creative problem-solving are certainly among the primary goals of a good education, but they are not developed casually in the course of an undirected exploration. Nor should we assume that there is an innate human propensity to rise to that challenge. Most of us are intellectually lazy about large spheres of the world around us. For every person who really wants to know how an automobile engine works, there must be a dozen of us who are content if it starts reliably when we turn the key. This is not necessarily bad. Life would be impossible if we could not take much around us for granted, and even new discoveries rest on the discoveries of others that we do not have to repeat.

Deconstructivism

This is the fundamental wrong-headedness of another classic description of education, Rousseau's Emile. Raised in isolation, denied the use of books and of direct instruction by his tutor, Emile is expected to learn by following his natural inclinations and responding to situations that his tutor secretly creates for him. The boy, Rousseau tells us, "instructs himself so much the better because he sees nowhere the intention to instruct him." His tutor "ought to give no precepts at all; he ought to make them be discovered."

Here is the authentic note of much current pedagogical advice. The article of faith widely held among educators, especially those who have themselves benefited from the most sophisticated education, is that the teacher should never impose anything on his students, nor suggest to them that there are fixed truths that are worth learning or seeking to discover. Instead he should closely observe the interests of his students and create situations in which they are challenged to use those interests as opportunities for learning. In responding to these challenges, the students will "construct" solutions and even meanings that are uniquely their own and will thus be more deeply and validly learned than any that might be suggested by the teacher or by the wider culture and tradition. In the process, students will become autonomous human beings, not the mere creatures of their culture, and will develop capacities of critical judgment that will enable them to participate in creating—"constructing"—a better world.

According to a recent account of "constructivism" in the 2000 yearbook of the National Society for the Study of Education:

> There is to be no notion of correct solution, no external standard of right or wrong. As long as a student's solution to a problem achieves a viable goal, it has to be credited. Nor can relevant educational goals be set externally; they are only to be encountered by the student . . . the constructivistic teacher is to make do without any concept of objective truth or falsehood.

"Even if it were possible to educate children in this way," philosopher Roger Scruton has written, "one thing is certain: that each generation would know less than the one before. . . . And that, of course, is Rousseau's underlying intention—not to liberate the child, but to destroy all intellectual authority, apart from that which resides in the self." As a result, Emile "is the least free of children, hampered at every point in his search for information," and "one can read *Emile* not as a treatise on education, but as a treatise against education." Rousseau's pupil could arrive at a quite incorrect understanding of many natural and social phenomena by relying naively on his experience alone.

Why should we concern ourselves with what Rousseau wrote almost two-and-a-half centuries ago—or indeed with what Plato wrote long before that?

Because education is an enterprise, more perhaps than any other religion, that is shaped by how we choose to think about it.

There is another tradition of thinking about education. It is expressed in the Hebrew scriptures and Jewish practice: "Why do we do these things?" The Passover questions are answered with a story about the experience of a people, a story that has sustained them and given moral direction and meaning to their lives. Does being taught a tradition and taught within a tradition prevent questioning? Of course not; it provides the content that makes questioning fruitful. It can also be found in the classical Greek concept of *paideia* as, in Michael Oakeshott's words, a "serious and orderly initiation into an intellectual, imaginative, moral and emotional inheritance."

"The knowledge-centered teacher," Scruton points out, "is in the business of passing on what he knows—ensuring, in other words, that his knowledge does not die with him." The teacher who loves his subject and cares about his students is concerned that the rising generation not know less than the one that preceded it.

Emancipation is among the elements of a good education; it can help to prepare the way for the exercise of freedom by removing barriers, but it does not of itself make a man or woman free. Education that supports individual freedom and a free society is induction into a culture, not as a straitjacket but as the context of meanings and restraints that make the exercise of real freedom possible. As Philip Rieff has noted, "A culture must communicate ideals . . . those distinctions between right actions and wrong that unite men and permit them the fundamental pleasure of agreement. Culture is another name for a design of motives directing the self outward, toward those communal purposes in which alone the self can be realized and satisfied."

It is for this reason that structural reforms supporting freedom and diversity in education are not enough; they must be paired with a willingness to confront the much more difficult issue of the purposes, the means, and the content of a good education. Diversity and choice must be paired with common standards, and the content of these must be rich and meaningful. This will require an effort for which the schooling we have received in recent decades almost unfits us, to rediscover and give new life and conviction to those elements of history and culture, the virtues, achievements, and consolations, that have at all times shaped and sustained civilization. This is not a plea for a narrowly Western nostalgia trip, but rather an insistence that only a recovery of the permanent things, of humanity's highest accomplishments, can serve as the basis for a worthy education.

Such a happy outcome would be helped along if opponents of school vouchers would refrain from scare tactics based on unfounded stereotypes about faith-based schooling. Schools that teach in ways shown to be harmful to children should be shut down, but the debate over how to organize a pluralistic education system is not helped by worst-case scenarios. Many Western democracies have faced this challenge successfully, finding an appropriate balance between the autonomy of schools and public accountability, and we can do so too, now that the Supreme Court majority has decided in favor of educational freedom.

Paul E. Peterson　　　　　　　　　　　　　➡ **NO**

Victory for Vouchers?

In the most anticipated decision of its recent term, the Supreme Court ruled, in the case of *Zelman v. Simmons-Harris*, that the school-voucher program in Cleveland, Ohio did not violate the Constitution's ban on the "establishment" of religion. Opponents of vouchers—i.e., the use of public funds to help families pay tuition at private schools, including religious schools—were predictably disappointed, but pledged to fight on. As Senator Edward M. Kennedy declared, "Vouchers may be constitutional," but "that doesn't make them good policy."

The policy's sympathizers, needless to say, saw the ruling in a different light. President Bush used the occasion of the Supreme Court's decision to issue a full-throated endorsement of vouchers. *Zelman*, he told a gathering in Cleveland, did more than remove a constitutional cloud; it was a "historic" turning point in how Americans think about education. In 1954, in *Brown v. Board of Education*, the Court had ruled that the country could not have two sets of schools, "one for African-Americans and one for whites." Now, he continued, in ruling as it did in the Cleveland case, the Court was affirming a similar principle, proclaiming that "our nation will not accept one education system for those who can afford to send their children to a school of their choice and one for those who can't." *Zelman*, according to the President, is *Brown* all over again.

But is it?

༺◈༻

Publicly funded school vouchers got their start in Milwaukee, Wisconsin in 1990. Established at the urging of local black leaders and Wisconsin Governor Tommy Thompson (now the Secretary of Health and Human Services), the program was originally restricted to secular private schools and included fewer than a thousand needy students. To accommodate growing demand, religious schools were later allowed to participate, an arrangement declared constitutional in 1998 by the Wisconsin Supreme Court. The Milwaukee program now provides a voucher worth up to $5,785 to over 10,000 students, amounting to more than 15 percent of the school system's eligible population.

In 1999, at the behest of Governor Jeb Bush, Florida also established a publicly funded voucher program, aimed at students attending public schools that failed to meet state standards. Though just two schools and fewer than a hundred students have participated in the program thus far, ten other schools, with thousands of students, will be eligible to participate this fall. (The Florida program is also noteworthy because it served as a model for the voucher-like federal scholarship program advocated by George W. Bush during the 2000 presidential campaign—a program subsequently abandoned by the administration in its push for an education bill.)

Though the Milwaukee and Florida programs had until recently received the most public attention, it was the program in Cleveland—the country's only other publicly funded voucher program of any size[1]—that won the opponents of vouchers their day before the Supreme Court. The Cleveland program is relatively small, providing a maximum of $2,250 a year to each of roughly 4,000 students. Parents use the vouchers overwhelmingly for religious schools, which in recent years have enrolled over 90 percent of the program's participants. This, according to lawyers for the teachers' unions, the most powerful foe of vouchers, constituted an obvious violation of the separation between church and state. And they prevailed twice in federal court, winning decisions at the trial and appellate level against Susan Zelman, Ohio's superintendent of public instruction and the official responsible for administering the Cleveland program.

But the five more conservative members of the Supreme Court were not persuaded. In his opinion for the majority in *Zelman*, Chief Justice William Rehnquist pointed to three well-known precedents—*Mueller* (1983), *Witters* (1986), and *Zobrest* (1993)—in which the Court had allowed government funds to flow to religious schools. What these cases had in common, he wrote, and what they shared with the Cleveland voucher program, was that public money reached the schools "only as a result of the genuine and independent choices of private individuals." Under Cleveland's program, families were in no way coerced to send their children to religious schools; they had a range of state-funded options, including secular private schools, charter schools, magnet schools, and traditional public schools. Considered in this wider context, the voucher program was, Rehnquist concluded, "entirely neutral with respect to religion."

The dissenters in *Zelman*, led by Justice David Souter, challenged the majority's reading of the relevant precedents—especially of *Nyquist* (1973), a ruling that struck down a New York State program giving aid to religious schools—and suggested that the choice in Cleveland between religion and non-religion was a mere legal fiction. They saved their most pointed objections, however, for what they saw as the likely social consequences of the ruling. The Court, Souter wrote, was promoting "divisiveness" by asking secular taxpayers to support, for example, the teaching of "Muslim views on the differential treatment of the sexes," or by asking Muslim-Americans to pay "for the endorsement of the religious Zionism taught in many religious Jewish schools." Justice Stephen Breyer suggested that the decision would spark "a struggle of sect against sect," and Justice John Paul Stevens wondered if the majority had considered the lessons of other nations' experience around the world, including "the impact of religious strife . . . on the decisions of neighbors in the Balkans, Northern Ireland, and the Middle East to mistrust one another."

⋅◦⟨◉⟩◦⋅

If judicial rhetoric is all that counts, the dissenters in *Zelman* had the better of it. In the majority opinion, by contrast, there is very little that rises to the level of *Brown's* often-cited language about the demands of American equality. Even observers pleased by the ruling were disappointed that the majority's opinion did not go much beyond showing how the facts of the case fit past precedents; no ringing declarations are to be found in Chief Justice Rehnquist's cautious prose.

Only in the concurrences written by two of the Justices does one get a sense of the wider issues at stake. Responding to the worries of the dissenters, Justice Sandra Day O'Connor pointed out that taxpayer dollars have long flowed to various religious institutions—through Pell Grants to denominational colleges and universities; through child-care subsidies that can be used at churches, synagogues, and other religious institutions; through direct aid to parochial schools for transportation, textbooks, and other materials; and, indirectly, through the tax code, which gives special breaks to the faithful. If government aid to religious institutions were such a problem, she suggested, wouldn't American society be torn already by sectarian strife?

What Justice O'Connor failed to answer was the dissenters' obvious disquiet—one shared these days by many Americans—at the prospect of public money going to support the teaching of extremist religious creeds. This is a reasonable concern—though it is hardly clear, as the Justices themselves might have argued, that the best tool for conquering intolerance born of religious zeal is for the government to impose secular enlightenment. The U.S. has achieved religious peace not by depending upon school-based indoctrination of any stripe but by ensuring that the members of all creeds have access to the democratic process and a robust private sphere in which to meet their particular needs.

As an educational matter, several well-designed studies have shown that students who attend private schools in the U.S. are not only just as tolerant of others as their public-school peers but are also *more* engaged in political and community life. Catholic schools have a particularly outstanding record, probably because for more than a century American Catholics have felt compelled to teach democratic values as proof of their patriotism. There are obviously extremist outliers among, for instance, some of the American *madrassas* discovered by journalists since September 11, but there is no reason to doubt that most of the country's religious schools are attempting to prove that they, too, can create good citizens.

As for *Brown* itself, only Justice Clarence Thomas, in his own stirring concurrence, pointed to it as an explicit precedent, quoting Frederick Douglass to argue that today's inner-city public-school systems "deny emancipation to urban minority students." As he observed,

> The failure to provide education to poor urban children perpetuates a
> vicious cycle of poverty, dependence, criminality, and alienation that
> continues for the remainder of their lives. If society cannot end racial
> discrimination, at least it can arm minorities with the education to
> defend themselves from some of discrimination's effects.

For Justice Thomas—as for President Bush, whose own remarks were undoubtedly influenced by these passages—vouchers are a civil-rights issue; they promise not to intensify religious strife, as the Court's dissenters would have it, but to help heal the country's most enduring social divide.

◦◦◉◦◦

Whether *Zelman* can in fact meet these high expectations remains very much to be seen. *Brown*, in principle, was self-enacting. Neither state legislatures nor local school boards could defy the ruling without running afoul of the law. George Wallace, Bull Connor, and many other Southern politicians were willing to do just that, but in the end, federal authorities imposed the Supreme Court's decision on the vested interests that opposed it.

Zelman is different. Though it keeps existing voucher programs intact, it does not compel the formation of new ones. Here the barricades to change remain extraordinarily high.

Public opinion does not pose the most serious obstacle; indeed, on this issue it is highly uncertain. Pollsters can get either pro-voucher or anti-voucher majorities simply by tinkering with the wording of their questions and the order in which they are asked. Nor, despite greater exposure for the issue, have the public's views evolved much in recent years; questions asked in 1996 generated basically the same results in 2001.

Vouchers suffer from graver problems among members of the political class. Whether in Congress or at the state level, substantial bipartisan support is usually necessary to get a piece of legislation through the various committees, past a vote in two chambers, and signed into law. For vouchers, such support has never materialized. Whatever the private opinions of Democrats, for most of them, it is political suicide to support vouchers publicly. Teachers' unions have long placed vouchers at the top of their legislative kill list, and they are a key Democratic constituency, providing the party with both substantial financing and election-day shock troops.

Nor can voucher proponents rely on whole-hearted support from the GOP. Most Republicans, especially social conservatives and libertarians who have read their Milton Friedman, support vouchers in principle. Still, an idea whose primary appeal is to black Americans, the most faithful of all Democratic voting blocs, is a hard sell among the Republican rank-and-file. Vouchers simply do not have much resonance with well-heeled suburbanites who already have a range of educational choices. When vouchers came up as state ballot questions in both California and Michigan two years ago, most Republican politicians found a way to dodge the issue—and the proposals lost badly.

Even if this political situation were to change, most states have constitutional restrictions of their own that may be invoked to scuttle attempts to provide vouchers for use at religious schools. Many of these provisions are so-called "Blaine" amendments, dating to the 19th century, when James Blaine, a Senator from Maine and a Republican presidential candidate, sought to win the anti-immigrant vote by campaigning to deny public funds to Catholic schools.

(Blaine is perhaps most famous for describing the Democrats as the party of "Rum, Romanism, and Rebellion.") In its classic version, the Blaine amendment read as follows:

> No money raised by taxation for the support of public schools, or derived from any public fund therefore, nor any public lands devoted thereto, shall ever be under the control of any religious sect; nor shall any money so raised or lands so devoted be divided between religious sects or denominations.

In a number of cases, state courts have interpreted Blaine amendments to mean nothing more than what is required, according to the Supreme Court, by the establishment clause of the First Amendment. On this view, vouchers are safe—but not every state judge necessarily shares this view. Such language—may prove to be a hurdle for the voucher program in Florida, where a trial court has now ruled that the law violates the state constitution. Depending on what finally happens at the state level, the Supreme Court may in time be asked to decide whether, on account of their nativist and anti-Catholic origins, the Blaine amendments themselves are unconstitutional.

❧

However much of these practical differences may separate *Zelman* from *Brown*, one powerful similarity remains: like the Court's famed ruling against segregation in the schools, the decision to allow vouchers means much more for black students and their families than for other Americans.

For decades, and despite a host of compensatory reforms the sizable gap in educational performance between blacks and whites has remained roughly the same. According to the National Assessment of Educational Progress, black eighth graders continue to score about four grade levels below their white peers on standardized tests. Nor is this gap likely to close as long as we have, in President Bush's words, "one education system for those who can afford to send their children to a school of their choice and one for those who can't."

When parents choose a neighborhood or town in which to live, they also select, often quite self-consciously, a school for their children. That is why various Internet services now provide buyers—and real-estate agents—with detailed test-score data and other information about school districts and even individual schools. But there is a catch: the mobility that makes these choices possible costs money. It is no accident that children lucky enough to be born into privilege also attend the nation's best schools.

African-Americans are often the losers in this arrangement. Holding less financial equity, and still facing discrimination in the housing market, they choose from a limited set of housing options. As a result, their children are more likely to attend the worst public schools. Richer, whiter districts rarely extend anything more than a few token slots to low-income minority students outside their communities.

It is thus unsurprising that blacks have benefited most when school choice has been expanded. In multi-year evaluations of private voucher programs in New York City, Washington, D.C., and Dayton, Ohio, my colleagues and I found that African-American students, when given the chance to attend private schools, scored significantly higher on standardized tests than comparable students who remained in the public schools. In New York, where the estimates are most precise, those who switched from public to private schools scored, after three years, roughly 9 percentage points higher on math and reading tests than their public-school peers, a difference of about two grade levels. If reproduced nationwide, this result would cut almost in half the black-white test-score gap. (Interestingly, there is no evidence that vouchers have improved the academic performance of students from other ethnic groups. In my own research, they had no impact, positive or negative, on the test scores of either whites in Dayton or Hispanics in New York City.)

These findings about the especially positive effects of private schools on African-American students are hardly isolated. One review of the literature, conducted by the Princeton economist Cecilia Rouse, concludes that even though (once again) it is difficult to discern positive benefits for white students, "Catholic schools generate higher test scores for African-Americans." Another, done by Jeffrey Grogger and Derek Neal, economists from the University of Wisconsin and the University of Chicago, finds little in the way of detectable gains for whites but concludes that "urban minorities in Catholic schools fare much better than similar students in public schools."

No less important, in light of concerns about the effect of vouchers on students "left behind," is that school choice also seems to improve the performance of students who remain in the *public* schools. The best data from Milwaukee show strong advances in test scores since the voucher program was put into place there ten years ago, especially at public schools in those low-income neighborhoods where the voucher option was available. As observers in Milwaukee have noted, it was only in the wake of the voucher program's expansion that the public-school system there began to adopt a series of apparently successful reforms.

We do not know precisely what accounts for the gains that black students have made by switching to private schools. The answer is certainly not money, since the private schools they attend are usually low-budget, no-frills operations. The most striking difference, according to my own research, lies in the general educational environment: the parents of these students who reported being much more satisfied with everything from the curriculum, homework, and teacher quality to how the schools communicate with the parents themselves. The classes tend to be smaller, they say, and there is less fighting, cheating, racial conflict, or destruction of property.

⚜

That vouchers can produce such results has been known for some time. The question now is whether the ruling in *Zelman* will have any impact on what the public and politicians think about the issue. If nothing else, the Court's authoritative pronouncement on the constitutionality of vouchers has already conferred new legitimacy on them. Newspaper editors and talk-show hosts have been forced to give the idea more respect, and political opponents cannot dismiss it so easily.

Still, the key to change lies within the black community, and especially with parents, who increasingly know that private schools provide a better education for their children. A 1998 poll by Public Agenda, a nonpartisan research group, found that 72 percent of African-American parents supported vouchers, as opposed to just 59 percent of white parents. A poll conducted two years later by the Joint Center for Political and Economic Studies had similar results, with just under half of the overall adult population supporting vouchers but 57 percent of African-American adults favoring the idea. Perhaps more to the point, blacks constituted nearly half of all the applicants for the 40,000 privately funded vouchers offered nationwide by the Children's Scholarship Fund in 1999, even though they comprised only about a quarter of the eligible population.

Even in the face of such numbers, it is too much to expect that men like Jesse Jackson and Al Sharpton will reconsider their virulent opposition to vouchers; their political tendencies are too well defined. But pressure to support school vouchers is building among black parents, and black leaders will have to act. Howard Fuller, the former superintendent of Milwaukee's public-school system, has formed the Black Alliance for Educational Options, a pro-voucher group that has mounted an effective public-relations campaign and is making waves in civil-rights circles. And young politicians like Cory Booker in Newark have begun to challenge their old-line, machine-style elders, using vouchers as a key dividing point. Responding to these currents—and to the decision in *Zelman*—the city council of Camden, composed entirely of black and Hispanic Democrats, passed a unanimous resolution in July urging the state of New Jersey to establish a voucher program for the city's dysfunctional public schools. Such examples are sure to multiply.

Not even the Supreme Court, it should be recognized, can make educational change come quickly in America. Though *Brown* was handed down in 1954, it took more than a decade before major civil-rights legislation was enacted; Southern schools were not substantially desegregated until the 1970's. Anyone writing about *Brown* ten years after its passage might have concluded that the decision was almost meaningless.

The same may be said about *Zelman* on its tenth anniversary. Perhaps the safest prediction is that, in four or five decades, American education will have been altered dramatically, in ways we cannot anticipate, by the parental demand for greater choice—a demand codified in *Zelman*. Many battles will be fought and lost along the way, to be sure, but the victories will accumulate, because choice, once won, is seldom conceded.

Note

1. New York City, Washington, D.C., and numerous other cities have well-developed *private* voucher programs designed to help low-income families; these currently serve over 50,000 students.

POSTSCRIPT

Has the Supreme Court Reconfigured American Education?

In "Privatizing Education: The Politics of Vouchers," *Phi Delta Kappan* (February 2001), Sheila Suess Kennedy identifies the partisans in the voucher wars. Pro-voucher groups include pro-market libertarians, business organizations, the Christian Right, and the Catholic Church. The anti-voucher side includes the education establishment (teachers' unions, in particular), civil libertarians, church/state separationists, and official African American organizations. Regarding this last group, Michael Leo Owens, in "Why Blacks Support Vouchers," *The School Administrator* (June 2002), states that although urban black America favors school vouchers, its leaders do not. He cites a 1999 survey showing that 68 percent of blacks favor vouchers whereas a similar percentage of black state and local officials do not support voucher plans. Apparently, despite their shortcomings, vouchers offer hope to poor families whose children are trapped in the nation's worst schools. On the contrary, Benjamin O. Canada, in "Black Leadership and Vouchers," *The School Administrator* (June 2002), contends that vouchers cannot systematically expand educational opportunities for blacks—they are a hoax. Interestingly, the first federally funded voucher program has been initiated in the predominantly black District of Columbia schools.

Clearly, the *Zelman* decision has rekindled the debate about breaking up the government monopoly in schooling and giving parents and children new options. So say Lawrence W. Reed and Joseph P. Overton in "The Future of School Choice," *USA Today* (January 2003), who assert, "The empowerment and transformation of parents into active agents is the foundation of educational choice theory." Reed and Overton further contend that the Supreme Court's momentous decision has opened the door to improving schools through the power of choice and competition. In time, they say, it will be seen as a pivotal ruling in the restoration of American education.

In contrast, Peterson's concerns are echoed in Steven Menashi's "The Church-State Tangle: School Choice and Religious Autonomy," *Policy Review* (August & September 2002), in which the author worries that "if voucher laws saddle private schools with the same regulatory regime that now hampers the public education system, school choice will prove an iatrogenic aggravation of the educational crisis."

For further slants on the issue, see the April 2002 issue of *Educational Leadership* and the Winter 2001 issue of *Education Next*. More recent sources are Benjamin Dowling-Sendor, "Revisiting the Voucher Debate," *American School Board Journal* (July 2006); "School Choice: A Progress Report," by Dan Lips and Evan Feinberg in *USA Today* magazine (January 2007); and Peter Schrag, "Vouchers: They're Baaaaaack!" *The Nation* (June 20, 2011).

ISSUE 8

Is No Child Left Behind a Flawed Policy?

YES: Frederick M. Hess and Chester E. Finn, Jr., from "Crash Course: NCLB Is Driven by Education Politics," *Education Next* (Fall 2007)

NO: Dianne Piché, from "Basically a Good Model," *Education Next* (Fall 2007)

ISSUE SUMMARY

YES: Frederick M. Hess and Chester E. Finn, Jr., review the development of the NCLB policy and conclude that political compromises have produced sputtering machinery and weak sanctions that require an extreme makeover.

NO: Dianne Piché, executive director of the Citizens' Commission on Civil Rights, supports the testing and accountability measures of the federal law as the best way to advance the interests of the poor and minorities.

Congress and the executive branch began wrestling with the reauthorization of the No Child Left Behind (NCLB) Act in 2007, and the issue was a central point of argument in the 2008 national, state, and local political campaigns. There are those who want sweeping changes and those who feel that any change would diminish the law's ambitious goal of raising standards of performance in American schools. Some criticize the unreasonableness of the law's specific demands, citing 2007 figures showing more than 4,500 schools serving over 2 million students failing to meet annual progress goals for four years or more. Wade A. Carpenter, in "The Other Side of No Child Left Behind," *Educational Horizons* (Fall 2006), states that he does not blame the Bush administration for its goals but blames it for its method, namely "test-driven minimalism, with the slower and resistant kids monopolizing the time of frustrated and surly teachers and the brighter kids sitting quietly, bored stupid."

The main points of dispute, as outlined in the *American School Board Journal* of January 2007, are the adequacy of federal funding, the mode of measuring yearly progress, the facilitation of school transfers (an option now taken by a very small percentage of parents of eligible students), the act of providing tutorial services, the recruitment of highly qualified teachers, and the problem of flexibility in dealing with special education students and English language learners. Supporters of NCLB argue that the law's core provisions are sound and point to significant gains in math and reading scores and new levels of achievement by minority students, as reported in the *Congressional Digest* of May 2008. In addition, a "blueprint" for strengthening the reform has been issued by the administration, emphasizing more rigorous coursework, new tools for chronically underperforming schools, and more options for families. Representative George Miller, a co-author of the law, has put forth some key changes, among them giving credit to schools that make progress, bringing employers and colleges together as stakeholders, and increasing attention to middle and secondary schools. U.S. Department of Education Secretary Margaret Spellings has stated that after decades of doling out federal dollars and hoping for the best, we are now expecting and getting results.

A 2007 report by Jennifer McMurrer of the Center on Education Policy, "Choices, Changes, and Challenges," recommends staggering testing requirements to include tests in other academic subjects, encouraging states to give adequate emphasis to art and music, and requiring states to arrange for an independent review of standards and assessments at least once every three years. Other constructive appraisals of NCLB can be found in "Ten Big Effects of No Child Left Behind on Public Schools" by Jack Jennings and Diane Stark Rentner in *Phi Delta Kappan* (October 2006) and in a forum of articles in the Fall 2007 edition of *Education Next*.

Under NCLB, the federal government has taken an increasingly active role in steering the public schools, perhaps more than at any time in the nation's history. Some see this as a federal takeover, a usurpation of local control. Stephen J. Caldas and Carl L. Bankston III, in "Federal Involvement in Local School Districts," *Society* (May/June 2005), state that "If districts are in accord with the goals of NCLB, then perhaps following the federal guidelines is not viewed as sacrificing local initiative for federal money. The sad truth is, however, that most districts cannot even imagine existence without the huge amount of federal aid they receive. Thus, they are rarely in a position to even ask themselves the hard question of whether or not following federal stipulations is what is best for their students or their communities." This problem is explored in depth by Phillip C. Schlechty in "No Community Left Behind," *Phi Delta Kappan* (April 2008). He contends that the most fundamental flaw in NCLB is that decisions regarding what the young should know and be able to do are removed from the hands of parents and local community leaders, and turned over to officials and experts located far from the schoolhouse door. This, Schlechty feels, "destroys one of the greatest resources the nation has in the struggle to maintain a sense of community in an increasingly globalized and impersonal world."

In the YES selection, Hess and Finn find the NCLB accountability system to be a faulty stitching together of otherwise plausible ideas with an overlay of unreasonable expectations, while in the NO selection, Dianne Piché defends NCLB as a boon to students historically shortchanged in our public schools.

YES ↩

Frederick M. Hess and
Chester E. Finn, Jr.

Crash Course: NCLB Is Driven by Education Politics

Enacted in 2001, the No Child Left Behind Act (NCLB) began with the resounding promise that every U.S. schoolchild will attain "proficiency" in reading and math by 2014. Noble, yes, but also naive, misleading, and in some respects dysfunctional. While nobody doubts that the number of "proficient" students in America can and should increase dramatically from today's woeful level, no educator believes that universal proficiency in 2014 is attainable. Only politicians promise such things. The inevitable result is weary cynicism among school practitioners and a "compliance" mentality among state and local officials.

In hindsight, NCLB's passage was less about improving schools or fostering results-based public sector accountability than about declaring fealty to a gallant but utopian ambition, one that the statute welded to a clumsy, heavy-handed set of procedural mandates.

NCLB is, in fact, a civil rights manifesto masquerading as an education accountability system. Its grand ambition provided a shaky basis for policy-making, rather as if Congress asserted in the name of energy reform that America will no longer need to import oil after 2014 or fought crime by declaring that by that date all U.S. cities would be peaceable kingdoms.

NCLB's particular brand of hubris has solid precedent. Picture John Kennedy pledging in 1961 that "America will get 75 percent of the way to the moon by decade's end." Or former President Bush and the governors solemnly declaring in 1990 that the U.S. would be 12th in the world in math and science by the year 2000. Indeed, it's practically un-American to aim for anything less than the top.

Moreover, NCLB's backers can legitimately argue that they had already spent nearly two decades asking state and local officials and education leaders to address mediocre school performance and stubborn race- and class-linked inequities in educational outcomes. In that light, the passion-drenched unseriousness infusing NCLB is forgivable, even honorable.

And NCLB indeed has virtues: it produced long-overdue school transparency, focused unprecedented attention on achievement, created urgency where lethargy had ruled, and offers valuable political cover to determined superintendents and principals.

Kennedy's promise was kept in just eight years, when it turned out that money, brainpower, and determination could surmount the technical challenges posed by a moon landing. The "first in the world" goal, however, was not attained and quickly became the stuff of mockery.

Invitation to a Backlash

The NCLB accountability system was adopted with scant attention to principles of sound public-sector accountability, how the statute's many pieces fit together, or whether they could be competently deployed through the available machinery. Meanwhile, the statute's rhetoric invites a backlash that may not only gut the law, but also discredit the increasingly fruitful goal-setting, school-changing, choice-conferring results that have marked education reform since 1983.

As the calendar rolls toward 2011 and 2012, and sharp increases in proficiency rates become necessary, the number of schools failing to make adequate progress will rise precipitously. Unless current standards are eased, thousands of schools that communities had long regarded as effective are going to be tarnished. Claims of moral urgency and vague paeans to accountability are unlikely to prove much of a match for community pride and fears for property values. Moreover, many of those schools, while doubtless less effective than they ought to be for at least some kids, are pretty decent and far better than the urban-disaster schools, where the case for mandated interventions is unarguable.

There's nothing wrong with lofty ambitions. Yet political compromises meant that NCLB's grand aspirations were saddled with sputtering machinery and weak sanctions. Few Americans realize that, for states to keep their Title I dollars, they need only to set goals, administer tests, report results, and see that districts intervene in specified ways in low-performing schools. NCLB doesn't actually mandate that kids *learn* anything. If the kids don't learn, or if their schools don't improve, no sanctions follow (save possible embarrassment) so long as officials comply with the procedural requirements. The money keeps on flowing.

NCLB's architects thought they were devising an elaborate plan to alter the behavior of thousands of schools and millions of educators, drawing on a mix of goals, rewards, sanctions, choices, and sunlight. They overlooked the fact that effective behavior-changing regimens are rooted in realistic expectations and joined to palpable incentives and punishments; NCLB provides none of these.

Aspirational Politics

The conventional account, as told by NCLB champions like Congressman George Miller, Senator Ted Kennedy, Secretary of Education Margaret Spellings, or advocates like the Education Trust or Citizens' Commission on Civil Rights, is that the law-capped a 12-year effort to advance education accountability from Washington. They attribute any apparent failures to implementation glitches, foot dragging by state and local officials, educator recalcitrance, or lack of funding.

In this telling, 1989's Charlottesville summit begat Bush's America 2000 plan, which begat conjoined twins—Clinton's Goals 2000 plan and Improving America's Schools Act (IASA)—which somehow begat NCLB, with each generation better able than its ancestors to drive education reform and boost student achievement.

That chronology is right, but the record of steady progress forward is questionable. An evolution of sorts did take place, with Uncle Sam's hand pressing down harder and harder and with ever more elaborate provisions meant to keep states, districts, and schools in line. Several pending reauthorization proposals—notably those from the Aspen commission chaired by former governors Tommy Thompson and Roy Barnes—would extend that pattern and press down harder still from Washington, with more rules, regulations, and commands.

That may well be what Congress ends up doing. But it is unlikely to work as intended, because it misdiagnoses the essential problem.

In promoting education reform during the 2000 campaign and after, President Bush fatefully chose to focus on compassionate moralism (e.g., "the soft bigotry of low expectations") rather than on reshaping the structures and incentives of K–12 schooling. In so doing, he reflected standard Washington practice: the rhetoric of education policy is more often about social justice than about incentives or instruction. Enlisting allies in the civil rights community who were eager to see improved outcomes for poor and minority students, Bush was able to forge a bipartisan coalition stronger than the status quo defeatism of the National Education Association.

What is remarkable is that, at the very moment of supposed conservative "victory" on federal education policy, the Bush administration embraced a moralistic conception of accountability and big-government enforcement rather than the pragmatic, incentive-focused model that had emerged from three decades of conservative critiques of grandiose Great Society designs.

It's a mistake to depict NCLB either as perfecting its statutory predecessors or as a coherent engine of behavior modification. NCLB's provisions are a hodgepodge of Texas precedents, "New Democrat" reforms, liberal nostrums, and proposals by countless constituencies, all superimposed on programmatic architecture and rules that had accumulated since Lyndon Johnson worked in the Oval Office.

Many Prototypes

Embedded within NCLB's accountability system are three distinct, discernible models of educational change that have been awkwardly welded together.

Model one would make transparent the performance of students across the nation, providing an X-ray to show parents, educators, and policymakers how different schools and groups are performing in key subjects. Model two would deploy "behavior modification" accountability methods, refined through decades of public sector reform, to force low-performing schools and districts to set goals, assess effectiveness, and do better. And model three would set "shoot-the-moon" targets and use the federal bully pulpit to exhort leaders in states and districts to improve.

Each of these approaches is plausible on its own terms. And each has a place in federal policy. *But they cannot reasonably be linked to one another,* as NCLB tries to do. They entail discrepant views of the federal role in education and employ discordant mechanisms. The result isn't working.

For example:

—The value of an "X-ray" of the nation's school performance has long been recognized. NCLB's dictate that all states regularly test students in key subjects marked a historic success. The accuracy of the picture is compromised, however, when this cross-sectional look at student achievement becomes the basis for gauging the performance of schools and educators, much less for triggering interventions or remedies. We don't judge doctors based on whether their patients are sick today but by how much patient health improves under their care. Judging professional performance on the basis of a one-moment-in-time X-ray encourages questionable behavior, leads states to play games with standards, and threatens to discredit the X-ray itself.

—Prodding public sector institutions to set goals, monitor performance, and then reward excellence and address mediocrity has been a signal success for reformers on both the left and the right. Decades of studied effort, touted in iconic books like *Reinventing Government* and championed through the 1990s by the Gore commission, make clear that sensibly structured accountability systems encourage self-interested workers to take goals seriously, focus on outcomes, and employ all the levers at their disposal to produce those outcomes. But we compromise such "behavior modification" when those on the ground view the targets as unattainable. If workers know they are unlikely to succeed, the goal becomes to avoid trouble when they fail. By making failure inevitable, unrealistic goals have the perverse effect of focusing employees on compliance and encouraging actions that will mask "failure."

—Bully pulpit exhortation is a legitimate role for federal officials. Dating at least to Bill Bennett's colorful tenure as secretary, the Department of Education has sometimes been a valuable podium from which to promote and energize school reform. Setting high bars and challenging state and local officials to meet them provides political cover to leaders, while lighting fires under laggards. It's great to shine a bright light on performance and then laud or shame schools, states, and districts based on that performance. Yet such efforts are discredited when they are based on X-rays ill-equipped to readily trace progress or when behavior modification schemes lead local officials and educators to react by devoting their energies to bureaucratic compliance on the one hand, and loophole exploitation on the other.

Rube Goldberg structures are generally unstable as well as unattractive, and the stability of this one is further menaced by the cracking foundation under it: education federalism circa 1965. NCLB's architects failed to appreciate how weakly that foundation supported even the lighter burdens of Goals 2000 and IASA, both passed in 1994. Those measures had taken for granted that the LBJ-era mechanisms for distributing federal dollars allocated for needy children via state and local education agencies were also suited to a regimen of school reform.

That hierarchy of responsibility—from Washington to state education department to local school system to school and finally to classroom—has been the basis of federal education policy since passage of the Elementary and Secondary Education Act. But it was never designed to support a results-based accountability system; repair schools or districts; function in an environment awash in charter schools, home schooling, and distance learning; or address the dysfunctions of the very agencies charged with its implementation.

Although IASA and Goals 2000 were not nearly as demanding as NCLB, close listeners could already hear the foundation cracking. Yet to our knowledge, none of NCLB's architects even paused to ask whether a hierarchy decently suited to distribute money via certain formulas could manage a very different and much more aggressive federal role or the exigencies of school improvement. To accomplish these tasks competently, the federal government would require much more direct authority over resources, assessments, low-performing schools, and interventions. By no means are we endorsing efforts to give the feds that kind of control. We are, however, noting that operating in a federal system without such grand powers requires that federal officials legislate and act with an eye to what they can and cannot constructively do. The seeming nonchalance with which NCLB's proponents tossed new responsibilities onto this precarious governmental base betrayed a dangerous unconcern.

Bundling together the X-ray assessment, behavior modification, and aspirational jawboning also presumes that federal intervention on all three counts was and is appropriate everywhere in the land. Not true, and another challenge to traditional notions of education federalism. In fact, several states, including Florida and Massachusetts, already had X-ray assessment or behavior modification systems more advanced than those required by NCLB. Moreover, the fact that these systems were not linked to a fixed date for universal proficiency was arguably a strength, not a problem.

What to Do

Can this law be saved? Yes, indeed, but only if we thoughtfully separate its key components from one another and from naively heroic expectations.

It is appropriate for Uncle Sam to demand that every state provide a fine-grained image of student achievement. It's reasonable also to insist that states develop sanctions, remedies, and interventions for schools and districts that are performing badly and not improving. Washington should indeed press states to track performance levels, but "adequate progress" should be based primarily on the academic value that schools add (i.e., the achievement gains their pupils make), not merely on the aggregate level at which students perform.

Moreover, states that are already moving on these fronts *do not need* federal intervention, much less cookie-cutter prescriptions. It's folly for Congress to draft school-level modifications; far better to require that lagging states act, then move to withhold funds—big bucks, including, if necessary, the whole Title I payment—from any that sit on their hands or post unacceptable results.

It's valuable, too, for Washington to set ambitious goals and exhort everyone to attain them. But the constructive way to do this is by promoting transparency, setting benchmarks, rewarding high achievers, pointing fingers at laggards, and clearing political obstacles. With a consistent metric, call it a national standard, accompanied by national tests, everyone's performance can be fairly tracked and compared. If the Jefferson School lags behind the Franklin School; if Hispanic youngsters in Tucson fall behind Hispanic pupils in San Antonio; if Springfield can't keep pace with Sacramento; if Ohio is making gains but Kentucky isn't, all these and more should be readily visible. Comparisons should be easy and swift. Washington can competently see to this. But it cannot competently micromanage what state, districts, or schools do. And it shouldn't try.

Even the Great Society's most daring and important victories avoided the sweeping hubris of NCLB. Neither the Civil Rights Act of 1964 nor the Voting Rights Act of 1965, both remembered now as towering triumphs, ever sought to change precinct-level behaviors. Backed by the National Guard and armed with clear, concrete, and fairly straightforward goals, federal officials focused entirely on forcing a limited number of recalcitrant states to adopt specific changes. This is the kind of role in which federal leadership has a reasonable record of success.

That accomplishment can happen in education, too, if we couple an emphasis on readily comparable gauges of performance and progress with real consequences for mediocrity and inertia.

NCLB could have a bright future, if it gets an extreme makeover.

Dianne Piché ➡ **NO**

Basically a Good Model

No Child Left Behind (NCLB) may be the most vilified act of Congress in modern times. Just about anybody can find something in the law to get worked up over: the testing rules, "highly qualified teachers," funding shortfalls and so on. It's great fodder for presidential candidates, too, one of whom recently went so far as to blame the childhood obesity problem on NCLB and to equate companies providing tutoring to low-income students to Halliburton. Funny thing is NCLB is actually doing some good things for real people, many of them students who historically have been shortchanged in our public schools.

I was an early, proud supporter of the law, and I still am. My civil rights colleagues and I fought for some of its tougher provisions, like accountability for subgroups of students, the 2014 proficiency deadline, requiring states to submit plans for the equitable assignment of teachers, and providing a way out for kids trapped in failing schools. By now, most of the criticism of NCLB—some legitimate but some ginned up by special interests opposed to real accountability—seems pretty old and tiresome.

Let's examine some of the grenades most commonly lobbed at NCLB. First, there is the oft-heard complaint that the measurement system for accountability is all wrong. Why? Because NCLB doesn't call for measuring students' growth from year to year. Instead, the measurement system in the law compares the proficiency levels of this year's 3rd graders to last year's 3rd graders. This is also called the "status model."

Suggesting that NCLB 1.0 is flawed because it did not explicitly provide, back in 2001, for "growth models" is like saying my 2001 desktop was a bad buy because in 2007 it can't run Windows Vista or streaming video. Virtually none of the states had the technology and other capacity to design and implement growth-measurement systems in the early years of this authorization. The fact that Education Secretary Margaret Spellings has approved only seven to date is not because she's not eager to see many states move in this direction. There simply aren't, even today, many states ready, willing, and able to carry out a credible, statistically sound growth-based accountability system.

Since 1994 the "status model" has been the accountability paradigm embedded in Title I, and in many state accountability systems as well. It was based, in part, on public health models that aspire, for example, to increase numbers of annual healthy births and immunized kindergarteners and decrease things like malnutrition, disease, and teen pregnancy. Significantly, it was not until sometime after NCLB's final passage that the noise level about the "status" model and the plea for growth measures became audible. And this was not because states suddenly had vast new capacity to measure growth. They didn't. Instead, increasingly, leaders of the education establishment (i.e., school boards, administrators, and the teacher unions) were doing their Adequate Yearly Progress (AYP) math in the context of the 2014 deadline. They rightly feared that, unlike the Clinton administration, the Bush administration was determined to enforce the law, particularly with regard to assessment and accountability. Simply put, they hoped that with a growth model, they might get credit for *some* amount of improvement in test scores, even if the requisite numbers of students were not actually proficient.

This political background is important context for the debate taking place in Congress. Virtually nobody disputes the merits of allowing states to base their accountability systems on the value a school or teacher adds to a student's knowledge and skills. But when it comes time for Congress to get down to actual legislative language, members will have to choose whether to open the door to all comers, including states with pitifully low standards (compared to those of the National Assessment of Educational Progress), deficient data and student-tracking systems, and a poor track record on including English language learners and students with disabilities. Or they can take the more prudent course, accede to the secretary's good judgment, and limit the "growth" option to those states that can demonstrate both the capacity and the rigor required to bring students to proficiency within a specified period. Thus, simply arguing "growth measures good, current law bad" may in the end not be very helpful to the deliberations on Capitol Hill and could well undermine the efforts of those who favor only those growth systems that can meet tough standards for rigor, reliability, and inclusion of all students.

Then there's the suggestion that the 2014 proficiency deadline is crazy. Says who? Certainly not the parents whose children attend persistently low-performing schools and for whom even one school year is too much time to lose.

Increasingly we are seeing high-poverty, high-minority schools across the country that are achieving outstanding academic success. In high-achieving schools, proficiency for all students is possible *this year*. Let's do what we can with NCLB to drive the dollars and incentives to the schools that are replicating the no-excuses approach to teaching the children of the poor.

Common Ground?

Perhaps surprisingly, my fellow forum authors and I agree on the importance of NCLB's core aspirations:

- Transparency and public reporting of student achievement data
- The need for high standards pegged to postsecondary education and careers
- Regular assessment in reading and math
- Accountability based on assessment results
- Options for parents.

We even agree on some of the more nuanced, yet potentially powerful, improvements Congress and states could enact to strengthen education reform:

- Differentiated consequences
- Continued efforts to measure growth from year to year
- Measuring effectiveness and attaching rewards/consequences for administrators and teachers.

Finally, we may actually agree on the most radical proposal from the standpoint of the more than 40-year history of the Elementary and Secondary Education Act (ESEA): Congress should not continue to subsidize failure after providing years of assistance and the opportunity to improve. There are a variety of ways to remove funding from chronically low-performing schools and transfer it to better schools (including moving the dollars in the figurative "backpacks" of the students) that merit serious consideration.

Our disagreements reflect our fundamentally different beliefs about the role of the federal government itself, particularly with respect to advancing the interests of the poor and minorities. Since when has leaving it all up to the states helped the poor and minorities achieve equality of opportunity? Not when it came to voting rules. Not when it came to public accommodations. Not when it came to desegregating schools in the aftermath of *Brown* v. *Board of Education*. And certainly not now, when the achievement gaps based on race and class are as virulent as ever, with only modest signs of abatement.

Of course, not everything is working perfectly yet. School choice and supplemental educational services were not high on the political priority list under the first Bush administration, but it does not follow that these two vital provisions for parents cannot be made to work. It often takes a period of years (sometimes even a complete authorization cycle) for a controversial new provision to take root. For example, most states did not pay much attention to the "accountability lite" provisions in the Clinton-era Improving America's Schools Act (IASA), nor did that administration do much to signal to states that it would enforce IASA's requirements for "corrective action" and school improvement. It took another authorization and a clear signal from the Bush administration that the federal government was serious about accountability in order for the states to come up with plans to hold their own schools and districts accountable.

Moreover, there are encouraging signs of bipartisan support for proposals to add some real teeth to the public school transfer options in NCLB. Currently, parents may choose a better school when their child's school fails to make AYP, but as the Lawyers' Committee for Civil Rights Under Law has called it, the choice option is "a right without a remedy." School districts implement the provision only halfheartedly and many argue a lack of space in successful schools. The interdistrict provisions in the law are weak, and charter options are not meaningful in states with arbitrary limits on new charter schools.

The Citizens' Commission on Civil Rights, along with the Aspen Institute's NCLB Commission and other proponents, have proposed tough new measures to guarantee public school choice to children who attend persistently low-performing schools. One proposal would deny states that do not provide parents and children with demonstrably better choices their Title I money. States would have the obligation to create and offer those children in the worst schools seats in better-performing schools. To increase seats, states could lift caps on the number of charter schools, expand successful schools, or provide for interdistrict transfers. A second proposal would require an "audit" to determine whether capacity in better schools actually exists and, if so, where. Finally, the Aspen Institute and a number of civil rights organizations favor enabling parents to take legal action when rights conferred under NCLB, like the right to place their child in a better-performing school, are violated. Congress should consider how best to target funding to the schools, leaders, and models that have the best record of success in high-poverty communities. But the bottom line is that unless and until the money is used to leverage dramatic change, there is unlikely to be any marked change. And without dramatic change, achievement gaps are unlikely to close any time soon. The status quo is a powerful player to be reckoned with in the struggle for educational equity.

The Pace of Reform

NCLB is in many respects the latest in a long line of efforts in the policy and legal arenas to promote equity and opportunity in the public schools, including desegregation cases, the Civil Rights Act of 1964, the original ESEA, and school finance and adequacy cases in the states.

How long does it take a cutting-edge civil rights law to "work"? Could a credible argument have been made in 1969, five years after passage of the Civil Rights Act, that the ambitious law was "not working" and therefore ought to be abandoned?

This particular legislation needs to be strengthened by ensuring high state standards, reliable assessments, realistic school-improvement measures, an equitable distribution of effective teachers, and real parental choice. Those of us—on the left, right, and middle—who believe in the transformative power of education need to draw more from the work of the increasing numbers of urban schools that are demonstrating *how* to succeed with large numbers of poor and minority students despite the odds. We need to learn from the contagious successes of outstanding public schools and choice programs like the Amistad Academy in Connecticut, the Green Dot schools in California, and the voluntary interdistrict transfer program in St. Louis.

Abandoning NCLB now would be the height of cynicism. Instead, like the civil rights movement itself, the education reform movement is in dire need of creative thinking, committed education leaders, and informed, involved parents—all united in our belief in the worth and value of every young life and each child's potential to learn and do great things.

POSTSCRIPT

Is No Child Left Behind a Flawed Policy?

"**N**CLB is influenced deeply by the market-based philosophies of its prime, neoconservative movers. Markets inherently create winners and losers. The rhetoric of leaving no child behind is belied by a system geared to a narrow standardization of goals that results in a diminished realm of opportunity to demonstrate accomplishment and achievement." These thoughts from Margaret McKenna and David Haselkorn, in "NCLB and the Lessons of Columbine," *USA Today* (May 2005) certainly run counter to the assessment offered by Dianne Piché. McKenna and Haselkorn believe that our national education policies are seriously misguided, based as they are on a long-discredited behaviorist view of human development prompted by extrinsic rewards and consequences rather than intrinsic motivation.

Another critic, Richard Rothstein, in "The Corruption of School Accountability," *The School Administrator* (June 2008), agrees with Nichols and Berliner that under NCLB reliance solely on flawed numerical measures to evaluate performance has corrupted schooling, causing an emphasis on drill, teaching to the test, and manipulating data. Similarly, W. James Popham in *America's Failing Schools: How Parents and Teachers Can Cope with "No Child Left Behind"* (2004) argues that the prescribed achievement goals are altogether unrealistic, that "the establishment of expectations that are unattainable will rarely spur people to perform at new levels of excellence." Other interesting articles on testing and accountability include Mark F. Goldberg, "The Test Mess," *Phi Delta Kappan* (January 2004) and "Test Mess 2: Are We Doing Better a Year Later?" *Phi Delta Kappan* (January 2005); Thomas Toch, "Turmoil in the Testing Industry," *Educational Leadership* (November 2006); Lawrence A. Uzzell, "Cheat Sheets: No Child Left Behind Has Taught Our Nation's Schools One Thing—How to Lie," *The American Spectator* (September 2005); and Richard Rothstein, "The Limits of Testing," *American School Board Journal* (February 2005).

Covering some other crucial related issues are these recommended articles: David Mathews, "The Public and the Public Schools: The Coproduction of Education," *Phi Delta Kappan* (April 2008); Paul D. Houston, "The Seven Deadly Sins of No Child Left Behind," *Phi Delta Kappan* (June 2007); and John Chubb and Diane Ravitch, "The Future of No Child Left Behind: End It? Or Mend It?" *Education Next* (Summer 2009).

ISSUE 9

Can Failing Schools Be Turned Around?

YES: Karin Chenoweth, from "It Can Be Done, It's Being Done, and Here's How," *Phi Delta Kappan* (September 2009)

NO: Andy Smarick, from "The Turnaround Fallacy," *Education Next* (Winter 2010)

ISSUE SUMMARY

YES: Karin Chenoweth, a senior writer with the Education Trust and author of *How It's Being Done*, describes strategies employed to bring about dramatic improvements in low-performing schools.

NO: Andy Smarick, a visiting fellow at the Thomas B. Fordham Institute, advocates the closing of failing schools to make room for replacements through chartering.

The question of how to best serve children of poverty has been wrestled with for decades and has become even more crucial during the recent economic downturn. The No Child Left Behind law, with its focus on test-performance improvement, has met with a good deal of negative reaction from front-line educators and academic theorists alike. Richard A. Gibboney, in his article "Why an Undemocratic Capitalism Has Brought Public Education to Its Knees: A Manifesto," *Phi Delta Kappan* (September 2008), put it this way: "Rather than support policies designed to reduce poverty and its toxic effects on the ability of children to succeed in school, our lawmakers are pursuing the misbegotten path of penalizing schools in poverty-stricken cities and rural areas for their failure to work educational miracles." Richard Rothstein poses the question "Whose Problem Is Poverty? in *Educational Leadership* (April 2008), offering an inventory of deficits experienced by the poor, including a lack of health care, more lead-poisoning, iron-deficiency anemia, family instability, more exposure to crime and drugs, fewer positive role models, and less exposure to culturally uplifting experiences.

Katherine Bradley, president of the CityBridge Foundation in Washington, DC, has stated that turning around chronically low-performing, high-poverty schools is the grittiest task that educators face. While the search is on to find a successful turnaround formula, Bradley, in a *Washington Post* (August 7, 2011) piece, expresses concern over a growing sentiment in favor of the "highly disruptive strategy of school closure and restart." Under No Child Left Behind policies, failing schools face the possibilities of "restructuring" whereby half or more of the teachers may be fired or a complete school shutdown after which the state may assume management or a replacement charter school may be authorized. In a June 29, 2010, opinion expressed on AOL News.com, Diane Ravitch pleaded "Don't Close Schools, Fix Them." She suggested that "every state should enlist a team of evaluators to visit every struggling school, document its problems, make recommendations and stay involved to make sure that the school gets the resources it needs to improve." Ravitch has concluded that "it may take courage to close schools, but it takes, experience, wisdom and persistence—as well as courage—to improve them and to strengthen families and communities." An elaboration of these views can be found in her Summer 2010 *American Educator* article entitled "In Need of a Renaissance: Real Reform Will Renew, Not Abandon, Our Neighborhood Schools."

Andy Smarick, former COO of the National Alliance for Public Charter Schools, has been among the leaders of the movement to develop a new type of system for urban public education, a system of charter schools. In "Wave of the Future," *Education Next* (Winter 2008), he admits that charter supporters, a "motley crew of civil rights activists, free market economists, career public-school educators, and voucher proponents," have yet to fashion a consistent vision. Some states have imposed caps on charter expansion and in some districts funding has been unequal. Often school boards, teachers unions, and school administrators have been antagonistic, but in some quarters collaborative relationships have emerged.

Advocates of internally turning around troubled schools, Deborah Meier, Laura Pappano, Karin Chenoweth, Katherine Bradley, Ruby Payne, and Pamela Cantor, among others, seem to agree on many of the guidelines for resuscitating failing schools, namely staff self-assessment, teacher collaboration replacing isolation, community-building, and serious inservice training. Karin Chenoweth's books, *It's Being Done: Academic Success in Unexpected Schools* (2007) and *How It's Being Done* (2009), provided a wealth of examples of regular neighborhood schools that did whatever it took to dramatically elevate student morale and achievement levels without resorting to magnet programs, charters, or outside management. Chenoweth's profiles revealed a pattern of high expectations for both teachers and students, wise use of time (with extra time devoted to low-performing students), and continual re-examination of practices, all occurring in an atmosphere of respect.

The YES and NO selections pit turnaround advocate Karin Chenoweth against charter proponent Andy Smarick in the search for the best way to deal with failing schools in high-poverty areas.

YES ↵

Karin Chenoweth

It Can Be Done, It's Being Done, and Here's How

For decades, a sense of powerlessness has permeated many schools and many educators. "There's not much we can do" has been the mantra of many teachers faced with students who arrive behind and seem to slip backward through their school years.

Maureen Downey of the *Atlanta Journal-Constitution* recently wrote about this phenomenon: "I am always taken aback when teachers tell me that their students are essentially unteachable, that there's little they can do to educate children who arrive at school unfed, unprepared, and unmotivated" (July 15, 2009).

Educators' sense of powerlessness has been bolstered by what seem like endless data demonstrating the correlation of achievement with poverty and race. Poor, black, and Hispanic students achieve at lower levels, on average, than middle-class white and Asian students in study after study, assessment after assessment, giving failure a sense of inevitability.

So what can we make of schools where those patterns are broken—schools where poor students read as well as middle-class students; where black and Hispanic students do math as well as or even better than white students in their states?

Take, for example, George Hall Elementary. Just a few years ago, the school was one of the lowest performing schools in Mobile, Alabama, and suffered mightily from disciplinary problems. With a student population almost entirely low-income and black, in an area of Mobile notorious for high crime rates and intergenerational poverty, its low performance and chaotic atmosphere weren't considered all that surprising. What was surprising was the attitude of its new principal, Agnes "Terri" Tomlinson, and her team after the school was reconstituted in 2004. (Reconstitution meant, in this case, that the entire staff reapplied for their jobs.)

"I knew achievement wouldn't be a problem," Tomlinson said.

Tomlinson, a veteran educator, was right: Once the school was doing what it should have been doing, students' academic achievement rose to a level more often associated with white, middle-class students. In fact, most George Hall students score above the national norm on the SAT 10 test.

George Hall isn't the only school that demonstrates the power that schools have to change the educational trajectory of their students. Graham Road Elementary in Falls Church, Virginia, is another. Once one of the lowest performing schools in Fairfax County, Graham Road is now one of the top schools in the state, outperforming many much wealthier schools. This, even though 80% of the students speak a language other than English at home because they mostly come from low-income families who recently immigrated to this country.

Yet another is P.S./M.S. 124 Osmond A. Church School in Queens, New York, where more than 80% of the students qualify for the federal free lunch program but perform at levels associated with much wealthier students. Still another is Capitol View Elementary in a low-income neighborhood of south-western Atlanta, where the students—almost all black—post student achievement that rivals the wealthiest schools in Georgia.

What's Different?

So the question is: What's done differently at George Hall, Graham Road, P.S./ M.S.124 Queens, Capitol View, and other schools where low-income children and children of color learn at high levels?

After spending the last few years visiting such schools and writing about what they do, I've come to the conclusion that they succeed where other schools fail because they ruthlessly organize themselves around one thing: helping students learn a great deal.

This seems too simple an explanation, really. But, by focusing on student learning and then creating structures that support learning, these schools have drastically departed from the traditional organizational patterns of American schools.

I sometimes think about what Wendy Wachtel, a math teacher at high-achieving Lockhart Junior High School where most students are low-income and Hispanic, told me: "It's not rocket science. You figure out what you need to teach, and then you teach it."

In contrast, consider a recent quotation in the *New York Times* from a teacher who teaches recent immigrants: "American students come to school with a lot of cultural knowledge," she said, "teachers assume they don't have to explain because their kids get it from growing up in this country, watching television or surfing the Internet."

Schools that successfully teach students of poverty and students of color do not begin with the assumption that there are things they don't have to explain. They begin by figuring out what children need to know and be able to do; they assess what their students already know and are able to do; they figure out how to move students from where they are to where they need to be; and then they analyze what students have learned and whether they need further instruction. They do this systematically grade by grade, class by class, student by student, month by month, and day by day, carefully and relentlessly. They know, as Marie Parker, an instructional coach at Graham Road, told me, "If we're not going to do it, who is?"

At Graham Road, for example, teachers go over every test with each student to discuss their wrong answers so that any misunderstandings can be addressed immediately and don't compound. When teachers met to discuss test results, they realized that their students needed to radically improve their vocabularies and their background knowledge. This, of course, is a common need among low-income students around the country.

To help build vocabulary and background knowledge, Graham Road teachers use the thousands of documentary videos that many schools can access. If teachers want children to read a particular book but know they won't understand the book's references to earthquakes and volcanoes, they have students visit the classroom's "background knowledge center"—otherwise known as the computer—to watch short documentaries on earthquakes and volcanoes. They do this because, as Molly Bensinger-Lacy, principal of Graham Road Elementary, said, "We have almost no kids who, if you haven't taught something, will get it."

George Hall uses field trips in the same deliberate, thoughtful way. Classes take field trips about once a month, and teachers think deeply about what vocabulary words and background knowledge students need to understand to get the most out of the trip to the state capital, the local zoo, the theater, or wherever they're going. Then, after the field trip is over, students post on the Internet the photos and videos that they have taken, together with written commentary. Teachers know many of their students have rarely left their neighborhoods and, in order to be educated, need exposure to the wide world. "They live 10 minutes from the bayou," one teacher told me. "But they've never even seen it—or been on a boat. We take them on a boat."

Provide Time for Teacher Learning

My point is not that every school should use videos or field trips or any other particular teaching method (though I do think both are kind of nifty). The point is that every school should engage in the kinds of deep discussion that Graham Road and George Hall faculties have when they meet together to study their state's standards (and, sometimes, other states' standards), think about what their students already know and are able to do, and decide what more they need to learn. During these discussions, they look at student achievement data, build curriculum maps, and develop benchmark assessments, grading rubrics, and lesson plans. Even more profoundly, they discuss why one teacher is having success teaching fractions while another is not, and what the more successful teacher can teach the less successful teacher.

Such discussions take time, which means that successful high-poverty and high-minority schools must build their schedules carefully in order to ensure that teachers have the necessary time to meet together.

Many of the successful high-poverty and high-minority elementary schools I've visited schedule "specials" in a way that enables grade-level teams to meet together during those times. That means all 1st graders go at the same time to art, music, computer, gym, or whatever other "specials" the school has. At Atlanta's Capitol View, students have, in addition to the specials every day, "back-to-back specials" once a week, permitting grade-level teachers to meet with the principal and assistant principal for almost two straight hours to discuss curriculum, instruction, achievement data, and all the other things that they need to discuss to ensure that their students learn to high levels. At secondary schools, teachers' "prep" periods are scheduled so teams or departments can meet together.

These scheduling practices are so simple and mundane that they hardly seem worth mentioning. But they're one of the many building blocks that help develop the kind of deep teacher collaboration that allows teachers to focus on student learning. This means these successful schools have directly addressed something that too often is overlooked in many discussions of student achievement—the American tradition of teacher isolation.

I should say the topic of teacher isolation is not overlooked in the academic literature of school reform. Richard Elmore, Michael Fullan, Mike Schmoker, and many more have written at length about the role teacher isolation has played in retarding student achievement. Robert Marzano, Rick and Becky DuFour, and many others have long preached the gospel of collaboration as a way to improve student achievement. And yet its importance has yet to permeate the national education discussion.

For the most part, schools are still organized on the principle that teachers close their doors and teach by themselves. But no teacher can be an expert in all aspects of the curriculum, all the possible ways to teach it, and every child who sits in his or her class. Although every teacher should have expertise that can be tapped by other teachers to improve their knowledge of their subject, pedagogy, and students, the traditional organization of schools doesn't allow teachers to pool their knowledge in a systematic, structured way.

Teacher Collaboration

Because they focus so closely on what students need to learn, successful high-poverty and high-minority schools operate as schools, not as a collection of isolated classrooms. That means, among other things, that they tackle such questions as discipline and teacher quality—problems that plague many low-performing schools—with schoolwide responses.

This is what I mean. I recently spent a day in a dysfunctional urban high school in which the staff had voted to prohibit students from wearing hats, hoods, or earphones. A common enough rule, but only a few administrators enforced it. Teachers who cared about the rule enforced it in their classrooms; teachers who didn't care or felt overwhelmed didn't bother. As a result, the rule was openly flouted, and teachers who valiantly tried to enforce the rule felt undermined and lonely. The school had an unlawful feel; the week before my visit, there had been three fires at the school.

The successful high-poverty and high-minority schools I've visited have very different atmospheres. If the school has a rule, every grownup in the school (and that includes nonteaching staff) enforces it because everyone has a stake in providing a safe, respectful, and comfortable environment in which students can learn.

Similarly, teachers who are working collaboratively help guard the quality of the teaching force in ways that are impossible when teachers work in isolation. Once teaching is public and collaborative—meaning that teachers work together to figure out what children need to learn and how to teach it—teachers who don't contribute or openly sabotage such efforts begin to stand out.

Von Sheppard—who as principal took Dayton's Bluff Achievement Plus Elementary from what was widely acknowledged in 2001 to be the worst school in St. Paul, Minnesota, to a well-organized, more-or-less average-achieving school in 2005—calls sabotaging teachers "toxic teachers" because they poison the atmosphere. As Dayton's Bluff developed a collaborative culture, he says, "the [other] teachers in the building began holding these teachers accountable. No one wanted to be associated with a toxic teacher." As a result, the toxic teachers left of their own accord—a fairly common experience in high-achieving high-poverty and high-minority schools.

By acting as a team, all the energy and expertise of the faculty and staff are concentrated, rather than dispersed, and can have a much bigger effect than is possible with the tradition of teacher isolation. That concentrated effect allows students—even students burdened by poverty and discrimination—to learn at much higher levels than has traditionally been expected.

Isolation Hurts Students

There is an interesting argument that has been waged in the education world that I suspect is well known to readers of the *Kappan,* and it goes along these lines: All the talk of a crisis in American education is overblown. There may be problems in some schools, but the problems are mostly concentrated in urban and rural schools and other schools where most of the children are low-income or minority. Most schools, the argument goes on to say, are just fine and serve students well. Besides, schools can affect student achievement only on the margins because so much depends on the social capital that students bring with them. The fact that high-minority and high-poverty schools have low achievement has more to do with the characteristics that students bring to school than with anything the schools do; thus anyone who cares about education should focus their attention not on school practices but on building the social capital of impoverished families.

I would make a different argument: The traditional organization of schools, which relies on isolated teachers doing their jobs with little interference and less support, means individual students are totally reliant on the knowledge and skills of their individual teachers. They (and their teachers) have little access to the broader expertise of a school's faculty or the accrued wisdom of the education field as a whole. Because middle-class students bring more social capital than students of poverty, this tradition of isolation, on average, hurts them less. That doesn't mean it doesn't hurt them, but their parents are more likely to notice a problem in decoding or in mastery of basic math facts and either demand more help or provide it at home, either themselves or with the help of outside tutoring. Their parents are also more likely to fill in the background knowledge that too often teachers assume their children have.

Poor students, on the other hand, are often terribly harmed by that isolation, in large part because their parents are less likely to notice deficits and less able to compensate for them. For the most part, parents living in poverty leave education to the schools—not because they don't care about their children's education but because they often don't feel competent to challenge the knowledge of teachers and because they're more likely to be overwhelmed with the daily logistics of life. This means low-income children are often completely reliant on their schools for their education.

When schools understand that and step up to the challenge—as George Hall, Graham Road, and many others have done—and set up the structures and systems that allow teachers to work together, even students burdened by poverty and discrimination can achieve remarkable success. That does not relieve us as a nation of the obligation to try to ensure that poverty becomes less common and less desperate. Nor does it relieve us of the obligation to provide low-income families with the social and health services that better allow children to learn. But it does require that we think deeply about how we organize schools.

But that raises something that George Hall's principal said to me. She and I were talking about how her students—most of whom live in isolated poverty—are now achieving at levels that in some ways exceed that of well-off, white students in wealthy parts of Mobile and elsewhere in Alabama. "It makes me wonder what they are doing in those schools," Tomlinson said. With students who have many more advantages than students at George Hall, few schools are outperforming George Hall. "I think they're coasting," she said.

I suspect a lot of schools are coasting on the advantages of their students. If they learned the lessons that high-performing schools that are also high-poverty and high-minority schools can teach us, our nation's academic achievement would soar.

Reference

Downey, Maureen. "Are They Unteachable?" *Atlanta Journal-Constitution*, June 15, 2009. www.ajc.com/opinion/content/opinion/stories/2009/06/15/learned_0615_2DOT.html

Andy Smarick   ⟶ **NO**

The Turnaround Fallacy

For as long as there have been struggling schools in America's cities, there have been efforts to turn them around. The lure of dramatic improvement runs through Morgan Freeman's big-screen portrayal of bat-wielding principal Joe Clark, philanthropic initiatives like the Gates Foundation's "small schools" project, and No Child Left Behind (NCLB)'s restructuring mandate. The Obama administration hopes to extend this thread even further, making school turnarounds a top priority.

But overall, school turnaround efforts have consistently fallen far short of hopes and expectations. Quite simply, turnarounds are not a scalable strategy for fixing America's troubled urban school systems.

Fortunately, findings from two generations of school improvement efforts, lessons from similar work in other industries, and a budding practice among reform-minded superintendents are pointing to a promising alternative. When conscientiously applied strategies fail to drastically improve America's lowest-performing schools, we need to close them.

Done right, not only will this strategy help the students assigned to these failing schools, it will also have a cascading effect on other policies and practices, ultimately helping to bring about healthy systems of urban public schools.

A Body at Rest Stays at Rest

Looking back on the history of school turnaround efforts, the first and most important lesson is the "Law of Incessant Inertia." Once persistently low performing, the majority of schools will remain low performing despite being acted upon in innumerable ways.

Examples abound: In the first year of California's Academic Performance Index, the state targeted its lowest-performing 20 percent of schools for intervention. After three years, only 11 percent of the elementary schools in this category (109 of 968) were able to make "exemplary progress." Only 1 of the 394 middle and high schools in this category reached this mark. Just one-quarter of the schools were even able to accomplish a lesser goal: meeting schoolwide and subgroup growth targets each year.

In 2008, 52 Ohio schools were forced to restructure because of persistent failure. Even after several years of significant attention, fewer than one in three had been able to reach established academic goals, and less than half showed any student performance gains. The *Columbus Dispatch* concluded, "Few of them have improved significantly even after years of effort and millions in tax dollars."

These state anecdotes align with national data on schools undergoing NCLB-mandated restructuring, the law's most serious intervention, which follows five or more years of failing to meet minimum achievement targets. Of the schools required to restructure in 2004–05, only 19 percent were able to exit improvement status two years later.

A 2008 Center on Education Policy (CEP) study investigated the results of restructuring in five states. In California, Maryland, and Ohio, only 14, 12, and 9 percent of schools in restructuring, respectively, made adequate yearly progress (AYP) as defined by NCLB the following year. And we must consider carefully whether merely making AYP should constitute success at all: in California, for example, a school can meet its performance target if slightly more than one-third of its students reach proficiency in English language arts and math. Though the CEP study found that improvement rates in Michigan and Georgia were considerably higher, Michigan changed its accountability system during this period, and both states set their AYP bars especially low.

Though alarming, the poor record for school turnarounds in recent years should come as no surprise. A study published in 2005 by the Education Commission of the States (ECS) on state takeovers of schools and districts noted that the takeovers "have yet to produce dramatic consistent increases in student performance," and that the impact on learning "falls short of expectations."

Reflecting on the wide array of efforts to improve failing schools, one set of analysts concluded, "Turnaround efforts have for the most part resulted in only marginal improvements. . . . Promising practices have failed to work at scale when imported to troubled schools."

Like Finding the Cure for Cancer

The second important lesson is the "Law of Ongoing Ignorance." Despite years of experience and great expenditures of time, money, and energy, we still lack basic information about which tactics will make a struggling school excellent. A review published in January 2003 by the Thomas B. Fordham Foundation of more than 100 books, articles, and briefs on turnaround efforts concluded, "There is, at present, no strong evidence that any particular intervention type works most of the time or in most places."

An EdSource study that sought to compare California's low-performing schools that failed to make progress to its low-performing schools that did improve came to a confounding conclusion: clear differences avoided detection. Comparing the two groups, the authors noted, "These were schools in the same cities and districts, often serving children from the same backgrounds. Some of them also adopted the same curriculum programs, had teachers with similar backgrounds, and had similar opportunities for professional development."

Maryland's veteran state superintendent of schools, Nancy Grasmick, agrees: "Very little research exists on how to bring about real sea change in schools. . . . Clearly, there's no infallible strategy or even sequence of them." Responding to the growing number of failing Baltimore schools requiring state-approved improvement plans, she said, "No one has the answer. It's like finding the cure for cancer."

Researchers have openly lamented the lack of reliable information pointing to or explaining successful improvement efforts, describing the literature as "sparse" and "scarce." Those attempting to help others fix broken schools have typically resorted to identifying activities in improved schools, such as bolstering leadership and collecting data.

However, this case-study style of analysis is deeply flawed. As the U.S. Department of Education's Institute of Education Sciences (IES) has noted, studies "that look back at factors that may have contributed to [a] school's success" are "particularly weak in determining causal validity for several reasons, including the fact that there is no way to be confident that the features common to successful turnaround schools are not also common to schools that fail."

Researchers have noted that the Department of Education has signaled its own ignorance about what to do about the nation's very worst schools. One study reported, "The NCLB law does not specify any additional actions for schools that remain in the implementation phase of restructuring for more than one year, and [the Department] has offered little guidance on what to do about persistently struggling schools." Indeed, the IES publication, "Turning Around Chronically Low-Performing Schools" practice guide, purportedly a resource for states and districts, concedes, "All recommendations had to rely on low levels of evidence," because it could not identify any rigorous studies finding that "specific turnaround practices produce significantly better academic outcomes."

Still in Its Infancy?

The prevailing view is that we must keep looking for turnaround solutions. Observers have written, "Turnaround at scale is still in its infancy," and "In education, turnarounds have been tried rarely" (see "The Big U-Turn," *features*, Winter 2009). But, in fact, the number and scope of fix-it efforts have been extensive to say the least.

Long before NCLB required interventions in the lowest-performing schools, states had undertaken significant activity. In 1989 New Jersey took over Jersey City Public Schools; in 1995 it took over Newark Public Schools. In 1993 California took control of the Compton Unified School District. In 1995 Ohio took over the Cleveland Metropolitan School District. Between 1993 and 1997 states required the reconstitution of failing schools in Denver, Chicago, New York City, and Houston. In 2000 Alabama took over a number of schools across the state, and Maryland seized control of three schools in Baltimore.

Since NCLB, interventions in struggling schools have only grown in number and intensity. In the 2006–07 school year, more than 750 schools in "corrective action," the NCLB phase preceding restructuring, implemented a new research-based curriculum, more than 700 used an outside expert to advise the school, nearly 400 restructured the internal organization of the school, and more than 200 extended the school day or year. Importantly, more than 300 replaced staff members or the principal, among the toughest traditional interventions possible.

Occasionally a program will report encouraging success rates. The University of Virginia School Turnaround Specialist Program asserts that about half of its targeted schools have either made AYP or reduced math and reading failure rates by at least 5 percent. Though this might be better than would otherwise be expected, the threshold for success is remarkably low. It is also unknown whether such progress can be sustained. This matter is particularly important, given that some point to charter management organizations Green Dot and Mastery as turnaround success stories even though each has a very short turnaround résumé, in both numbers of schools and years of experience.

Many schools that reach NCLB's restructuring phase, rather than implementing one of the law's stated interventions (close and reopen as a charter school, replace staff, turn the school over to the state, or contract with an outside entity), choose the "other" option, under which they have considerable flexibility to design an improvement strategy of their own (see "Easy Way Out," *forum*, Winter 2007). Some call this a "loophole" for avoiding tough action.

Yet even under the maligned "other" option, states and districts have tried an astonishing array of improvement strategies, including different types of school-level needs assessments, surveys of school staff, conferences, professional development, turnaround specialists, school improvement committees, training sessions, principal mentors, teacher coaches, leadership facilitators, instructional trainers, subject-matter experts, audits, summer residential academies, student tutoring, research-based reform models, reconfigured grade spans, alternative governance models, new curricula, improved use of data, and turning over operation of some schools to outside organizations.

It's simply impossible to make the case that turnaround efforts haven't been tried or given a chance to work.

A Better Mousetrap?

Despite this evidence, some continue to advocate for improved turnaround efforts. Nancy Grasmick supports recognizing turnarounds as a unique discipline. Frederick Hess and Thomas Gift have argued for developing school restructuring leaders; Bryan Hassel and Emily Ayscue Hassel have recommended that states and districts "fuel the pipeline" of untraditional turnaround specialists. NewSchools Venture Fund, the Education Commission of the States, and the research firm Mass Insight have offered related turnaround strategies.

And the Obama administration too has bought into the notion that turnarounds are the key to improving urban districts. Education secretary Arne Duncan has said that if the nation could turn around 1,000 schools annually for five years, "We could really move the needle, lift the bottom and change the lives of tens of millions of underserved children." In the administration's 2009 stimulus legislation, $3 billion in new funds were appropriated for School Improvement Grants, which aid schools in NCLB improvement status. The administration requested an additional $1.5 billion for this program in the 2010 budget. This is all on top of the numerous streams of existing federal funds that can be—and have been—used to turn around failing schools.

The dissonance is deafening. The history of urban education tells us emphatically that turnarounds are not a reliable strategy for improving our very worst schools. So why does there remain a stubborn insistence on preserving fix-it efforts?

The most common, but also the most deeply flawed, justification is that there are high-performing schools in American cities. That is, some fix-it proponents point to unarguably successful urban schools and then infer that scalable turnaround strategies are within reach. In fact, it has become fashionable among turnaround advocates to repeat philosopher Immanuel Kant's adage that "the actual proves the possible."

But as a Thomas B. Fordham Foundation study noted, "Much is known about how effective schools work, but it is far less clear how to move an ineffective school from failure to success. . . . Being a high-performing school and becoming a high-performing school are very different challenges."

In fact, America's most-famous superior urban schools are virtually always new starts rather than schools that were previously underperforming. Probably the most convincing argument for the fundamental difference between start-ups and turnarounds comes from those actually running high-performing high-poverty urban schools. Groups like KIPP (Knowledge Is Power Program) and Achievement First open new schools; as a rule they don't reform failing schools. KIPP's lone foray into turnarounds closed after only two years, and the organization abandoned further turnaround initiatives. Said KIPP's spokesman, "Our core competency is starting and running new schools."

A 2006 NewSchools Venture Fund study confirmed a widespread aversion to takeover-and-turnaround strategies among successful school operators. Only 4 of 36 organizations interviewed expressed interest in restructuring existing schools. Remarkably, rather than trusting successful school operators' track records and informed opinion that start-ups are the way to go, Secretary Duncan urged them to get into the turnaround business during a speech at the 2009 National Charter Schools Conference.

The findings above deserve repeating: Fix-it efforts at the worst schools have consistently failed to generate significant improvement. Our knowledge base about improving failing schools is still staggeringly small. And exceptional urban schools are nearly always start-ups or consistently excellent schools, not drastically improved once-failing schools.

So when considering turnaround efforts we should stop repeating, "The actual proves the possible" and bear in mind a different Kant adage: "Ought implies can."

If we are going to tell states and districts that they must fix all of their failing schools, or if we are to consider it a moral obligation to radically improve such schools, we should be certain that this endeavor is possible. But there is no reason to believe it is.

Turnarounds Elsewhere

Education leaders seem to believe that, outside of the world of schools, persistent failures are easily fixed. Far from it. The limited success of turnarounds is a common theme in other fields. Writing in *Public Money & Management*, researchers familiar with the true private-sector track record offered a word of caution: "There is a risk that politicians, government officials, and others, newly enamored of the language of failure and turnaround and inadequately informed of the empirical evidence and practical experience in the for-profit sector . . . will have unrealistic expectations of the transformative power of the turnaround process."

Hess and Gift reviewed the success rates of Total Quality Management (TQM) and Business Process Reengineering (BPR), the two most common approaches to organizational reform in the private sector. The literature suggests that both have failed to generate the desired results two-thirds of the time or more. They concluded, "The hope that we can systematically turn around all troubled schools—or even a majority of them—is at odds with much of what we know from similar efforts in the private sector."

Many have noted that flexibility and dynamism are part of the genetic code of private business, so we should expect these organizations to be more receptive to the massive changes required by a turnaround process than institutions set in what Hess calls the "political, regulatory, and contractual morass of K–12 schooling." Accordingly, school turnarounds should be more difficult to achieve. Indeed, a consultant with the Bridgespan Group reported, "Turnarounds in the public education space are far harder than any turnaround I've ever seen in the for-profit space."

Building a Healthy Education Industry

We shouldn't be surprised then that turnarounds in urban education have largely failed. The surprise and shame is that urban public education, unlike nearly every other industry, profession, and field, has never developed a sensible solution to its continuous failures. After undergoing improvement efforts, a struggling private firm that continues to lose money will close, get taken over, or go bankrupt. Unfit elected officials are voted out of office. The worst lawyers can be disbarred, and the most negligent doctors can lose their licenses. Urban school districts, at long last, need an equivalent.

The beginning of the solution is establishing a clear process for closing schools. The simplest and best way to put this into operation is the charter model. Each school, in conjunction with the state or district, would develop a five-year contract with performance measures. Consistent failure to meet goals in key areas would result in closure. Alternatively, the state could decide that districts only have one option—not five—for schools reaching NCLB-mandated restructuring: closure.

This would have three benefits. First, children would no longer be subjected to schools with long track records of failure and high probabilities of continued failure.

Second, the fear of closure might generate improvement in some low-performing schools. Failure in public education has had fewer consequences (for adults) than in other fields, a fact that might contribute to the persistent struggles of some schools. We should have limited expectations in this regard, however. Even in the private sector, where the consequences for poor performance are significant, some low-performing entities never become successful.

Third, and by far the most important and least appreciated factor, closures make room for replacements, which have a transformative positive impact on the health of a field. When a firm folds due to poor performance, the slack is taken up by the expansion of successful existing firms—meaning that those excelling have the opportunity to do more—or by new firms. New entrants not only fill gaps, they have a tendency to better reflect current market conditions. They are also far likelier to introduce innovations: Google, Facebook, and Twitter were not products of long-standing firms. Certainly not all new starts will excel, not in education, not in any field. But when provided the right characteristics and environment, their potential is vast.

The churn caused by closures isn't something to be feared; on the contrary, it's a familiar prerequisite for industry health. Richard Foster and Sarah Kaplan's brilliant 2001 book *Creative Destruction* catalogued the ubiquity of turnover in thriving industries, including the eventual loss of once-dominant players. Churn generates new ideas, ensures responsiveness, facilitates needed change, and empowers the best to do more.

These principles can be translated easily into urban public education via tools already at our fingertips thanks to chartering: start-ups, replications, and expansions. Chartering has enabled new school starts for nearly 20 years and school replications and expansions for a decade. Chartering has demonstrated clearly that the ingredients of healthy, orderly churn can be brought to bear on public education.

A small number of progressive leaders of major urban school systems are using school closure and replacement to transform their long-broken districts: Under Chancellor Joel Klein, New York City has closed nearly 100 traditional public schools and opened more than 300 new schools. In 2004, Chicago announced the Renaissance 2010 project, which is built around closing chronically failing schools and opening 100 new public schools by the end of the decade.

Numerous other big-city districts are in the process of closing troubled schools, including Detroit, Philadelphia, and Washington, D.C. In Baltimore, under schools CEO Andrés Alonso, reform's guiding principles include "Closing schools that don't work for our kids," "Creating new options that have strong chances of success," and "Expanding some programs that are already proving effective."

Equally encouraging, there are indications that these ideas, which once would have been considered heretical, are being embraced by education's cognoscenti. A group of leading reformers, the Coalition for Student Achievement, published a document in April 2009 that offered ideas for the best use of the federal government's $100 billion in stimulus funding. They recommended that each state develop a mechanism to "close its lowest performing five percent of schools and replace them with higher-performing, new schools including public charter schools."

A generation ago, few would have believed that such a fundamental overhaul of urban districts was on the horizon, much less that perennial underperformers New York City, Chicago, and Baltimore would be at the front of the pack with much of the education establishment and reform community in tow. But, consciously or not, these cities have begun internalizing the lessons of healthy industries and the chartering mechanism, which, if vigorously applied to urban schooling, have extraordinary potential. Best of all, these districts and outstanding charter leaders like KIPP Houston (with 15 schools already and dozens more planned) and Green Dot (which opened 5 new schools surrounding one of Los Angeles's worst high schools) are showing that the formula boils down to four simple but eminently sensible steps: close failing schools, open new schools, replicate great schools, repeat.

Today's fixation with fix-it efforts is misguided. Turnarounds have consistently shown themselves to be ineffective—truly an unscalable strategy for improving urban districts—and our relentless preoccupation with improving the worst schools actually inhibits the development of a healthy urban public-education industry.

Those hesitant about replacing turnarounds with closures should simply remember that a failed business doesn't indict capitalism and an unseated incumbent doesn't indict democracy. Though temporarily painful, both are essential mechanisms for maintaining long-term systemwide quality, responsiveness, and innovation. Closing America's worst urban schools doesn't indict public education nor does it suggest a lack of commitment to disadvantaged students. On the contrary, it reflects our insistence on finally taking the steps necessary to build city school systems that work for the boys and girls most in need.

POSTSCRIPT

Can Failing Schools Be Turned Around?

Public schools in high-poverty areas, especially those in large urban centers, have historically suffered from neglect and underfunding. Recent budget short-falls and declining enrollments have accelerated school closures in Chicago, Detroit, New Orleans, New York, Cleveland, Milwaukee, St. Louis, Kansas City, and Denver, creating what Monica Martinez characterizes as "Learning Deserts" in her February 2011 *Phi Delta Kappan article*. Those who champion the turnaround strategy believe that closing schools only contributes to the abandonment of urban communities, Martinez states. Others, who embrace charter alternatives, see hope in organizations attracting outside funding "to build portfolios of schools that encompass a variety of educational approaches offered by different vendors in an attempt to address intractable problems in public schools."

An analysis that goes beyond the turnarounds versus charters issue is presented in Jung-ah Choi's "Reading Educational Philosophies in *Freedom Writers*," *The Clearing House* (May/June 2009). The author extracts four basic philosophical elements that steered the inner-city teacher's success in the film *Freedom Writers*. They were the following: rewriting the curriculum, treating students as creators of knowledge, classroom community-building, and seeing teaching as self-realization. This entails a refusal to mechanically follow the prescribed curriculum, no longer treating students as mere recipients of knowledge, moving toward a more egalitarian relationship between teachers and students, and elevating the "job" of teaching to a teaching "career."

Another slant on the issue concentrates on the wider social factors impinging upon school quality. This is treated in a Winter 2010 *Education Next* forum titled "Poor Schools or Poor Kids?" The forum features interviews with Joe Williams of the Education Equality Project and Pedro Noguera of A Broader, Bolder Approach to Education. Among other provocative viewpoints worth considering are the following: "Tackling the Toughest Turnaround—Low-Performing High Schools." *Phi Delta Kappan* (February 2011) by Daniel L. Duke and Martha Jacobson; "Is Education the Cure for Poverty?" *The American Prospect* (May 2007) by Jared Bernstein; "Are Teachers Responsible for Low Achievement by Poor Students?" *Kappa Delta Pi Record* (Fall 2009) by David C. Berliner; and "Hidden Assumptions, Attitudes, and Procedures in Failing Schools," *Educational Horizons* (Winter 2008) by Betsy Gunzelmann.

Books dealing with the issue and its surrounding social context are Laura Pappano's *Inside School Turnarounds* (2010), Kathryn M. Neckermann's *Schools Betrayed* (2007), Jamie Vollmer's *Schools Cannot Do It Alone* (2010), and David Whitman's *Sweating the Small Stuff: Inner-City Schools and the New Paternalism* (2008).

ISSUE 10

Are Local School Boards Obsolete?

YES: Marc Tucker, from "Changing the System Is the Only Solution," *Phi Delta Kappan* (March 2010)

NO: Diane Ravitch, from "Why Public Schools Need Democratic Governance," *Phi Delta Kappan* (March 2010)

ISSUE SUMMARY

YES: Marc Tucker, president of the National Center on Education and the Economy, calls for shifting the running of public schools to the states, allowing local boards to focus solely on the improvement of learning.

NO: Education historian Diane Ravitch feels that a movement of control to the state level or to the mayor's office will undermine democratic deliberation and move toward a top-down business model.

The American "system" of public schools is one of the most decentralized in the world. Historically, there has been no centralized ministry of education as is the case in many European countries, no national curriculum, no national standards, no national examinations. According to *School: The Story of American Public Education* (2001), edited by Sarah Mondale and Sarah B. Patton (and aired as a PBS special program), by the late nineteenth century local school board membership in the United States was "the largest group of public officials in the world. Education historian Diane Ravitch characterized the developmental years of public schooling as a time when local boards made all of the important decisions about curriculum and personnel, teachers had minimal training, state departments of education had little or no control over local school districts, and federal officials "merely collected and disseminated statistics." Some politically appointed boards were guilty of nepotism and "cronyism" and even those elected by the people (often in low-turnout contests) operated the schools with great frugality and often imposed "provincial ideas and standards." Some boards were taken over by fringe political groups that banned supposedly offensive books (a practice still going on today) and forced teachers to use outdated but "approved" curriculum materials.

The twentieth century saw increasing consolidation of small districts and the assertion of more power by state authorities. By the midpoint of the century political support of federal aid to the nation's public schools grew, culminating in the 1965 Elementary and Secondary Education Act which earmarked poverty-area schools and improvement of math and science instruction, among other things. The current manifestation of this act is No Child Left Behind. With the establishment of the U.S. Department of Education by the Carter administration, the expansion of federal authority over what is legally a state function was set in motion. The fact that some local school boards have not been able to lift student performance levels or close achievement gaps among racial or ethnic groups has opened the door to increased federal and state control. In some large cities, such as Boston, Chicago, Detroit, and New York, mayors have asserted control, This phenomenon is detailed in *When Mayors Take Charge: School Governance in the City* (2009), edited by Joseph P. Viteritti. The shift in power from local school boards to higher levels of government is also treated in Paul E. Peterson's *Saving Schools: From Horace Mann to Virtual Learning* (2010).

The diminishment of local school board power has been welcomed in some quarters. In "First, Kill All the School Boards," *The Atlantic* (January/February 2008), Matt Miller of the Center for American Progress bemoans the fact that the American obsession with local control still dominates our schools, an artifact of our Colonial past, an iconic symbol of democratic American learning. Miller quotes Mark Twain: "In the first place, God made idiots. This was for practice. Then He made School Boards." He concludes that we should continue the move toward nationalizing our schools even though it goes against every cultural tradition we have. And as this sentiment gains ascendency, school board members, stressed by the weight of federal mandates and regulations, are developing a sense of caution and powerlessness.

A variety of views in support of local school boards were expressed in the March 2010 issue of *Phi Delta Kappan*. In "School Boards: A Neglected Institution in an Era of School Reform" Michael D. Usdan argues that if comprehensive national reforms are to be sustained they will need the support and understanding of local authorities, school boards that are here to stay at least for the immediate future. In "School Boards: Why American Education Needs Them" Michael A. Resnick and Anne L. Bryant see local boards as essential in the task of connecting federal and state laws and strategies with the "real and diverse world of local people in a way that is close to the community and accountable to it."

The YES and NO articles are also from the March 2010 *Phi Delta Kappan*. In the YES article, Marc Tucker wants states to staff the schools and to form partnerships of teachers to run them. In the NO article, Diane Ravitch warns that elimination of local school boards will end budgetary transparency and obliterate a needed forum for parents.

YES ↵

Marc Tucker

Changing the System Is the Only Solution

Long ago, I was a member of the school board in my home town. I've been an observer of school governance in the United States ever since. I come away from these experiences humbled by memories of the countless unpaid hours of hard work put in by people, often good friends, on school boards across the country, people whose contribution to the improvement of the schools is obvious and vital. But I'm also haunted by other observations.

In many suburban and rural districts, board members are made to feel that they have no business involving themselves in educational issues, which, they are told, ought to be the province of the professionals. In districts of all sizes, it is assumed that boards will have a major say in who is hired and who cannot be fired, with all the opportunities for the exchange of favors those relationships imply. Others run for the opportunity to control the letting of contracts by the district, often one of the largest organizations in town, with all the opportunities for the exchange of favors that implies. Although management is often success-ful at keeping school board members away from strictly educational decisions, school board members almost everywhere have strong incentives to microman-age in other arenas and to serve as advocates for individual parents and staff members in ways that time and again defeat sound management of the schools. For a very long time, superintendents were hired based on considerations other than their record in improving student performance and were fired despite their strong history of improving student performance, and that is still true in all too many districts. To a degree that still might shock many voters, the arguments about school policy are arguments among adults about which adults get what benefits from the school system, not about how to make the most of the district's resources to improve the achievement of students.

Most school board members, superintendents, teachers, and union chiefs are doing the best they can. But they're caught in a system that is dysfunctional.

The problems I just pointed to are not the inevitable consequence of living in a democracy. There are other, better ways to run school districts.

Change Hiring Practices

First, states, not local districts, should hire and employ teachers. That's the only way to break the connection between teacher quality and local tax-able wealth. Until that connection is broken, this country will never have an education system that provides a fair chance to all children. Furthermore, if the state employs the teachers, the people who hope to control the patronage system will no longer run for school board.

This also means that bargaining teacher contracts would no longer be a local district responsibility. Instead, bargaining would occur at the state level. This would place both partners in the bargaining on a more even level than is often the case with local bargaining.

Bargaining would focus on pay and working conditions, and those would be narrowly defined. The teacher partnerships that are described below would determine the actual working conditions, just as is the case in other professional partnerships.

Changing teacher employment, of course, changes the role of teacher associations. At the state level, teacher associations would do more than hold on to their union role; they would also assume a new role. Like most other state and national professional associations, the teacher associations would become a principal source for continuing professional development for educators, providing an unending program of courses and seminars for professional teachers across the country. That is what other professional associations do, besides representing their members in Washington and state capitals.

New Role for School Boards

Second, school boards should get out of the business of running schools and focus on improving student learning.

In my scenario, local school districts would no longer own schools. Instead, school boards would contract with third parties to run their schools. These third parties would be partnerships of teachers, organized as companies. These partnerships of teachers would compete with each other to run the schools in the district.

Partnerships that win the right to run a school would receive a performance contract from the district. That contract would specify what and how much students should learn in order to be ready for college when they graduate. The contract would specify how much money the school would receive if students achieve at that level by the end of the year. The contract also would specify a higher level of student achievement that would trigger a bonus payment to the school. Likewise, the contract would spell out the consequences if student performance falls below a specified level after a certain number of years. The consequences should include losing the contract and opening up the competition process anew. The value of the contract doesn't need to depend entirely on student performance as measured by examinations, but that performance would count for a lot.

Partnerships that win these contracts would get a lump sum to run the school. That sum would include the money needed to fund most of the services now provided by the district. The school could buy services from the district, or it could buy services from other providers. The partnership would have an enormous incentive to get the best services for the lowest cost because the personal income of the members of the partnership would depend on it.

The lump sum payment would include an amount for the space needed to run the school. Districts could lease their school buildings to the partnerships, but the partnerships could also lease them from others or create corporations to get mortgage loans to build the buildings and then lease the buildings back from these corporations. The lump sum payments to the partnerships would also include the money required for building maintenance, utilities, and so on.

No Longer a Stepping Stone

In the world I have in mind, people who run for school boards hoping to use the position as a stepping stone to higher office and to gain control of vital community economic functions for their own advancement would no longer do so because the board would no longer control many jobs or services or supply contracts.

Those who run for school board to make a contribution to improving student performance would be more likely to do so because that would be the primary function of the board and they would see that they would have a much improved chance of being joined by other similarly motivated people. Similarly, people who want their schools to reflect the particular needs and character of their community would be more likely to run because formulating the criteria for the school performance contracts would be an important role of the board and a great opportunity to help define what the community wants in its schools, not as a rhetorical exercise, but as the pivot point for contract requirements. School boards would be the sounding board for the community on the strengths and weaknesses of the partnerships providing the school services and would be in the best position to communicate to those providers what they need to do if they want to continue to serve. This emphasis on performance and responsiveness would be the heart of the job. In this system, micromanagement and grandstanding would not be rewarded, but patient service to the community and a genuine contribution to the steady improvement of school performance would.

District staffs would be much leaner, especially in large districts. Much more of the available funds would go to the schools. Teachers would have an incentive to increase class size because the fewer the teachers employed at the school, the more each teacher will be paid, but they would not have an incentive to increase class size to a point where it lowered student performance because their pay would be based on that performance.

The teachers would not put up with work rules that lowered their productivity, because doing so would lower their paycheck. Teachers running the schools would have an incentive to hire the very best teachers and to get rid of teachers who couldn't cut it. They'd also have an incentive to work as hard as they could to get the best results they could for the students. And they'd look for the best value for their money when buying services for the school.

Funding Schools

Principals would no longer have an incentive to spend half their time downtown lobbying the central office for resources, because a formula would determine school funds and those funds would be distributed by the state to the school in one lump sum. The formula would ensure that schools with large proportions of poor, minority, and handicapped children would get substantially more than schools with less challenged populations. The best teachers and principals, instead of fleeing the schools that need them the most, would have an incentive to serve in those well-funded schools.

Districts would be obligated to make sure that there were sufficient places for all the students who needed places. The competitive, data-based market, combined with the performance contracts themselves, would create schools that were constantly seeking to improve their performance year in and year out. The fact that schools serving students from low-income families and other categories of disadvantaged students would get substantially more money than schools with more advantaged student bodies would ensure that these students would be served by high-quality school operators. It would be very hard for low-quality school operators to survive in this environment.

Parents would be seen as customers instead of being viewed as annoying amateurs and persistent rule-breakers where their children's interests are concerned. They would be courted. Teachers would take the time and trouble to help parents learn how to support their children because they would understand the importance of parental encouragement and involvement in learning.

In this system, the district central staff would be responsible for running the performance management system, which anyone with experience with such systems in private industry will tell you is very demanding. It requires clear specification of what is wanted by the community from its schools, with clear measures, the development of high-quality requests for proposals, active recruitment of potential contractors, a careful review of proposals and effective negotiations over the contracts awarded, the constant collection and monitoring of performance data of all kinds, guidance to the contractors intended to help them perform well, and appropriate action when they do not. Many districts will also want to remain active providers of the myriad services that schools need, and they will certainly be able to do so, provided that they can do so effectively and efficiently in the new competitive climate. And the district will still play an important mediating role between the community at large and its schools, on many fronts.

Conclusion

This vision is very different from the current reality. You may not be very comfortable with it. Before you reject it, though, I urge you to stop and think. The American way of governing our schools is almost unique in the industrialized world. So is our high cost and relatively poor performance. Do you really think things are fine just as they are? If you do not like my proposals, what would you do?

Diane Ravitch

NO

Why Public Schools Need Democratic Governance

Every time some expert, public official, or advocate declares that our public schools are in crisis, stop, listen, and see what he or she is selling. In the history of American education, crisis talk is cheap. Those who talk crisis usually have a cure that they want to promote, and they prefer to keep us focused on the dimensions of the "crisis" without looking too closely at their proposed cure.

The crisis talkers today want to diminish the role of local school boards and increase the privatization of public education. They recite the familiar statistics about mediocre student performance on international tests, and they conclude that bold action is needed and there is no time to delay or ponder. Local school boards insist on deliberation; they give parents and teachers a place to speak out and perhaps oppose whatever bold actions are on the table. So, in the eyes of some of our current crop of school reformers, local school boards are the problem that is blocking the reforms we need. The "reformers" want action, not deliberation.

Local school boards have not been enthusiastic, for example, about privatization of public schools. More often than not, they're skeptical that private entrepreneurs will be more successful running schools than experienced educators. Nor are they eager to open charter schools, which drain away resources and students from the regular schools and have the freedom to remove the students who are most difficult to educate. Local school boards have also been an obstacle to those who want to replace experienced principals and teachers with enthusiastic neophytes.

Local school boards are right to be wary of the latest fad. Our education system tends to embrace "reforms" too quickly, without adequate evidence of their value. Here's just one example from the many I could cite. In 1959, James Conant, the president of Harvard University, led a campaign against small high schools. He said they were inefficient and unable to supply a full curriculum. He called for consolidation of small districts and small high schools, so we could have the advantages of scale. Conant was featured on the cover of *Time*, and suddenly large high schools were the leading edge of reform. In our own time, the Bill & Melinda Gates Foundation poured $2 billion into breaking up large high schools and turning them into small high schools. Now, the Gates Foundation has decided that wasn't such a good idea, and it's off on another tangent, offering rewards to districts that evaluate teachers by their students' test scores.

Today, the public schools once again have a plethora of critics. Some say that public education itself is obsolete. There is a large and growing movement to dismantle public education. Some critics want to get rid of public education and replace it with a completely choice-based system of vouchers and charter schools. Proponents of this view say the market and choice are the only mechanisms that will produce high achievement. Government, they say, has failed. They believe—naively, I think—that in an open market, good schools would thrive and bad ones would die. Personally, I think this is a ludicrous analysis to apply to public education, which is a public good, not a private good or a commodity. As a society, we have a legal, moral, and social responsibility to provide a good public school in every neighborhood and not to leave this vital task to the free-market and not to take unconscionable risks with the lives of vulnerable children.

First Line of Defense

The local school boards are the first line of defense for public education. Critics know this. In 2008, an article in *The Atlantic* was titled "First, Kill All the School Boards." It was written not by a right-wing extremist or a libertarian, but by Matt Miller of the Center for American Progress, whose president, John Podesta, led the Obama transition team. Miller argued that local control and local school boards are the basic cause of poor student performance. He said the federal government should take control of the nation's schools, set national standards, eliminate teacher tenure, and tie teacher pay to student performance. In an ideal world, he wrote, we would scrap local boards and replace them with mayoral control, especially in urban districts. This one act of removing all democratic governance, he claimed, would lead to better education.

This argument lacks logic and evidence. Some localities have high achievement, some have low, and the difference is economics and demography, not democracy. There is not a shred of evidence in Miller's article or in the research literature that schools improve when democratic governance ends.

In a similar vein, *Tough Choices or Tough Times*, a report prepared by the New Commission on the Skills of the American Workforce, proposed turning over all public schools to private managers. The role of school boards would be limited to approving performance contracts with these independent managers, monitoring their performance, and closing schools that didn't meet their goals. Under this proposal, signed by many of our most eminent leaders, local government would get out of the business of running public schools. In effect, every school would be a privately managed school.

Why would schools get better if they're managed by private companies? What secret do private sector organizations have that hasn't been shared with state and local education leaders? What's the logical connection between privatization and quality education? Why are they so certain that any privately managed school will be better than any regular public school?

The recommendation for universal privatization is irresponsible. You don't rip apart a vital part of the nation's social fabric—its public schools—because it sounds like a good idea. You don't destroy democratic governance of public education because of a hunch.

New York Experience

As it happens, New York City has already created a test case of what happens when the local school board is rendered toothless. In 2002, the state legislature turned over control of the school system to the city's newly elected mayor, Michael Bloomberg. The legislation continued a central board, but abolished the city's 32 local school boards. The central board, however, consisted only of appointees who serve at the pleasure of the person who appointed them. Of its 13 members, eight serve at the pleasure of the mayor, and the remaining five serve at the pleasure of the borough presidents who appointed them.

The mayor immediately demonstrated that the new central board was of no importance. He renamed it the Panel for Educational Policy. When he introduced its members at a press conference, he made clear that they would not be speaking out on anything. He said, "They don't have to speak, and they don't have to serve. That's what 'serving at the pleasure' means" (Hernandez 2009). On a rare occasion, when two of his appointees planned to vote against his plan to end social promotion for 3rd graders, he fired them and replaced them on the same day. This central board, which was supposed to provide oversight and a check on the mayor's extraordinary power over the schools, was reduced to a rubber stamp.

Only one borough president appointed a representative who dared to ask questions. Patrick J. Sullivan, a business executive, was appointed to the central board in 2007 as a parent member. Before his term began, he sat in on a meeting and watched the board approve a $17 billion budget, a major labor contract, and a new database costing $80 million, all in less than an hour. He observed that, "The Panel for Educational Policy seemed more a misplaced relic of the Brezhnev-era Soviet Union than a functioning board of directors overseeing the education of 1.1 million children" (2009).

The board exists to do whatever the mayor and chancellor want, not to exercise independent judgment. Sullivan reported that board members seldom had presentation materials in advance. Votes are cast before hearing public comments, not after, as is typical of other public boards. Although the law specified that the board would meet at least once a year in executive session, no such meeting was held in Sullivan's first two years on the board. Time and again, when controversial issues came up, Sullivan was the only dissenting voice on the panel.

When mayoral control of the schools came up for reauthorization before the New York state legislature in 2009, the mayor waged a heavily financed campaign to maintain his complete control of the school system. His advocacy group received millions of dollars from the Bill & Melinda Gates Foundation, the Broad Foundation, and other foundations. On one point, the mayor drew a line: He did not want any board members to serve for a fixed term, even if he appointed them. They must continue to serve at his pleasure. When Citizens Union, a respected civic organization, was considering the possibility of issuing a statement on behalf of fixed terms, it received a personal letter from U.S. Secretary of Education Arne Duncan, opposing fixed terms for any appointees and insisting that the mayor could be effective only if he had complete control.

Because New York City no longer has an independent board of education, it no longer has democratic control of its public education system. There is no forum in which parents and other members of the public can ask questions and get timely answers. Major decisions about the school system are made in private, behind closed doors, with no public review and no public discussion.

Because New York City no longer has an independent board of education, there are no checks or balances, no questioning of executive authority. A contract was awarded for nearly $16 million to the business consulting firm of Alvarez & Marsal to review operations and cut spending. This firm rearranged the city's complex school bus routes and stranded thousands of young children on one of the coldest days of the year without any means of getting to school. Some of the chaos they created might have been averted had there been public review and discussion of their plans. No one was held accountable for their mistakes; they were not chastised, and their contract was not terminated.

Similarly, the Department of Education imposed a grading system on every school in the city. In the name of accountability, each school is given a single letter grade from A to F, not a report card. The grade depends mainly on improvement, not on performance. Some outstanding schools, where more than 90% of the students meet state standards, got an F because they didn't make progress, while some really low-performing schools, even persistently dangerous ones, got an A because they saw a one-year gain in their scores. This approach was imposed without public discussion or review. The result was a very bad policy that stigmatizes some very good schools and helps none. The lesson is, or should be, that public discussion can prevent or mitigate policy errors.

In the absence of an independent board, there is no transparency of budget. There is no public forum in which questions are asked and answered about how the public's money is spent. Consequently, the number and size of no-bid contracts for consultants and vendors have soared into the hundreds of millions of dollars, with no public review or oversight. The education budget has grown from $12 billion annually to nearly $22 billion.

In the absence of a school board to oversee the actions of the executive, there is no accountability. The mayor can do as he wishes in the schools. The chancellor can adopt any policies he wishes; he serves at the pleasure of the mayor and answers to no one else. When a school fails or many schools fail, only the principal is held accountable. Those at headquarters who impose policies and programs are never held accountable.

All this unchecked authority has been used to turn New York City's public schools into a demonstration of choice and free markets in education. Children may choose among 400 or so high schools. They may choose from among

100 charter schools. If the school is successful or popular, students must enter a lottery or go onto a waiting list. In many of the poorest neighborhoods, the number of charter schools has increased, and many have been given space in neighborhood public schools. New York City might be the only district in the nation that places charter schools in public school buildings, taking away space previously allocated to art rooms, music rooms, computer rooms, and other activities. Parents and teachers have protested, but the mayor continues to place charters in public school buildings. By the end of the mayor's third term, there may be neighborhoods that have no public schools, just charters to which students seek entry.

The mayor has promised to open yet another 100 charter schools because he believes that schools should function like a marketplace, with choice and competition. Parents must struggle to get their child into the right high school, the right middle school, or the right charter school. Sustaining and improving regular public schools, neighborhood public schools, has low priority in the new world of the business model in education.

This business model has impressed the Obama Administration. Secretary Duncan has strongly endorsed mayoral control as a means to improve achievement, even though the results of the National Assessment of Educational Progress suggest caution: Two of the three lowest-performing districts in the nation (Cleveland and Chicago) are controlled by their mayors, while the highest performing districts (Charlotte and Austin) are managed by school boards. The Obama Administration has also required states to remove their caps on charter schools to be eligible for its $4.3 billion "Race to the Top" fund. In this time of budget cutting, every district wants new funding. But the price may be too high if public education is placed in jeopardy.

The business model assumes that democratic governance is a hindrance to effective education. It assumes that competition among schools and teachers produces better results than collaboration. It treats local school boards as a nuisance and an obstacle rather than as the public's representatives in shaping education policy. It assumes that schools can be closed and opened as if they were chain stores rather than vital community institutions.

By endorsing mayoral control and privatization, the Obama Administration is making a risky bet.

References

Hernandez, Javier C. "Schools Panel Is No Threat to the Mayor's Grip." *The New York Times*, April 23, 2009: A1.

Miller, Matt. "First, Kill All the School Boards." *The Atlantic* (Jan-Feb 2008).

Sullivan, Patrick J. "Inside the Panel for Educational Policy." *NYC Schools Under Bloomberg and Klein*, ed. Diane Ravitch. New York: Lulu.com, 2009.

POSTSCRIPT

Are Local School Boards Obsolete?

Assuming that local school boards are destined for either a diminished or altered role in governance in coming years, do the ideas of Marc Tucker and Diane Ravitch hold any promise of mutual accommodation? Would Tucker's relief of school boards' management functions allow them to perform the community tailoring of external demands that Ravitch sees as important? Can current frailties of school board operations be corrected? In "Weighing the Case for School Boards: Today and Tomorrow," *Phi Delta Kappan* (March 2010), Frederick M. Hess points to four indictments: (1) a lack of voter attention makes it difficult to hold board members accountable, (2) electoral apathy allows mobilized constituencies to exert disproportionate influence, (3) elected boards often lack coherence and continuity, and (4) boards operate in isolation from a city's political and civic leaders.

In the near future increased attention will be given to the appropriate roles of the federal government, state and local governments, and representative school boards in the improvement of the nation's schools. Chester E. Finn, Jr., in "How to Run Public Schools in the 21st Century," *Education Next* on the web (June 27, 2011), identifies four major problems that must be recognized and dealt with (1) "local" has gradually become a less accurate way to describe, much less to organize, public education; (2) the dream of keeping education out of politics has turned into a nightmare; (3) keeping K-12 education separate from the rest of the public sector does more harm than good; and (4) our inherited structures presuppose a qausi-monopoly over K-12 education. These and similar issues are handled in a variety of ways in "Can We Live Without Federal Involvement?" *School Administrator* (June 2010) by Steve Atwater, who sees the federal role as being a support agency concentrating on turning around low-performing schools; in "Federal Involvement in Local School Districts," *Society* (May/June 2005), by Stephen J. Caldas and Carl L. Bankston III, and in "Governance as a Profession," *American School Board Journal* (February 2010), by Rick Maloney, who says that our nation's schools deserve professional leadership at the policy-making level.

Further ideas can be gleaned from these sources: Gene I. Maeroff, "School Boards in America: Flawed But Still Significant," *Phi Delta Kappan* (March 2010) in which he seeks ways to revitalize local boards while acknowledging their limited autonomy; a pair of articles in *Education Next* (Summer 2004), "Lost at Sea" by Chester E. Finn, Jr. and "Steering a True Course" by Sarah C. Glover; and two books, *Besieged: School Boards and the Future of Education Politics* (2005) edited by William G. Howell and *The Essential School Board Book* (2009) by Nancy Walser.

Internet References . . .

Federation for American Immigration Reform (FAIR)

Offers materials concerning school overcrowding, budget straining, and other effects of policies favoring undocumented immigrants.

http://www.fairus.org

American Federation of Teachers

Addresses key issues affecting the professional lives of teachers and puts forth resolutions on public policy.

http://www.aft.org

Pre-K Now

Offers reports and fact sheets on the universal preschool movement.

http://preknow.org

Privatization Approaches

Covers controversies over privatization, vouchers, and charter schools.

http://hypertextbook.com

Circle of Inclusion

Offers materials and methods for serving learners with disabilities in inclusive school settings.

http://www.circleofinclusion.org

National Center on Time & Learning

Updates nationwide developments in the time-expansion movement and offers access to its extensive database.

http://www.timeandlearning.org

Partnership for 21st Century Skills

Provides news on nationwide developments and suggests tools and resources for action in local school districts. Includes interactive guide.

http://p21.org

National Association for Single-Sex Public Education

Advocacy group presenting the case for single-sex schools and classes.

http://singlesexschools.org

Current Specific Issues

*T*his unit probes specific questions currently being discussed by educators, policy-makers, and parents. In most cases these issues are grounded in the more basic questions explored in Units 1 and 2. Views are expressed by a wide variety of writers, including Supreme Court Justices Brennan, Burger, Souter, and Thomas, David L. Kirp, Douglas J. Besharov, Chris Whittle, Henry Levin, Mara Sapon-Shevin, Wade A. Carpenter, Peter Meyer, Vincent A. Anfara, Jr., Lowell Monke, Andrew Coulson, Louis Malfaro, Chris Gabrieli, Larry Cuban, Andrew J. Rotherham, Daniel T. Willingham, and Diana Senechal.

- Are Undocumented Immigrants Entitled to Public Education?
- Has the Time Arrived for Universal Preschool?
- Is Privatization the Hope of the Future?
- Is the Inclusive Classroom Model Workable?
- Do Teachers Unions Stymie School Reform?
- Can Merit Pay Accelerate School Improvement?
- Are Single-Sex Schools and Classes Effective?
- Can Zero Tolerance Violate Students Rights?
- Do American Students Need More Time in School?
- Do Computers Negatively Affect Student Growth?
- Is the "21st Century Skills" Movement Viable?

ISSUE 11

Are Undocumented Immigrants Entitled to Public Education?

YES: William J. Brennan, Jr., from Undocumented Children Deserve Equal Protection (June 15, 1982)

NO: Warren Burger, from The Decision Distorts the Function of the Court (June 15, 1982)

ISSUE SUMMARY

YES: Justice William Brennan argues that the action of the Texas state legislature to authorize local school districts to deny enrollment in public schools to children not "legally admitted" to the country violates the Fourteenth Amendment.

NO: Chief Justice Warren Burger, in dissent, counters that the Court has no business assuming a policymaking role simply because the legislative branches of government fail to act appropriately.

The situation regarding the treatment of immigrants who are not authorized to be here has deteriorated in the last few years. The period has been marked by congressional inaction on immigration policy, acceleration of authorities' raids on businesses harboring undocumented workers, actions of local governments seeking to reverse the impact of immigrants, and the increase in fearfulness in immigrant communities. According to some sources, about 70 percent of the undocumented immigrants have been residing here for at least five years and identify themselves as Americans, making the sudden enforcement of existing laws rather problematic. Approximately 5 percent of the American workforce consists of undocumented immigrants, and only 66,000 visas are currently available for immigrant unskilled workers, a number considered laughable by some.

There are those who want to arrest and deport all these people. There are those who want to work out some sort of amnesty program. Tom Bethell, in "Freedom of Immigration Acts: A Special Report," *The American Spectator* (September 2007) states "My sense is that ending the contribution of the illegals to the U.S. economy would have an effect comparable to that of a major tax increase. Possibly there would be a real economic contraction. Without an expanding, dynamic economy, America would soon be in a great mess."

Beyond such broad economic concerns lies the situation of the children of undocumented immigrants who may or may not be availing education and other social services during their stay in the United States.

The National Association for Bilingual Education has estimated that over one million children, aged 5–19, are the offspring of parents who are undocumented immigrants. Some groups have pressured schools to turn away such children in spite of the Supreme Court's decision in *Plyler v. Doe* that protected them from exclusion. Since that 5-4 decision, public schools across the nation have been obligated to enroll children regardless of their immigration status. Mary Ann Zehr, in "Amid Immigration Debate, Settled Ground: High Court's School Access Ruling Endures as a Quiet Fact of Life," *Education Week* (June 12–13, 2007), cites a number of attempts to counteract the Court's ruling. In 1994, California voters tried to deny a K–12 education and other public services to undocumented immigrants in Proposition 187, which stipulated that "no public elementary or secondary school shall admit, or permit the attendance of, any child who is not a citizen of the United States, an alien lawfully admitted as a permanent resident, or a person who is otherwise authorized under federal law to be present in the United States." The Proposition was thrown out by a federal court and the appeal process fizzled. In 1996, there was an unsuccessful attempt by a California congressman to attach an amendment to federal legislation that would allow states to pass laws similar to that disallowed by *Plyler v. Doe*. In 2004, an Arizona ballot measure denied adults the opportunity to get a free K–12 education, thus partially diminishing the impact of the *Plyler v. Doe* ruling.

In an article commemorating the 25th anniversary of *Plyler,* Sarah Karlin, in "The Invisible Class," *American School Board Journal* (November 2007), says that challenges still persist for undocumented students who secure a high school diploma. They cannot receive federal financial aid for higher education, and most are not offered in-state tuition. A 2007 National Survey of Latinos by the Pew Hispanic Center shows that they are "feeling a range of negative effects from the increased public attention and stepped-up enforcement measures that have accompanied the growing national debate over illegal immigration." Federal policies to strictly enforce laws by workplace crackdowns could certainly have a long-term impact on children whose family life may be compromised.

The landmark case, *Plyler, Superintendent, Tyler Independent School District, et al. v. Doe, Guardian, et al.* involved a Texas statute that withheld from local school districts any state funds for the education of children who were not "legally admitted" into the United States and that authorized local school districts, like that in Tyler, to deny enrollment to such children. The majority and dissenting opinions in that case are herein presented.

YES ↵ William J. Brennan, Jr.

Undocumented Children Deserve Equal Protection

JUSTICE BRENNAN delivered the opinion of the Court.

The question presented by these cases is whether, consistent with the Equal Protection Clause of the Fourteenth Amendment, Texas may deny to undocumented school-age children the free public education that it provides to children who are citizens of the United States or legally admitted aliens.

I

Since the late 19th century, the United States has restricted immigration into this country. Unsanctioned entry into the United States is a crime, and those who have entered unlawfully are subject to deportation. But despite the existence of these legal restrictions, a substantial number of persons have succeeded in unlawfully entering the United States, and now live within various States, including the State of Texas.

In May, 1975, the Texas Legislature revised its education laws to withhold from local school districts any state funds for the education of children who were not "legally admitted" into the United States. The 1975 revision also authorized local school districts to deny enrollment in their public schools to children not "legally admitted" to the country. These cases involve constitutional challenges to those provisions.

Plyler v. Doe

This is a class action, filed in the United States District Court for the Eastern District of Texas in September 1977, on behalf of certain school-age children of Mexican origin residing in Smith County, Texas, who could not establish that they had been legally admitted into the United States. The action complained of the exclusion of plaintiff children from the public schools of the Tyler Independent School District. The Superintendent and members of the Board of Trustees of the School District were named as defendants; the State of Texas intervened as a party-defendant. After certifying a class consisting of all undocumented school-age children of Mexican origin residing within the School District, the District Court preliminarily enjoined defendants from denying a free education to members of the plaintiff class. In December 1977, the court conducted an extensive hearing on plaintiffs' motion for permanent injunctive relief.

From Supreme Court of the United States, June 15, 1982, parts I–VI.

In considering this motion, the District Court made extensive findings of fact. The court found that neither 21.031 nor the School District policy implementing it had "either the purpose or effect of keeping illegal aliens out of the State of Texas." Respecting defendants' further claim that 21.031 was simply a financial measure designed to avoid a drain on the State's fisc [treasury], the court recognized that the increases in population resulting from the immigration of Mexican nationals into the United States had created problems for the public schools of the State, and that these problems were exacerbated by the special educational needs of immigrant Mexican children. The court noted, however, that the increase in school enrollment was primarily attributable to the admission of children who were legal residents. It also found that while the "exclusion of all undocumented children from the public schools in Texas would eventually result in economies at some level," funding from both the State and Federal Governments was based primarily on the number of children enrolled. In net effect then, barring undocumented children from the schools would save money, but it would "not necessarily" improve "the quality of education." The court further observed that the impact of 21.031 was borne primarily by a very small subclass of illegal aliens, "entire families who have migrated illegally and—for all practical purposes—permanently to the United States." Finally, the court noted that, under current laws and practices, "the illegal alien of today may well be the legal alien of tomorrow," and that without an education, these undocumented children, [a]lready disadvantaged as a result of poverty, lack of English-speaking ability, and undeniable racial prejudices, . . . will become permanently locked into the lowest socio-economic class.

The District Court held that illegal aliens were entitled to the protection of the Equal Protection Clause of the Fourteenth Amendment, and that 21.031 violated that Clause. Suggesting that "the state's exclusion of undocumented children from its public schools . . . may well be the type of invidiously motivated state action for which the suspect classification doctrine was designed," the court held that it was unnecessary to decide whether the statute would survive a "strict scrutiny" analysis because, in any event, the discrimination embodied in the statute was not supported by a rational basis. The District Court also concluded that the Texas statute violated the Supremacy Clause.

The Court of Appeals for the Fifth Circuit upheld the District Court's injunction. The Court of Appeals held that the District Court had erred in finding the Texas statute pre-empted by federal law. With respect to equal protection, however, the Court of Appeals affirmed in all essential respects the analysis of the District Court, concluding that 21.031 was "constitutionally infirm regardless of whether it was tested using the mere rational basis standard or some more stringent test."

In re Alien Children Education Litigation

During 1978 and 1979, suits challenging the constitutionality of 21.031 and various local practices undertaken on the authority of that provision were filed in the United States District Courts for the Southern, Western, and Northern Districts of Texas. Each suit named the State of Texas and the Texas Education

Agency as defendants, along with local officials. In November 1979, the Judicial Panel on Multi-district Litigation, on motion of the State, consolidated the claims against the state officials into a single action to be heard in the District Court for the Southern District of Texas. A hearing was conducted in February and March 1980. In July 1980, the court entered an opinion and order holding that 21.031 violated the Equal Protection Clause of the Fourteenth Amendment. The court held that "the absolute deprivation of education should trigger strict judicial scrutiny, particularly when the absolute deprivation is the result of complete inability to pay for the desired benefit." The court determined that the State's concern for fiscal integrity was not a compelling state interest; that exclusion of these children had not been shown to be necessary to improve education within the State; and that the educational needs of the children statutorily excluded were not different from the needs of children not excluded. The court therefore concluded that 21.031 was not carefully tailored to advance the asserted state interest in an acceptable manner. While appeal of the District Court's decision was pending, the Court of Appeals rendered its decision in No. 80-1538. Apparently on the strength of that opinion, the Court of Appeals, on February 23, 1981, summarily affirmed the decision of the Southern District. We noted probable jurisdiction, and consolidated this case with No. 80-1538 for briefing and argument.

II

The Fourteenth Amendment provides that "[n]o State shall . . . deprive any person of life, liberty, or property, without due process of law; nor deny to any person within its jurisdiction the equal protection of the laws." Appellants argue at the outset that undocumented aliens, because of their immigration status, are not "persons within the jurisdiction" of the State of Texas, and that they therefore have no right to the equal protection of Texas law. We reject this argument. Whatever his status under the immigration laws, an alien is surely a "person" in any ordinary sense of that term. Aliens, even aliens whose presence in this country is unlawful, have long been recognized as "persons" guaranteed due process of law by the Fifth and Fourteenth Amendment. Indeed, we have clearly held that the Fifth Amendment protects aliens whose presence in this country is unlawful from invidious discrimination by the Federal Government.

Appellants seek to distinguish our prior cases, emphasizing that the Equal Protection Clause directs a State to afford its protection to persons within its jurisdiction while the Due Process Clauses of the Fifth and Fourteenth Amendments contain no such assertedly limiting phrase. In appellants' view, persons who have entered the United States illegally are not "within the jurisdiction" of a State even if they are present within a State's boundaries and subject to its laws. Neither our cases nor the logic of the Fourteenth Amendment supports that constricting construction of the phrase "within its jurisdiction." We have never suggested that the class of persons who might avail themselves of the equal protection guarantee is less than coextensive with that entitled to due process. To the contrary, we have recognized that both provisions were fashioned to protect an identical class of persons, and to reach every exercise of state authority. . . .

In concluding that "all persons within the territory of the United States," including aliens unlawfully present, may invoke the Fifth and Sixth Amendments to challenge actions of the Federal Government, we reasoned from the understanding that the Fourteenth Amendment was designed to afford its protection to all within the boundaries of a State. Our cases applying the Equal Protection Clause reflect the same territorial theme . . .

There is simply no support for appellants' suggestion that "due process" is somehow of greater stature than "equal protection" and therefore available to a larger class of persons. To the contrary, each aspect of the Fourteenth Amendment reflects an elementary limitation on state power. To permit a State to employ the phrase "within its jurisdiction" in order to identify subclasses of persons whom it would define as beyond its jurisdiction, thereby relieving itself of the obligation to assure that its laws are designed and applied equally to those persons, would undermine the principal purpose for which the Equal Protection Clause was incorporated in the Fourteenth Amendment. The Equal Protection Clause was intended to work nothing less than the abolition of all caste-based and invidious class-based legislation. That objective is fundamentally at odds with the power the State asserts here to classify persons subject to its laws as nonetheless excepted from its protection.

⌘

Use of the phrase "within its jurisdiction" thus does not detract from, but rather confirms, the understanding that the protection of the Fourteenth Amendment extends to anyone, citizen or stranger, who is subject to the laws of a State, and reaches into every corner of a State's territory. That a person's initial entry into a State, or into the United States, was unlawful, and that he may for that reason be expelled, cannot negate the simple fact of his presence within the State's territorial perimeter. Given such presence, he is subject to the full range of obligations imposed by the State's civil and criminal laws. And until he leaves the jurisdiction—either voluntarily, or involuntarily in accordance with the Constitution and laws of the United States—he is entitled to the equal protection of the laws that a State may choose to establish.

Our conclusion that the illegal aliens who are plaintiffs in these cases may claim the benefit of the Fourteenth Amendment's guarantee of equal protection only begins the inquiry. The more difficult question is whether the Equal Protection Clause has been violated by the refusal of the State of Texas to reimburse local school boards for the education of children who cannot demonstrate that their presence within the United States is lawful, or by the imposition by those school boards of the burden of tuition on those children. It is to this question that we now turn.

III

The Equal Protection Clause directs that "all persons similarly circumstanced shall be treated alike." But so too, "[t]he Constitution does not require things which are different in fact or opinion to be treated in law as though they were the same." The initial discretion to determine what is "different" and what is "the same" resides in the legislatures of the States. A legislature must have substantial latitude to establish classifications that roughly approximate the nature of the problem perceived, that accommodate competing concerns both public and private, and that account for limitations on the practical ability of the State to remedy every ill. In applying the Equal Protection Clause to most forms of state action, we thus seek only the assurance that the classification at issue bears some fair relationship to a legitimate public purpose.

But we would not be faithful to our obligations under the Fourteenth Amendment if we applied so deferential a standard to every classification. The Equal Protection Clause was intended as a restriction on state legislative action inconsistent with elemental constitutional premises. Thus we have treated as presumptively invidious those classifications that disadvantage a "suspect class," or that impinge upon the exercise of a "fundamental right." With respect to such classifications, it is appropriate to enforce the mandate of equal protection by requiring the State to demonstrate that its classification has been precisely tailored to serve a compelling governmental interest. In addition, we have recognized that certain forms of legislative classification, while not facially invidious, nonetheless give rise to recurring constitutional difficulties; in these limited circumstances we have sought the assurance that the classification reflects a reasoned judgment consistent with the ideal of equal protection by inquiring whether it may fairly be viewed as furthering a substantial interest of the State. We turn to a consideration of the standard appropriate for the evaluation of 21.031.

A

Sheer incapability or lax enforcement of the laws barring entry into this country, coupled with the failure to establish an effective bar to the employment of undocumented aliens, has resulted in the creation of a substantial "shadow population" of illegal migrants—numbering in the millions—within our borders. This situation raises the specter of a permanent caste of undocumented resident aliens, encouraged by some to remain here as a source of cheap labor, but nevertheless denied the benefits that our society makes available to citizens and lawful residents. The existence of such an underclass presents most difficult problems for a Nation that prides itself on adherence to principles of equality under law.

The children who are plaintiffs in these cases are special members of this underclass. Persuasive arguments support the view that a State may withhold its beneficence from those whose very presence within the United States is the product of their own unlawful conduct. These arguments do not apply with the same force to classifications imposing disabilities on the minor children of such illegal entrants. At the least, those who elect to enter our territory by stealth and in violation of our law should be prepared to bear the consequences, including, but not limited to, deportation. But the children of those illegal entrants are not comparably situated. Their "parents have the ability to conform their conduct to societal norms," and presumably the ability to remove themselves from the State's jurisdiction; but the children who are plaintiffs in these cases "can affect neither their parents' conduct nor their own status." Even if the State found it expedient to control the conduct of adults by acting against their children, legislation directing the onus of a parent's misconduct against his children does not comport with fundamental conceptions of justice.

Of course, undocumented status is not irrelevant to any proper legislative goal. Nor is undocumented status an absolutely immutable characteristic since it is the product of conscious, indeed unlawful, action. But 21.031 is directed against children, and imposes its discriminatory burden on the basis of a legal characteristic over which children can have little control. It is thus difficult to conceive of a rational justification for penalizing these children for their presence within the United States. Yet that appears to be precisely the effect of 21.031.

Public education is not a "right" granted to individuals by the Constitution. But neither is it merely some governmental "benefit" indistinguishable from other forms of social welfare legislation. Both the importance of education in maintaining our basic institutions, and the lasting impact of its deprivation on the life of the child, mark the distinction. The "American people have always regarded education and [the] acquisition of knowledge as matters of supreme importance." We have recognized "the public schools as a most vital civic institution for the preservation of a democratic system of government," and as the primary vehicle for transmitting "the values on which our society rests." "[A]s . . . pointed out early in our history, . . . some degree of education is necessary to prepare citizens to participate effectively and intelligently in our open political system if we are to preserve freedom and independence." And these historic "perceptions of the public schools as inculcating fundamental values necessary to the maintenance of a democratic political system have been confirmed by the observations of social scientists." In addition, education provides the basic tools by which individuals might lead economically productive lives to the benefit of us all. In sum, education has a fundamental role in maintaining the fabric of our society. We cannot ignore the significant social costs borne by our Nation when select groups are denied the means to absorb the values and skills upon which our social order rests.

In addition to the pivotal role of education in sustaining our political and cultural heritage, denial of education to some isolated group of children poses an affront to one of the goals of the Equal Protection Clause: the abolition of governmental barriers presenting unreasonable obstacles to advancement on the basis of individual merit. Paradoxically, by depriving the children of any disfavored group of an education, we foreclose the means by which that group might raise the level of esteem in which it is held by the majority. But more directly, "education prepares individuals to be self-reliant and self-sufficient participants in society." Illiteracy is an enduring disability. The inability to read and write will handicap the individual deprived of a basic education each and every day of his life. The inestimable toll of that deprivation on the social, economic, intellectual, and psychological well-being of the individual, and the obstacle it poses to individual achievement, make it most difficult to reconcile the cost or the principle of a status-based denial of basic education with the framework of equality embodied in the Equal Protection Clause. What we said 28 years ago in Brown v. Board of Education (1954), still holds true:

> Today, education is perhaps the most important function of state and local governments. Compulsory school attendance laws and the great expenditures for education both demonstrate our recognition of the importance of education to our democratic society. It is required in the performance of our most basic public responsibilities, even service in the armed forces. It is the very foundation of good citizenship. Today it is a principal instrument in awakening the child to cultural values, in preparing him for later professional training, and in helping him to adjust normally to his environment. In these days, it is doubtful that any child may reasonably be expected to succeed in life if he is denied the opportunity of an education. Such an opportunity, where the state has undertaken to provide it, is a right which must be made available to all on equal terms.

B

These well-settled principles allow us to determine the proper level of deference to be afforded 21.031. Undocumented aliens cannot be treated as a suspect class because their presence in this country in violation of federal law is not a "constitutional irrelevancy." Nor is education a fundamental right; a State need not justify by compelling necessity every variation in the manner in which education is provided to its population. But more is involved in these cases than the abstract question whether 21.031 discriminates against a suspect class, or whether education is a fundamental right. Section 21.031 imposes a lifetime hardship on a discrete class of children not accountable for their disabling status. The stigma of illiteracy will mark them for the rest of their lives. By denying these children a basic education, we deny them the ability to live within the structure of our civic institutions, and foreclose any realistic possibility that they will contribute in even the smallest way to the progress of our Nation. In determining the rationality of 21.031, we may appropriately take into account its costs to the Nation and to the innocent children who are its victims. In light of these countervailing costs, the discrimination contained in 21.031 can hardly be considered rational unless it furthers some substantial goal of the State.

IV

It is the State's principal argument, and apparently the view of the dissenting Justices, that the undocumented status of these children vel non establishes a sufficient rational basis for denying them benefits that a State might choose to afford other residents. The State notes that while other aliens are admitted "on an equality of legal privileges with all citizens under nondiscriminatory laws," the asserted right of these children to an education can claim no implicit congressional imprimatur. Indeed, in the State's view, Congress' apparent disapproval of the presence of these children within the United States, and the evasion of the federal regulatory program that is the mark of undocumented status, provides authority for its decision to impose upon them special disabilities. Faced with an equal protection challenge respecting the treatment of aliens, we agree that the courts must be attentive to congressional policy; the exercise of congressional power might well affect the State's prerogatives to afford differential treatment to a particular class of aliens. But we are unable to find in the congressional immigration scheme any statement of policy that might weigh significantly in arriving at an equal protection balance concerning the State's authority to deprive these children of an education.

⋅⟨◉⟩⋅

We are reluctant to impute to Congress the intention to withhold from these children, for so long as they are present in this country through no fault of their own, access to a basic education. In other contexts, undocumented status, coupled with some articulable federal policy, might enhance state authority with respect to the treatment of undocumented aliens. But in the area of special constitutional sensitivity presented by these cases, and in the absence of any contrary indication fairly discernible in the present legislative record, we perceive no national policy that supports the State in denying these children an elementary education. The State may borrow the federal classification. But to justify its use as a criterion for its own discriminatory policy, the State must demonstrate that the classification is reasonably adapted to "the purposes for which the state desires to use it." We therefore turn to the state objectives that are said to support 21.031.

V

Appellants argue that the classification at issue furthers an interest in the "preservation of the state's limited resources for the education of its lawful residents." Of course, a concern for the preservation of resources standing alone can hardly justify the classification used in allocating those resources. The State must do more than justify its classification with a concise expression of an intention to discriminate. Apart from the asserted state prerogative to act against undocumented children solely on the basis of their undocumented status—an asserted prerogative that carries only minimal force in the circumstances of these cases—we discern three colorable state interests that might support 21.031.

First, appellants appear to suggest that the State may seek to protect itself from an influx of illegal immigrants. While a State might have an interest in mitigating the potentially harsh economic effects of sudden shifts in population, 21.031 hardly offers an effective method of dealing with an urgent demographic or economic problem. There is no evidence in the record suggesting that illegal entrants impose any significant burden on the State's economy. To the contrary, the available evidence suggests that illegal aliens underutilize public services, while contributing their labor to the local economy and tax money to the state fisc [treasury]. The dominant incentive for illegal entry into the State of Texas is the availability of employment; few if any illegal immigrants come to this country, or presumably to the State of Texas, in order to avail themselves of a free education. Thus, even making the doubtful assumption that the net impact of illegal aliens on the economy of the State is negative, we think it clear that "[c]harging tuition to undocumented children constitutes a ludicrously ineffectual attempt to stem the tide of illegal immigration," at least when compared with the alternative of prohibiting the employment of illegal aliens.

Second, while it is apparent that a State may "not . . . reduce expenditures for education by barring [some arbitrarily chosen class of] children from its schools," appellants suggest that undocumented children are appropriately singled out for exclusion because of the special burdens they impose on the State's ability to provide high-quality public education. But the record in no way supports the claim that exclusion of undocumented children is likely to improve the overall quality of education in the State. As the District Court in No. 80-1934 noted, the State failed to offer any "credible supporting evidence that a proportionately small diminution of the funds spent on each child [which might result from devoting some state funds to the education of the excluded group] will have a grave impact on the quality of education." And, after reviewing the State's school financing mechanism, the District Court in No. 80-1538 concluded that barring undocumented children from local schools would not necessarily improve the quality of education provided in those schools. Of course, even if improvement in the quality of education were a likely result of barring some number of children from the schools of the State, the State must support its selection of this group as the appropriate target for exclusion. In terms of educational cost and need, however, undocumented children are "basically indistinguishable" from legally resident alien children.

Finally, appellants suggest that undocumented children are appropriately singled out because their unlawful presence within the United States renders them less likely than other children to remain within the boundaries of the State, and to put their education to productive social or political use within the State. Even assuming that such an interest is legitimate, it is an interest that is most difficult to quantify. The State has no assurance that any child, citizen or not, will employ the education provided by the State within the confines of the State's borders. In any event, the record is clear that many of the undocumented children disabled by this classification will remain in this country indefinitely, and that some will become lawful residents or citizens of the United States. It is difficult to understand precisely what the State hopes to achieve by promoting the creation and perpetuation of a subclass of illiterates within our boundaries, surely adding to the problems and costs of unemployment, welfare, and crime. It is thus clear that whatever savings might be achieved by denying these children an education, they are wholly insubstantial in light of the costs involved to these children, the State, and the Nation.

VI

If the State is to deny a discrete group of innocent children the free public education that it offers to other children residing within its borders, that denial must be justified by a showing that it furthers some substantial state interest. No such showing was made here. Accordingly, the judgment of the Court of Appeals in each of these cases is Affirmed.

➡ **NO**

The Decision Distorts the Function of the Court

CHIEF JUSTICE BURGER, with whom JUSTICE WHITE, JUSTICE REHNQUIST, and JUSTICE O'CONNOR join, dissenting.

Were it our business to set the Nation's social policy, I would agree without hesitation that it is senseless for an enlightened society to deprive any children—including illegal aliens—of an elementary education. I fully agree that it would be folly—and wrong—to tolerate creation of a segment of society made up of illiterate persons, many having a limited or no command of our language. However, the Constitution does not constitute us as "Platonic Guardians" nor does it vest in this Court the authority to strike down laws because they do not meet our standards of desirable social policy, "wisdom," or "common sense." We trespass on the assigned function of the political branches under our structure of limited and separated powers when we assume a policymaking role as the Court does today.

The Court makes no attempt to disguise that it is acting to make up for Congress' lack of "effective leadership" in dealing with the serious national problems caused by the influx of uncountable millions of illegal aliens across our borders. The failure of enforcement of the immigration laws over more than a decade and the inherent difficulty and expense of sealing our vast borders have combined to create a grave socioeconomic dilemma. It is a dilemma that has not yet even been fully assessed, let alone addressed. However, it is not the function of the Judiciary to provide "effective leadership" simply because the political branches of government fail to do so.

The Court's holding today manifests the justly criticized judicial tendency to attempt speedy and wholesale formulation of "remedies" for the failures—or simply the laggard pace—of the political processes of our system of government. The Court employs, and in my view abuses, the Fourteenth Amendment in an effort to become an omnipotent and omniscient problem solver. That the motives for doing so are noble and compassionate does not alter the fact that the Court distorts our constitutional function to make amends for the defaults of others.

I

In a sense, the Court's opinion rests on such a unique confluence of theories and rationales that it will likely stand for little beyond the results in these

From Supreme Court of the United States, June 15, 1982, parts I–II.

particular cases. Yet the extent to which the Court departs from principled constitutional adjudication is nonetheless disturbing.

I have no quarrel with the conclusion that the Equal Protection Clause of the Fourteenth Amendment applies to aliens who, after their illegal entry into this country, are indeed physically "within the jurisdiction" of a state. However, as the Court concedes, this "only begins the inquiry." The Equal Protection Clause does not mandate identical treatment of different categories of persons.

The dispositive issue in these cases, simply put, is whether, for purposes of allocating its finite resources, a state has a legitimate reason to differentiate between persons who are lawfully within the state and those who are unlawfully there. The distinction the State of Texas has drawn—based not only upon its own legitimate interests but on classifications established by the Federal Government in its immigration laws and policies—is not unconstitutional.

A

The Court acknowledges that, except in those cases when state classifications disadvantage a "suspect class" or impinge upon a "fundamental right," the Equal Protection Clause permits a state "substantial latitude" in distinguishing between different groups of persons. Moreover, the Court expressly—and correctly—rejects any suggestion that illegal aliens are a suspect class, or that education is a fundamental right. Yet by patching together bits and pieces of what might be termed quasi-suspect-class and quasi-fundamental-rights analysis, the Court spins out a theory custom-tailored to the facts of these cases.

In the end, we are told little more than that the level of scrutiny employed to strike down the Texas law applies only when illegal alien children are deprived of a public education. If ever a court was guilty of an unabashedly result-oriented approach, this case is a prime example.

(1)

The Court first suggests that these illegal alien children, although not a suspect class, are entitled to special solicitude under the Equal Protection Clause because they lack "control" over or "responsibility" for their unlawful entry into this country. Similarly, the Court appears to take the position that 21.031 is presumptively "irrational" because it has the effect of imposing "penalties" on "innocent" children. However, the Equal Protection Clause does not preclude legislators from classifying among persons on the basis of factors and characteristics over which individuals may be said to lack "control." Indeed, in some circumstances persons generally, and children in particular, may have little control over or responsibility for such things as their ill health, need for public assistance, or place of residence. Yet a state legislature is not barred from considering, for example, relevant differences between the mentally healthy and the mentally ill, or between the residents of different counties, simply because these may be factors unrelated to individual choice or to any "wrongdoing." The Equal Protection Clause protects against arbitrary and irrational classifications, and against invidious discrimination stemming from prejudice and hostility; it is not an all-encompassing "equalizer" designed to eradicate every distinction for which persons are not "responsible."

The Court does not presume to suggest that appellees' purported lack of culpability for their illegal status prevents them from being deported or otherwise "penalized" under federal law. Yet would deportation be any less a "penalty" than denial of privileges provided to legal residents? Illegality of presence in the United States does not—and need not—depend on some amorphous concept of "guilt" or "innocence" concerning an alien's entry. Similarly, a state's use of federal immigration status as a basis for legislative classification is not necessarily rendered suspect for its failure to take such factors into account.

The Court's analogy to cases involving discrimination against illegitimate children is grossly misleading. The State has not thrust any disabilities upon appellees due to their "status of birth." Rather, appellees' status is predicated upon the circumstances of their concededly illegal presence in this country, and is a direct result of Congress' obviously valid exercise of its "broad constitutional powers" in the field of immigration and naturalization. This Court has recognized that in allocating governmental benefits to a given class of aliens, one "may take into account the character of the relationship between the alien and this country." When that "relationship" is a federally prohibited one, there can, of course, be no presumption that a state has a constitutional duty to include illegal aliens among the recipients of its governmental benefits.

(2)

The second strand of the Court's analysis rests on the premise that, although public education is not a constitutionally guaranteed right, "neither is it merely some governmental 'benefit' indistinguishable from other forms of social welfare legislation." Whatever meaning or relevance this opaque observation might have in some other context, it simply has no bearing on the issues at hand. Indeed, it is never made clear what the Court's opinion means on this score.

The importance of education is beyond dispute. Yet we have held repeatedly that the importance of a governmental service does not elevate it to the status of a "fundamental right" for purposes of equal protection analysis. In San Antonio Independent School Dist. v. Rodriguez (1973), JUSTICE POWELL, speaking for the Court, expressly rejected the proposition that state laws dealing with public education are subject to special scrutiny under the Equal Protection Clause. Moreover, the Court points to no meaningful way to distinguish between education and other governmental benefits in this context. Is the Court suggesting that education is more "fundamental" than food, shelter, or medical care?

The Equal Protection Clause guarantees similar treatment of similarly situated persons, but it does not mandate a constitutional hierarchy of governmental services. JUSTICE POWELL, speaking for the Court in San Antonio Independent School Dist., put it well in stating that to the extent this Court raises or lowers the degree of "judicial scrutiny" in equal protection cases according to a transient Court majority's view of the societal importance of the interest affected, we "assum[e] a legislative role and one for which the Court lacks both authority and competence." Yet that is precisely what the Court does today.

The central question in these cases, as in every equal protection case not involving truly fundamental rights "explicitly or implicitly guaranteed by the Constitution," is whether there is some legitimate basis for a legislative distinction between different classes of persons. The fact that the distinction is drawn in legislation affecting access to public education—as opposed to legislation allocating other important governmental benefits, such as public assistance, health care, or housing—cannot make a difference in the level of scrutiny applied.

B

Once it is conceded—as the Court does—that illegal aliens are not a suspect class, and that education is not a fundamental right, our inquiry should focus on and be limited to whether the legislative classification at issue bears a rational relationship to a legitimate state purpose.

The State contends primarily that 21.031 serves to prevent undue depletion of its limited revenues available for education, and to preserve the fiscal integrity of the State's school-financing system against an ever-increasing flood of illegal aliens—aliens over whose entry or continued presence it has no control. Of course such fiscal concerns alone could not justify discrimination against a suspect class or an arbitrary and irrational denial of benefits to a particular group of persons. Yet I assume no Member of this Court would argue that prudent conservation of finite state revenues is per se an illegitimate goal. Indeed, the numerous classifications this Court has sustained in social welfare legislation were invariably related to the limited amount of revenues available to spend on any given program or set of programs. The significant question here is whether the requirement of tuition from illegal aliens who attend the public schools—as well as from residents of other states, for example—is a rational and reasonable means of furthering the State's legitimate fiscal ends.

Without laboring what will undoubtedly seem obvious to many, it simply is not "irrational" for a state to conclude that it does not have the same responsibility to provide benefits for persons whose very presence in the state and this country is illegal as it does to provide for persons lawfully present. By definition, illegal aliens have no right whatever to be here, and the state may reasonably, and constitutionally, elect not to provide them with governmental services at the expense of those who are lawfully in the state. In De Canas v. Bica (1976) we held that a State may protect its "fiscal interests and lawfully resident labor force from the deleterious effects on its economy resulting from the employment of illegal aliens." And only recently this Court made clear that a State has a legitimate interest in protecting and preserving the quality of its schools and "the right of its own bona fide residents to attend such institutions on a preferential tuition basis." The Court has failed to offer even a plausible explanation why illegality of residence in this country is not a factor that

may legitimately bear upon the bona fides of state residence and entitlement
to the benefits of lawful residence.

It is significant that the Federal Government has seen fit to exclude illegal aliens from numerous social welfare programs, such as the food stamp
program, the old-age assistance, aid to families with dependent children, aid
to the blind, aid to the permanently and totally disabled, supplemental security income programs, the Medicare hospital insurance benefits program, and
the Medicaid hospital insurance benefits for the aged and disabled program.
Although these exclusions do not conclusively demonstrate the constitutionality of the State's use of the same classification for comparable purposes, at
the very least they tend to support the rationality of excluding illegal alien
residents of a state from such programs so as to preserve the state's finite revenues for the benefit of lawful residents.

The Court maintains—as if this were the issue—that "barring undocumented children from local schools would not necessarily improve the quality
of education provided in those schools." However, the legitimacy of barring
illegal aliens from programs such as Medicare or Medicaid does not depend on
a showing that the barrier would "improve the quality" of medical care given
to persons lawfully entitled to participate in such programs. Modern education, like medical care, is enormously expensive, and there can be no doubt
that very large added costs will fall on the State or its local school districts as
a result of the inclusion of illegal aliens in the tuition-free public schools. The
State may, in its discretion, use any savings resulting from its tuition requirement to "improve the quality of education" in the public school system, or to
enhance the funds available for other social programs, or to reduce the tax burden placed on its residents; each of these ends is "legitimate." The State need
not show, as the Court implies, that the incremental cost of educating illegal
aliens will send it into bankruptcy, or have a "grave impact on the quality of
education"; that is not dispositive under a "rational basis" scrutiny. In the
absence of a constitutional imperative to provide for the education of illegal
aliens, the State may "rationally" choose to take advantage of whatever savings will accrue from limiting access to the tuition-free public schools to its
own lawful residents, excluding even citizens of neighboring States.

Denying a free education to illegal alien children is not a choice I would
make were I a legislator. Apart from compassionate considerations, the long-
range costs of excluding any children from the public schools may well out-
weigh the costs of educating them. But that is not the issue; the fact that there
are sound policy arguments against the Texas Legislature's choice does not
render that choice an unconstitutional one.

II

The Constitution does not provide a cure for every social ill, nor does it vest
judges with a mandate to try to remedy every social problem. Moreover, when
this Court rushes in to remedy what it perceives to be the failings of the political processes, it deprives those processes of an opportunity to function. When
the political institutions are not forced to exercise constitutionally allocated

powers and responsibilities, those powers, like muscles not used, tend to atrophy. Today's cases, I regret to say, present yet another example of unwarranted judicial action which in the long run tends to contribute to the weakening of our political processes.

Congress, "vested by the Constitution with the responsibility of protecting our borders and legislating with respect to aliens," bears primary responsibility for addressing the problems occasioned by the millions of illegal aliens flooding across our southern border. Similarly, it is for Congress, and not this Court, to assess the "social costs borne by our Nation when select groups are denied the means to absorb the values and skills upon which our social order rests." While the "specter of a permanent caste" of illegal Mexican residents of the United States is indeed a disturbing one, it is but one segment of a larger problem, which is for the political branches to solve. I find it difficult to believe that Congress would long tolerate such a self-destructive result—that it would fail to deport these illegal alien families or to provide for the education of their children. Yet instead of allowing the political processes to run their course—albeit with some delay—the Court seeks to do Congress' job for it, compensating for congressional inaction. It is not unreasonable to think that this encourages the political branches to pass their problems to the Judiciary.

The solution to this seemingly intractable problem is to defer to the political processes, unpalatable as that may be to some.

POSTSCRIPT

Are Undocumented Immigrants Entitled to Public Education?

The provocative Web site of illegal immigrants (www.illegalaliens.us) proclaims that calling an illegal immigrant an "undocumented worker" is like calling a burglar an uninvited houseguest. Hostile attitudes such as this seem to be on the rise as the impact of increasing numbers of immigrants in a broad spectrum of American communities is being felt. In her 1997 book, *Made in America: Immigrant Students in Our Public Schools,* Laurie Olsen candidly discussed situations faced by most of the immigrants. She concluded that "few immigrants get the preparation they need academically . . . that they are largely precluded from access to the curriculum that their English-fluent and U.S.-born schoolmates receive. And as they begin to develop some fluency in English, they learn that it is not the only requirement for being accepted in their new land. They begin to see that to become American is to take one's place on the 'racial map' of our nation." The book chronicles life in a richly multicultural school environment that, ironically, does not produce wider choices and "more appreciation and support for multiple human identities."

This exploration of the deeper problems of immigrants, documented and undocumented alike, can be found in the Winter 2008 issue of *Theory into Practice* featuring articles on the theme "Immigrant Families and U.S. Schools." Included are "Beyond a 'Culture Clash' Understanding of Immigrant Experiences" by Bic Ngo, "Listening to Hyphenated Americans: Hybrid Identities of Youth from Immigrant Families" by Nina Asher, and "Demographic Data and Immigrant Student Achievement" by Lesa M. Clarkson. Another source of facts and figures is Lawrence Hardy's *Education Vital Signs 2007,* published by the National School Boards Association, especially the chapter on "The New Americans: Educating All Children—Regardless of Status."

"Anti-Immigration Legislation, Social Justice, and the Right to Equal Educational Opportunity" by Loucas Petronicolos and William S. New in the *American Educational Research Journal* (Fall 1999) offers a conceptual analysis of policies that seek to exclude undocumented youths from public education. Also of special interest are "Build Fences or Open Doors?" by John Kavanagh and Martin Lancaster in *Community College Journal* (April/May 2008) and "Fighting for Immigrant Rights" by Scott LaFee in *The School Administrator* (November 2007).

Journal theme issues of special note are "Immigration and Diversity," *American School Board Journal* (September 2008) and "The Politics of Immigrant Education," *Theory into Practice* (Autumn 2009).

ISSUE 12

Has the Time Arrived for Universal Preschool?

YES: David L. Kirp, from "The Kids-First Agenda," *Big Ideas for Children: Investing in Our Nation's Future* (First Focus, 2008)

NO: Douglas J. Besharov and Douglas M. Call, from "The New Kindergarten," *The Wilson Quarterly* (Autumn 2008)

ISSUE SUMMARY

YES: David L. Kirp, a professor of public policy and author of *The Sandbox Investment,* calls for expansion of federal support for universal preschool and other child care services.

NO: Professor Douglas J. Besharov and research associate Douglas M. Call of the University of Maryland School of Public Policy examine the development of child care programs and conclude that the case for universal preschool is not as strong as it seems.

In an article titled "Preschool Education: A Concept Whose Time Has Come," *Principal* (September/October 2005), W. Steven Barnett, director of the National Institute for Early Education Research, states that "no area in education has grown like preschool in recent decades." Preschool education received a powerful boost when the federal Head Start program was launched in 1964, but major barriers in affordability and accessibility for those not eligible for Head Start have slowed the movement.

Individual states have moved toward providing preschool programs in recent years. Oklahoma and Georgia have led the country in offering voluntary programs for four-year-olds. Florida, New York, North Carolina, and Massachusetts have moved toward universally available programs. However, neither Georgia or Oklahoma has experienced significant improvement in students' academic performance. According to The Heritage Foundation's *Backgrounder* (May 14, 2009), 80% of children in preschool are in programs run by private providers and who would likely be displaced or burdened with heavy regulation if federal support is vastly expanded.

But the Obama administration has pushed for major increases in federal subsidies, with some commentators saying that this effort is second only to universal health care on the liberal policy agenda. In "Protect Our Kids from Preschool," *The Wall Street Journal* (August 22, 2008), Shikha Dalmia and Lisa Snell of the Reason Foundation claim that our understanding of preschool effects is in its infancy, that kids with attentive parents might well be better off spending more time at home during their formative years, and that "the last thing that public policy should do is spend vast new sums of taxpayer dollars to incentivize a premature separation between toddlers and parents." In agreement with this position, Lindsey Burke of the Heritage Foundation states, "While proponents of universal preschool often cite the findings of small, high intervention programs, it is unlikely that any large-scale implementation of universal preschool could mimic their conditions and would thus fail to produce the results promised by proponents."

Among the advocates of universal preschool is the Pew Center of the States with its Pre-K Now campaign. This organization monitors progress in all states and makes recommendations for strengthening the movement. In spite of recent growth, less than 30 percent of three- and four-year-olds are served in publicly funded early education, according to a 2009 report by the Pew Center. The report calls for a new strategy of collaboration with community-based partners (child care centers, Head Start programs, and faith-based organizations, for example) to enhance access and choice. Sara Mead of the New America Foundation is concerned that a major spike in federal funding may get ahead of the capacity to deliver high-quality programs. She calls for expedited alternative routes to Pre-K teaching, creation of research-based Early Education Academies in neighborhoods now served by low-performing schools, and improvement of articulation between Pre-K programs and the elementary school curriculum. Mead, in "A Case for Pre-K," *The American Prospect Online* (July 18, 2007), states that David L. Kirp and other advocates of universal preschool see it "not as an end in itself but as the groundwork for a more ambitious effort to expand public and social services for children."

In an article in *The Washington Post* (May 15, 2009), "Slow the Preschool Bandwagon," Chester E. Finn, Jr. warns that everybody should pause before embracing universal preschool since "it dumps 5-year-olds, ready or not, into public school classrooms that today are unable even to make and sustain their own achievement gains, much less to capitalize on any advances these youngsters bring from preschool. He concludes that "done right, preschool programs can help America address its urgent education challenges, but today's push for universalism gets it almost entirely wrong."

In the following articles Kirp makes a case for both universal preschool and expanded child development action, while Besharov and Call sound cautionary warnings.

YES ↵

David L. Kirp

The Kids-First Agenda

To say that, when it comes to children's issues, Washington has been asleep at the switch, is much too kind.

Since 2004, as First Focus's 2008 report on the children's budget shows, kids have been losing out to seniors, wealthy taxpayers, and everyone else. A single penny out of every new nondefense dollar is being spent on children's programs; the overall share of federal nondefense spending on kids has dropped by 10 percent; and while other discretionary spending on social initiatives has grown 8 percent, children's programs have been cut by 6 percent. What makes this malign neglect especially infuriating is the impeccable evidence that kids are the best social investment the government can make.

Washington's dereliction is not only a matter of dollars and cents, but the fact that the government has not figured out how to spend its money wisely. The Bush administration's signature initiative, the No Child Left Behind Act, has been a debacle. The promised increased in education funding never materialized, and neither did the predicted improvement in reading and math test scores. What is more, the narrow-gauge, high-stakes testing regimen has distorted educational priorities, giving an entirely new meaning to the practice of teaching to the test.

The lion's share of federal dollars pays for child care, and if that money were well-spent it could make a huge difference. The most famous example, the Abecedarian Program, delivered intensive support to poor children starting a few months after birth. A study done a generation later showed that Abecedarian participants had higher IQs, stayed in school longer and held down better jobs. The annual rate of return over the course of those children's lives is an impressive 7 percent.

Federal policy-makers have ignored such evidence—the rationale for funding child care is not helping kids but expanding the workforce. Child care, as conceived in Washington, is simply a cheap way to park infants and toddlers while their mothers are on the job. There is no Abecedarian—and precious few slots in the considerably less expensive Early Head Start program, despite solid evidence of its success. What is available, whether at child care centers or from the kindly lady down the block, is usually mediocre—and one out of every eight licensed child care centers has been rated "unsafe." Kids do benefit from the sense of self-sufficiency that their parents gain when they are working. But these ill-conceived, on-the-cheap ventures do not help kids. In fact, the worst of them can do harm. Some youngsters who spend long days in impoverished environments become more aggressive.

In the impoverished world into which these children have been dumped, aggression becomes a *Lord of the Flies* survival tactic.

Washington operates too many mini-programs, mostly well-intentioned, but few of them demonstrably effective. The laundry list—everything from educating homeless children to making schools safe and drug-free—has grown haphazardly, with little understanding of what will have the biggest impact. Early Head Start limps along with barely half a billion dollars—essentially a rounding error in the federal budget—and can serve just 2.4 percent of poor children. Meanwhile programs such as teacher quality grants, on which $3 billion is being spent, prosper despite a lack of evidence that, as currently structured, they are worth the investment.

Since the mid-1990s, all the action has taken place outside the Beltway. Forty-one states now support prekindergarten. Public-private partnerships such as Ounce of Prevention have devised exemplary models for infant and toddler care. Foundations have underwritten promising experiments such as the Harlem Children's Zone and the Nurse-Family Partnership. But among Washington lawmakers there is little discussion of which programs need to be overhauled (whether, for instance, Head Start can learn something from the best state-funded preschools), which initiatives should be merged to streamline bureaucracy, and which ought to be dropped. A top-to-bottom rethink of what Washington is doing seems, well, unthinkable.

The public is miles ahead of the politicians. "Overwhelmingly, Americans care about meeting the needs of children," Democratic pollster Geoff Garin has written. And because of their "strong sense of obligation to give children a good start in life" many citizens see the un-benign neglect of children as a "crisis." A new poll commissioned by Every Child Matters, a Washington advocacy group, finds that a sizeable percentage of voters—notably the swing voters—rank increasing the Head Start budget and guaranteeing health care to all children above paying more for homeland security or farm support. The belief that child-rearing ought to be left entirely to parents is being replaced by an ethic of empathy—an acknowledgement that, while parents play a pivotal role, the polity must become a "good steward."

The old saw that children don't matter because they don't vote and don't consume no longer holds true. Governors from both sides of the political aisle—among them Tim Kaine (Virginia), Bobby Jindal (Louisiana), Phil Bredesen (Tennessee), Richard Riley (Alabama), Ted Strickland (Ohio), and Rod Blagojevich (Illinois)—have made children's needs a priority. Politically, they have done well by doing good. The kids-first agenda is the proverbial $20 bill that economists insist cannot be—but is—lying on the sidewalk, awaiting a politician on the national scene to pick it up. Imagine the impact of a kids-first presidential address, delivered with even a fraction of the eloquence of Barack Obama's meditation on race.

The Kids-First Agenda

- Offer help to families from the start.
- Give families the opportunity for top-quality zero-to-five care and education.
- Promote safe and strong communities, with schools as their hub.
- Provide kids the support of a stable, caring adult.
- Support families that save for their children's future.

What is needed in 2008 is not utopian dreaming but "pragmatopia"—a doable agenda that carries the promise of benefiting all children while narrowing race and class gaps. With a new administration in place, Washington is likely to address the basics—guaranteeing health care to all children (which requires only a modest expansion of the overwhelmingly popular Children's Health Insurance Program); liberalizing the child tax credit to reach the poorest 10 million children whose families pay no taxes and so get nothing, and the 10 million youngsters whose families do not earn enough to benefit from the full credit; rewriting the No Child Left Behind Act to make its testing regimen more attentive to thinking and emotional well-being than to parroting; and improving public education with matching grants for states that couple higher salaries with more rigorous training and greater accountability.

The kids-first agenda builds on these basics. It specifies five powerful ideas that, taken together, confront an array of children's needs from birth through adolescence. These ideas, a few of which show good promise of success, are based on solid research. That is crucial, since at present, a host of untested ideas—as well as a goodly number of demonstrably failed ideas—compete with known successes for scarce dollars and attention. The result is Gresham's Law in action: bad initiatives, usually inexpensive and slickly promoted, drive out the good. The kids-first agenda does not focus on K-12 education, since ideas for revamping—or blowing up—the public schools are already thick on the ground. Instead, it specifies what is needed to pull off what University of Chicago economist James Heckman calls "a policy of equality of opportunity in access to home environments *(or their substitutes)."*

Modest expectations are in order, since new ideas, however carefully thought through and faithfully put in place, cannot guarantee that lives turn out well. But the kids-first agenda goes a long way toward assuring that all children, whatever their social circumstances, are treated decently. While that may sound like mommy-state-ism run amok, it makes good economic sense. Not only does the kids-first agenda promote the cognitive skills that can lead to decent jobs and effective membership in the society, it also encourages the acquisition of "soft" skills—perseverance, dependability, consistency, and the ability to keep one's emotions in check—that report cards used to call "working and playing well with others." These non-cognitive abilities have a powerful effect on which teenagers can find jobs, avoid cigarettes and drugs, keep from becoming pregnant, and stay out of jail.

Anticipating a new political regime, the children's advocacy groups are dusting off their wish lists. The most predictable objection to the Kids-First agenda is that it does not include x or y or z initiative. No short list can hope to cover everything, and there is room for full-throated debate about what should be on it. But the pragmatopia agenda must be short because a flood of competing proposals only assures failure. And it must be based on what is best, not for the politicians, bureaucrats, or professionals, but for the kids.

1. Offer Help to Families from the Start

As every parent appreciates, raising kids is hard work. Its importance in shaping children's lives cannot be exaggerated, because parents are youngsters' first and most influential teachers and their emotional buttress—what sociologist Christopher Lasch memorably called a "haven in a heartless world." This is complicated stuff, and many mothers and fathers will value help that begins during pregnancy and continues through the first years of an infant's life. This used to be the province of mothers and grandmothers, but with so many splintering families and single-family households, as well as a deeper understanding of all that is involved in being a good parent, such support can be invaluable.

First-time, poor mothers, especially teenage moms, are likely to be under the greatest stress and the least equipped to cope. They can benefit particularly from a top-notch program, the best of which is the Nurse-Family Partnership. Beginning with home visits during pregnancy, the intention is to build long-term, trusting relationships between these new young moms and highly-trained nurses. (It is considerably harder to get fathers involved.) Mothers who participate are less likely to need social services such as Medicaid and food stamps, less likely to expose their children to abuse, and less likely to have additional children during their teen years. Their children pick up language more quickly, do better in school and, as teenagers, are less likely to get in trouble with the law. Those positive outcomes translate into $5.70 in benefits for every $1 invested. The Nurse-Family Partnership is a good illustration of why quality, though expensive, is what makes the critical difference: The identical program did not have any impact when carried out by paraprofessionals. What began three decades ago as a three-city experiment now operates in 22 states, and within a decade it will expand to reach 150,000 mothers and their children. While that is impressive, the Nurse-Family Partnership only reaches 3 percent of the target population. There is a political lesson to be gleaned from the success of the pre-K movement: Good ideas need powerful advocates.

Many mothers, not just those who are poor, will fare better if they do not have to go it alone. Second and third children often pose new challenges, and middle class moms can be just as ill-prepared as their poorer sisters. We would do well to follow Vermont's lead and make sure that every new mother receives least one home nurse visit. Promising and widely-used initiatives such as Parents as Teachers, which combines group support with one-on-one relationships, have a broader reach. The effect of such programs is likely to be cumulative: As more parents become actively engaged, more children become better off; as good parenting becomes the norm, a critical mass of knowledgeable parents makes for a better community.

The essential bond between a parent and a child would be stronger if the parent with primary child-rearing responsibility didn't have to return to work soon after giving birth. Even though unpaid leave is guaranteed by federal law, few parents have been able to take advantage of the opportunity, since most cannot do without a salary. Logically, four to eight weeks of paid leave is an idea that should appeal to conservatives as well as liberals because it enables parents to raise their infants. At-home care during the first months significantly lowers the rate of infant mortality, and that adds to its moral and economic appeal. California offers workers up to eight weeks to care for a newborn or a sick relative. The federal government should give incentives to states that do the same.

2. Give Families the Opportunity for Top-Quality, Zero-Five Care and Education

Oceans of ink have been spilled addressing the issue of reforming schools— understandably so, since children spend so many hours of their lives there— but what transpires before kids enter kindergarten makes a bigger difference. By their fourth birthday, children from professional families have heard 30 million more words than youngsters whose mothers are on welfare, while the four year old from a professional family has a bigger vocabulary than the mother who is on welfare.

In a kids-first society, every child would have access to good care and education from birth to the age of five. Infants and toddlers are natural explorers whose brains are developing at a phenomenal rate, and in the right setting they can flourish. And they are social beings who learn from example. Geneticists report that while the genetic potential of well-off children has been maxed out, IQ differences among poor children overwhelmingly depend on whether they have grown up in a world that is stable or chaotic, nurturing or punishing.

The best-studied early education program, Abecedarian, which began at infancy and extended through the first years of school, cost about $14,000 a year for each child. That amount is not surprising when you consider that the infant-adult ratio was three-to-one. But it is not necessary to spend that much money to make a meaningful difference.

Early Head Start delivers an array of services, including health care, as well as play-centered education and parent outreach. It costs about $9,000, and the research finds a significant impact.

Even if Washington expands Early Head Start so that all eligible children can participate, millions of youngsters who are not living in dire poverty, but whose parents cannot afford decent early education, are still left out. North Carolina's Smart Start has the right idea, one that other states are picking up: Spend public dollars to underwrite higher-quality early education, explain to parents why quality makes a difference, give them options, and let the market do the rest. Instead of building something brand new, that is the approach that Washington should underwrite with incentive grants.

Preschool for three- and especially four-year-olds has lately become popular. No wonder. The landmark studies report returns on investment as unbelievably high at 17:1 for Perry Preschool. While a scaled-up venture of a high-quality pre-K would yield a considerably lower return—RAND Corporation estimated a 2.7:1 return for a statewide preschool initiative in California—that is still impressive, as are new data from Tulsa, Oklahoma's pre-K program. Those returns signify better lives: more children graduating from high school, going to college, getting decent jobs, remaining healthy, and staying out of jail.

Put pre-K together with nurse-family partnerships and care that is as good as Early Head Start and the cumulative effects logically multiply. In Minneapolis, Federal Reserve economist Art Rolnick is testing this approach. High-quality nurse home visiting for poor mothers and scholarships for carefully vetted pre-K programs make a powerful dose of two proven strategies. Give poor kids access to decent elementary schools, with good teachers and a proven curriculum, and there will be still greater gains to report.

As with every kids-first initiative, pre-K will succeed only if it is topnotch. Studies show what "quality" means: engaged parents and small classes so that well-trained teachers can pay attention to each kid. The best teaching uses kids' play as its starting point. It concentrates less on drilling children in the alphabet than on engaging their social and emotional lives: learning to wait in line, to share, to keep their tempers in check, letting them tell their stories. That quality does not come cheap. Perry Preschool cost about $12,000, and despite the benefits such an investment would yield, that is more money than the government is likely to commit. The Chicago Child-Parent Centers, which have been running for 40 years with remarkable success, cost $8,500, about $2,000 more than Head Start, but less than what many public schools spend on elementary school students.

The federal government should not pick a single winner. Instead, it should follow the same approach as in early education: Help states that offer incentives to strengthen pre-K programs and give parents information that makes them informed consumers.

3. Promote Safe and Strong Communities, with Schools as Their Hub

A decade ago, Judith Harris made headlines with her claim in *The Nurture Assumption* that children's peers, not their parents, shape how they grow up. Like so many single-factor explanations, this one proves too simple. But Harris is onto something important. Community characteristics can affect children's health, their readiness for school, and the likelihood that they will commit crimes. What factors other than sheer poverty make the biggest difference is a conundrum with which researchers have long grappled. But when Harvard sociologist Robert Sampson compared the lives of black children growing up in "concentrated disadvantage" with those who lived in more stable neighborhoods, he found the impact of that experience—the cumulative effect of neighborhood conditions on parenting and school quality as well as children's levels of distrust and fear for their own safety—is equal to an entire year of school.

One response that has been tested with mixed success is to take children out of the places that produce bad outcomes and put them and their families in environments that produce better ones. But the moving van is not a solution, since poor neighborhoods are not going to disappear. A kids-first agenda needs to reach kids where they live and to develop place-based solutions.

In most communities, the school makes a natural hub that has the potential to go far beyond teaching the three Rs, as mandated by the No Child Left Behind Act, or even nurturing the growth of the mind. It can bring together parents, kids, and the child-serving agencies and everything from sports clubs to health clinics. That is the strategy of the Schools of the 21st Century, a model devised by Edward Zigler, Head Start's first director. Those schools house child care, health care, after-school and summer programs under one roof. More than 1,000 of these schools are operating across the country. The evidence suggests that they work. Not only do kids do better on standardized tests, they are also physically and emotionally better off.

The Harlem Children's Zone, the brainchild of charismatic educator Geoffrey Canada, has a bolder vision: to build a cocoon for children from birth to age 20 in one of the country's toughest neighborhoods. It has seeded a 97-block area with an array of initiatives that would be the envy of most places. There is something for almost every child and young adult, including pre-K with a 4:1 adult-child ratio, a "Baby College" for young parents, a charter school for elementary and middle school youngsters, an arts program, after-school tutoring and an investment club for high school students, and tech training for young adults.

Canada would like to see similar ventures in other beleaguered cities, and several places, among them Los Angeles and Baltimore, are giving consideration to emulating the model. While the complexity of the enterprise and the character of its force-of-nature founder make replication especially challenging, the reach of its ambition—the commitment to turn a mean-streets neighborhood into one that is truly kids-first—is what makes the Harlem Children's Zone so exciting. Other place-based models deserve a look. Britain's Sure Start, which began a decade ago in the poorest neighborhoods, offering everything from child care to medical check-ups for young children, has gone nationwide because of parent demand. Similarly, Best Start LA, now getting off the ground in Los Angeles, aims to bring together an array of services for parents, infants, and toddlers.

While these community-building ideas are promising, there is no solid evidence of their long-term effects, no Nurse-Family Partnership studies for neighborhood ventures. Still, it is not too early for Washington to become a partner in underwriting and studying promising initiatives—funding 20 "children's zones," perhaps, as Barack Obama has proposed, as well as assisting school districts that operate "Schools of the 21st Century." The dream is powerful and the logic persuasive. Children start forming ties based on love and trust at home. Child care and preschool, and later the school and the neighborhood, build on that foundation. At each of those critical stages, government can help out.

4. Provide Kids the Support of a Stable, Caring Adult

Ask anyone who works with kids what they need most and the answer is almost always the same: a mentor, a stable and caring adult, someone with the know-how to help a youngster navigate the twisting and sometimes treacherous pathway from early childhood to adulthood. As Generations United, a Washington, DC nonprofit, points out, many baby-boomer retirees do not want to spend their retirement on the golf course.

The century-old Big Brother-Big Sister program has shown that it can boost school attendance and achievement and reduce juvenile crime. There are 250,000 adults in the program. It merits public support so that it can expand. The Senior Grandparents Program, a federal enterprise established in 1965, offers services that range from caring for premature infants to mentoring troubled teens. Its current budget, just $68 million, supports 168,000 children, or less than $500 per child, and there is a waiting list of youngsters needing such help.

In San Diego, a more ambitious model is a work in progress. There, bridging the generational divide is not a one or two hour-a-week activity, but is woven into the fabric of government. Kids' impact is the watchword: Housing for seniors is built on the grounds of an elementary school, Alzheimer's patients are spending time with toddlers in child care centers, and public space is being designed to be child-friendly. The government is looking at the world through kids-first lenses—that is an approach worth replicating with federal support.

5. Support Families that Save for Their Children's Future

The income gap between rich and poor is sizeable and growing. The asset gap, the amount of money that is in the piggybank, is far larger. It also matters more, because it is nearly impossible to spend one's way out of poverty. One way to narrow that gap is for the government to start savings accounts for America's 4.2 million newborns. A kids' saving account plan would give families and children a kick-start in preparing for what is down the road. It is a nest egg built on compound interest that can help to pay for college or job training.

The children's savings account not only puts dollars and cents behind society's commitment to the well-being of the next generation, it also encourages families—especially poor families—to see the payoff from investing in their children's well-being. The best evidence that it works comes from Britain, where 3.2 million accounts have been established since the program was launched in 2001. Three-quarters of these accounts have been invested in stock market funds, and one out of four families has added its own money to the kitty. To encourage parents, as well as neighbors, church, and community groups to chip in, Washington should match additional contributions made by families with limited means.

When Hillary Clinton floated this plan last fall, she was pilloried and quickly backed down. But there is no reason why, as in Britain, the idea's appeal should not transcend party lines. For liberals, it is a step toward equity. Conservatives should find it attractive because it fosters a new generation of capitalists.

From the Kids-First Agenda to Facts on the Ground: Holding Government Accountable

"End child poverty by 2020" was British Prime Minister Tony Blair's bold pledge in 1997, renewed by Gordon Brown this year. Not only did this become the metric that drove policy, it also became a measure of accountability. The press continues to scrutinize the government's success in meeting interim goals, and that oversight by the Fourth Estate has kept the pressure on.

In this country, the Annie E. Casey Foundation's "Kids Count" report highlights differences among the states on a number of measures including child poverty, infant mortality, premature births, teen births, and high school dropouts, while the Education Trust plays a similar role with respect to public education. These foundations are performing a great service, but this is really a job for the government. A national Kids-First Commission would collect information on key indicators, expanding the Casey Foundation's list to include such items as the percentage of children enrolled in prekindergarten, performance on the National Assessment of Educational Progress, and juvenile crime rates. An annual report could spur competition among the states. That is what has happened when states receive grades on "report cards" issued by Pre-K Now, a Washington advocacy group, and are rated by the National Institute for Early Education Research. In Oklahoma, after that state received high marks and flattering national media attention, preschool became a source of state pride, even among conservatives who had strongly opposed it. The same thing happened this year in Alabama, when the state, not usually known as socially progressive, received kudos. A federal seal of approval—or a failing grade—would have an even bigger effect.

The Kids-First Commission would also be charged with seeking out initiatives that have a profound payoff, such as assuring that all children who need them have a pair of glasses; that good dental treatment be made universally available; that pregnant women be screened for HIV (if an expectant mother is treated during the last few weeks of pregnancy with an antiviral drug her child will likely not carry the virus); and that youngsters in the inner cities, where asthma is endemic, receive needed attention.

A "kids' impact" statement also warrants testing. Its purpose is not to add another layer of paperwork, but to encourage agencies to view their programs in a new light. It might encourage HUD to underwrite more cross-generation housing, for instance, or prompt the Health and Human Services Department to join forces with the Education Department in supporting school-based health programs.

For too long, Washington has been an idea-free zone when it comes to children. Thinking "kids first" would change that—and it could change the arc of children's lives as well.

Douglas J. Besharov
and Douglas M. Call

NO

The New Kindergarten

In her Christmas 2007 campaign ad, Hillary Clinton was shown arranging presents labeled "Universal Health Care," "Alternative Energy," "Bring Troops Home," and "Middle-Class Tax Breaks." She then paused, looking somewhat puzzled, before delivering the punch line: "Where did I put universal pre-K?"

"Universal pre-K" has become a politically popular campaign cause. Clinton is no longer a candidate, of course, but Barack Obama has promised an ambitious pre-kindergarten agenda; John McCain's advisers have hinted that he will do the same. And why not? The rhetoric surrounding pre-K programs is quite extraordinary: They close the achievement gap between low-income children and their more affluent peers; they prepare all children, including middle-income children, for school; and they provide financial relief to working mothers who have been paying for child care.

Yet as the Clinton TV spot unwittingly suggested, universal pre-K programs do not have an obvious place in today's crowded child-care world. Sometimes called "the new kindergarten," pre-K is in most cases just what its name implies: a year of publicly funded half-day school before kindergarten—for all children, regardless of whether their mothers work and regardless of family income. Pre-K has hardly enjoyed a universal embrace. Twice in recent history, attempts to create similar national programs foundered on controversy and went down to defeat. In California, voters recently turned their backs on a statewide plan.

In a 2006 referendum, the Golden State's voters rejected universal "free" preschool by a margin of three to two. Proposition 82, "Preschool for All," was backed by the activist actor-director Rob Reiner and the California Teachers Association; it would have given all California four-year-olds "equal access to quality preschool programs" for three hours a day for about eight months a year—to be paid for by a 1.7 percentage-point increase in the tax rate for single individuals making more than $400,000 and couples making more than $800,000 (almost a 20 percent tax increase, by the way). Although attendance was theoretically voluntary, the proposition would have effectively withdrawn government subsidies from other forms of care, so that families needing or wanting a free or subsidized program would have had no choice but to use their local school's pre-K.

The referendum sparked a statewide debate that went beyond the typical mix of platitudes, generalizations, and exaggerations. Yes on 82, the prime sponsor of the referendum, repeated the oddly precise claim of RAND researchers that "every dollar California invests in a quality, universal preschool program

From *The Wilson Quarterly*, Autumn 2008, pp. 28–35. Copyright © 2008 by Wilson Quarterly. Reprinted by permission.

will return $2.62 to society because of savings from reduced remedial educa-
tion costs, lower high school dropout rates, and the economic benefits of a
better-educated work force."

Opponents pointed out, however, that more than 60 percent of California
four-year-olds were already in a child-care center, a nursery school, or Head
Start, and that the new program would have subsidized the middle-class families now paying for child care while, in the words of a *Los Angeles Times* editorial, establishing "a cumbersome bureaucracy . . . under the state Department
of Education, which has done a disappointing job with K–12 schools."

Strangely, the overwhelming rejection of universal pre-K by the voters
of our largest state has had no discernible impact on the national debate. It's
not that California just happened to have more preschool programs than the
rest of the country. Nationwide, about 74 percent of four-year-olds now spend
time in some form of organized child care.

⁕

To understand what is going on, a little history will help. Beginning in the
1950s, a steadily higher proportion of married women with children took jobs
outside the home. Between 1950 and 1970, the proportion of *married* mothers in
the work force doubled, rising from about 20 percent to about 40 percent. (Single mothers have always had little choice but to work, or go on welfare.) In 1971,
spurred by this change, as well as the emerging women's movement, a group
of liberal Democrats led by Walter Mondale (D.-Minn.) in the Senate and John
Brademas (D.-Ind.) in the House pushed the Child Development Act through
Congress. It was an expansive measure, designed to create a federalized system of
child development services. Children were to be enrolled regardless of whether
their mothers worked and needed child care, on the ground that all children
would benefit from a government-supervised child development effort.

Initially, key senior officials in the Nixon administration supported the
measure, seeing child care as an important component of their approach to
welfare reform. But after some uncertainty, President Richard M. Nixon vetoed
the bill, famously criticizing its "communal approaches to child rearing over
[and] against the family-centered approach." His veto—and the specter of
"communal" child rearing—not only killed the bill but took the political wind
out of the child-care issue for a decade. Mondale himself became alarmed by
the backlash even in his politically liberal home state.

Most liberal commentators have seen only conservative politics in the
Nixon veto, but even many supporters of a federal child-care program thought
the bill was deeply flawed, in ways that its congressional backers may not
have understood. The legislation would have jumped past the states to fund
hundreds if not thousands of "prime sponsors" (mostly local governments and
nonprofit organizations)—all to be selected by officials of the U.S. Department
of Health, Education, and Welfare. The prime sponsors were, in turn, supposed to establish local "child development councils" composed of parents,
children's services specialists, and community activists. These local entities
would then fund as many as 40,000 individual providers.

If this web of federally administered, community-based programs sounds like an echo of the War on Poverty, that's because it sprang from the same social agenda—and many of the same activists. They distrusted state and local governments and wanted "community groups" in control. The bill's supporters boasted that this nationwide cadre of well-funded organizations would be a strong political force for their favored causes. Maurien McKinley of the Black Child Development Institute explained: "It is to the advantage of the entire nation to view the provision of day care/child development services within the context of the need for a readjustment of societal power relationships. . . . As day care centers are utilized to catalyze development in black and other communities, the enhanced political and economic power that results can provide effective leverage for the improvement of the overall social and economic condition of the nation."

In the next three-plus decades, child-care advocates struggled to come up with a formula that would be more attractive to voters, but they repeatedly overestimated support for government-provided child care for middle-class children and underestimated the desire of parents for choice and flexibility.

In the years after Nixon's veto, tens of millions of American mothers entered the labor force. By the 1990s, about 70 percent of married mothers had left full-time child rearing for jobs outside the home, and child-care options had proliferated. According to the National Institute for Early Education Research (NIEER), about 74 percent of all four-year-olds are in "formal" child-care centers for at least part of the day, while the remainder are in "informal" arrangements, a category that includes care by anybody from their parents or relatives to the lady down the street.

Married mothers entered the labor force in waves. First came married women with older children, who were in school anyway and often could take care of themselves after school. Then came those with young children, who needed someone else to care for them. In 1975, only 34 percent of mothers with a child under age three worked outside the home; by 1990, 54 percent did. Moreover, new mothers are quick to return to work. About seven percent do so within one month of their child's birth, and about 41 percent within three months.

Some think that American mothers are in the process of completely abandoning their traditional child-rearing role, but the picture is more mixed. The influx of married women with children into the labor force largely came to a halt in the 1990s. About 30 percent of all mothers today still do not work outside the home. Include those who work only part time—most often less than 20 hours a week—and you will find that almost 50 percent of all mothers, and almost 60 percent of those with a child under three, are not in the full-time labor force.

Although some of these women might take full-time jobs if child care were free, most have decided to delay returning to the labor force until their children are older. In fact, even though they do not "need" child care, about half of stay-at-home mothers place their children in a preschool or nursery school (for at least a year) because they want them to be with other children in a structured learning environment. For these mothers, government-funded pre-K might be a welcome financial break, but it would have little or no educational effect.

Except among women on welfare, the great increase in working mothers had taken place by the late 1980s, when child-care advocates made their second major push for a universal program. In 1987, the Act for Better Child Care Services, or the "ABC bill," as its supporters happily dubbed it, was introduced in Congress. Like the legislation Nixon had vetoed 15 years earlier, the ABC bill sought to create a nationwide system of child development services.

This time, however, there was no Great Society model; the states would administer the program, although they were to be guided by local advisory councils. Each year, the states would distribute $4.6 billion as grants to child-care centers or, in some circumstances, as vouchers to eligible families. Families would be eligible to receive assistance on a sliding scale if their income did "not exceed 115 percent of the State median income for a family of the same size." In high-income states such as Connecticut and New Jersey, that meant a family of four with an income of more than $100,000 would have been eligible. Nationally, the average income cutoff for eligibility for a family of four was about $79,000. (Unless otherwise indicated, all dollar amounts in this essay are in 2007 dollars.)

The ABC bill seemed headed for easy passage until controversy broke out among its liberal backers over a new provision barring the states from expending child-care money for "sectarian purposes or activities." In other words, no money for child care by religiously oriented organizations—even though 28 percent of all center-based programs in 1990 were operated by religious groups—unless they removed all elements of religiosity from their premises.

That provision was a late addition to the bill, apparently at the urging of the National Education Association and the National Parent Teacher Association. These organizations were interested less in the theory of church-state relations than in maximizing the money available for public schools and their employees. And they worried that by using vouchers (thus avoiding strictures against federal aid to religious institutions), the bill would create a precedent for vouchers in K–12 education. Many of the advocacy groups that originally supported the ABC bill—especially those representing religiously based providers, such as the U.S. Catholic Conference and its allies—were incensed.

While the fight over aid to sectarian programs festered for almost two years, another, and ultimately more significant, rift developed among the Democrats who controlled Congress. Key leaders in the House, led by Thomas Downey (D.-N.Y.) and George Miller (D.-Calif.), decided that any new child-care bill should provide greater assistance to low-income families rather than attempt to start a universal child development system, as the ABC bill would. It is unclear whether they opposed a universal federal program in principle—as Marian Wright Edelman of the Children's Defense Fund charged—or were simply being pragmatic. Their own explanation was that a universal system was unlikely to be funded (at least in any meaningful way) and that, in the meantime, low-income families needed help.

Meanwhile, Congress had passed legislation that encouraged mothers to leave welfare for work. Downey, Miller, and their allies wanted to "make work pay" for these mothers—by providing government-funded child care and by supplementing low earnings through an expanded Earned Income Tax Credit (EITC).

In 1990, Congress and President George H. W. Bush finally agreed on a law, much different from the original 1987 ABC bill, that created a $1.3 billion annual program called the Child Care and Development Block Grant and a new half-billion–dollar entitlement for families "at risk" of becoming welfare recipients. It also doubled the EITC, from $11.9 billion in 1990 to $24.6 billion in 1993.

It is difficult to judge what would have happened had the original ABC bill become law, but the narrower Downey-Miller approach was a boon to low-income families. The EITC is now a $45 billion-a-year program, providing financial assistance to more than 23 million families. And the administrative structure it created—especially child-care vouchers—became the basis of the massive expansion of child-care funding six years later under President Bill Clinton's 1996 welfare reform law. That year, the Republican Congress—pushed hard by the Clinton administration—decided that if mothers were expected to work, the government should help pay for child care—the same argument that had appealed to Republicans as far back as the Nixon administration. In only five years, from 1996 to 2000, federal and related state child-care spending almost doubled, rising from $7 billion to $13.6 billion. Add in funding for Head Start, and the total rose from $11.7 billion to $19.9 billion. Spending has remained relatively flat since then.

The result has been an unprecedented increase in the number of children in government-subsidized child care. But more needs to be done. Only half of all eligible four-year-olds with low-income working mothers (and only 18 percent of those under age two) receive child-care aid.

Both the Child Development Act of 1971 and the ABC bill of 1987 foundered, in part, on the seemingly wide political opposition to a universal child-care program that ignores the immediate needs of low-income families. But rather than learn from this lesson, advocates are pushing yet again for a universal program. This time, the selling point is "school readiness" rather than child development, and the focus is only on placing four-year-olds in public schools. But the result is the same: a middle-class–oriented program that does not meet the needs of low-income families.

Advocates claim that pre-K programs do not have to be in schools, and that they would be happy to see existing child-care centers improved with pre-K funds (though that would leave out sectarian programs). But the "quality" requirements these programs impose, such as college degrees and specialized credentials for teachers, are, in the words of *The Los Angeles Times,* "written in such a way to favor programs at public schools."

In any event, given the strong political support for universal pre-K from teachers' unions and the allied educational establishment, it should not be surprising that most state pre-K money has gone to new programs in public schools. In the 2003–04 school year, about 90 percent of children supported by pre-K funds were enrolled in public schools.

Why add a new, school-based program for four-year-olds when, as we have seen, about 70 percent of all three- and four-year-olds nationwide *already* spend at least some time in some form of center-based child care or Head Start? Wasn't this goal of universality the political and programmatic hurdle that brought down California's Proposition 82? Would it not be sounder policy to expand the programs that already exist?

Perhaps the politicians supporting universal pre-K do not know the extent of existing preschool services. (That seems to have been the case in California.) After all, like the rest of us, they are constantly exposed to a barrage of complaints about the inadequacy of child-care services. And some governors seem to have been persuaded that a pre-K program would raise test scores, thus helping to prevent the financial penalties for failing to meet the standards of the No Child Left Behind Act.

The advocates of universal pre-K, however, know exactly what they are doing. In public, they justify creating a new program by claiming—often with some hyperbole—that existing programs are of such poor quality that displacing them will be a net good. Thus, Nathan James, a spokesman for Rob Reiner, asserted that as few as 25 percent of the four-year-olds in day care were in quality programs. Care for the others "could be baby-sitting or throwing a kid in front of a TV set," he said.

That kind of exaggeration—with its remarkable suggestion that the majority of parents hand their children over to dreadful caregivers—distracts attention from the real question: Would it not make more sense to improve the existing programs than to start up a fresh group of efforts whose quality is far from guaranteed? For example, "Project Upgrade" (funded by the U.S. Department of Health and Human Services) used rigorous evaluation techniques to test a revised curriculum for child-care centers in Florida. It raised test scores on at least some elements of cognitive development as much as the best state pre-K programs—at a much lower cost. (Because pre-K pays teacher-level salaries, on an hourly basis it costs about 50 percent more than center-based care.)

In private, advocates give a more plausible explanation. They say that the phrases "universal preschool" and "universal pre-K" are meant to suggest the extension of public education. The idea is to finesse the major reasons why past efforts to enact a universal child-care program failed. If pre-K is just adding another year to schooling, then it is not taking over child rearing (a prerogative carefully guarded by American parents). And if it is an education program, it might attract the children of stay-at-home mothers and would certainly justify taxpayer spending on middle-class and more affluent families. (After all, schools are free to all, regardless of income.)

Justifying free pre-K is politically important because, contrary to what the news media imply, two-parent families in which the mother works are actually much wealthier than those with stay-at-home mothers. As *The Los Angeles Times* complained, universal pre-K makes a "taxpayer-funded preschool available to middle-class and rich families, which can easily afford it." Although other factors are involved, consider that in 2006 the median income for households with two earners was $76,635, almost 40 percent more than that for married-couple households with only one earner ($55,372).

The key to this "pre-K is just another year of school" argument is the claim that, unlike Head Start, pre-K programs provide educational benefits to all children, not just the disadvantaged. "All children make phenomenal gains" in pre-K, claims Libby Doggett, executive director of the advocacy group Pre-K Now. Rob Reiner told the National Governors' Association that pre-K programs produce a "huger impact" on how all children do "in school and later on in life."

At first glance, the idea that starting school a year earlier would boost the learning of middle-class children might make sense. (Let's pass on the worry that many experts have about the negative impact of starting formal education too soon.) We want our children to do the best they can in school, so, presumably, the earlier they start preparing for school, the better.

Unfortunately, no scientifically rigorous evidence supports the claims of pre-K's impact on middle-class children. James Heckman, a University of Chicago Nobel laureate in economics, is one of the strongest voices in favor of early education for low-income children, but here is what he says about applying the model to the middle class: "Advocates and supporters of universal preschool often use existing research for purely political purposes. But the solid evidence for the effectiveness of early interventions is limited to those conducted on disadvantaged populations." As Bruce Fuller, an education professor at the University of California, Berkeley, and author of *Standardized Childhood* (2007), explains, "For middle-class kids the quality of preschool centers would have to approach a nirvana-like condition to present radically richer environments than the majority of middle-class homes, or home-based caregivers."

It's not that knowledgeable pre-K backers don't know this. Fuller reports on a conversation he had with one of the key foundation funders of the pre-K movement: "When I asked [universal pre-K] benefactor Sue Urahn of the Pew Charitable Trusts why government should subsidize preschools for all families, rich or poor, she acknowledged that 'you probably won't get the degree of benefit for middle-class children that you would for poor kids.' But, she added, universality may bolster the political will to widen children's access to, and to improve the quality of, preschool."

So that's the strategy: promise the middle class a free lunch. Thus far, it seems to be working. Each year sees an increase in the number of children in pre-K programs. In the 2006–07 school year, the NIEER reports, 14 states had 25 percent or more of all four-year-olds in pre-K, and three states had reached 50 percent.

In most places, pre-K programs are simply being added to the mix of pre-school programs, with little or no attempt to coordinate them with existing child-care programs or Head Start. The eventual goal, apparently, is to have universal pre-K programs substitute for all programs that now serve four-year-olds.

But is it the right strategy? What about the nearly 500,000 four-year-olds in Head Start? And what about the almost 1.6 million four-year-old children of full-time working women—children who need more than part-time care while their mothers are on the job?

༺❀༻

Pre-K is already eating into Head Start enrollments. Last year, Congress responded to what was called "underenrollment" by allowing Head Start grantees to enroll more infants and toddlers, and to raise income eligibility ceilings. This is, at best, a temporary fix to a long-term problem.

Nonprofit and for-profit child-care centers face a subtler threat. Full-time working mothers who use pre-K (whether because of its presumed quality or because it is free) no longer need their services. And because pre-K fills only a few hours of each day, these mothers tend to patch together some combination of before– and after–pre-K activities for their children. Because they generally cannot use child-care centers for this purpose, children are more likely to wind up in informal care, provided by neighbors, relatives, and others—the very care that pre-K advocates criticize most.

When researchers studying New York State's universal pre-K program raised the possibility that pre-K programs "could negatively impact the enrollment of four-year-olds at nonpublic child-care centers and preschools," a pre-K advocate asked, "Is this necessarily an all-negative outcome?"

Or perhaps advocates would prefer the Oklahoma solution. Using mostly federal funds, the state simply pays child-care centers for a full day for each child, even if the child is only present for four hours. (This practice is documented in government reports, but the folks in Washington either don't know or don't care about it.)

Another troubling aspect of the pre-K movement is that it is a retreat from parental choice in early childhood arrangements, an approach that has been nurtured since the passage of the block grant bill in 1990. Since then, more than $100 billion in child-care subsidies has been distributed through vouchers—with nary a problem—while low-income parents have had the freedom to choose the providers they want, largely without government constraints. (Even unlicensed providers can be used in most states.) But parents in neighborhoods served by pre-K have only one choice: send their children to the public program or dig into their pockets to send them to one of their own choosing.

Vouchers are controversial for K–12 education, but they have been widely accepted in the child-care world—because the context is so different. Remember, the children involved are three-year-olds and four-year-olds. Even some strong critics of vouchers for the schools, such as John Witte, a political scientist at the University of Wisconsin, Madison, have concluded that *for preschool programs* a "voucher system seems to be the best choice to maximize opportunity and equity and educational efficiency."

Besides encouraging responsive programming and service improvement, vouchers provide a high degree of flexibility needed to accommodate the disparate needs of families. Some parents want, or need, only half-day care; some need evening or after-hours care; others need full-day care, perhaps with extended hours. Some parents want their children cared for by other family members; some want to use neighbors; others want a nursery school; still others prefer a care center, perhaps in a church. Some parents may want all their children of different ages in one place; others may not care. Some parents will want their children close to home; others will want them close to work. The variations are almost infinite. Accommodating such variation is all but impossible in a top-down, pre-K regime.

Perhaps most troubling, universal pre-K does little, if anything, to solve the most vexing educational problem facing America: the achievement gap that puts low-income, mostly minority children so far behind more fortunate children. On a host of important developmental measures, low-income children suffer large and troubling social and cognitive deficits compared with others. This translates into a lifelong achievement gap that curtails the educational attainment, employment opportunities, and earnings potential of large numbers of children—especially among African Americans, Latinos, and other disadvantaged minorities.

·◦✿◦·

The achievement gap has many causes, from the poverty stemming from a history of discrimination and restricted opportunity to the child-rearing styles of many disadvantaged families. Cause and effect are intermingled in multiple and controversial ways. Early childhood education is a potentially important remedy to some of these problems, but the plain fact is that the family is the primary teacher of young children—and compensatory programs face a much larger challenge than pre-K advocates' rhetoric commonly suggests. What parents do (and do not do) counts much more than any early education program.

Debate rages about how best to close the achievement gap, but all specialists agree that to be successful, programs must be focused on the children's deep needs and be intense enough to make a difference. That means multiple years of educational and support services for the parents as well as the children—and that simply is not something pre-K and its three or four hours of school-based services will provide.

Some observers think that, if pre-K programs really worked for the middle class, they would widen the achievement gap. Bruce Fuller points out, "The well-orchestrated universal preschool campaign at once says their silver bullet will help all kids and close early achievement gaps. That's pretty difficult to pull off. It means that children from middle-class and wealthy families will accelerate in their development, and then poor kids will accelerate even more."

Perhaps sometime in the future all American children will be in free child care, at least by the time they are four years old. But we seem far from that goal. One research group estimates that a universal pre-K system would cost roughly $55 billion a year, more than six times the roughly $9 billion the federal and state governments now spend on four-year-olds. If past estimates for the costs of other social programs are any guide, it would not be unreasonable to double that forecast.

Universal pre-K might be a boon to the middle class—depending on whether, in the end, it is their tax dollars that pay for it—but it would still leave unmet the much more serious needs of low-income children. Half of all eligible low-income working mothers still do not receive child-care subsidies. Would it not be wiser policy to help them purchase better child care than to channel more funding into pre-K programs that serve higher-income children whose parents do not necessarily work?

Twice before, efforts to create a universal program stalled in Washington. But this round's education-based strategy may work. Although it failed with the voters of California, special interests hold much greater sway in the nation's capital. So, to answer Hillary Clinton's question: Universal pre-K is caught in the midst of middle-class and interest-group politics. As usual, the most disadvantaged children may lose out.

POSTSCRIPT

Has the Time Arrived for Universal Preschool?

Lisa Snell, in an October 31, 2008 web posting, "Preschool's Failures: Where Are the Long-term Benefits?" cites evidence that the high-quality preschool program in Tennessee produced no statistical achievement difference between those who attended preschool and those who did not. In Oklahoma, where preschool had been in place for 18 years, math and reading scores are still below the national average. In his recently published book, *Reroute the Preschool Juggernaut* (2009), Chester E. Finn, Jr. attempts to stifle the momentum of the universal preschool campaign spearheaded by secretary of education Arne Duncan, David L. Kirp, Libby Doggett of Pre-K Now, W. Steven Barnett, and others. Precisely as these strategists intend, he claims, "many Americans are coming to believe that pre-kindergarten is a good and necessary thing for government to provide; indeed that not providing it will cruelly deprive our youngest residents of their birthrights, blight their educational futures, and dim their life prospects." The result, he contends, has been strong public support for the movement with little consideration of how it will be paid for.

Further expansion of Douglas Besharov's concerns about the movement can be found in "Preschool Puzzle: As State After State Expands Pre-K Schooling, Questions Remain," *Education Next* (Fall 2008) and in his testimony of June 27, 2007 before the Joint Economic Committee of the U.S. Congress. In these documents Besharov addresses the problem of whether a preschool program can reduce the racial/ethnic achievement gap and the issue of who should receive expanded funding for early care and education.

An even-handed appraisal of the issue can be found in "Invest in Early Childhood Education," *Phi Delta Kappan* (April 2009) by Sharon Lynn Kagan and Jeanne L. Reid and in "Preparing for Change: A Case Study of Successful Alignment Between a Pre-K Program and K-12 Education," *Childhood Education* (Spring 2009) by Christopher Brown and Brian Mowry. Other worthwhile sources on the topic are "Pre-K 101," *Education Next* (Summer 2007) by Stephen Goldsmith and Nina S. Rees, which argues for parental choice; "Preschool Is School, Sometimes," *Education Next* (Winter 2007) by Robert C. Pianta; "Changing the Odds," *Educational Leadership* (October 2007) by Susan B. Neuman; and Bruce Fuller's book, *Standardized Childhood* (2007). The May 2010 issue of *Phi Delta Kappan* offers nine articles on universal preschool. Also of interest is "The Promise of Preschool: Why We Need Early Education for All," *American Educator* (Spring 2010), by W. Steven Barnett and Ellen Frede.

ISSUE 13

Is Privatization the Hope of the Future?

YES: Chris Whittle, from "Dramatic Growth Is Possible," *Education Next* (Spring 2006)

NO: Henry Levin, from *"Déjà Vu* All Over Again?," *Education Next* (Spring 2006)

ISSUE SUMMARY

YES: Chris Whittle, founder and CEO of Edison Schools, contends that public school systems still operate in an eighteenth-century mindset and offers an "independent learning" model as a replacement.

NO: Professor of economics and education Henry Levin criticizes the assumptions on which Whittle bases his prediction of successful operation of schools by for-profit management organizations such as Edison.

Nobel prize–winning economist Milton Friedman, in an article appearing in *The Washington Post* on February 19, 1995, put forth the idea that the American system of public education needs to be radically reconstructed. Specifically, he stated that this could be achieved "only by privatizing a major segment of the educational system—i.e. by enabling a private, for-profit industry to develop that will provide a wide variety of learning opportunities and offer effective competition to public schools." He conceded that this reconstruction must be gradual, that it cannot come overnight.

This theoretical base provided a springboard for a number of entrepreneurial ventures. Chris Whittle has led two major efforts to participate in such a reconstruction: Channel One and the Edison Project. The former places computer networks in schools to provide news programs accompanied by targeted advertising. The service now reaches about one-sixth of public school students. The Edison Project, as of the 2006–07 school year, reaches about 285,000 students in 19 states, the District of Columbia, and the UK, according to its Web site.

Meanwhile, the National Education Association (NEA) has taken a firm stance in regard to such inroads in the public domain. Their position on the matter is clear: "In public schools today, little is safe from commercialization and privatization." For many decades, private companies have contracted to perform various support functions in transportation, maintenance, and food services. In recent years, there has been a growth in private sector involvement in administrative and instructional functions for individual schools and entire school districts. The NEA fears that these movements, combined with a steady growth of corporate commercial activities within public schools, amount to an attempted private sector takeover of the entire system.

Edison Schools, Inc. has become the nation's largest for-profit manager of public schools. These schools place a heavy emphasis on teamwork and employ a "distributive leadership" model, dividing teachers into teams, each with a lead teacher who runs staff meetings, holds demonstrations, and handles discipline problems. Edison principals are supervised by a regional manager, are often guided by a mentor, and are assisted by a financial manager. In a January 1997 article in *The School Administrator*, "The Edison Project Founder's Musings on American Schooling," Chris Whittle optimistically predicted "the merging of public education and entrepreneurism, the convergence of caring and capital, and the coming together of local control and national resources" that may reward shareholders and will definitely benefit children, teachers, parents, and the nation. In the years following this statement, the enterprise fell on hard times as contracts were lost and its stock price plummeted. In 2003, however, Edison was bailed out by an investment firm representing the Florida pension fund that, perhaps ironically, serves teachers who are mostly opposed to privatization, according to an article by David Moberg, "How Edison Survived," *The Nation* (March 15, 2004). That influx of capital and some successes in Philadelphia breathed new life into Edison.

The February 2007 issue of *Phi Delta Kappan* features a lively exchange on private educational management organizations between Peter Campbell, Missouri state coordinator for the Assessment Reform Network, and John E. Chubb, chief education officer of Edison. In his article, "Edison Is the Symptom, NCLB Is the Disease," Campbell contends that Edison Schools, operating primarily in inner-city poverty areas, are characterized by harsh discipline, a rigid basic curriculum paced by tests, and the use of non-unionized teachers. Chubb's point-by-point refutation emphasizes that Edison brings scientific research and nationwide experience to otherwise failing schools.

In the articles paired here, Chris Whittle expresses hope that private ventures will radically reform America's schools, while Henry Levin argues that Whittle's scenario ignores contrary evidence about the complexities of school reform.

YES ↵

Chris Whittle

Dramatic Growth Is Possible

Until Thomas Friedman recently discovered otherwise, we believed the world was round. We also thought that phone calls had to travel through Ma Bell wires, and that your operator would be in Des Moines, not in New Delhi. Remember when we had just three daily television news programs, one with father Walter, and all at precisely the time when only our grandmothers could watch? And are you bothered that now anyone can see what's on your rooftop or in your driveway, anytime, via Google Earth? Does all this change, turmoil, even progress, concern you? Is your world being rocked?

Don't worry; if you need a fetal-like retreat to times gone by, there is a place you can find respite: *your childhood school is still here.* Even if the old buildings are gone, your old daily routine within them has been superbly, if unconsciously, preserved to a degree that would make King Tut beam brighter than the gold in his tomb. And not only can *you* return to your school-day experience just by visiting your children's schools; at the rate change is occurring in education, your great-grandchildren will attend the same ones!

The point is simple: how we educate our children today is remarkably similar to how we educated them decades ago. Perhaps more than any other modern-day institution, schooling is nearly impervious to change. If our "old school design" was working with a high degree of consistency and reliability, such inflexibility might be fine. But decades of facts say that it isn't fine. Results from the most recent National Assessment of Educational Progress (NAEP) show that roughly 15 million American children—more children than reside in all of England—are achieving below basic levels of literacy and numeracy. If the scale of this number concerns you, you should find it even more troubling that it has been that way for decades. And our problems don't stop with the children most in need. Even our best students are falling behind, in international comparisons and at home. Among the "talented tenth," those in the top 10 percent of NAEP test-takers, reading scores have dropped four points since 1971, and math scores have not budged since they were first measured in 1978.

Simply put, we are not making the grade *at the bottom or the top.*

Why Things Stay the Same

Why does America seem so unresponsive? Let me suggest three reasons.

First, because "numb" is the root word of numbers. We have lost our outrage (if indeed we ever had it) about the deplorable statistics . . . Education inadequacy is not sexy. Illiteracy is not sudden in its cause nor quick with its solution and thus lacks the "production values" highly desired by our ratings-craved media. Illiteracy can't compete with Katrina, 9/11, Iraq, or even a good Supreme Court nomination fight. Sure, there's the obligatory annual story in most news vehicles about "our education crisis," but contrast that to, say, round-the-clock, multiple-week coverage of a devastating hurricane. Our sound bite-oriented media find it far too complex to connect what is going on in our schools with the possibility of a 21st-century, full-eclipse of the American economy, imported from the Pacific Rim. Let C-SPAN or PBS do that kind of dull coverage.

A second reason is the colossal, $400 billion per year status quo that makes the military-industrial complex look nimble by comparison.

The third reason for our inaction is even more important: *America does not believe there is a "next" generation of schools.* What, we think, could be *that* different in schools of the future? We might change the calendar around, pay teachers a little more, update the curriculum, but none of those things is that big a deal. After all, schools are schools are schools.

A Failure of Imagination

I've now been involved in the world of public education for 15 years, as the founder and CEO of Edison Schools, one of the country's first private companies to take on the challenge of improving public schools. If Edison, which now works in various ways in nearly 1,000 schools and serves more than 300,000 students, were a public school district, I would be one of the longest-serving heads of a major school system in the United States (average tenure for the superintendent of a major system is less than four years). I've seen and heard a lot. And one of the things I've seen is stunningly uncharacteristic of America, earth's creative capital. We've had a national failure of imagination when it comes to what our schools can and should be. We don't *believe* there is anything particularly new to discover in schooling, so, as a society, we don't set out to find it. Columbus believed. NASA believed. When it comes to schools, we don't. For sure, there are pioneers here and there, but our national mindset does not embrace the possibility that our schools could be and should be radically different.

Instead, because "the way school is" was imprinted on all of us with Intel-like precision by our own 12 years of schooling, America believes that schools are governed by a set of immutable, almost physical, laws, which include:

1. In schools, adults must supervise children virtually all of the time (Dickens would feel right at home).

2. The school day must be rigidly organized, generally chopped up into 45-minute or one-hour blocks (changing this to longer periods of time was, some years back, viewed as a grand breakthrough).
3. The smaller the number of children in a class, the better the education results (never mind if a smaller class might mean a teacher who is paid less and is less prepared).
4. Adults must run all aspects of the school—and do all the work within it (that many teenagers now work after school and on weekends is a fact to ignore).
5. There are no efficiencies, economies, or new qualities to be found in "design breakthroughs"; greater spending is the only way to improve education (disregard more or less flat education results after two decades of real-dollar annual spending increases).

What if *all* of the above "truths" are incorrect—truths that we will some day regard as myths, artifacts of a forgotten era? What if we approached the organization of a school *without* any of these "truths" as cornerstones? Where might simple logic and our own real-life experiences take us?

Let me suggest what some of the new truths of school design might be:

1. Learning accomplished through individual effort, or through working in small teams, is as "sticky" (well retained) as that served up in a classroom group, no matter what its size.
2. Learning can come in many forms, and the size of the learning group can vary greatly without any penalization of effect.
3. Children are capable of tremendous focus and responsibility, and they can be taught these traits at a much younger age than many people might think.
4. Variety matters in learning; too much of any one thing, like sitting passively in a classroom for 12 years, has rapidly diminishing returns; and lack of variety negatively affects teachers as much as children.
5. Students can teach as well as learn. Has your child ever taught you anything? Has one of your older children ever taught something to one of your younger ones?

The Future

Working from these potential new "truths," let's imagine what a school of the future might look like. In fact, in key respects, the best school of the future might share some aspects of the school of the past, the 19th-century past that existed in many places of America up to the 1920s: the schoolhouse where older students were instructors, teaching under the guidance of a highly qualified adult. Indeed, we can reconstruct a school of the past that is appropriate to the modern era, where teachers' salaries are competitive with other professions, where students are taught by older peers under the supervision of master teachers who can use technology for pedagogical purposes.

Suppose, for example, that beginning in the 1st grade children spent an hour a day learning on their own, not under the direct supervision of a teacher (although perhaps watched over by an older peer). Let's presume that by the

3rd grade, the amount of time students were "on their own" increased to two hours per day. By the 6th grade and throughout middle school, let's assume that only half of a student's time was spent in what we now think of as a classroom. Finally, imagine that by high school only one-third of a student's time was in a traditional classroom setting. If this sounds overly radical, consider that many college students are in class fewer than 15 hours a week, half the time of a high-school senior. College freshmen are only 90 days older than high-school seniors. Did something magical occur in that short period to make them more capable of independent learning? Remember that fully half of all high-school seniors enter college.

If students are not in a classroom, where are they? Sleeping at their desks? Playing video games on school computers? Well, the answer is that they are learning—just not at that very moment with a teacher, just not in a class, but still "in school." More often than not, they will be reading! Educators believe deeply that students should read, but there is very little time in the school day for that to happen. And after a long day at school and with other homework and important activities, how much time is realistically available in the evening? They also will be working with a small group of other students. And they might be on their computers, writing, researching, exploring, mining that almost endless, great new ethereal library—the Internet. All the while, they will be monitored by their somewhat older peers, just as graduate students supervise and aid undergraduates in college environments. Though they will not be in class half of their day, they will be in a school building all of it.

ON THE HENRY LEVIN COMMENTARY

Editors' note: Since Henry Levin considered, in some detail, the record of Edison Schools in his essay on the future, Chris Whittle responds here to Levin's essay.

Henry Levin's essay criticizes the involvement of the private sector in public education, Edison Schools, and my vision of public education's future. These responses to selected points are intended to provoke thought on the overall thrust of his argument.

Economies of Scale. Superintendents struggling with the *loss of scale* resulting from enrollment declines would strongly disagree with Levin's contention that there are few economies of scale in education. Economies of scale occur at the *system* level—not the school level. As in well-run, large, public-school systems, Edison's central costs have improved significantly, in percentages, over time, which is a key reason Edison is now profitable.

Academic Results. Levin calls Edison's academic results "mediocre" and cites a recent RAND report and his view of results in Baltimore and Philadelphia. Readers can draw their own conclusions with data in hand, but this much we know: In the fall of 2002, Edison was assigned to manage 20 schools in Philadelphia with an average proficiency of only 6 percent. Proficiency has nearly *quadrupled* in 36 months. These schools—among the district's most challenging—have kept pace with a district achieving the highest gains among America's major urban systems. Edison was recently asked to manage two additional schools in Philadelphia.

Since the fall of 2000, Edison has managed three schools in Baltimore. The average ranking of those schools in 2000 was 101 out of 117 district schools. Today, their average ranking is *57 out of 115 schools*, with one school going from 107th to 24th. Our contract there was recently extended.

The RAND report says, "From 2002 to 2004, average proficiency rates in currently operating Edison schools increased by 11 percentage points in reading and 17 percentage points in math. Meanwhile, average proficiency rates in a matched set of comparison schools increased by lesser amounts, 9 percentage points in reading and 13 percentage points in math (although the Edison advantage is statistically significant only in math)."

Greater Funding. Levin incorrectly says that Edison receives more funding than typical public schools. Edison on average receives resources *below* those of public schools in the cities where it works. Exceptions are rare. An excellent report from the Thomas B. Fordham Foundation Institute shows charter-school funding well below comparable public school funding.

The Model. Levin uses a 40-year-old study to support his view that our current education model cannot be changed. However, a miraculous technological leap occurred on the way to the 21st century: the invention of the Internet and the PC. Levin correctly states that early uses of such technologies in classrooms have not worked well, but Wright's first flight did not go very far either.

Hope vs. Pessimism. Mr. Levin foresees the "struggle of incremental reforms in a system designed to conserve rather than transform society." While America's public educators want to conserve democracy and freedom, they do *not* want an education design that dooms 15 million children to near illiteracy. We *can* change this outcome by transforming a model that may have once served us well but is now out of date.

—Chris Whittle

Many educators reading this are probably saying, perhaps in less kindly terms, "This idea is hopelessly naive. Students cannot be entrusted with their own education; they cannot be expected to manage their own time. Students don't understand the importance of education and, therefore, can't be expected to manage it."

My response: schools have failed to make students the masters of their own learning, and we have the results to show for it. We are still operating in an 18th-century mindset, believing that these young, half-civilized things called children must be literally whipped into shape, if not with a stick then with a never-ending schedule. If students don't understand the importance of education enough to take charge of their own, it is because the schools we have designed don't spend any real time helping them understand this.

A huge side benefit of this "independent learning" model—and I am talking here mainly about middle- and high-school programs—is that it would *double* teachers' compensation in the United States. If students spent half as much time in class, then half as many teachers would be needed. And we could pay those remaining twice as much—without increasing taxes by one cent.

I introduce the concept of large-scale, independent learning in America's middle- and high-school communities and the corresponding increase in teachers' pay to suggest that there may be a more powerful school design "out there" that is radically different from what we now know. My example is only one idea of what education might be like. There are many more concepts worthy of serious consideration and development. However, most of these will never achieve meaningful scale unless America takes a fundamentally different approach to how it brings about change in its schools.

Focus on Education

This year, the federal government will spend $27 billion on healthcare research and development (R&D) through the National Institutes of Health. The Department of Defense recently invested $9 billion just on the prototype of the next generation of fighter planes. These investments are precisely why we have one of the finest health-care systems on the globe (providing our citizens one of the longest life spans of any country) and an unparalleled military. We have exceptional health care and national security because we constantly *invest in change*—above and beyond what we spend to merely operate our military and health-care systems. Our health care and national security may not be perfect, but there is little question about our international placement in these fields.

By contrast, we invest virtually nothing in changing our schools. Education research-and-development spending at the federal government level is 1/100th of what we spend in health care. Why, then, are we surprised when our K–12 schools are far from the envy of the world? We spend a staggering sum, $400 billion a year, to run the schools we inherited from one hundred years ago. At the same time, we are investing, by modern R&D standards, only a pittance ($260 million) to design and test the next generation of schools. As a result, we get exactly what we pay for—out-of-date school designs.

Our local school districts don't have the scale to take on these R&D initiatives. The private sector of K–12 education, which is still in a fledgling stage, does not have the resources, either. And if you expect philanthropy to come to the rescue, think again. The endowment of just one Ivy League college is more than ten times all the annual giving to our public schools. Only one institution in America has the scale required to fund the invention of our next generation of public schools: our federal government. If 15,000,000 less-than-literate students are not enough to move it to action, let's hope, for the sake of our children, that the looming threat of second-class economic citizenry in the 21st century does the trick.

Henry Levin

➡ **NO**

Déjà Vu All Over Again?

My vision of where education will be—and where it must be—overlaps with Chris Whittle's to some extent. But it also differs in significant ways. Whittle's essay, drawn from his cheerful book (*Crash Course*), tells us that most of our education troubles will be over in just a quarter century. I disagree. His assumptions often differ markedly from the available evidence on what works and ignore the complexity of the witches' brew of politics, unions, bureaucracies, immigration, economics, and the social sciences. He implies that his vision is inexorable when it is merely wishful.

Chris Whittle's projection for 2030 is an elaborated echo of the 1990s, when for-profit education-management organizations (EMOs) proposed a mission and rationale for transforming American education. The standard fare promoted by those EMOs and their venture-capital sources was that the education industry was the next big opportunity for private capital, following the profitable example of the earlier HMO transformation of health care.

The lead financial actor at the beginning of that EMO era was Merrill Lynch, advisor to Whittle's company, Edison Schools. Merrill Lynch published *The Book of Knowledge*, a 193-page report on the $740 billion education and training market. Distributed widely to potential investors, *The Book* identified five "Big Ideas" that would transform the education and training industry over the next decade. But the book's story begins with the ostensible failure of public education and its rapidly rising costs, mediocre student achievement results, poor high-school graduation rates, and limp international rankings. The reason given for this miserable showing was the inefficiency of government.

Business enterprise efficiency would rescue the schools through organizational improvements; selection, training, assessing, and rewarding of principals and teachers on the basis of performance; and adoption of promising education technologies. Sophisticated business projections were conjured to assure potential investors that these enterprises would be highly profitable (doing well) while serving society (doing good).

The Wrong Assumptions

Not all has gone well, and Edison is a good case study, having lost more than six hundred million dollars of its investors' funding. Edison has one of the most complete models among the EMOs. It has truly attempted to deliver a quality school, but the evidence on raising student achievement shows no

From *Education Next*, Spring 2006, pp. 21–24. Copyright © 2006 by Education Next. Reprinted by permission of Hoover Institution, Stanford University.

revolution in results. According to a recent evaluation by the RAND Corporation and comparisons in Philadelphia and Baltimore, Edison's record is not very different from that of similar public schools, though it has received greater funding than its public counterparts.

Somehow, in projecting to the future, Whittle posits a large number of changes in the basic institutions for delivering education, education research, and education personnel, based on the "success" of the EMOs, especially Edison. And despite the financial losses and mediocre achievement results, he believes that schools should be turned over to large businesses—with "economies of scale." Teachers' salaries would be double those of today to obtain the best professional talent; new training institutions for principals would arise through collaborative efforts of top business and education schools to churn out exemplary leadership; and government would increase funding for education research by a factor of ten or more.

The Whittle scenario also assumes that school districts would retain only a tiny percentage of federal, state, and local revenues, perhaps 1 percent, and limit themselves to "monitoring and quality-control" oversight of schools; private contractors would receive the other 99 percent. National and international education firms will compete for these contracts, and their retention by the district will depend on their performance. Teachers will be chosen by contracted schools, but will be employees of both districts and contractors (opening up districts to liability for personnel whom they neither select nor supervise). Teachers' salaries will reach numbers like $130,000 (adjusted for inflation) at the highest ranks. Principals will earn up to $250,000 with a base of 60 percent of this amount and the remainder in bonuses.

Back to the Future

The complete shift of schools to for-profit contractors seems to be based on the old business claims of the 1990s and Whittle's selective interpretation of Edison's record. It is also based on the argument that the contracting firms will benefit from economies of scale that are unavailable to the average school district in the United States. This is a strange and stubborn argument for Edison, which persistently claimed that annual losses in the tens of millions of dollars were due to insufficient numbers of schools. Subsequent expansions led only to larger losses.

Research has shown that beyond very small schools and school districts, there are few opportunities for economies of scale in education because most of the costs increase with enrollments and are not fixed costs that decline with additional clients. In fact, the number of teachers and other employees per student has increased in recent decades. Further, size tends to depersonalize education. As a consequence, the leading edge of school reform is the promotion of smaller rather than larger units.

Whittle supports his assertion on scale economies with a table (page 180 in his book) that contrives the appearance of economies of scale by comparing a school district spending $28 million in 2030 with a hypothetical contractor receiving $25 billion in revenues. The table purports to show where contractors would experience scale economies and how they would yield a profit of

10 percent of revenues. As Yogi Berra would say, It's *déjà vu* all over again. It hasn't worked in the past; there's no reason to believe it will work in 2030.

Even more puzzling is how schools would prosper with half the teaching personnel. According to Whittle, this would be done largely through replacing teachers with student labor. Educators have long argued for greater participation of students in the education process, but not as a way of reducing costs. Four decades ago, noted economist William Baumol argued that the idea of reducing costs in education and similar labor-intensive industries by substituting capital for labor or less-skilled labor for higher-paid professionals was impractical, at best. According to Baumol, education, by its very nature and its intransigence to change (whether public or private), is a teacher-intensive activity and so cannot benefit from standard approaches to increasing productivity. Equally, it is not possible to eliminate half of the opera singers in a classical opera or to replace two members of a string quartet with music synthesizers as a cost-effective way of improving quality. To this point no one has succeeded in disproving Baumol's thesis, nor has anyone discovered methods of providing the same education with half the number of teachers.

What Else Won't Work

Whittle's prime example of assigning students to peer tutoring is already used widely in public schools. I don't know a single situation where this method has reduced teachers' responsibilities. It is a form of supplementary instruction for selected students who are far behind other students (particularly for those with learning disabilities), not a substitute for regular teachers. And peer tutoring is not "free." The cost of effective peer tutoring is higher than alternatives, such as computer-assisted instruction or smaller class sizes or longer school days, because of the needs for adult personnel to coordinate, train, and monitor the student tutors. If peer tutoring has the capability of replacing half of our teachers, why wait until 2030?

Whittle suggests that charters and EMOs would do well to establish demonstration schools to show how we can use student chores to reduce the teachers by half. But it is remarkable that at present he can promise a sweeping future based on this phenomenon without dredging up even a single example as a proof of its existence.

Whittle also assumes (in his book) that the "wireless revolution" will contribute to independent learning and a reduction in the need for teachers. But even if this claim were supported by evidence, the record shows that technology did not reduce teacher cost significantly enough to make Edison profitable or to create superior student achievement. Larry Cuban's history of the overblown promises of education technology (in his 2001 book *Oversold and Underused: Computers in the Classroom*) provides a concrete picture of why we cannot count on technology. Of course, even as astute an observer as Bertrand Russell got this wrong in predicting in 1933 that instruction by motion pictures would require only large auditoriums with low-paid classroom monitors. Whittle is in good company in his zeal for a strategy that has always generated more vision than reality.

In his infomercial on behalf of for-profit education enterprises, there is a technological determinism that assumes no opposition from or conflict with special interests such as teacher unions, administrators, and education bureaucracies. Every projected change is in the interest of all groups, a harmonious solution to what ails the schools. Even teacher organizations that would lose half of their membership and half of their collegial help at the school site will capitulate to the siren song of higher salaries. And new approaches to teacher training will enable them to get better results with half of the labor force and student assistance.

What Can and Should Be Done?

Whittle's assertion of the dominant role of for-profit firms in 2030 and the feasibility of halving the teaching force are not demonstrated to be feasible or desirable. Of course, the education system will be pressed to improve, especially on behalf of children from families in poverty, minorities, and immigrants, who will eventually compose a key component of the labor force. We will also need to find ways to ensure that all students master basic skills and that a substantial portion master the thinking skills and collaborative methods that will ensure a productive polity and prosperous economy. It should be noted that there has never been a golden age in education in which these goals were met, and the future will represent a struggle of incremental reforms in a system designed to "conserve" rather than transform society.

What types of reforms?

I agree completely with Whittle that we must improve the selection and training of teachers and principals, and increase funding for education research. Raising teachers' salaries is absolutely necessary to get the best talent into teaching. At the same time, the system needs better career ladders for teachers and far more effective approaches to selection, mentoring, and evaluation in order to enlist such talent productively. Teacher turnover, a high-cost item, must be reduced. Almost half of the teachers in Ohio's charter schools quit their schools in the four-year period between 2000 and 2004, in comparison with about 8 percent in conventional public schools and 12 percent in high-poverty, urban public schools, suggesting that new organizations are not a magic formula for school stability. Although technology is unlikely to replace many teachers, it is still a powerful tool for raising education quality by providing a vehicle for topic enrichment, student research, more challenging student projects, and greater student engagement. At the same time, the education community must be open to new forms of enterprise wherever it can make a contribution, such as contracting of specific instructional services, teacher cooperatives, and information technologies that enhance evaluation of students' knowledge and capabilities.

If present evidence is to be used, two potent contributions to raising student achievement will be widespread: effective preschool programs for all children and intensive interventions that build capacities of families to support the education of their children. I believe that both of these will be prevalent by 2030 because they show evidence of great promise even today. If I had my druthers, I would also add that education of at-risk students will shift from remediation and "drill and kill" to enrichment and acceleration, as we have tried to accomplish with the Accelerated Schools Project over the past two decades. The instructional approaches used in the best gifted and talented programs, with their emphasis on engagement, depth, and real-world applications, reinforce both basic skill development and more advanced learning. And the implementation of powerful and widespread approaches to building parents' capacity to support out-of-school learning will gain support from community organizations.

Where will the money come from? By recouping funds that are "lost" to society because of poor education we can easily fund the improvements. Recent work by economists and other academic researchers—some of it presented at a recent symposium at Columbia University ("The Social Costs of Inadequate Education")—concluded that such investments have large payoffs in raising national income and tax revenues and reducing the cost of public services. For example, improvements in the availability and quality of preschool education would save large expenditures on special education and grade retention and improve high-school graduation rates and college attendance, especially among the poor, minorities, and immigrants. Just the loss in state and federal tax revenues from the 23 million high-school dropouts has been estimated at $50 billion a year. High-school dropouts pay about one-half the taxes of high-school graduates, and about one-third the taxes of those with more than a high-school diploma. Public health costs for the estimated 600,000 high-school dropouts in 2004 totaled about $58 billion. Some $10 billion could be saved each year in public assistance through universal high-school graduation; a mere 10 percent increase in the high-school completion rate would shave about $14 billion from the cost of crime. By investing in more productive educational practices, we can recoup magnitudes of investment that can easily fund the improvements set out above. And we don't have to wait until 2030.

POSTSCRIPT

Is Privatization the Hope of the Future?

Which is more "democratic": a public school system serving all equally but controlled by a governmental and professional bureaucracy, or a privatized system offering choice and variety but controlled by business interests seeking profits? This question is addressed by Randy Hewitt in "Human Capital as the *Summum Bonum* of Public Education: Past and Present," *The Educational Forum* (Winter 2007); by Kenneth J. Saltman in his 2007 book *Capitalizing on Disaster: Taking and Breaking Public Schools*; in John E. Chubb's "Privatization: A Solution for School Inequities?" *Reason* (October 2001); and in *Educational Entrepreneurship: Realities, Challenges, Possibilities* (2006) by Frederick M. Hess.

The largest-scale privatization of public school management undertaken to date has been in Philadelphia where, as of 2005, seven private companies, including Edison, were operating 45 previously poorly performing schools. Analyses of this endeavor may be found in Lauren Morando Rhim's "School Restructuring in Philadelphia: Management Lessons from 2002 to 2005," an Education Commission of the States case study (2005), and Suzanne Blanc and Elaine Simon's "Public Education in Philadelphia: The Crucial Need for Civic Capacity in a Privatized Environment," *Phi Delta Kappan* (March 2007).

Another aspect of the privatization issue is the increasing encroachment of commercial interests in a wide range of school activities. April Moore, in "A Balancing Act," *American School Board Journal* (May 2007), examines corporate support and commercial infringement. She finds that there are many examples of successful school-business partnerships, but she expresses concern that a recent study found that corporate advertising is part of daily life in more than 80 percent of the nation's public schools. Alex Molnar of Arizona State University's Commercialization in Education Research Unit has identified and monitored eight categories of corporate involvement: sponsorship of programs and activities, exclusive agreements, incentive programs, appropriation of space, sponsored educational materials, electronic marketing, privatization, and fund-raising. His concerns have been documented in *Giving Kids the Business: The Commercialization of America's Schools* (1996), *Virtually Everywhere: Marketing to Children in America's Schools* (2004), and "The Commercial Transformation of Public Education" in the *Journal of Education Policy* (September 2006).

[Of special note on the basic topic are Andy Smarick's "Wave of the Future: Why Charter Schools Should Replace Failing Urban Schools," *Education Next* (Winter 2008) and Paul E. Peterson and Matthew M. Chingos, For-Profit and Nonprofit Management in Philadelphia Schools," *Education Next* (Spring 2009).]

ISSUE 14

Is the Inclusive Classroom Model Workable?

YES: Mara Sapon-Shevin, from "Learning in an Inclusive Community," *Educational Leadership* (September 2008)

NO: Wade A. Carpenter, from "The Other Side of Inclusion," *Educational Horizons* (Spring 2008)

ISSUE SUMMARY

YES: Professor of inclusive education Mara Sapon-Shevin presents a redefinition of the inclusive classroom and offers specific strategies for bringing it about in practice.

NO: Associate professor of education Wade A. Carpenter expresses concerns about the inclusive ideology's uncritical infatuation with socialization.

The Education for All Handicapped Children Act of 1975 (Public Law 94-142), which mandated that schools provide free public education to all students with disabilities, is an excellent example of how federal influence can translate social policy into practical alterations of public school procedures at the local level. With this act, the general social policy of equalizing educational opportunity and the specific social policy of ensuring that young people with various physical, mental, and emotional disabilities are constructively served by tax dollars were brought together in a law designed to provide persons with disabilities the same services and opportunities as nondisabled individuals. Legislation of such delicate matters does not ensure success, however. Although most people applaud the intentions of the act, some people find the expense ill-proportioned and others feel that the federal mandate is unnecessary, heavy-handed, and ill-funded.

Some of the main elements of the 1975 law were that all learners between the ages of 3 and 21 with handicaps—defined as students who are hearing impaired, visually impaired, physically disabled, emotionally disturbed, mentally retarded, or have special learning disabilities—would be provided a free public education, that each would have an individualized program jointly developed by the school and parents, that each student would be placed in the least restrictive learning environment possible, and that parents would have approval rights in placement decisions.

The 1990 version of the law, the Individuals with Disabilities Education Act (IDEA), has spawned an "inclusive schools" movement whose supporters recommend that no students be assigned to special classrooms or segregated wings of the school. According to advocates of this view, "the inclusion option signifies the end of labeling and separate classes but not the end of necessary supports and services" for all students needing them.

The primary justification for inclusion has traditionally resided in the belief that disabled children have a right to and can benefit from inclusion in a regular educational environment whenever possible. French sociologist Emile Durkheim felt that attachment and belonging were essential to human development. If this is the case, then integration of young people with disabilities into regular classrooms and into other areas of social intercourse would seem to be highly desirable.

According to Richard A. Villa and Jacqueline S. Thousand in "Making Inclusive Education Work," *Educational Leadership* (October 2003), in some schools inclusion means the mere physical presence or social inclusion in regular classrooms of students with disabilities while in others it means modification of content, instruction, and assessments to enable these students to engage in core academic experiences. Villa and Thousand see inclusion as a general education initiative, not just an add-on unrelated school reform. Karen Agne, in "The Dismantling of the Great American Public School," *Educational Horizons* (Spring 1998), takes a dim view of inclusion and cites examples of classroom disruption, frazzled teachers, and disproportionate expenditures of time and money (citing, for example, a single disabled child being granted over $140,000 per year to meet his special needs). She is especially concerned with disregard of gifted students and the fact that disabled students do not get appropriate academic development in regular classrooms.

In a 2007 book, *Widening the Circle: The Power of Inclusive Classrooms*, Mara Sapon-Shevin puts forth the proposition that the entire classroom, viewed as a learning community, will benefit from a welcoming approach to all students assumed to be full members of the community, perhaps with modifications, adaptations, and extensive support. She frames inclusion in terms of social justice, an excellent idea sometimes badly implemented.

In the articles presented here Mara Sapon-Shevin offers details of her expanded theory of inclusion which develops students who are comfortable with differences, skilled at confronting challenging situations, and aware of human interconnectedness and Wade A. Carpenter offers a pungent, mostly negative, appraisal of the inclusion effort, drawing parallels with another "right-thing-to-do" campaign, desegregation.

YES ↩   Mara Sapon-Shevin

Learning in an Inclusive Community

Schools are increasingly acknowledging the heterogeneity of their student populations and the need to respond thoughtfully and responsibly to differences in the classroom. It's understandable that educators often feel overwhelmed by growing demands for inclusion, multicultural education, multiple intelligences, and differentiated instruction to deal with the growing diversity.

But what if including all students and attending thoughtfully to diversity were part of the solution rather than part of the task overload? What if we put community building and the emotional climate of the classroom back at the center of our organizing values? What if we realized that only inclusive classrooms can fully support the goal of creating thoughtful, engaged citizens for our democratic society?

Redefining the Inclusive Classroom

Alter years of struggle about the politics and practice of inclusion and multicultural education, it's time we understand that inclusive, diverse classrooms are here to stay. But inclusion is not about disability, and it's not only about schools. Inclusion is about creating a society in which all children and their families feel welcomed and valued.

In truly inclusive classrooms, teachers acknowledge the myriad ways in which students differ from one another (class, gender, ethnicity, family background, sexual orientation, language, abilities, size, religion, and so on); value this diversity; and design and implement productive, sensitive responses. Defining inclusion in this way requires us to redefine other classroom practices. For example, *access* can mean, Is there a ramp? But it can also mean, Will letters home to parents be written in a language they can understand?

Differentiated instruction can mean allowing a nonreader to listen to a book on tape. But it can also mean organizing the language arts curriculum using principles of universal design, assuming and planning for diversity from the beginning rather than retrofitting accommodations after the initial design.

Positive behavior management can be a system of providing support to students with diagnosed emotional problems. But it can also mean ongoing community building, classroom meetings, cooperative games, and a culture of appreciation and celebration for all students.

What does it mean to think inclusively, and how can this framework enhance the learning of all children? There are many lessons that inclusive education settings can teach us. Here are just a few.

Comfort with Diversity

In our increasingly diverse world, all people need to be comfortable with diversity. Inclusion benefits all students by helping them understand and appreciate that the world is big, that people are different, and that we can work together to find solutions that work for everyone.

Inclusion teaches us to think about *we* rather than *I*—not to ask, Will there be anything for me to eat? but rather to wonder, How can we make sure there's a snack for everyone? Not, Will I have friends? but rather, How can I be aware of the children here who don't have anyone to play with? When we are surrounded by people who are different from us, we are forced to ask questions that go beyond the individual and address the community. When we have friends who use wheel-chairs, we notice that there are steep stairs and no ramps. When we have friends who wear hearing aids, we listen differently to comments like "What are you, deaf or something?" When we have friends with different skin colors, we become more alert to racist and exclusionary comments. When we have friends from different religious backgrounds, we are more aware that the decorations in the mall are about only one religion.

In the absence of diversity, it's hard to learn to be comfortable with difference. The white college-age students I teach are often confounded about how to talk about people of color: "Is the right term *African American* or *black*? What if the person is from Jamaica or Haiti? How do I describe people?" Similarly, many adults are nervous about interacting with people with disabilities, unsure whether they should offer help or refrain, mention the person's disability or not.

The only way to gain fluency, comfort, and ease is through genuine relationships in which we learn how to talk to and about people whom we perceive as different, often learning that many of our initial assumptions or judgments were, in fact, erroneous. The goal is not to make differences invisible ("I don't see color"; "It's such a good inclusive classroom, you can't tell who the kids with disabilities are") but to develop the language and skill to negotiate diversity. Classrooms cannot feel safe to anyone if discussions of difference are avoided, discouraged, or considered inappropriate.

I am always delighted, and a bit stunned, when I see young people easily negotiating conversations about difference that would have been impossible a decade ago and that are still out of reach for many of us. I recently witnessed a discussion of different kinds of families during which children from ages 5 to 8 spoke of adoption, same-sex parents, known and unknown donors, and the many ways they had come to be members of their family. These students, growing up in an inclusive, diverse community, will not need a book that says,

"There are many kinds of families." That understanding is already part of their lived experience.

As a teacher, you can successfully facilitate discussions like this by doing the following:

- Familiarize yourself with the current terminology and debates about what people are called: Do Puerto Ricans call themselves *Latino*? Why is the term *hearing impaired* preferred by some but not all "deaf" people? If there are disagreements about terms—for example, some people prefer the term *Native American* and some *Indian*—find out what that conversation is about. Model appropriate language when discussing differences in the classroom.
- Provide multiple opportunities for talking about diversity When a news story is about a hurricane in Haiti, pull down the map: Where is that country? What languages do the people there speak? Do we have anyone at our school from Haiti?
- If you hear teasing or inappropriate language being used to discuss differences, don't respond punitively ("I don't ever want to hear that word again!"), but don't let it go. As soon as possible, engage students in a discussion of the power of their language and their assumptions. Teach students the words *stereotype, prejudice,* and *discrimination* and encourage them to identify examples when they see them: "On the commercial on TV last night, I noticed that all the people they identified as 'beautiful' were white."

Inclusion is not a favor we do for students with disabilities, any more than a commitment to multicultural education benefits only students of color. Inclusion is a gift we give ourselves: the gift of understanding, the gift of knowing that we are all members of the human race and that joy comes in building genuine relationships with a wide range of other people.

Honesty About Hard Topics

Inclusion not only makes students better educated about individual differences, but also provides a place to learn about challenging topics. In inclusive classrooms, teachers and students learn to talk about the uncomfortable and the painful.

Often, as adults, we don't know what to do when we are confronted by people and situations that frighten, surprise, or confound us. Children, through their eagerness to engage with the world and seek answers to their questions, can learn important repertoires of communication and interaction in inclusive settings: How can I find out why Michelle wears that scarf on her head without hurting her feelings? How can I play with Jasper if he doesn't talk? Learning how to ask questions respectfully and how to listen well to the answers are skills that will provide a smoother entry into the complexities of adulthood.

In one school, a young boy who required tube feeding provided the opportunity for all the students to learn not only about the digestive system but also about ways to help people while preserving their dignity and autonomy. In another school, a child whose religion kept him from celebrating birthdays and holidays gave other students the opportunity to not only learn about different religions but also brainstorm ways of keeping Jonah a valued and supported member of the classroom. And when a young Muslim child was harassed on the way home from school in the months after the attack on the World Trade Center, the whole class was able to engage in an important discussion of racism and being allies to those experiencing prejudice and oppression.

A student in one classroom was dying of cancer. The teachers, rather than excluding the student and avoiding the subsequent questions, helped all the other students stay informed and involved in his life (and eventually, in his death). With close communication with parents, the teachers talked to students about what was happening to Trevor and how they could support him: "Of course we would miss you if you died." "Yes, it's very, very sad." "No, it's not fair for a 6-year-old to die; it doesn't happen very often." On days when Trevor was in school and feeling weak, the students took turns reading to him. On days when he was not able to come to school, they wrote him notes and made cards. When he died, many of them went to the funeral. Tears were welcomed and tissues were widely used; the teachers were able to show their sadness as well. Teachers had to be thoughtful about discussions of religious beliefs in order to be inclusive: "Yes, some people believe in heaven, and they think that's where Trevor is going."

Although no parents would want their children to have to deal with the death of a classmate, the sensitivity and tenderness of the experience helped bond the class and enabled students to connect to both the fragility and the sacredness of life. When they experience death again later in their lives, they will have some understanding of what it means to offer and receive support and will be able to seek the information and caring they need for their own journeys.

In inclusive classrooms, I have seen students learn to support a classmate with cerebral palsy, become allies in the face of homophobic bullying, and help a peer struggling with academic work. All of these were possible because the teachers were willing and able to talk to the students honestly about what was going on, creating a caring, supportive community for all students rather than marginalizing those who were experiencing difficulty.

Mutual Support

Sadly, teasing and exclusion are a typical part of many students' school experience. Bullying is so common that it can become virtually invisible. But inclusive classrooms foster a climate in which individual students know they will not be abandoned when they experience injustice. Inclusion means that we pay careful attention to issues of social justice and inequity, whether they appear at the individual, classroom, or school level or extend into the larger community.

I have used Peggy Moss's wonderful children's book *Say Something* (Tilbury House, 2004) to engage students and teachers in discussions about what we do when we see someone being picked on. In the book, a young girl goes from witnessing and lamenting the mistreatment of her classmates to taking action to change the patterns she observes.

TEN STRATEGIES FOR CREATING A POSITIVE, INCLUSIVE CLASSROOM

1. Make time for community building throughout the year. Time spent building community is never wasted.
2. Proactively teach positive social skills: how to make friends, how to give compliments, what to do if someone teases you or hurts your feelings. Don't wait for negative things to happen.
3. Be explicit in explaining to your students why treating one another well and building a community is important. Use key terms: *community, inclusion, friends, support, caring, kindness.* Don't let those words become empty slogans; give lots of examples of positive behaviors.
4. Adopt a zero-indifference policy. Don't ignore bullying in the hope that it will go away. Don't punish the participants, but be clear about what is acceptable. Say, "I don't want that word used in my classroom. It hurts people's feelings and it's not kind."
5. Share your own learning around issues of diversity and inclusion. When students see that you are also learning (and struggling), they can share their own journeys more easily. Tell them, "You know, when I was growing up, there were some words I heard and used that I don't use anymore, and here's why." "You know, sometimes I'm still a little uncomfortable when I see people with significant physical differences, but here's what I've been learning."
6. Think about what messages you're communicating about community and differences in everything you do, including the books you read to your students, the songs you sing, what you put on the walls, and how you talk about different families and world events.
7. Seize teachable moments for social justice. When students say, "That's so gay," talk about the power of words to hurt people and where such oppressive language can lead. When a student makes fun of another student, talk about different cultures, norms, and experiences.
8. Provide lots of opportunities for students to work together, and teach them how to help one another. End activities with appreciation circles: "What's something you did well today?" "How did Carlos help you today?"
9. Don't set students up to compete with one another. Create an atmosphere in which each student knows that he or she is valued for something.
10. Keep in mind that your students will remember only some of what you taught them but everything about how they felt in your classroom.

This book and similar materials encourage students to talk about the concept of courage, about opportunities to be brave in both small and large ways, and about how they can make a difference.

Inclusive classrooms give us many opportunities to be our best selves, reaching across our personal borders to ask, Do you want to play? or Can I help you with that? Our lessons about how we treat one another extend beyond the specificity of rules (Don't tease children with disabilities) to broader, more inclusive discussions: How would you like to be treated? What do you think others feel when they're left out? How could we change this activity so more kids could play? How do you want others to deal with your challenges and triumphs, and what would that look like in our classroom?

Teachers in inclusive classrooms consider helping essential. The classroom becomes a more positive place for everyone when multiple forms of peer support—such as peer mentoring and collaborative learning—are ongoing, consistent, and valued. Rather than saying, "I want to know what you can do, not what your neighbor can do," inclusive teachers say, "Molly, why don't you ask Luis to show you how to do that," or "Make sure everyone at your table understands how to color the map code."

Inclusive settings provide multiple opportunities to explore what it means to help one another. By challenging the notion that there are two kinds of people in the world—those who need help and those who give help—we teach all students to see themselves as both givers and receivers. We recognize and honor multiple forms of intelligence and many gifts.

Courage to Change the World

When students develop fluency in addressing differences, are exposed to challenging issues, and view themselves as interconnected, teachers can more easily engage them in discussions about how to improve things.

Having a personal connection profoundly shifts one's perception about who has the problem and who should do something about it. When students have a classmate who comes from Mexico and is undocumented, discussions of immigration rights, border patrols, and fair employment practices become much more real. When students have learned to communicate with a classmate with autism, they understand at a deep level that being unable to talk is not the same as having nothing to say. When a classmate comes from a family with two mothers, reports of gay bashing or debates about marriage rights become more tangible.

A powerful way to combat political apathy is by helping young people make connections between their lives and those of others and giving them opportunities to make a difference in whatever ways they can. Although it's certainly possible to teach a social-justice curriculum in a fairly homogeneous school, inclusive classrooms give us the opportunity to put social-justice principles into action. In inclusive classrooms, students can *live* a social-justice curriculum rather than just study it.

Inclusive classrooms that pay careful attention to issues of fairness and justice bring to the surface questions that have the potential to shift students' consciousness now and in the future: Who gets into the gifted program, and how are they chosen? How can we find a part in the school play for a classmate who doesn't talk? Why do people make fun of Brian because he likes art and doesn't like sports? How can we make sure everyone gets to go on the field trip that costs $20?

Inclusive classrooms put a premium on how people treat one another. Learning to live together in a democratic society is one of the most important goals and outcomes of inclusive classrooms. How could we want anything less for our children?

Wade A. Carpenter

 **NO**

The Other Side of Inclusion

According to the big shot running the meeting the other day, anyone who questions inclusion is a candidate for commitment. Our special education textbook is almost as supercilious: "Inclusion is a belief system shared by every member of a school as a learning community . . . about the responsibility of educating all students so they reach their potential." It is precisely this kind of simplistic triumphalism that makes it next to impossible to improve practices that are sadly insufficient. So yes, I question it.

Unlike the aforementioned true believer, the textbook goes on to admit that the real world is not quite so tidy and to cite a few sources that show problems:

> In today's schools, what is considered inclusive practice varies widely depending on the clarity of state and local policies related to inclusion, the resources available to foster such practices, teacher and administrative understanding and commitment, and parent and community support.[1]

Ya' think?

If inclusion means on one hand the latest good-willed attempt to solve the problem of what to do for our extreme cases—our privileged, our victims, our victimizers, and our unfortunate—by careful placement and enhanced resources, then I'm for it. But let's acknowledge the reports indicating that this problem is still pretty intractable, and try to do something sensible about it.[2]

If, on the other hand, inclusion means that every kid should be confined for the greater part of the day with students requiring extraordinary attention (much less every psycho, free rider, and drug dealer), then no, I'm not for it, *and the law does not require it.*[3] Our textbook finally acknowledges that inclusion

> does not mean that every student is educated with peers at all times, but it does mean that the responsibility of discovering effective means for all students to learn together is taken very seriously and deviations from this approach are made with reluctance and only after careful deliberation.[4]

From *Educational Leadership*, Spring 2008, pp. 134–138. Copyright © 2008 by Wade A. Carpenter. Reprinted by permission of the author.

With that caveat I have no quarrel. We know that the old special education models did not work adequately, and I'm glad they have been discarded. I believe full inclusion is the right thing to do. Nonetheless, in nearly every conversation I have with practicing teachers, they express frustration and sadness, usually without prompting of any sort, over students questionably included or included in large classes with inadequate support. In nearly every observation I conduct, I see other kids bored stiff; they could have been challenged and could excel or even come to love learning, except that the teacher is pressured to focus on the "bubble kids" most likely to show substantial improvement on test scores. I also see far too many kids who think they can get by with insubstantial and careless work, and they are probably right. If inclusion for students with disabilities is combined with weak administrative support on behavior problems and modest intellectual goals for everyone, the process is unlikely to work. Making this right-thing-to-do even more problematic is that we are trying to include an extraordinary range of abilities, advantages, disadvantages, and handicaps while also trying to keep the criminals and those who hate school (for no matter how good a reason) in school.

I've seen this situation before, in my generation's struggles with another right-thing-to-do that has, until now, been sacrosanct: desegregation. If by desegregation one meant the morally necessary attempt to resolve three hundred years of racial injustice, to promote domestic tranquility, and to guarantee a decent chance at the American dream to decent people of all races, then I'm for it. In fact, I spent the greater part of my career working awfully hard to make it work, occasionally putting myself at considerable physical risk. By the twentieth century our society had been so morally corrupted and impoverished by generations of racism and discriminatory schooling that we rightly put freedom of association in abeyance, or at least reduced it considerably. But how far can we take that reduction in the twenty-first century and still call ourselves "the land of the free"?

Leveling downward is not compatible with education, either, by any definition of the word to which I care to subscribe. If by desegregation we mean the socially toxic result of miseducating kids of whatever race to the level of the street-corner hustler or the semiliterate Ku Kluxer, then no, I'm not for it at all. I did my high school teaching in Charlotte, North Carolina, the "home" of busing, in the 1970s and '80s, and I witnessed firsthand the results of doing the right thing badly; now I read that just about everything we accomplished for desegregation back then has been undone.[5] For many years I was a good soldier and kept my mouth shut. I'm too old for that stuff now.

Part of the problem, I think, was that we were desegregating without any regard whatsoever for whether or not that particular child belonged in that particular class. I well remember the sweet little old lady from downstairs coming into my classroom at the beginning of every semester with her clipboard, and moving kids—lots of them—to and from advanced and low-level classes *simply to comply with the court order.* You, you, and you are now slow learners. Sorry. You, you, and you are now advanced. Congratulations.

I believe the other problem with desegregation, and now inclusion, lies in an uncritical infatuation with socialization, resulting in a seduction pulled off with an awful cynicism.[6] To quote British philosopher Michael Oakeshott:

> Modern governments are not interested in education: they are concerned only to impose "socialization" of one kind or another upon the surviving fragments of a once considerable educational engagement. . . . [This is] the alternative to education, invented for the poor as something instead of virtually nothing.[7]

While the rationale for both desegregation and inclusion is multi-faceted, nuanced, and intellectually and morally compelling, most of the evidence for their effectiveness has been built around socialization, and socialization done poorly, at that. Discrimination may or may not be an evil, depending on how it's done, but indiscriminate inclusion may bring with it an evil far worse, and I fear it will hurt the kids with disabilities, probably even worse than their nondisabled classmates.

"Socialization" is important, but it is not unproblematic. A facile "They're all equal in God's sight" from developmentally delayed social gospelers just won't do, nor will an equally facile "They all have to learn to get along with all kinds of people" from historically bypassed egalitarians. Most children are perfectly capable of learning about a sewer without having to roll around in one, so it stands to reason that they can also learn about felons without having to sit beside them eight hours per day, one hundred eighty days per year, for twelve (or more) years. Our society has not yet provided enough support or alternatives for exceptional kids, nor has it learned how to discriminate *well*.[8] To make inclusion work beyond the merely "adequate," we need to provide more attractive alternatives for those kids who don't want to be in schools and who detract from the education of those who do. We need to give teachers more support and give the kids more teachers—I would suggest no more than fifteen kids per class in inclusive settings. Blithely asserting that "individualization," "inclusive practices," or a bigger "bag of tricks" will solve the problem of extreme cases applies methodological Band-Aids to political diseases, places undue burdens (including a deeply unfair load of guilt) on conscientious and overloaded teachers, and ultimately hurts far too many kids.[9] As with segregation, this is not a methods problem; it is a policy problem. "Best practices" should never be a bureaucratic placebo for bad policy. A naive notion of equality and socialization is no more helpful than is a bigoted attitude toward diversity and social mobility. Contrary to some egalitarians, a good society rightly honors those who through intelligent good will, artistic talent, athletic prowess, or plain honest hard work make our lives better. Conversely, a good society shelters *all* children from being held down by conservative elitists, held back by liberal egalitarians, or held up by criminals. Benjamin Barber elegantly describes a kinder view of equality:

> When democratic citizenship insists on leveling, it demands that slaves be emancipated, not that masters be enslaved; that suffrage be granted to the dispossessed, not taken from the powerful; that I win the exercise of my rights, not that you lose the exercise of yours.[10]

Contrary to some devotees of socialization, schools are not likely to fix every kid, and not every kid belongs in a school. Unless we figure that out, we will find ourselves increasingly burdened by schools in which nobody belongs, and as usual, the exceptional will be victimized even more savagely, because they are more vulnerable. The thrust of this column is simple: *inclusion is not likely to work if we insist on including the victimizers with the victims.*

Equality and socialization should accompany—not replace—judgment and education. To substitute the former for the latter, or vice versa, is an unsafe practice, pure and simple. No child should be denied the benefits of our education, but many do not deserve the burdens of our schooling—as it is currently practiced.

Notes

1. Marilyn Friend, *Special Education: Contemporary Perspectives for School Professionals.* 2nd ed. (Boston: Pearson/Allyn Bacon, 2008), pp. 20, 21.

2. Start with Friend, then go to the USDOE's site and take up with . . ., and then surf from there. Be forewarned, however: although the research is pretty solid that inclusion seldom hurts and often helps students with disabilities, and may have affective and social benefits for all, the research "suggesting" that it doesn't hurt "the other kids" academically is dated, limited, and unconvincing. Those who even think about it generally finesse the issue. And even its most enthusiastic proponents do not approve of inclusion without adequate support systems—including alternative systems for those who resist schooling and make it difficult for others. And that is my beef. See also Debbie Staub, *Inclusion and the Other Kids* (Newton, Mass.: National Institute for Urban School Improvement, 1999), ERIC ED 439206.

3. "All children have the right to learn together"; "[t]here are no legitimate reasons to separate children for their education. Children belong together—with advantages and benefits for everyone. They do not need to be protected from each other" (Organization for Inclusion, Acceptance, and Respect, "Questions and Answers about Inclusion" . . .). Such statements are sentimentalist rubbish. Ask any cop, social worker, or even bullying victim whether protection from *some* children is needed. And that kind of bogus "rights talk" just trivializes worthy and weighty matters: one could just as easily invent a "right" to learn separately, a "right" to attend the college or university of one's choice, or even a "right" to live in a smoke-free city. I found it interesting to hear not long ago that Estonia has declared Internet access a "fundamental human right." It may indeed be very desirable, but compared to life, liberty, and the pursuit of happiness . . . c'mon, folks, get a grip.

4. Friend, *Special Education,* 21.

5. My own experience gives me enough lamentable war stories from "back then," and Ann Doss Helms's articles in my hometown *Charlotte Observer* about post-desegregation outcomes are depressing reading. For broader perspectives and some precise figures, see the NAEP reports on the racial gaps at . . .; the Uniform Crime Statistics published yearly by the FBI at . . .; the drug-abuse figures and the teenage-pregnancy figures released by the

U.S. Department of Health and Human Services at . . .; and the findings of the Guttmacher Institute at. . . . Maybe I have to confess that although my generation of teachers did a good job with a lot of individual kids, societally we may have been a disaster.

6. Most of us are probably aware that St. Peter left half the statement unsaid: Love may indeed cover a multitude of sins, but infatuation can lead to a lot more. I Peter 4:8.

7. Timothy Fuller, ed. *Michael Oakeshott on Education* (New Haven:Yale, 1989), p. 86.

8. "Enough support or alternatives": my best suggestion at this point is in Wade A. Carpenter (2007): "For Those We Won't Reach: An Alternative" in *Educational Horizons* 85 (3): 146–155.

9. "Methodological Band-Aids . . . political diseases": an intentional mixed metaphor. I'm not disputing the need for better teaching methods for intellectually challenged and behaviorally challenging children; I am asserting that they may be necessary, but they are unlikely to be sufficient.

10. Benjamin R. Barber, *An Aristocracy of Everyone: The Politics of Education and the Future of America* (New York: Oxford University Press, 1992), p. 6. Allow me to add the suggestion that an aristocracy of everyone is the only democracy worth living in.

POSTSCRIPT

Is the Inclusive Classroom Model Workable?

One wit has stated that P.L. 94-142 was really a "full employment act for lawyers." Indeed, there has been much litigation regarding the identification, classification, placement, and specialized treatment of disabled children since the introduction of the 1975 act. The 1992 ruling in *Greer v. Rome City School District* permitted the parents to place their child, who has Down syndrome, in a regular classroom with supplementary services. Also, the decision in *Sacramento City Unified School District v. Holland* (1994) allowed a girl with an IQ of 44 to be placed in a regular classroom full time, in accordance with her parents' wishes (the school system had wanted the student to split her time equally between regular and special education classes). These cases demonstrate that although the aspect of the law stipulating parental involvement in the development of individual educational programs can invite cooperation, it can also lead to conflict.

Teacher attitude becomes a crucial component in the success or failure of placements of disabled students in regular classrooms. Teacher training institutions have tried to incorporate "special education" material into the preparation of regular classroom teachers, but many of these teachers find themselves at a loss when it comes to dealing with and assisting children with special needs. Some articles dealing with this and related problems are "Disruptive Disabled Kids: Inclusion Confusion," *School Board News* (October 1994) by Diane Brockett and "Discipline Procedures with Students with Disabilities," *The Clearing House* (January/February 2000), by Jean Mueth Dayton.

Of special interest are "The Oppression of Inclusion," *Educational Horizons* (Fall 2000), by David Aloyzy Zera and Roy Maynard Seitsinger; "Americans with Disabilities: Are They Losing Ground?" *The Clearing House* (January/February 2002), by Nathan L. Essex; "More Choices for Disabled Kids," *Policy Review* (April & May 2002), by Lewis M. Andrews; and Lisa Snell's "Special Education Confidential," *Reason* (December 2002).

More recent material may be found in Thomas Hehir, "Confronting Ableism," *Educational Leadership* (February 2007); Joetta Sack-Min, "The Issues of IDEA," *American School Board Journal* (March 2007); Cynthia G. Simpson, Rebecca McBride, Vicky G. Spencer, John Lowdermilk, and Sharon Lynch, "Assistive Technology: Supporting Learners in Inclusive Classrooms," *Kappa Delta Pi Record* (Summer 2009); and Rachel Hughes, "Learning Disabilities and Social Inclusion," *Journal of Intellectual Disability Research* (June 2009).

ISSUE 15

Do Teachers Unions Stymie School Reform?

YES: Andrew Coulson, from "A Less Perfect Union," *The American Spectator* (June 2011)

NO: Louis Malfaro, from "Lessons on Organizing for Power," *American Educator* (Fall 2010)

ISSUE SUMMARY

YES: Andrew Coulson, director of the Center for Educational Freedom at the Cato Institute, contends that the NEA and AFT monopolize public school operations, resulting in a collapse of productivity.

NO: Louis Malfaro, an AFT vice president, sees the teachers unions as uniquely able to build productive relationships and exert positive influence on the improvement of teaching and learning.

The vast majority of public school teachers in the United States belong to the National Education Association (NEA) or the American Federation of Teachers (AFT), powerful unions that engage in collective bargaining, lobbying, and political action. While they clearly and effectively represent the interests of educational professionals at all levels, they have come under increasing scrutiny regarding their role in influencing the quality of public schooling and, in particular, the improvement of student academic performance.

The NEA, founded in 1857 as the National Teachers Association, was for many years controlled by school administrators and was disdainful of the younger AFT, a teachers-only group affiliated with the AFL-CIO. The AFT, begun in 1916, negotiated contracts with local school boards and, as it became more powerful, was not reluctant to use the threat of strikes to strengthen its demands. In recent decades the NEA has adopted union tactics and has also built one of the richest political action committees in the nation, wielding considerable power at the federal level.

The initial onslaught against teacher union power was led by William J. Bennett when he was the secretary of education in the Reagan administration. Bennett charged that "almost without fail, wherever a worthwhile school proposal or legislative initiative is under consideration, those with a vested interest in the educational status quo will use political muscle to block reform." Another union critic, Myron Lieberman, stated in 1998 that all public sector unions are adamantly opposed to smaller government, lower taxes, and privatization efforts. The economic downturn that began in 2008 has rekindled anti-union sentiments, with political leaders in many states and localities demanding concessions from public sector unions and, in some cases, seeking to curtail collective bargaining rights.

Public opinion samples taken in 2011 have found that while teachers are held in reasonably high regard their unions are seen as capable of doing bad as well as good. As reported by Alexandra Rice in *Education Week* (August 24, 2011) a recent poll shows that the public wants to find and retain high-quality teachers who are compensated on the basis of experience, academic degrees, and principal evaluations, with student test scores seen as less important. This would seem to put the public in accord with a basic union position on teacher retention. Education historian Diane Ravitch, in "Why Teacher Unions Are Good for Teachers—and the Public," *American Educator* (Winter 2006–2007), states that the unions protect teachers' rights, support professionalism, and check administrative power. It is her view that the unions, despite attacks by zealous politicians, "will continue to be important, vital, and needed so long as they speak on behalf of the rights and dignity of teachers and the essentials of good education."

Education columnist Thomas Toch, in "The Teacher Union's Odysseus," *Phi Delta Kappan* (September 2011), reports that both the AFT and NEA have issued position statements that "break sharply with teacher unions' long-standing focus on job protection" by advocating "rigorous teacher evaluations linked to student learning and quicker dismissals of underperformers." AFT president Randi Weingarten, Toch says, has assumed a leading role among teacher unionists in acknowledging that the unions have lost some public support in recent years. Weingarten believes that an emphasis on teacher quality and education reform can outflank those who want to bust up the unions or at least greatly reduce union power.

A number of books have explored the historical development of unionism in the teaching profession, offering divergent perspectives on the current scene. Peter Brimelow's *The Worm in the Apple: How Teacher Unions Are Destroying American Education* (2003) makes the case that union-fashioned agreements have stifled innovation and risk-taking reforms that would raise the level of student performance. Terry Moe's *Special Interest: Teachers Unions and America's Public Schools* (2011) charts the growth of union power and its consequences. Steven Brill's *Class Warfare: Inside the Fight to Fix America's Schools* (2011) advocates expansion of charter schools unfettered by union influence.

In the following selections Andrew Coulson of the Cato Institute specifies the sources of increased union power in recent decades and suggests ways to rein in that power, while union official Louis Malfaro details his personal story of union affiliation in the state of Texas and the positive lessons he has learned along the way.

YES ⤺

Andrew Coulson

A Less Perfect Union

Student achievement at the end of high school has stagnated or declined, depending on the subject, since we started keeping track around 1970. Over that period, the cost of sending a child through the K-12 public system tripled, even after adjusting for inflation. Public school employee unions, the National Education Association and American Federation of Teachers, are partly to blame for this, but the attention focused on collective bargaining in particular has been misplaced. The unions' success in driving up costs and protecting even low-performing teachers stems less from their power at the bargaining table than from the monopoly status of their employer. Taxpayers, and most families, have no place else to go.

In his post-apocalyptic film *Sleeper*, Woody Allen explained the apocalypse with the line: "a man named Albert Shanker got hold of a nuclear warhead." This was in 1973, when Shanker headed New York City's muscle-flexing teachers' union. In those days, the goals of school employee unions were widely understood: uniformly better compensation, greater job security, and reduced workloads for their members. That's what labor unions are for. If NEA and AFT leadership failed to pursue those goals, their members would replace them with people who would.

But for a while, during the sustained economic growth of the '80s, '90s, and early '00s, the public ceased to think very much about these unions as unions. The NEA and AFT have often portrayed themselves as selfless champions of children, who sought only to improve the quality of American education. It's hard to say how widely their PR puffery was believed, but certainly it was the dominant framing in the media and was seldom challenged by more realistic appraisals. (Except, ironically, by Shanker himself, who once declared that he would "start representing schoolchildren" when they "start paying union dues.")

Since the late fiscal unpleasantness began in 2008, all that has changed. It has changed because the money has run out. Think of public schooling as a game of Monopoly in which one of the players, the unions, owns 90 percent of the properties (9 out of 10 American students attend public schools). The other players, taxpayers, have some cash and a few properties of their own, but they can't make it around the board without paying ever-increasing union rents—just as, in real life, taxpayers must continue funding public schools no matter how much they cost. They can survive for a while, of course, and while they do the unions reap handsome rewards. Eventually, though, the taxpayers run out of money. Game over.

In the board game, we'd call the unions the "winners." In reality, their victory is Pyrrhic. They've been so successful in protecting their members' jobs (including those of the mediocre and inept), raising salaries and benefits, and reducing workloads (by inducing more hiring to lower the student/teacher ratio), that they have precipitated budget crises all over the country, derailing their own gravy train.

Consider the numbers. Since 1970, the inflation-adjusted cost of putting a child through the K-12 public school system has risen from $55,000 to $155,000. Over the same period, the *quality* of that education has stagnated in math and reading and declined in science.

Where has all that extra money gone, if not toward improving quality? Some has fueled higher salaries and benefits for teachers, who enjoy total compensation 42 percent higher than their private-sector colleagues. More has gone into expanding the public school workforce. Astonishingly, employment in public schools has grown *10 times* faster than enrollment over the past four decades.

So while every other service or product has gotten better, more affordable, or both, public school productivity has collapsed. It is now costing us more to teach kids less. If our schools had merely maintained the level of productivity they enjoyed in 1970—not improved as other fields have, just held their ground—American taxpayers would be saving roughly $300 billion a year. In California alone, the $26 billion budget deficit would be instantly wiped out and replaced with a $10 billion surplus.

How did this happen? How did unions grow the public school workforce so much faster than enrollment? For those familiar with the overall trend in unionization, their feat at first seems miraculous. Because while the teachers unions were growing extravagantly, unions nationwide were shriveling up. In the private sector, union membership declined from 31 percent to less than 7 percent of the workforce since 1960. Among public school employees, it doubled from 35 percent to 70 percent over the same period.

Upon reflection, it isn't hard to explain this divergence. In the private sector, unionization is self-regulating. In the public sector, it is not. When a business makes excessive concessions to a union and is thereby forced to raise prices above those of its competitors, it loses customers. As it loses customers, it lays off workers, eroding the union's power. If this situation continues, the business fails and the union members who sought above-market compensation lose their jobs. Overly aggressive unions thus price their own workers out of the workforce. Conversely, less aggressive unions have little appeal to workers because they offer costs (in the form of dues) without value (in the form of above-market wages or benefits).

The easier it is for consumers to shop around, the less value unions can add, because consumers can more easily place their orders with competitors. And thanks to advances in technology comparison-shopping has been getting progressively easier for decades. That's made it increasingly difficult for private sector unions to win above-market wages or benefits.

More than that, the heightened competitiveness of modern markets has meant that the interests of workers and management are more closely aligned than ever. A business that tried to raise profits by paying below-market wages would risk losing its best employees to its competitors or to businesses in related fields, injuring its productivity and ultimately its profitability.

None of this has been lost on the workers themselves. As the usefulness of private sector unions has declined, so has their membership.

But what happens in an industry in which one producer is able to give its product away for "free," draws its revenues from compulsory taxation, is able to hide the full cost of its operations from the public, and is legally required to remain in business? Obviously the unions representing workers in that industry can win substantially above-market compensation and pad their membership dramatically without fear of putting themselves out of business in the short or even the medium term. That, of course, is what has happened in our nation's state-run school systems. The self-regulating aspects of union action in competitive markets do not exist in the public sector.

But after nearly half a century, public school employee unions have finally begun to suffer from their own success. State-run schooling has become so profligate under their ministrations that America can no longer afford it. In an effort to moderate the teachers unions' voracious consumption of tax dollars, governors and legislators in several states have sought to curtail their collective bargaining powers. So it's useful to ask: what role have these powers actually played in the unions' ability to drive up spending?

When I reviewed the scholarly evidence on this question for the *Cato Journal* last year, I was surprised to discover that the answer is: not much. Depending on the study, the existence of collective bargaining has little or no impact on school district spending. The real mechanism by which unions have driven up their membership and compensation has been lobbying in state and federal legislatures and packing school boards with their supporters.

The public school employee unions have been the single biggest political contributors at the federal level over the past 20 years. The $56 million they've spent is roughly equal to the combined contributions of Chevron, Exxon Mobil, the NRA, and Lockheed Martin.

But it is at the state level that their lobbying efforts are focused, because that is the level at which the nation's public school monopolies are legally enshrined. So long as they protect that monopoly on roughly $600 billion in tax dollars, they will face no meaningful competition, and so long as they are without competition, they will be able to secure wages, benefits, and staffing levels far above what a competitive market would bear.

In New York State, for example, teachers unions spent $6.6 million on political activities in 2008. The year before, they paid $571,012 to a single luxury hotel, the Desmond, in the state capital of Albany, to facilitate their lobbying efforts. Those efforts have sought to limit competition from charter and private schools and raise public school spending. They've been largely successful. New York is by no means exceptional in this regard: California's teachers unions accounted for half of the state's total initiative campaign expenditures in the first five months of 2009.

At the local school board level, teachers union power can be even greater. Education journalist Joe Williams reported that "United Teachers Los Angeles had such a tight grip on its school board in 2004 that union leaders actually instructed [board members] on important policies and made no attempt to hide their hand signals to school board members during meetings."

Given the fact that political lobbying and the capture of school boards have been the means by which teachers unions have won their above-market concessions, and that collective bargaining *per se* seems to have played a relatively minor role in their success, it seems unlikely that curtailing collective bargaining will return fiscal sanity to American education.

Others have argued that the balance of power can be restored if states stop automatically garnishing teachers' paychecks in the amount of compulsory union dues and sending the money to the unions. If unions are forced to collect the money themselves, they reason, it will make it harder for them to raise the vast sums they've been spending on political action. This view relies on the improbable assumption that public school employees are ignorant of their own interests. Given their huge wage and benefit advantage over the competitive private sector, union dues are the safest and best investment most public school employees could hope to make. At the moment, dues are returning around 2,000 percent annually (public school teachers enjoy a $17,000 annual compensation premium over their private sector counterparts, and dues run only about $800). Where else could they get a return like that without the use of firearms?

If curbs on collective bargaining and mandatory government dues collection won't rein in the unions' budget-busting political action, what will? The answer is to take advantage of the same freedoms and incentives that have prevented unions from going off the rails in the private sector: give parents and taxpayers real choice, and give public schools real competition.

At present, private schools are at a massive disadvantage to state-run schools because the latter have a monopoly on $13,000 per pupil of government spending annually. That makes it hard for parents, and impossible for taxpayers, to seek out private sector alternatives to the state-run schools. And contrary to widespread perception, public schools spend roughly 50 percent more, on average, than do private schools—including all sources of revenue, not just tuition.

The simplest way to simultaneously give taxpayers and parents educational choice is to cut the taxes on families that pay for their own children's education. Such cuts, called "direct" or "personal use" education tax credits, already exist on a small scale in Iowa and Illinois. If adopted in other states and increased in value they would bring the option of independent, privately operated schools within reach of most Americans. And since the credits need not cover the full cost of private school tuition, the migration from public to independent schools would save taxpayers a great deal of money.

Effective as they are, such direct credits have an obvious limitation: they can only help parents with non-negligible state/local tax liabilities. Most lower-income families owe little in taxes and so wouldn't benefit, leaving them stuck in the deficient, inefficient, state schools. Fortunately, there is a simple solution: cut taxes on individuals and businesses who pay tuition for *other* people's children. Seven states already have such programs, including Arizona, Pennsylvania, and Florida. Called "scholarship donation" tax credits, they cut the taxes on those who donate to non-profit Scholarship Granting Organizations (SGOs). The SGOs, in turn, help families pay for K-12 independent schooling.

What makes scholarship tax credits unique among school choice programs serving low-income children is that they offer choice not just to parents but to taxpayers themselves. No one is compelled to donate to an SGO, and if you choose to do so you select the organization that receives your funds. Think that the organization you're currently supporting is no longer helping families as effectively as it should? You can send your money elsewhere. This forces the SGOs to compete with one another in terms of efficiency and service to families, just as other charitable organizations must.

Combining these two types of tax credits and allowing them to expand in response to public demand would end the unions' half-century stranglehold on education funding. As in every other field, the public would finally be able to seek out the best, most cost-effective providers. The result would be the same in education as it has been in other fields: in the presence of efficient markets, salaries and benefits would depend on performance. The best teachers would easily command much larger salaries than the largest any public school teacher enjoys today. In sectors of the education industry that already operate within the free enterprise system, such as the Asian after-school tutoring market, the top teachers reach tens of thousands of students via web lectures and earn millions of dollars a year (yes, *millions*) thanks to profit sharing with their employers. Schools that charged more than their competitors for a similar or lower-quality education would lose students and fail. With the end of the state school monopoly, unions would no longer be able to bleed taxpayers for above-market compensation.

Educational freedom would thus end the reign of state school employee unions as a powerbroker in American politics. The Democratic Party would be hardest hit. The NEA has given $30 million in federal campaign contributions since 1990, 93 percent of which has gone to Democrats or the Democratic Party. The AFT has contributed $26 million to federal campaigns, of which 99 percent has gone to Democrats.

This perhaps explains why Democratic lawmakers from Indiana and Wisconsin fled their states this spring, in an effort to block legislation that was expected to curb teachers' union power. And it perhaps explains why President Obama, Education Secretary Arne Duncan, and congressional Democrats killed a small private school choice program in Washington, D.C. (which was subsequently reinstated by Republicans in April as part of the budget agreement).

If Democrats continue to cling to the union-dominated state school monopoly as their salvation, they will ride it, like the Titanic, beneath the waves. It is a ship with a yawning gash beneath the waterline. Most elected Democrats, from President Obama on down, want to deal with that catastrophe by shoveling more money into the furnaces. The longer they do this, the less time they'll have to abandon ship when they realize, belatedly, that the system is doomed.

Sooner or later, the public will no longer be able to maintain school employees in the numbers or in the manner to which they have become accustomed. Our state school monopoly is simply not sustainable, and as Herbert

Stein observed, "things that can't go on forever . . . don't." When Americans finally discard this system, they will look around to see who fought to preserve it until the last possible moment. If the answer is "Democrats," it will not only be the Democratic Party that is hurt.

Single-party government has not tended to equate to good government. If Republicans enjoy unitary control of Congress and the presidency for some years while Democrats search for a new base of political support, we will not be blessed by a period of cautious, limited government. But Democrats can avert their own irrelevance by acknowledging today the inherent defects of the union-captured monopoly school system, and championing educational freedom in its place. This would give them a platform they could successfully take to voters: educational excellence, educational freedom, fiscal sanity. A platform they could be proud of.

There are indications that such a shift is possible. Florida has the largest private school choice program in the nation—a scholarship donation tax credit serving 33,000 students, which is set to grow by 25 percent annually in the coming years. It received a single Democratic vote when enacted in 2002. Today it enjoys the support of half the state's Democratic caucus. Hopefully, Democrats nationwide will take Florida as a model. The alternative, for themselves and the nation, is bleak.

Louis Malfaro

Lessons on Organizing for Power

School systems sometimes make promises they have no intention of keeping. Other times, they can deliver a world of opportunities to our neediest children. They may or may not want to listen to parents or even teachers, but school systems always attend to the demands of the most powerful individuals and institutions in their communities. For the last 20 years, I've been working and organizing to build power through my local union—Education Austin.

Over the summer, as I made the transition from being president of Education Austin to being secretary-treasurer of the Texas AFT, I spent some time reflecting on how union locals—especially locals like mine in states without collective bargaining—build power. Not power for its own sake, but power to work with school districts, policymakers, and institutions on an equal footing, to advance an agenda of issues for members and the children they serve. I don't have a list of lessons learned or a set of simple steps to follow. What I have is a story. It's my story and the story of my union's struggle to give educators a place at the table.

Teaching and Learning the Hard Way

I started teaching in 1987 at Blackshear Elementary School in Austin, Texas, as a second-grade bilingual teacher. Just eight years earlier, Austin had been ordered by the U.S. Supreme Court to bus students; it was one of the last major urban school districts to come under a court-ordered desegregation plan. The district complied, busing students at all levels beginning in 1980. In 1986, a new school board was elected on a let's-get-rid-of-busing platform. By then, the courts had pretty much gotten out of the business of desegregation. The school district was allowed to reinstitute neighborhood elementary schools, as long as it agreed to make certain accommodations for 16 high-poverty "priority" schools—including that they would be staffed by experienced and exceptional principals and teachers.

I arrived on the scene excited to be assigned to Blackshear Elementary, one of the 16 priority schools, where more than 95 percent of the students received free or reduced-price lunch. As a new teacher, I looked forward to being surrounded by veteran colleagues who would mentor and support me as I learned my new craft.

Reprinted with permission from the Fall 2010 issue of *American Educator,* the quarterly journal of the American Federation of Teachers, AFL-CIO.

As it turned out, of the five of us assigned to second grade, four had never taught a lick. Our lone veteran colleague had fewer than five years under her belt. I received a quick lesson in how public school systems can work: promises made to communities (and courts) are not always kept.

At about this time, I was solicited through the mail by the Association of Texas Professional Educators, an anti-collective bargaining, anti-union teacher association. Its flier said, "We believe that strikes should be saved for the grand old game of baseball." Over 20 years later, I still recall the steam coming out my ears as I read this paean to passivity. Where I grew up, in Pennsylvania, my teachers were unionized and union workers at Bethlehem Steel forged the beams of the Golden Gate Bridge. I had learned my history too. Reading *The Jungle* in my public high school opened my eyes to an American history rife with abuse of the American worker. I knew that the labor movement played a very significant role in protecting workers' rights and promoting high-quality public schools.

In most states, the right of school employees to union representation is no longer a stirring issue for educators, but in Texas, state law prohibits collective bargaining. Unlike some southern states where the historical practice is to not engage in collective bargaining, in Texas, it is downright illegal, statutorily prohibited not only for teachers but for virtually all public employees (with a few exceptions for public safety workers). When I moved to Texas, I realized that as far as rights on the job are concerned, the lock had been turned back to pre-1960s America.

When I received the anti-union flier, I cursed the ignorance of it, but I didn't sit in the shadows swearing at the darkness. A few weeks later, I was contacted by the AFT affiliate, the Austin Federation of Teachers, Local 2048. I breathed fire into the phone about the flier I'd received. There was an organizer at my school the next day to sign me up as a new member.

The union, for me, was and continues to be a vehicle for forming relationships with people who share my interests and concerns. Within the first year, I signed up to be the building representative—there were only three AFT members at the school! In fact, although there were two AFT affiliates within the school district, a certified teacher local and a PSRP (paraprofessional and school-related personnel) local, the teacher local had fewer than 300 members spread across 80 schools.

The big group in town was the NEA affiliate. If somebody from there had talked to me first, it's likely that I would have signed up with the NEA. As with the AFT, the NEA's positions on a lot of issues were similar to mine. Over time, I found that our local union was the little-but-loud group—the real union—so I embraced it.

One of my first initiatives as a building representative was to survey the 16 "priority" schools to find out if they had received the promised master teachers or any of the other promised resources. None of the 16 schools had received the experienced teachers. They did get other things, like reduced class sizes and a little extra money to take kids on field trips. So the district hadn't completely failed, but on the critical issue of quality teachers, nothing had been done. There certainly was quality teaching going on in those 16 schools, but there were many, many greenhorns like me with precious little support.

My first year, I literally got a cardboard box full of teacher's editions of textbooks and was turned loose with 15 second-graders. Nobody came into my room for weeks. Weeks turned into months, and I kept thinking to myself, "I can't believe they just put me in here with these kids! I've never taught before, and nobody is coming in here to see how I'm doing!" To make matters worse, I was the only bilingual second-grade teacher in my school, so I was the only person teaching my specific curriculum to kids in Spanish (their primary language) and English. It was an isolating experience.

Desperate, I eavesdropped on the four-year veteran's classroom, which wasn't difficult because our rooms were divided by a folding wall. During my planning period, I parked myself right next to the thin wall and, while grading papers, listened to her teach, to her pace and how she interacted with the kids. Aside from what I had learned from my student teaching, I really didn't know a lot about what I was supposed to be doing.

Nevertheless, I had the same experience many young, energetic teachers have. I fell in love with my students and their families. I poured in many hours and was astounded at how much I learned about children, and at how quickly my children learned. I went into teaching to work with poor, immigrant kids. I knew I would encounter a lot of really bright kids, but I was amazed by the children's capacity and potential. I ran an afterschool Shakespeare club for a couple of years in which we produced elementary school versions of several dramas, including *A Midsummer Night's Dream* and *Romeo and Juliet*.

Despite the lack of mentoring and support, teaching was a great experience for me. It renewed my faith in the importance of public schools, especially for kids whose parents are immigrants or did not go to college. Working in a classroom every day puts one in touch with the unbridled potential that children bring with them to school. Yet, too often, school systems don't invest adequately in teachers, who, like students, fail to reach their potential as a result. They never become as good at teaching as they could be because they haven't been equipped. I think I was an example of how that happens. I was hard working, I was well intentioned—and I'm not saying I didn't have success in the classroom. But I had so much more to learn. My school district did not have a mentoring or induction program, or a well-articulated professional development program, although I did receive some good training here and there. How much more quickly could I have improved with a real expert by my side, and how would that have affected my students?

The union, in contrast, provided a great deal of leadership training. Even though we were a small local, we were part of a bigger network of local AFT affiliates around Texas. I enjoyed meeting other teachers' union leaders from around the state and hearing about their struggles. The Texas AFT had a very strong leadership development program, with summer training that covered how to run a local, the nuts and bolts of what a local should do: advocacy, organizing, grievance handling, internal and external communications, and consultation (which, as I'll explain later, is as close as we have gotten to collective bargaining).

By 1992, I was on the executive board of the Austin Federation of Teachers. We were still the little 300-member, lean, mean fighting machine. Our local president decided abruptly that she didn't want to continue to serve, and the board, which we jokingly renamed "the junta," managed the local for the remainder of that school year.

That was the end of my fifth year in the classroom. I had been accepted into the graduate program at the Lyndon B. Johnson School of Public Affairs at the University of Texas. My plan was to take a leave of absence from school to earn a master's degree in public policy. The board members, thinking that I'd have more free time as a graduate student than they would as classroom teachers, asked me to run for president.

I agreed and was elected president of the local—a job that came with many hours of work and a whopping $50 a week stipend. For two years, I studied state governance, school finance, and other aspects of public policy. Meanwhile, every Monday night I was down at the school board meetings, and all week in the afternoons (when not in class) I was making fliers and visiting schools. Fortunately, it wasn't long before the Texas AFT assigned a staff person to my local.

At the end of graduate school, I had the choice between selling securities or becoming the local president full time, released from teaching. Although I received a very attractive offer from a major investment house, there was never a question in my mind about where I belonged.

Building Power

My time in the classroom taught me there was a need for powerful institutions that could hold the district accountable to its students, staff, and community. But as the new leader of a very small affiliate, I actually felt a little resentment as I listened to Albert Shanker—the iconic president of the national AFT—say that fixing schools and providing professional development are union work. I kept thinking to myself: "In Austin, we don't even have the basic right of recognition. How can we have a meaningful role in any quality-of-education initiative when they don't even recognize us?"

Still, I reflected on the locals doing professional issues work: they were the big locals that had grown enough to negotiate with the district as a peer. They could make demands and back them up with people and money. I began to see a sequence for the union's work. First, we had to build power, and then we could tackle our priorities. So we focused hard on growing the union and talking to teachers about our rights on the job. We also fought for better pay and health care choices.

Unlike my experience as a teacher, in my union work I was anything but isolated. In 1994, my local was awarded an AFT organizing grant, and we hired two organizers. We merged with the local AFT PSRP affiliate, which was called the Allied Education Workers, and Julie Bowman (the then-PSRP local president who now directs leadership development at the Texas AFT) became my copresident.

For five years, we went into schools and work sites, and we organized teachers and school support staff. We built a great local, we elected school board members, we recruited new members, we conducted surveys to find out what motivated our members, and we waged campaigns to improve pay and working conditions.

During this time, my sister began her teaching career in a suburban Philadelphia school district. I used her family as an example when I talked to Austin's school board. My brother-in-law and my nieces and nephews all had health coverage through my sister's teaching job, but in Austin we didn't receive any health coverage for our families. And I would ask: "Why are teachers in some states paid well and treated decently? Why are we so stingy here? Why do you think 18 percent of the staff leaves every year?" We differentiated ourselves from the nonunion teacher groups by explaining that collective bargaining had helped school employees win basic workplace dignity as well as decent pay, pensions, and health benefits. And we kept building a strong organization.

At the heart of that organization were—and still are—the words printed on the original charter the AFT gave us in 1970: "Democracy in Education, Education for Democracy." Our union is an autonomous government of school employees. It is democratic, its leaders are elected, and it is governed by a constitution. What separates democracies in the world from tyrannies of the left and the right is the ability of individuals to associate freely and to speak freely—the basics contained in the Bill of Rights.

Can you imagine employers discouraging their employees from voting? People would be outraged. Yet, that is exactly what employers do when they discourage employees from associating with one another and from forming unions. Protecting our rights, whether at work or in our neighborhoods, is an act of preserving the very underpinnings of democracy. The institutions that make up what we call civil society in this country are fragile and often under attack. Ernesto Cortes Jr. of the Industrial Areas Foundation has pointed out that mobility, technology, and changes in the way we live, work, and associate have transformed human relationships. The neighborhoods where everyone knew one another—went to school together, worked in the same factory, worshipped together—have given way to a more dislocated society. We have to find new ways to build community, and the places we must look to do that are our schools, our workplaces, our neighborhoods, and our places of worship. The ability to associate freely with your coworkers, to organize, and to bring forward common interests and concerns is fundamental to the health and well-being of American democracy.

These notions of building power were in the forefront of my mind as I thought about how to continue growing my local in the late 1990s. At the national level, the AFT and the NEA were talking about merging, but Texas remained one of the few areas of the country where AFT and NEA locals were still fighting each other. San Antonio's representation fight in the mid-'90s was especially bitter. The AFT wrested representation away from the NEA affiliate, but it took a tremendous expenditure of time, money, and energy from both sides.

In Austin, Julie Bowman and I had been paying a lot of attention to the NEA affiliate, partly because we were raiding its members, but partly because we were beginning to question our tactics. If we take all the members from one group and move them into another group, we wondered, have we really made progress in terms of organizing? So we started talking to the NEA affiliate, informally at first, to imagine having one big organization. Soon we had a committee that met quarterly. Eventually we conducted a retreat with both locals' boards.

The negotiations with the NEA local were like a courtship, but in reality we were working on two fronts. Even as we were arguing for the merger, our local worked independently to challenge the NEA's status as the consultation representative with the district. Although collective bargaining is illegal in Texas, school boards are allowed to set up "consultation" mechanisms to take input from their employees. Consultation can't result in a contract, but agreements can be struck and the school board can adopt them as it would any other policy. Austin's school board had a longstanding consultation policy that named the NEA affiliate as the teacher consultation representative. Our AFT affiliate convinced the board to change the policy to require a vote of the employees to elect the representative. We then told the NEA local that we intended to challenge its bid to become the representative—but that we would rather join together and create a new organization instead.

Initially, the NEA local's leaders thought we were trying to take consultation away from them. We told them we didn't want to take it away, we wanted to share it. Since both groups understood that we needed one voice speaking for all employees, we came together to create a single union.

With the date for the election for the consultation representative having been set by the school board, we all felt pressure to bring our courtship to a close. The national AFT and NEA brought in high-powered facilitators from Harvard Law School. With their help, using an accelerated six-month process, we went from rival organizations to allied groups with a merger agreement. Then it took another three months to educate the broader membership and take a vote on both sides.

We started the school year in 1999 with a new superintendent, a new merged union called Education Austin, and a consultation election in which Education Austin was overwhelmingly elected. It was the first time school employees in Austin had ever had the ability to vote on a representative. Our combined membership surged over the next couple of years because people who'd been on the fence about joining were energized by our unity. The funny thing about bringing together two organizations that share a common set of values and goals is that, at the grass-roots level, it inherently makes sense to the members. We surveyed members on both sides, and they overwhelmingly supported unification. They clearly wanted one big, strong organization.

The merger agreement called for a three-year transition in which we had a tripartite presidency of Julie Bowman, who was our PSRP president (the NEA affiliate did not have a PSRP division); Brenda Urps, the NEA local president; and myself. After three years, the tripartite presidency ended and I ran unopposed to be the president of Education Austin.

There were plenty of kinks to work out, but we have thrived as the first merged local affiliate in Texas. Amazingly, San Antonio followed us a couple of years later. Members there realized the only alternative to fighting was to figure out how to follow our path. Other smaller districts around the state also pulled together, although many parts of Texas remain a battleground for the AFT and the NEA.

During our merger talks, we understood that if coming together were just about becoming bigger, then despite what we say in Texas, bigger wouldn't necessarily be better. This new organization needed to actually be better than either of its predecessors. The merger process helped us define what a "better" union should look like. Probably the most important improvement was working to more fully engage our members. We agreed to create structures through which more members would not just pay dues and answer surveys, but would also become actively involved in the union, in politics, in professional issues, in the consulting process with the school district, and in outreach to the community. Today, we have a large group of political action leaders, and myriad standing committees on issues such as early childhood education, special education, assessment, and transportation.

Soon after the merger, Austin Interfaith (a community organization affiliated with the Industrial Areas Foundation and made up of about 30 congregations, schools, and unions) asked our union to join them. The group saw the newly unified Education Austin as a power within the school district and the city. Being a part of Austin Interfaith has helped our union develop and work more broadly to build power. We have borrowed extensively from its organizing style. Education Austin's organizing model asks each individual: What are you interested in? What problems could we work together to solve? Are you willing to form relationships with other teachers and school employees to work on those problems? This approach has defined the union and been very productive. It has also challenged our leaders to take on issues like health care, immigration, housing, and other issues that aren't school issues per se, but that do affect our students and members. Now, our work is expanding again: Education Austin was recently awarded an AFT Innovation Fund grant to work with Austin Interfaith to do community school organizing. Austin Interfaith has a track record of successful school organizing, having worked in the 1990s to organize the parents, teachers, and community at 16 high-needs schools.

Taking Up Shanker's Challenge

Right after the merger and consultation representative election in 1999, Education Austin focused on basic pay and health insurance issues. We negotiated decent pay raises. We persuaded the district to adopt an internal minimum wage for workers, so even the custodial and food service staff start off at a living wage. We also negotiated leave benefits and training for employees. Then we began a long, hard push to include professional issues in our official consultation with the district.

I remember reading a "Where We Stand" column in which Al Shanker bemoaned the fact that when fighting to win collective bargaining, teachers and their unions were accused of only caring about their own pay and benefits—not caring about kids. But, Shanker said, when they won bargaining and tried to negotiate things that would be good for students, like reduced class sizes, they were told that it was not their concern. In city after city, management only wanted to bargain wages, hours, and working conditions. Shanker rightly pointed out the hypocrisy of calling teachers' unions self-interested while restricting what they could negotiate to wages and benefits.

In Austin, the same thing happened when we tried to introduce ideas that would be good for kids and for school quality, such as mentoring programs for new teachers and high-quality professional development for all teachers. We were told those things are management's prerogative. I remember the chief academic officer telling us, "I'll meet with you on the side about that, but we're not going to do that during consultation." It was frustrating.

One of the areas that we really had to fight hard on for many years was assessment, and in particular practice testing. Our district, like many districts over the last 10 years, ratcheted up the amount of time teachers are required to do practice testing with kids. We were told to administer beginning-, middle-, and end-of-year benchmark tests, plus six-week and nine-week tests. Some schools also gave three-week tests, and even weekly tests. None of these were teacher-made assessments. They were all designed to estimate how students would do on the end-of-year state assessment. One of our strongest committees in the last several years has been the over-testing committee. But until very recently, we were rebuffed every year, even though our proposals were reasonable requests, supported by a majority of teachers, to make some of the tests optional.

Recently, with our new superintendent, Meria Carstarphen, we were able to create a labor-management committee to review the district's testing regime. After a full year of work, we arrived at an agreement to significantly reduce the amount of practice testing and to spend another year designing meaningful formative assessments that will take up less class time and better guide instruction. This sort of labor-management partnership would have been unthinkable a decade ago, but with greater power and the political sophistication (on both sides) to engage around tough issues, we have improved the ability to get things done.

Compensation is another example of a difficult issue where labor-management collaboration has had some success. In 2006, we signed a two-year pay agreement, an unprecedented event because normally our pay negotiations are linked to the annual adoption of the budget. Teacher and support staff received raises of 11.5 percent over two years, and an extra $4 million was set aside for development of a new alternative compensation plan that the union and district would design together. The compensation committee was jointly chaired by the human resources director, a business leader, and me. We already knew that we had strong resources from the AFT and the NEA, which both sent staff with experience in developing alternative compensation systems to help us. Many members got involved as the union worked with the district to create a large steering committee plus a smaller design committee. Our teachers helped the district understand that just paying more wasn't going to change anything—teachers needed better support and the right tools to improve.

The result of several years' worth of research, learning together, and work was the Austin Independent School District REACH program, which is now entering its fourth year as a pilot at 15 of our schools. In order to become a pilot site, two-thirds of the teachers had to vote in favor of participating.

REACH provides full-time mentors for teachers in their first three years, support for national board certification, schoolwide performance bonuses based on student growth on the state's reading and math assessments, and individual teacher bonuses based on teacher-developed student-learning objectives. We're comfortable with this approach to alternative compensation because teachers are well supported and the alternative pay is on top of the regular salary schedule. It was important to us to recognize and encourage teacher collaboration, so the state assessment results are only used for school-wide incentives. Instead of looking at current achievement, the district looks at year-over-year growth of the same students and compares it with the growth in 40 similar schools. Bonuses are awarded to schools that rank in the top quartile on growth in reading and/or math. We were also careful in designing the individual incentives: they are teacher selected student-learning objectives, and they are developed by all teachers in every subject and grade, so that the art teacher, French teacher, librarian, gym teacher, band teacher, pre-K teacher, etc., all set goals based on their students and the curriculum they teach.

REACH has started to create a culture of looking at data, setting measurable goals, and assessing personal and group performance. But that's only part of what makes it effective. The other part—probably the more important part—is the mentoring. All of the full-time mentors have completed the AFT's Foundations of Effective Teaching professional development course. The first year, the union paid to send about seven people to the training. The district was so impressed by its quality that it paid the full cost for both the union and the district—around $30,000—in the second year.

When we designed REACH, our plan was to offer all pilot schools the alternative compensation, but to provide full-time mentoring only in the highest-needs schools (i.e., those with the highest concentrations of low-income students and English language learners). We quickly learned that mentoring should be offered to all pilot schools because all new teachers, not just those in our most challenging schools, are really interested in receiving extensive support and feedback. In addition, we found that mentoring new teachers is a huge relief to our senior teachers, who no longer felt pressured to assist their new colleagues. In fact, some senior teachers are seeking out the mentors because they want extra support too, especially in designing their student-learning objectives.

Going forward, all REACH schools will have the same supports, but the highest-needs schools will have added monetary incentives for teachers that include bigger performance bonuses and a retention stipend. For first-through third-year teachers, the retention stipend is $1,000. For those who have been in the school more than three years, it's $3,000. Use of a retention stipend is supported by research conducted by our district that links longevity at the school site with increased student performance.

This is the final year of the REACH pilot. We are still collecting data to determine program effectiveness, but there are some positive early results. We are hoping to expand the program to almost 40 schools, mainly our highest-needs schools.

Interestingly, working on the REACH program has deepened the union's relationship with the entire human capital development wing of the school district. The district now has a chief human capital officer who pays close attention to teacher leadership, professional development, the REACH program, and the development of a new, much more robust teacher induction program for the whole district.

REACH has also built our relationship with the chamber of commerce and the business community. The business community loves performance pay—but our business leaders have also appreciated that the program is a labor-management partnership. They've been real boosters and have supported raising the tax rate to help fund the program.

Developing Leaders

Being a local union leader is transformative because it forces you to be political. You must engage with power wherever it is. One mistake I've seen new local presidents make is not grasping the difference between being political and being partisan. Being political is not just about winning elections. It's about reading the newspaper every day. It's about knowing what's going on in your community. It's about listening to your members. It's about developing other leaders. It's about building webs of relationships within the organization and the community that allow you to reach out and be influential. Even in the absence of collective bargaining, good leaders can still build power.

Linda Bridges, the president of the Texas AFT, is a terrific example of acting politically to build power. When she was still the president of the AFT local in Corpus Christi, she successfully ran the mayor's campaign. She was a pioneer in the field of labor-management collaboration (without the safety or structure of a collective bargaining agreement) and won the prestigious Saturn Award for her local. Among many other responsibilities, she served on the board of the local community college and was president of the Coastal Bend Labor Council. She built relationships that in turn built the union. She understood that she had power because of the people standing behind her, and she used that power to build her strength and the strength of the organization.

As a local leader, I tried to follow Linda's lead, to be political but not partisan. When the new superintendent, Meria Carstarphen, came to town last year, I threw my arms around her, in a manner of speaking. I attended all the forums for staff and the community to get to know her. The school board, with whom we had already built a relationship, brought her to our office her first day on the job. Soon thereafter, she announced plans to hold a big convocation with all 11,000 district employees. I asked to get up on stage with her and talk to the district's employees. Although she spoke for an hour and I spoke for 10 minutes, there were only three people on that stage at the event: the president of the school board, the superintendent, and the union president (me). I was there for two reasons. First, my members put me there; they built the power and the strength to enable me to make the demand to be on stage. Second, I asked to be there. I insinuated myself into that situation. Woody Allen said that 80 percent of success is showing up. Sometimes it's awkward and uncomfortable. But if you think and behave politically, if you are able to engage power by offering something and demanding something, and if you are not afraid to show up and not shut up, there are few limits to what you can get done if you have organized people standing with you.

One way to stay focused on the political and on building a broad base of support for the union is to ask a simple question: whom am I developing? It's a question all leaders and organizers should ask themselves constantly. It is not simply a matter of succession, as in "whom am I preparing to someday take my job." Whether you're staying or going, whether you're short term or long term, whether you're a building representative or a local president, you are only as effective as the other leaders you bring with you. I wish I had figured that out much earlier because I would have achieved more and maybe not had to work quite so awfully hard.

In organizations like ours, leadership is everything. But leadership isn't the person sitting at the top. Leadership is the relationships with other people, both inside and outside the union—relationships that bring people along, develop their talents, and tie them to one another through shared interests and a common understanding of what they want to see happen and what they are willing to do to make it happen.

My union includes members who lived in Section 8 housing, who were afraid to go to their children's school because they didn't think they belonged, but who now look mayors and senators and superintendents in the eye and talk to them about their interests and needs, and their community's needs. Some of these leaders have been cultivated by me and by other union organizers. Some of them have come through Austin Interfaith's leadership training. Seeing people grow into strong leaders makes me realize that, although our society is built on the notion of egalitarianism, we don't get social equity unless we teach people how to organize and exercise power. Building power through organizing makes the ideal of egalitarianism a reality.

In our local union, we are instituting a culture among our staff and our leaders to have deliberate conversations with others, to figure out who they are and what makes them angry and what they care about. This is the heart of effective organizing. There is power in knowing other people's stories. It opens up an understanding of what people's needs are, what their interests are, and what's motivating them. A strong organization doesn't just get people to sign up for a march; it knows what brought them to the march, why they chose to march instead of spending time with their family or going fishing. All people are motivated by strong experiences that have shaped them. The union's ability to tap into that, to build relationships and get people to know each other, sets us apart from other kinds of institutions and is our key to building leaders and power. In turn, our success at cultivating new leaders and building power will be directly proportional to our success at achieving our goals as a union.

POSTSCRIPT

Do Teachers Unions Stymie School Reform?

Teacher Unions Are Dead! Long Live Teacher Unions!" shouts Thomas Toch in the December 2010/January 2011 issue of *Phi Delta Kappan* in which he concludes that with millions of members and vast political networks the unions are the most powerful force in American education, but they will have to make peace with reform. Long-held positions on merit pay, tenure, seniority, teacher evaluation, and charter schools will have to be modified. While the positions offered in the Coulson and Malfaro articles seem fairly rigidly antithetical, one can discern some evidence of possible convergence when the welfare of students is placed before them. Both would do well to address the "Four Myths About Teachers" described by Ilana Garon in *Dissent* (Summer 2011). Myth No. 1: The big problem with U.S. education is the teachers. Myth No. 2: Charter schools are better than regular public schools. Myth No. 3; Unions stand in the way of all that is good in education because they keep unfit teachers in their jobs. Myth No. 4: Tenure makes it so that teachers become complacent because it's difficult to fire them since they have no motivation to improve their performance.

An interesting juxtaposition of views is presented in a post by Frederick Hess of *Education Next* on June 13, 2011 titled "Moe v. Meier on Teacher Unions." Hess reports on a panel discussion of Moe's book *Special Interest*. Moe sees "reform unionism" as a pipe dream and contends that school improvement must be driven by incentives to improve student test performance. Panelist Deborah Meier counters that Moe's critique rests on the notion that test scores can usefully measure teacher effectiveness.

Worldwide comparisons of student test performance often show Finland at or near the top. An article in the September 2011 *Smithsonian* by Lynnell Hancock points out that the people in the government agencies overseeing Finnish schools are educators, not politicians and that the teachers union is extremely strong there. A question remains: Does the Finnish union operate differently from ours? If so, what can we learn?

Alternative views on the basic issue and sub-issues include these: Joel Klein, "Scenes from the Class Struggle," *The Atlantic* (June 2011); Katherine Mangu-Ward, "Education Showdown: The Irresistible Force of School Reform Meets the Immovable Object of Teachers Union," *Reason* (May 2011); Evan Thomas and Pat Wingert, "Why We Can't Get Rid of Failing Teachers," *Newsweek* (March 15, 2010); Philip Mattera, "Public Employees and the Public Interest," *Social Policy* (Spring 2011); and Mike Antonucci, "The Long Reach of Teachers Unions," *Education Next* (Fall 2010).

ISSUE 16

Can Merit Pay Accelerate School Improvement?

YES: **Steven Malanga**, from "Why Merit Pay Will Improve Teaching," *City Journal* (Summer 2001)

NO: **Stuart Buck and Jay P. Greene**, from "Blocked, Diluted, and Co-opted," *Education Next* (Spring 2011)

ISSUE SUMMARY

YES: Steven Malanga, a senior fellow of the Manhattan Institute, draws on examples from the corporate world and from public school systems in Cincinnati, Iowa, and Denver to make his case for performance-based merit pay for teachers.

NO: Professor of education reform Jay P. Greene and doctoral fellow Stuart Buck recognize the theoretical and empirical reasons for expecting merit pay to have a positive impact but contend that the prospects are not promising for a variety of reasons.

T he issue of merit pay, or pay-for-performance, for teachers is certainly not new, but as Steven Malanga, one of the combatants presented in the pairing offered here, says, it is "one of the bitterest controversies in today's school reform debate." The current push to improve public education, particularly in impoverished areas, and to hold individual schools more accountable for achieving desired results has rekindled the argument over merit pay as a replacement for a reward system based primarily on seniority and earned course credits.

Although some forms of merit plans were widely used in the early part of the twentieth century, the economic depression of the 1930s prompted conversions to uniform pay scales. Teachers' unions, which gained strength throughout the remainder of the century, were not supportive of incentive pay schemes. They expressed doubts about the fairness of various evaluation methods and concerns about possible threats to collegiality and the standardization of teaching practices. Since the 1980s, and particularly since the passage of the "No Child Left Behind" legislation, pressure for an accountability system containing specific rewards for teachers and schools that meet desired outcomes has vastly increased.

The matter of how to appropriately and fairly evaluate teacher perform-ance remains a major stumbling block in the adoption of merit-pay plans. Local socioeconomic factors and the unevenness of support structures among school systems and states add complexity to the process. According to Sandra McCollum, in "How Merit Pay Improves Education," *Educational Leadership* (February 2001), merit-pay programs are often discontinued because of one or more of the following reasons: they are unfairly implemented, teachers' unions refuse to endorse them, they create poor teacher morale, legislators who support them leave office, and they are simply too costly and difficult to administer.

An economist's view is offered by Darius Lakdawalla in "Quantity Over Quality," *Education Next* (Fall 2002). He contends that schools have been hiring more teachers in an effort to reduce class sizes but have not been rewarding them for quality performance. In the past few decades, serious opportuni-ties outside teaching have opened up, and school systems have not risen to challenge the competition. The problem of retaining and attracting top-quality teachers is addressed in Marge Scherer, "Improving the Quality of the Teaching Force: A Conversation With David C. Berliner," *Educational Lead-ership* (May 2001). Berliner states that 7 of 23 nations surveyed exceed the United States in starting salaries for teachers and that 9 of 21 nations exceed the United States in top teacher salaries. In the realm of pay, status, and work-ing conditions, says Berliner, "The U.S. is saying to its educators that they are not really important; if we thought they were important, we'd pay them a larger share of our gross domestic product, as other nations do." Yet Berliner is also worried that a merit-pay plan based primarily on student achievement could lead to teachers' doing the wrong thing in their classrooms—cheating and narrowing the curriculum.

Some guidelines for the fair evaluation of teacher performance are put forth by Thomas R. Hoerr in "A Case for Merit Pay," *Phi Delta Kappan* (Decem-ber 1998). In Hoerr's view, there must be trust between the administration and the faculty, judgments must be treated with confidentiality, there must be recognition that both what is valued and how it is measured will vary by context, and teachers who do not perform satisfactorily and do not respond to supportive intervention should not be rehired. Getting rid of ineffective teachers, however, is so arduous and expensive that many school systems do not attempt it. So says Peter Schweizer in "Firing Offenses," *National Review* (August 17, 1998). He analyzes the companion issue of teacher tenure, a sys-tem that was originally designed to protect the best teachers from wrongful termination but that Schweizer says now protects the worst teachers from rightful termination.

In the following selections, Steven Malanga argues that merit pay is essential to meaningful teacher evaluation and school improvement, while Buck and Greene catalog the factors militating against successful implementa-tion of any pay for performance policy.

YES ⬅

Steven Malanga

Why Merit Pay Will
Improve Teaching

One of the bitterest controversies in today's school-reform debate is merit pay—rewarding teachers not for seniority and the number of ed-school credits they've piled up, as public schools have done since the early 1920s, but for what they actually achieve in the classroom. Education reformers argue that merit pay will give encouragement to good teachers and drive away bad ones, and thus improve under-performing public schools. But most teachers' unions adamantly oppose the idea. We don't have reliable means to measure a teacher's classroom performance, the unions charge, so merit plans will inevitably result in supervisor bias and favoritism: "Just too many cliques in the system," one teacher typically complains in a recent survey.

Nowhere is the incentives debate raging more fiercely than in New York City, where teachers' contract negotiations have been at an impasse for months. Mayor Rudolph Giuliani has demanded that merit pay for individual teachers be part of any deal; the teachers' union response (at least so far): fuhgeddaboudit.

Missing from the argument, though, are lessons from the private sector, where sophisticated, effective performance-based compensation has been *de rigueur* since the 1980s—part and parcel, experts believe, of corporate America's hugely successful restructuring. Also ignored are experiments with comprehensive merit-pay plans that are under way in a few innovative school districts across the country—districts burdened with much less political resistance than Gotham.

⋅⟨۞⟩⋅

To get a sense of what merit pay could do for the public schools, consider the benefits it has showered on American industry over the last two decades. Before the eighties, merit pay in U.S. firms—if it existed at all—was pretty simple: the boss gave you a fat bonus if you (or your unit) met sales or production goals. But as international economic competition pummeled them in the early 1980s, U.S. corporations, desperate to regain their competitiveness, began to experiment with measuring individual worker performance. They established pay incentives to improve it in formerly hard-to-measure categories of output

From *City Journal*, vol.11, no. 3, Summer 2001. Copyright © 2001 by the Manhattan Institute, Inc. Reprinted by permission of City Journal.

and in previously intangible areas like customer service or product quality. Of course, the bottom line was still the bottom line, but these intangibles, companies now reasoned, mattered to the long-term economic health of the firm, even if they didn't show up right away in the quarter-by-quarter numbers.

Familiar today, the new performance criteria—and the multi-faceted compensation plans built on their foundation—were strikingly original at the time. Retailers hired "mystery" shoppers to check out how employees treated customers, and based salaries, in part, on what they found. Businesses built into sales contracts "integrity" clauses that gauged not just how many widgets an employee sold but how long clients stuck with him. Banks remunerated loan officers not just for the lending they brought in but for the long-term quality of their loan portfolios. Some auto dealers tied part of salesmen's pay to how customers rated them in follow-up surveys. Companies combined these kinds of individualized incentives with rewards for everybody if the whole firm did well. Airlines, for example, gave the entire crew bonuses if the fleet's on-time performance improved.

Predictably, when U.S. businesses first introduced these innovations, workers grumbled, especially in heavily unionized industries like auto manufacturing, where any change threatened cushy labor arrangements. "They said that you couldn't measure some things, that the pay systems were too subjective, that supervisors were too subjective—in short, everything that teachers today are saying," observes Alan Johnson, a New York-based compensation consultant. Many efforts stumbled at first, too, and companies had to discard or overhaul them. Creating effective programs, it became clear, would not be an overnight fix. "Even today, with all we know, it takes three years to start up an effective incentive-pay program," cautions Martha Glantz, a compensation expert with Buck Consultants in Manhattan. "You can spend the first year just deciding what the company's goals and missions are, and collecting the data."

But American firms, needing to change or perish, forged ahead, winning over employees who liked the challenge of incentive pay and, through trial and error, developing pay plans that worked. By the mid-1990s, half of all major American corporations used such incentives. "It's no longer credible to say you can't measure something or that the only thing you can measure is a simple output," says Johnson. Merit pay played a crucial role, most observers believe, in generating the zooming productivity gains and superior product quality that American firms began recording in the late 1980s and that have been central to the nation's economic prosperity ever since.

⁀⊙⁀

The public education monopoly has long resisted merit pay with the same ferocity with which private-sector workers at first greeted it. Opponents have constantly invoked previous attempts that failed—though their only examples have been two experiments that are over 100 years old, and another from the 1960s, before modern notions of performance pay emerged. The conventional wisdom among educators had long been that any attempt to pin down exactly what makes for good teaching, let alone measure and reward it fairly, was doomed to fail. "There was a general feeling that you were either gifted as a teacher or you weren't, and that good teaching wasn't something you could define," says Charlotte Danielson, an expert on teaching at the Educational Testing Service in New Jersey. As a last-ditch defense, some educators even argued that factors outside school, especially a student's socioeconomic and family situation, had a much greater impact on student performance than teachers did, so that using merit pay based on student performance to promote good teaching, even if it could be defined, wasn't fair. The unasked question was why teachers should ever receive salary hikes if what they do doesn't matter.

Over the last decade, these views have utterly collapsed, undermining the intellectual case—weak as it was—against merit pay. A key figure has been University of Tennessee statistician William Sanders, who discovered how to measure a teacher's effect on student performance. Rather than try to filter out the myriad sociological influences on pupils, a nearly impossible task, Sanders used complex statistical methods to chart the progress of students against themselves over the course of a school year and measure how much "value" different teachers added. Now called the Tennessee Value-Added Assessment System, Sanders's approach proved what every parent already knew: not only did teachers matter, but some were lots better than others. Other education experts, including Danielson, author of several popular books on pedagogy, developed widely accepted criteria to judge good teaching, which put paid to the absurd notion that it was too elusive to define.

If the 1990s helped re-establish the centrality of teaching in the education debate, however, that victory hasn't melted away the teachers' unions' political opposition to merit pay. Even so, a small number of school systems across the country, under intense pressure from parents, politicians, and administrators to improve student performance, have turned to merit pay to promote better teaching. And, after some give-and-take, they've managed to get the teachers' unions on board.

Cincinnati's public school system, the first to experiment with performance incentives, persuaded its teachers' union in 1997 to do a test run of merit pay. Two years later, a ten-school pilot program, designed by administrators and teachers, got under way. Essential to union support was the pilot's proposed use of peers to evaluate teachers. "The peer evaluators, who have no stake in how teachers are judged, are important to the perception of the fairness of the system," observes Kathleen Ware, associate superintendent of Cincinnati schools. Using Danielson's criteria of good teaching—they include class preparation and clarity of presentation—the principals and peer evaluators devoted 20 to 30 hours to assessing every teacher in the ten chosen schools. Based on how they scored, teachers then wound up in one of five salary categories, with "novices" making the least money and "accomplished" teachers the most.

The pilot proved successful. A majority of teachers involved found it fair and judged the standards used as appropriate for the whole school district. The city's board of education adopted it in the spring of 2000, and, in a subsequent election, union members signed on. Teachers will go through evaluations every five years, though those looking to move up quickly can request an appraisal after just two years. New teachers and one-fifth of all experienced teachers [had] evaluations done [in 2001], but no one [started] getting paid under the new system until 2002.

Unfortunately, Cincinnati's new program doesn't directly use student test scores in its evaluations. Bringing in scores would have generated too much union hostility for the plan to gain acceptance, reports school superintendent Steven Adamowski. And in all likelihood, tying pay solely to test scores is a bad idea; nobody would call meritorious a teacher who boosted scores but left his students psychological wrecks because of his bullying. Yet leaving tests out altogether also makes no sense. After all, what better way to determine how well students are doing—the only reason for the concern over teaching quality in the first place—than test scores? Cincinnati's program recognizes this implicitly. The district will monitor test results of students whose teachers score the highest ratings. If those students don't show substantial improvement, school officials will toughen the program's standards. In addition, the district will rely on student tests to award bonuses to all teachers in a school whose kids take big strides.

❧

One major benefit of merit systems is that they enable schools to pay teachers—especially young and ambitious teachers—fatter salaries. That's the overriding rationale behind Iowa's new incentives program, enacted by the state legislature to keep better-paying nearby states from spiriting away top teachers. The state has anted up $40 million for salary increases, but, in a program similar to Cincinnati's, Iowa will now evaluate teachers thoroughly to make sure the extra dough goes only to the good classroom performers, not the duds. "We believe this system will help us retain the best people by re-professionalizing teaching," enthuses John Forsyth, chief executive of the Des Moines-based Wellmark Blue Cross and Blue Shield. Forsyth helped the state dream up the new system, looking to the market for inspiration. "We know good teachers make a difference," he continues, "and we're going to pay those who do make a difference." How much more reasonable this is than the New York union's claim that, because a few city teachers jump to higher-paying suburban schools each year, all teachers—the good and the bad alike—need equal raises to make them stay.

In Iowa's new system, good teachers will now be able to reach higher salary levels much earlier in their careers than before. "The private pay consultants who looked at our old seniority system thought it must have been designed specifically to keep teacher pay low and save school districts money," says Ted Stilwill, director of Iowa's Department of Education. "The only way for teachers to get paid more under that system was for them to stick it out for years." As in Cincinnati, union opposition means that Iowa won't rely on test scores to evaluate teachers—at least not directly. But in addition to paying teachers based on their performance evaluations, the state will also offer modest yearly bonuses to all teachers in a school whose students do well on standardized tests, with the biggest bonuses going to the school's best instructors, rather than all teachers getting equal rewards.

Helping to develop Iowa's plan has been an eye-opener for the state's education chief. "Private-sector compensation experts taught me that businesses use pay as a way of getting everyone to follow common goals," Stilwill says. "Being in the public sector most of my life, I never understood that."

⋅⟐⋅

Though Cincinnati and Iowa have skirted the controversy of using student test scores, Denver is confronting it head-on. The city has launched two pilot plans that link pay directly to scores. One pilot program uses student scores in standardized tests of basic skills; another relies on scores in specific subjects. Principals and teachers agree at the beginning of the school year on what kinds of improvements in test scores they'll shoot for and then face evaluation at the end of the year to see if they've met their goals. Denver is also instituting a third merit-pay pilot program that instructs teachers in the principles of good teaching and then evaluates their teaching skills and rewards them accordingly. Denver will later measure how their students perform on tests to see if its criteria for good teaching really produce results. Through these experiments, Denver hopes to figure out what motivates teachers best and what works best for students.

Denver's teachers' union, surprisingly, has contributed mightily to developing the pilots; the head of the project's design team, Brad Jupp, is a union negotiator. He says the union is participating because the demand to make schools more accountable is so intense that teachers would rather help create performance systems than have them imposed from above. "If you believe that your union members are doing a good job—and we do—then you want a system that accurately measures that," says Jupp.

Experiences from the private sector suggest that it will take several years before these imaginative programs work out all their kinks. In the meantime, controversy will dog the new programs. Critics will pounce on their every mistake as evidence that paying teachers for performance is a bad idea. And unions are likely to push for watered-down plans in order to deflect criticism without giving up too much.

This last is exactly what's happening in New York. The teachers' union has offered the mayor a compromise: pay every teacher in a school or district a bonus if the school's or district's test scores rise. A trial run of such a system, supported by Gotham's business community, is under way in two urban districts; other states, including California and Georgia, already have school-based bonuses.

But group bonuses will never substitute adequately for true performance pay, compensation experts believe, since they don't single out good and bad teachers. All they're likely to do is to frustrate first-rate teachers working in schools with mediocre staffs. "If you have four workers doing well in a unit that is not otherwise performing, over time those four will leave the company and go somewhere that they can be rewarded for their superior work," says consultant Glantz. And since schoolwide bonuses don't put any pay at risk—poor performance doesn't mean less money—they won't help rid schools of lousy teachers either. By contrast, teachers who score poorly in, say, Cincinnati, now find themselves shunted into the lowest salary level, discouraging them from sticking around. Mayor Giuliani, rightly, has rejected the union's offer.

Of course, smaller cities like Cincinnati are far removed from the we don't-do-windows union obstructionism of a New York or a Los Angeles. For 15 years, Cincinnati's teachers' union has accepted some kind of peer evaluation of teachers; it's easily one of the nation's most flexible teachers' unions. Unions in New York and Los Angeles, conversely, have fought almost every education reform tooth and nail. Last year in Los Angeles, thousands of teachers ferociously protested against a proposed merit-pay plan, eventually killing it. Moreover, in the current public school monopoly, there's nothing really comparable to the outside economic pressure that forced American industry to develop its merit programs—one more argument for school choice.

Without individualized merit pay, teacher evaluations will remain perfunctory at best. Today, New York principals fail less than 1 percent of all teachers in annual evaluations. New York hopes to get principals to crack down on bad teaching by rewarding them financially when their schools do well. That will eliminate one of the main objections to teacher merit pay—that it leads to supervisor favoritism: even if a principal hates an effective teacher's guts, he's not going to want to lose someone who's helping him sweeten his own salary. But until teachers are part of any performance-pay system, the impact of such innovations will be severely limited—and students will continue to get shortchanged, regardless of how much their teachers take to the bank.

Stuart Buck and Jay P. Greene

→ **NO**

Blocked, Diluted, and Co-opted

As education policy churns through fad after fad, merit pay is really hot right now. The U. S. Department of Education asked states to include proposals for implementing teacher merit pay—pay based on classroom performance—in their 2010 applications for Race to the Top (RttT) monies, and many applicants promised action on this front. In Washington, D.C., former schools chancellor Michelle Rhee negotiated a strikingly original merit-pay plan, despite strong union opposition. According to the latest *Education Next* poll, public support for merit pay gained significant ground over the past year and now outdistances opposition by a 2:1 margin.

Replacing the standardized salary schedule, where the only factors that determine teacher salaries are the number of years on the job and academic credentials, seems a worthwhile goal. In theory, pay-for-performance plans both provide a clear monetary incentive to teachers to find the best way to motivate and instruct their students and, over the longer term, attract and retain those more-effective teachers who wish to work in a field that rewards professionals for the quality of their efforts. But enacting high-quality performance pay plans in the United States is easier said than done. Last year, the Florida legislature enacted one of the more stringent proposals any state has ever attempted—only to have the bill vetoed by Governor Charlie Crist as a way of jump-starting his ultimately doomed bid to become Florida's first independent U.S. senator. That is not the only time a merit pay bill has seemed on the verge of success, only to founder or be undermined by the need to compromise. In general, merit pay plans are more likely to be symbolic than substantive and more likely to be promised than delivered.

Most often, they are not even promised. Even if one counts the most token of performance pay plans, they are to be found in no more than 500 school districts out of some 14,000 districts nationwide, a mere 3.5 percent of the total.

When new merit-pay plans are proposed, teachers unions often block their enactment or water down their provisions. In Cincinnati and Philadelphia, for example, merit pay policies were blocked just before they were about to be implemented. Denver's Professional Compensation for Teachers (ProComp) plan, widely heralded as the leading national example of performance pay, awards more money for earning another degree than for demonstrated

From *Education Next,* vol. 11, no. 2, Spring 2011, pp. 27–31. Copyright © 2011 by Education Next. Reprinted by permission of Hoover Institution, Stanford University.

performance in the classroom. In Houston, merit was defined so broadly that it included an overwhelming majority of the teachers. In Florida, Iowa, and Texas, the legislatures have encouraged local districts to enact performance pay plans. But unions have been able to dissuade local districts from participating in the state-authorized programs. Only a handful of Florida districts participate in merit pay, for example, even though state funds cover the cost of the initiative.

A strong, well-designed merit-pay plan requires more than offering a bonus to high-performing teachers while paying the remainder according to the standard schedule. To be truly effective, pay for performance must mean in education what it does in other industries—salary increases for the successful, and salary reductions, even dismissals, for poor performers. State laws governing teacher tenure in most states make implementation of such plans unlikely.

All of this leads us to measured skepticism about the merit of merit pay, unless it is coupled with school choice innovations hefty enough to instigate sustained competition among schools and school sectors. Only then would local districts have the incentive to both lobby states for changes in state laws and to negotiate tough contracts with teacher unions. Only then would they find it important, if merely to retain their student enrollments, to structure their pay systems so as to attract top-notch employees and give them strong incentives to strive for excellent performances.

But we have covered a lot of ground very quickly. Let's step back and consider carefully the propositions we have set forth.

Does It Work?

High-quality research on this topic within the United States is sparse and results are mixed. Matt Springer and his colleagues at Vanderbilt released a study recently on a well-designed randomized trial of a merit pay experiment in Nashville. The program involved bonuses of up to $15,000, which would presumably be large enough to affect individual incentives. Yet virtually no effect was seen on test scores (outside of 5th-grade math, an effect that disappeared for those same children the next year). That said, the Nashville study did not examine long-term effects on the composition of the teacher workforce.

The Bloomberg administration in New York City made headlines in late 2007 by announcing a pilot merit-pay initiative, the School-Wide Performance Bonus Program. The New York City Department of Education randomly assigned eligible schools to treatment or control groups, which has enabled scholars to conduct rigorous evaluations. Early results with respect to student achievement are not promising overall, although the program appears to have had a positive impact in schools with fewer teachers. The researchers theorize that the group benefit feature of the merit pay program made it unlikely that it would have an impact on teacher behavior in any but the smallest schools.

The international evidence on performance pay is more encouraging, including a recent worldwide look that indicates that students learn more in countries with performance pay plans, all other known factors held constant. Ludger Woessman looked at 27 Organisation for Economic Cooperation and Development (OECD) countries and found that students in countries with some form of performance pay for teachers score about 25 percent of a standard deviation higher on the international math test than do their peers in countries without teacher performance pay.

Union Roadblocks

If merit pay seems promising (and certainly not harmful), convincing tests of its performance are difficult to undertake within the United States, simply because merit pay proposals typically end up being blocked, co-opted, or diluted by established interests. Admittedly, it is not easy to identify the various instances where merit pay has been proposed but then blocked from enactment, and therefore we cannot provide an explicit enumeration. In all likelihood, most potential proposals are never articulated, simply because likely sponsors regard the cause as hopeless. When 96.5 percent of all districts rigidly follow a standard salary schedule, it takes an energetic and devoted innovator to brave the odds and try to break from tradition nonetheless.

Still, there are several telling examples of established interests blocking merit pay proposals. Governor Mitt Romney proposed merit pay in Massachusetts back in 2005–06, as part of an education budget that included tens of millions in new spending. That proposal went down to defeat; as the *Lowell Sun* reported, "the Massachusetts Teachers Association [MTA] and United Teachers of Lowell opposed the idea. Catherine Boudreau, president of the MTA, called teacher bonuses 'inequitable and divisive.'"

Philadelphia tried to institute a pilot merit-pay program in 2000, but later ditched the initiative, "calling it too expensive, too difficult to administer, and a failure at giving teachers useful feedback" according to the *Philadelphia Inquirer*. Then, in 2006, Philadelphia received a $20.5 million grant from the U.S. government to develop a merit pay program. Said the *Inquirer*, "At the time, the federal grant was announced with much fanfare—the union would be the district's partner, officials said, ensuring the plan would succeed where others failed. But the deal fell apart." The local union abandoned the program in the face of a "surprise $180 million budget deficit," and the district gave the money to charter schools instead.

Another example comes from Cincinnati. That city's merit-pay plan proposed in 2002 was overwhelmingly voted down by teachers (1892 to 73), even though it did not base bonuses on student test scores. As *Education Week* noted, the plan "was based on an extensive evaluation system, which determines whether teachers advance in five career categories. . . . The evaluations entail multiple classroom observations by fellow teachers and administrators and portfolios that include logs of parent contacts, lesson plans, student work, and more." *Education Week* quoted a former associate superintendent of the

Cincinnati schools, who blamed the proposal's failure on the fact that it "would have applied to nearly all teachers, rather than allowing veterans the choice of opting into the new system."

In Alabama, the state's "Race to the Top" application originally proposed merit pay and a "new salary schedule that would give more money to math, science and special-education teachers," but that portion of the application was deleted, reported the *Press-Register* (Mobile), "after Alabama Education Association leader Paul Hubbert wrote state Superintendent Joe Morton a letter . . . opposing them"

If special interests fail to block a merit pay program, they may still be able to make it temporary. A Little Rock, Arkansas, performance-pay program lasted only three years and was not renewed by the local school board, despite evidence of positive effects on student achievement in math, reading, and language. Similarly, the Alaska School Performance Incentive Program was canceled after three years.

Special interests are also able to repeal merit pay based on putative budgetary constraints. The state of North Carolina suspended incentive awards to high-performing schools in 2008–09 due to budget problems. Winston-Salem/Forsyth County, North Carolina, suspended its bonus program due to budget difficulties as well.

Unions have been similarly successful at preventing local districts from participating in statewide programs, as the experience in Florida, Iowa, and Texas shows. Florida's "Merit Award Program" provides state money to local school districts. According to the Florida Department of Education, "Each district will determine an amount equal to at least 5% and no more than 10% of that district's average teacher salary to be awarded to all of the top performing personnel in the district, regardless of years of experience." Even though this program involves free money from the state for districts to hand out to teachers, the political forces opposing merit pay were able to prevent 88 percent of Florida districts from participating in 2009.

Similarly, Iowa's statewide Career Ladder and Pay-for-Performance grant program was passed in 2007, but only 3 Iowa districts, out of 360, bothered to apply. Only 20 percent of Texas districts opted into the District Awards for Teacher Excellence program in 2009–10. In other words, as a result of political opposition, the vast majority of school districts, even in conservative Texas, turned down extra money from the state rather than adopt merit pay.

Merit Pay in Name Only

When interest groups succeed in diluting or co-opting a merit pay plan, the plan ends up rewarding teachers mostly or entirely for inputs (e.g., professional development, graduate degrees, national certification) rather than for outputs (test scores, graduation rates, or even supervisor assessments).

One example is Arizona's Classroom Site Fund (CSF), a mandatory statewide program that involved a couple of new taxes. Districts had to "allocate forty per cent of the monies for teacher compensation increases based on performance and employment related expenses, twenty per cent of the monies for teacher base salary increases and employment related expenses and forty per cent of the monies for maintenance and operation purposes."

According to a 2010 report from the Arizona Auditor General, out of 222 districts receiving CSF funding, the auditor could identify only 29 "with strong performance pay plans that did a good job of linking teacher performance pay to student achievement." The report noted that "allowing districts the freedom to determine performance pay goals can help gain district and teacher buy-in," but that such freedom "has also led to inconsistent performance pay plans and to situations in which teachers receive similar performance pay for significantly different levels of effort and related performance results."

One example from the auditor's report deserves to be highlighted:

> One district awarded performance pay to eligible employees if freshman students' algebra test scores increased by at least 10 percent between a pre- and post-test. The actual increase in test scores was almost 90 percent. Since the pre-test is given to freshman students who have never been exposed to algebra and the post-test is given to them after receiving a full year of algebra instruction, it should be expected that scores would increase significantly more than 10 percent.

In other words, algebra teachers were being rewarded merely for getting students to learn 10 percent more about algebra than they knew before studying that subject at all. This is not a high hurdle to clear.

Denver's ProComp program has been heralded as a political and policy success. Then Senator Barack Obama said, "Cities like Denver have already proven that by working with teachers, this can work, that we can find new ways to increase pay that are developed with teachers, not imposed on them and not just based on an arbitrary test score." But the Denver ProComp program may be less than meets the eye. For one thing, it exempts teachers hired before January 1, 2006, from having to join, which means that the vast majority of teachers whose pay depends on seniority rather than on merit are able to keep their old pay structure in place. And if older teachers opt to enter the Pro-Comp program, they keep their old base salary; the ProComp program merely offers them a chance for bonuses on top of that old salary.

The ProComp program also rewards the old definition of "merit" more immediately and to a greater extent than it does anything that improves student achievement. The largest monetary award is for earning a graduate degree: a $3,300 permanent salary increase plus a tuition or student loan subsidy of $1,000 per year for up to four years. By comparison, teachers receive a one-time award, not a bump up in base salary, of up to $2,403.26 if their students exceed "district expectations" for student growth.

Moreover, as Paul Teske, a principal evaluator of the ProComp program, noted in the *Christian Science Monitor*, bad teachers face no penalty under the ProComp or similar merit-pay programs: "I guess your salary stays low, and maybe that sends the message that you should look at another career. But ProComp doesn't directly address that."

The federal Teacher Incentive Fund (TIF) provides grants to school districts that promise to develop merit pay programs "for raising student achievement and for taking positions in high-need schools." Currently, the Department of Education's website lists 33 TIF grantees, including some small districts and a few major city districts. But these programs may also end up being diluted or co-opted.

For example, the TIF program in Charlotte-Mecklenburg (North Carolina) includes substantial bonuses for professional development, working at hard-to-staff schools or in hard-to-staff subjects, and for taking on leadership roles. To the extent the program involves student achievement, it bases awards on "student learning objectives" as "created by individual teachers, with the approval of site-based administrators"; these objectives "will be measured by a combination of existing assessment instruments, and teacher designed tools," as well as by state standardized tests. The superintendent of Charlotte-Mecklenburg schools recently announced a plan to bring performance pay to the entire district.

Perhaps it is desirable to have teachers receive more professional development, work in hard-to-staff schools or subjects, and assume leadership roles, but these are inputs, not student outcomes. The bulk of the Charlotte-Mecklenburg TIF program, like many such programs, is MPINO—merit pay in name only.

Some locales have diluted the merit pay concept by making the bonuses to teachers small and setting the bar for receiving the bonuses low, thereby converting merit pay into something approximating an across-the board pay raise.

For example, the Texas Educator Excellence Grant (TEEG) program began in 2006–07 and ended after the 2008–09 year; it was funded at approximately $100 million per year. After analysts at the National Center on Performance Incentives (NCPI) reported no positive effects on student test scores, the *Dallas Morning News* declared the program a failure. NCPI report coauthor Lori Taylor speculated that "one possible cause of the program's failure was that bonuses were relatively small and were given to most teachers at each school—about 70 percent—so that the incentive for individual teachers to push for higher scores was 'relatively weak.' In addition, campuses that qualified already had to be higher performers, so it was difficult to register much improvement."

The same thing seems to be happening in Houston, where a merit pay program has existed since January 2007. The district announced financial awards totaling $40.4 million in 2010. The district's webpage notes, "in all, 15,688 HISD employees received performance pay [in 2010], ranging from $25 to $15,530. That's 88 percent of eligible HISD employees."

Minnesota's oft-heralded "Q Comp" program offers yet another example of a "merit pay" program that ends up as an across-the-board pay raise. As the *Minneapolis Star Tribune* recently reported, "In 22 school districts whose Q Comp practices were analyzed by the *Star Tribune* in 2009, more than 99 percent of teachers in the program received merit raises during the preceding school year. Only 27 of the roughly 4,200 teachers eligible did not get a pay raise."

The New York City School-Wide Performance Bonus Program mentioned above may also have been undermined by its structure. Some 180 schools were eligible in the 2007–08 school year for a collective $14 million in bonuses, or $3,000 per union teacher, if they met test score goals established by the district. In a key factor that enabled the plan to draw union support, committees composed of a principal, a person of the principal's choosing, and two union representatives were allowed to decide how the bonuses should be distributed at any given school. Researchers identified a number of drawbacks to the program design, including the possibility that bonuses based on school-wide improvements weaken the incentives for individual teachers to increase their efforts.

Making Merit Pay Work

The prospects for merit pay are not promising, despite both theoretical and empirical reasons for expecting that the programs would produce positive results for students. Our findings are consistent with the theory that school districts are not primarily educational institutions where policies are organized around maximizing student achievement. Instead, they are best understood, at least when it comes to compensation policies, as political entities shaped by powerful interest groups, including organized groups of employees.

Viewed in that light, it is unsurprising that public school systems have relatively little interest in authentic merit-pay programs. If some teachers could earn improvements in their wages and working conditions from their own efforts rather than from the efforts of their organized representatives or affiliated politicians, then more-effective teachers would have little reason to support the unions financially or politically. Their interests would be at odds with those of less-effective teachers. In short, the single salary schedule by which almost all public school teachers are paid is essential to the financial and political power of established interests.

One way to diminish the power of established interests and permit the adoption and implementation of merit pay is to expand choice and competition in education. If students choose their school, those schools have incentives to adopt and implement policies and practices that will improve their quality and attract students as well as the resources they generate. If merit pay systems help attract and motivate effective teachers, schools in a more competitive environment will have incentives to adopt those systems. They are more likely to design and maintain merit pay systems in a sensible way, since their revenue depends on it.

Schools that already compete for students appear more open to including merit pay in their personnel policies. According to University of Washington's Daniel Goldhaber and his colleagues, charter schools are more likely than traditional public schools to use merit pay. Michael Podgursky, professor of economics at the University of Missouri, looked at data from the 1999–2000 Schools and Staffing Survey and found that when school administrators were asked whether they used salaries to reward "excellence," only 6 percent of traditional public school administrators answered yes, while "the rates for charter (36 percent) and private schools (22 percent) were much higher." Even those charter and private schools without a formal performance-pay plan are typically able to offer higher salaries to teachers they hope to retain and, as important, to readily dismiss teachers deemed ineffective.

Attaching continued employment and level of compensation to job performance is something that frequently occurs among private enterprises in competitive markets. The difficulty with merit pay in education is that it attempts to simulate a market-based practice in a nonmarket environment. None of the forces that cause organizations to seek effective merit pay systems, or to maintain and alter them effectively over time, exist in public education.

Imposing merit pay on an unwilling education system is like trying to get kids to eat their vegetables when the kids are 25 years old and stronger than their parents. No matter how nutritious green beans may be, powerful adults who don't want to eat them can usually keep them off their plates and can almost always keep them out of their mouths.

POSTSCRIPT

Can Merit Pay Accelerate School Improvement?

After the Soviet Union's challenge to America's technological superiority manifested itself in the late 1950s, financial incentives were given to present and recruited teachers of math and science under a federal initiative. Currently, the "crisis" focus is on underperforming public schools located primarily in districts with high percentages of minority students. Some critics have made the argument that a maximum federal effort should be directed at schools with the greatest need in order to close the existing achievement gaps. This idea is elaborated upon by Cynthia D. Prince in "Attracting Well-Qualified Teachers to Struggling Schools," *American Educator* (Winter 2002). "Today," she explains, "both the ATF [American Federation of Teachers] and the NEA [National Education Association] favor offering locally-developed financial incentives to qualified teachers who choose to work in hard-to-staff schools."

In "The Teacher Shortage: A Case of Wrong Diagnosis and Wrong Prescription," *NASSP Bulletin* (June 2002), Richard M. Ingersoll offers an analysis of reasons why large numbers of qualified teachers are departing their jobs for reasons other than retirement. In "Why Are Experienced Teachers Leaving the Profession?" *Phi Delta Kappan* (September 2002), Barbara Benham Tye and Lisa O'Brien report on their survey of teachers who have already left the profession and those who are considering leaving. They found that those who had left ranked the pressure of increased accountability (high-stakes testing and standards) as the number one reason. Salary considerations ranked seventh. Of those who were considering leaving, however, salary considerations ranked first.

A stinging indictment of merit pay can be found in Maurice Holt's "Performance Pay for Teachers: The Standards Movement's Last Stand?" *Phi Delta Kappan* (December 2001). In it, Holt states, "Having done their best to demoralize schools and give the phrase 'testing to destruction' a new meaning, there's one last aspect of civilized education that the Standardistos have in their sights: the sense of trust and cooperation among teachers." Their ammunition: "competitive salary structures."

Further resources on the topic of merit pay for teachers include Lawrence Hardy, "What's a Teacher Worth?" *American School Board Journal* (August 2002); . . . Cynthia D. Prince, "Higher Pay in Hard-to-Staff Schools: The Case for Financial Incentives," *The School Administrator* (June 2002); . . . Sam Coleman, "Fault Lines in Merit Pay," *Rethinking Schools* (Summer 2008); and Jacob Vigdot, "Scrap the Sacrosanct Salary Schedule," *Education Next* (Fall 2008).

ISSUE 17

Are Single-Sex Schools and Classes Effective?

YES: Peter Meyer, from "Learning Separately: The Case for Single-Sex Schools," *Education Next* (Winter 2008)

NO: Vincent A. Anfara, Jr. and Steven B. Mertens, from "Do Single-Sex Classes and Schools Make a Difference?" *Middle School Journal* (November 2008)

ISSUE SUMMARY

YES: Journalist Peter Meyer examines the history of single-sex schools and recent concerns about "shortchanging" girls and the "crisis" in boys' education and lauds the current resurgence of single-sex schooling.

NO: Associate professor of education Vincent A. Anfara, Jr. and assistant professor of education Steven B. Mertens review research on student culture, academic climate, and attitudinal effects, concluding that the benefits of single-sex schooling remain unclear.

Gender has always been a factor in education policies and practices, both in the United States and around the world, both historically and today. Thomas Jefferson, our first "education president" deemed it appropriate to recommend three years of schooling for females to prepare them for marriage and motherhood. "Domestic arts" and "home economics" were for many decades cornerstones of the education of girls. Law schools and medical schools were predominantly male preserves historically. As recently as 1970 less than 1 percent of medical and law degrees were earned by women. The Title IX provisions passed by Congress in 1972, prohibiting discrimination on the basis of gender, opened the door of opportunity for women in professional preparation and athletic endeavors.

The 1992 study sponsored by the American Association of University Women, "How Schools Shortchange Girls," found pervasive gender bias in textbooks and classroom procedures that limited the development of girls' potential. Shortly afterward, two books, *Failing at Fairness: How America's Schools Cheat Girls* by Myra and David Sadker and Judy Mann's *The Difference: Growing*

Up Female in America, provided ideological and research-based support for the AAUW findings. Education historian Diane Ravitch at the time conceded that a gender bias is embedded in the popular culture but contended that since great strides have been made to redress patterns of historical discrimination in the schools federal gender equity legislation is not needed.

More recently attention has been paid to the ways in which boys are victimized during their school experiences. In 2000, Christina Hoff Sommers, in her book *The War Against Boys: How Misguided Feminism Is Harming Our Young Men*, declared that the typical boy is behind the typical girl in reading and writing, is less committed to school, and is less likely to go to college. In early 2006, *Newsweek* magazine featured a cover story on "The Boy Crisis," claiming that at every level of schooling boys are falling behind. Brain researcher Michael Gurian, author of *Boys and Girls Learn Differently* and *The Mind of Boys*, claims that boys make up 90 percent of discipline referrals, 70 percent of learning disabled children, and two-thirds of children on behavioral medication.

The most recent wrinkle in the on-going concern about gender factors in schooling is the movement toward single-sex classes and single-sex schools. New regulations issued by the U. S. Department of Education in 2006 have clarified the legal status of this approach. This makes it easier to establish single-sex schools than to form single-sex classes within co-educational facilities and it exempts charter schools from all stipulated requirements. A major force in the campaign to expand single-sex instruction is the National Association for Single-Sex Public Education headed by Dr. Leonard Sax. The most vocal opposition has come from the American Civil Liberties Union, the National Organization for Women, and the American Association of University Women. Emily Martin of the ACLU Women's Rights Project has said that the new regulations contradict Title IX which prohibits exclusion on the basis of gender alone. She states that schools may now "separate girls and boys for virtually any reason . . . including outdated and dangerous gender stereotypes."

Leonard Sax, in "Single-Sex Education: Ready for Prime Time," *The World & I* (August 2002), states that it is a new era in American education, that for the first time in our history an explicit legal provision exists affirming the value of single-sex schooling. Rosemary Salomone, author of *Same, Different, Equal* (2005), says that families of all incomes should at least have the option of one-sex schools. In *Successful Single-Sex Classrooms* (2009), Michael Gurian contends that such classrooms allow teachers to construct a brain-friendly environment for both boys and girls.

Among the basic concerns of the opposition are the conflict with the "separate educational facilities are inherently unequal" principle, the lack of supportive research, and the perpetuation of sex stereotyping.

In the following articles Meyer presents his arguments for single-sex education and Anfara and Mertens raise crucial points of caution.

Learning Separately: The Case for Single-Sex Schools

Susan Vincent reached into the cage and pulled out a small yellow bird, saying, "This is Kiwi. He loved us, but he was lonely." It is a lovely spring day in Spanish Harlem on the Upper East Side of Manhattan and Vincent, a former children's clothing designer turned award-winning high-school science teacher, is explaining some facts about the facts of life. "We had to get Kiwi a mate. It was a perfect way for the girls to learn something about nature, about birds, about"—she smiles, holding little Kiwi up—"about the birds and the bees."

It was, as they say in the field, "a teachable moment." And for Vincent it was much more teachable because all of her 10th-grade students were girls. "There was no giggling and whispering, no holding back," she recalls. "The girls gathered round and we talked about the mating habits of birds and they asked good questions and learned a lot. Boys would have been a big distraction."

It seems so logical. Separate boys and girls so they can get their work done. It was clear to me and my classmates 40 years ago, as we gazed out the window during English class in our all-boys high school (a Catholic seminary) and watched the teenage kids from town "making out" on a stone wall; at least it was clear to Father Ignatius, who would threaten a "bastinado with salt rubbed in the wounds" if we didn't focus on the sentence that needed diagramming.

"We can concentrate a lot better without boys," is a comment I heard dozens of times in the course of researching this story. Boys seem less sure of the benefits. "Yeah, it's okay," says a student at the private all-boys Roxbury Latin School, outside of Boston. . . . But the headmaster, Kerry Brennan, is certain: "Young men are able to focus much more ably on academics without the girls."

Rosemary Salomone, professor of law at St. John's University and author of the 2003 book *Same, Different, Equal: Rethinking Single-Sex Schooling,* agrees: "Many students in single-sex classes report feeling more comfortable raising their hands and expressing uncertainty regarding a lesson or topic without fear of embarrassment or teasing from the opposite sex."

The fact that researchers like Salomone are talking about single-gender education represents a sea change in attitudes—and policies and practices, a change that was formalized by the historic rewriting of Title IX of the federal Education Amendments in 2006. The new rules give local districts the option of offering single-gender public schools and programs for the first time in more than 30 years. The regulations permit single-sex classrooms when districts "provide a rationale," "provide a coeducational class" as well, and "conduct a review every two years." Districts may operate a single-sex school as long as they provide equal services either in a coed school or a school for the opposite gender. Charter schools are exempt from all restrictions. Prior to these changes, educators lived in a vague legal world, at the mercy of a Supreme Court decision (the 1996 Virginia Military Institute [VMI] case, *United States v. Virginia*), which required an "exceedingly persuasive justification" of anyone wanting to set up single-sex schools or classes.

As late as 1990, James Coleman remarked that that it was considered suspect to even study the question of single-sex schooling. The famous University of Chicago sociologist noted that there were times when "a societal consensus" dictates that "one institution is *right*" and, he concluded, "coeducation is such an institution."

At the time, Coleman was writing to introduce a pioneering book on the subject, *Girls and Boys in School: Together or Separate?* by Providence College sociologist Cornelius Riordan. The questions Riordan was asking—"just what are the consequences of single-sex and coeducational schools for those who pass through them? Specifically, what are the intellectual consequences, the psychological consequences, and the social consequences?"—had not been asked, or answered, before. Coleman attributed the research failure to "the force of conventional values." Riordan's research compared outcomes for graduates of single-sex Catholic schools with those for graduates of coed Catholic schools. He found that single-sex schooling helps to improve academic achievement, with benefits greater for girls than boys, and that underprivileged children derived the most benefit. His book concluded that we had to "give students some measure of access to single-sex education."

Going, Going, All but Gone

While there are no reliable counts of single-gender schools in the first half of the 20th century, best estimates are that most were schools for white boys. Many of the girls' schools that did exist early on served as "finishing" schools rather than preparation for college. Coleman wrote, "Single-sex school was, at the outset, schooling for boys. Schooling for girls was an afterthought, either in single-sex institutions of their own, or with boys, where small numbers made single-sex institutions inefficient. Boys' schools, however, were dominant, and the elimination of single-sex schooling could be seen as elimination of that dominance."

In the 1960s and 1970s, the civil rights and feminist movements combined their equality crusade fervor to "open" previously exclusive men's schools to women, and white schools to blacks. Public single-gender schools were all but eliminated in the process. Boston Latin, one of the oldest and most prestigious public schools in America, succumbed to coeducation in 1972, the same year that Congress passed Title IX mandating equal education for the sexes. Central High School in Philadelphia, founded in 1838, may have been the last all-boys public school in America when it finally went coed in 1983.

Although insulated from laws governing public schools, private schools felt the pressure as well, and many single-gender institutions, often fighting for economic survival, opened their doors to both sexes after 1970. For example, the Nichols School for boys in Buffalo, founded in 1892, accepted girls in 1973. Tabor Academy in Marion, Massachusetts, began in 1876 with male and female students, was a school for boys by the 1950s, and became coed again in 1979.

Yale went coed (in 1969), as did dozens of colleges and universities. The wave of coeducation sentiment was intense: even institutions that had arisen to offer women opportunity they couldn't get in a man's world were closed. In barely more than two decades, from 1960 to 1980, over half of the 268 women-only colleges in America closed, and many others went coed. By 1993, according to the National Institute on Postsecondary Education, Libraries, and Lifelong Learning, there were just 83 women-only colleges.

"Single-sex schooling seemed to be dying a slow but certain death," writes Salomone. Coeducational institutions were considered "more socially appropriate, liberating, and enlightened."

There was ample evidence to justify feminists' skepticism about single-gender education, since for many decades (even centuries) such schooling was meant only to reinforce gender stereotypes and prejudices. "Only in recent decades have societies seriously begun to unlock the full potential of girls," wrote David Von Drehle in *Time* magazine last summer, "but the cultivation of boys has been an obsession for thousands of years."

Tinkering Around the Coed Edges

Once single-sex schools were knocked out of the ring, the gender fights occurred almost exclusively inside the coed arena. The American Association of University Women (AAUW) published a series of studies in the 1990s called *Shortchanging Girls, Shortchanging America,* which highlighted the fact that girls aged 9 to 15 suffered from lower self-esteem, less willingness to stand up for their views with teachers, and lower interest in science and mathematics than boys. The AAUW report sparked an intense national debate, with its findings that girls were disadvantaged in classrooms by, among many inequities, being called upon less frequently and encouraged less than male students.

Great efforts were made to make schools more girl-friendly—introducing new math and science curricula and teaching methods, for example—which seemed to succeed only in creating a "boys crisis." "[B]oys rather than girls are now on the short end of the gender gap in many secondary school outcomes," said Cornelius Riordan in 2000. "Currently, boys are less likely than girls to be in an academic (college preparatory) curriculum. They have lower educational and occupational expectations, have lower reading and writing test scores, and expect to complete their schooling at an earlier age". . . .

The problem has gotten so far out of hand—schools have become, some argue, anti-boy—that *Time* put Von Drehle's report on the cover with the provocative headline, "The Myth About Boys." The writer paints a bleak picture of the state of boys in our current school system. He recounts meeting Christina

Hoff Sommers, author of *The War Against Boys*. "She ticked through a familiar, but disturbing indictment," Von Drehle writes. "More boys than girls are in special education classes. More boys than girls are prescribed mood-managing drugs. This suggests to her (and others) that today's schools are built for girls, and boys are becoming misfits."

In *Same, Different, Equal,* Rosemary Salomone concludes, "The data demonstrate that the prevailing system of education (overwhelmingly mixed-sex) is failing boys as well as girls, if in different ways, regardless of resource allocations."

Back from the Brink

Initial efforts to revive single-gender public education were done in by "conventional values," buttressed by what was then a sturdy Title IX ethos. "During the early 1990s a number of school leaders tried to set up single-sex schools or single-sex classes," Riordan recalls. "That was happening in Detroit, in Ventura, California, in Rochester, and other places. In all of those cases—it was a sad story—they were driven out or shut down by principals and teachers and parents. The one in Detroit went to court, but for the most part they were shut down by political pressure and threats of legal action."

Both Riordan and Salomone say 1996 was a turning point in the single-gender school wars. In June of that year, the Supreme Court declared VMI's all-male admissions policy unconstitutional while noting the advantages of single-gender education. All the justices—from Ruth Bader Ginsburg to Antonin Scalia—agreed that single-sex education offers positive educational benefits. In writing the majority opinion, Justice Ginsburg, a long and tireless advocate for gender equality, noted that "single-sex education affords pedagogical benefits to at least some students" and concluded, "that reality is uncontested in this litigation."

A few weeks after the Supreme Court ruling, Community School District 4 in New York City announced the opening of The Young Women's Leadership School (TYWLS) in East Harlem. . . . While it was the VMI case that got most of the nation's attention by seeming to strike a final blow against single-gender schooling in the United States, TYWLS seems to have won the day. The girls' school now has two schools in Queens, and one each in the Bronx and Philadelphia.

"Twenty years ago, all-girl schools seemed headed for extinction, a footnote in the story of American education," writes Ilana DeBare, author of *Where Girls Come First,* an account of public and private schools for girls going back into the 1800s. "Today they are experiencing an extraordinary renaissance. Between 1991 and 2001, more than 30 new girls' schools opened throughout the United States from Harlem to Silicon Valley, Atlanta to Seattle."

According to Leonard Sax, executive director of the National Association for Single Sex Public Education, in 1995 there were just 3 single-gender public schools in the United States; by 2007 there were 86, with an additional 277 public schools offering all-girls or all-boys education programs within their coeducational buildings.

This reversal of fortune has been spurred in part by "a growing body of research that single-gender, especially at the middle school level, works," says South Carolina Superintendent of Education Jim Rex, who campaigned on a platform that included making single-gender schools an option in every school district in the state.

Kathy Piechura-Couture, a professor at the Institute for Educational Reform at Stetson University in Deland, Florida, has studied children at the Woodward elementary school in Deland, which has had separate classes for boys and girls for three years. She concluded that boys and girls are different enough that they demand, or should be offered, separate schools. "We looked at gain scores and concluded that there is a significant difference for boys when put in separate classes," says Piechura-Couture. Over the years, she explains, other researchers have discovered a significant number of differences between boys and girls that affect their learning abilities at any given time. "Girls have better hearing than boys, for instance," she says. "So, if you have a room full of girls you don't have to yell."

A research review undertaken by the American Institutes for Research in 2005 culled the most reliable studies from a decade of research on single-sex education. Most of the research had been done on Catholic schools and more on girls' schools than on schools for boys. The review found that roughly one-third of studies favored single-sex schools on measures of short-term academic accomplishment. The researchers characterized most of the remainder as finding no difference or having null findings. They found little support, however, for coeducational schooling being more effective. This, argue proponents of single-sex schools, suggests that parents should at least be given a choice.

More Is Equal

The resurgence of single-sex schooling has also been the result of hard-fought battles to recapture the benefits of difference and take advantage of educational choice. The rewriting of Title IX addressed confusion created by the restrictions in the original 1972 statute and the support for single-sex education in the No Child Left Behind Act of 2001. Among proponents of the changes were Senators Hillary Clinton, Kay Bailey Hutchison, and Dianne Feinstein—women who have arrived, both Clinton and Feinstein via single-sex schools. Senator Hutchison, a product of coed schooling, in a 2001 *American University Law Review* article wrote, "Talk to students and graduates of single-sex schools (mostly private or parochial), and almost all will say with gusto that they were enriched and strengthened by their experience. . . . Study after study has demonstrated that girls and boys in single-sex schools are academically more successful and ambitious than their coeducational counterparts. Minority students in single-sex schools often show dramatic improvements in attitudes toward school, greater interest among girls in math and science, and dramatically fewer behavior problems."

It is true, as Salomone says, that sometimes "same is equal," other times "different is equal," and still other times, "more is equal." Part of what single-sex schools do is redress historic and historical inequities; another part is minimizing the distractions that come from mixing the sexes; and a final ingredient is addressing gender differences in learning. James Coleman, who died in 1995, probably would have appreciated the cultural shifts that have made the single-sex school take on new meaning, since he was one of the first modern academics to propose that coed schools offered a false promise of equality. As those who have studied the racial educational gaps in our public elementary and secondary schools have noticed, throwing children together does not solve the problems of dominance; it can, in fact, exacerbate them. The two notions of peer effects—race and gender—have been joined as more and more attention is being paid to "black boys" and schools that cater to them. That is surely what Tom Carroll, chairman of the Brighter Choice Charter Schools in Albany, New York, has proved. . . . Increasingly, the single-sex school movement is seen, as Martin Luther King III told an Albany audience celebrating Brighter Choice, as a means of "liberation—liberation from prejudice, liberation from socially imposed limitations, and liberation of the dignity, capabilities, and potential for excellence that dwells in the heart of every human being." Choice is opportunity. The choice of single-sex education is affirmative action for the sexes.

In a front-page story, the *New York Times* called the 2006 amendments to Title IX "the most significant policy change on the issue" in more than 30 years. The decision, of course, came with what Martin Davis of the Thomas B. Fordham Institute characterized as "a flood of criticisms from women's groups and some civil rights organizations." But the dire predictions about the resegregation of public schools and turning back the clock on civil rights gains for women never materialized. And while various groups threatened legal actions, none have materialized. It is a new world, especially for women, and serious educators seem to realize that single-sex schools and classrooms are not a threat, but another arrow in the quiver of education quality.

. . .

Vincent A. Anfara, Jr.
and Steven B. Mertens

→ **NO**

Do Single-Sex Classes and Schools Make a Difference?

Until the late 19th century, education in the United States was single-sex education. Coeducation gradually entered the American educational landscape in the late 1800s (Bureau of Education, 1883; Butler, 1910; Kolesnik, 1969), and since that time, single-sex education mainly has been confined to private and denominational (mostly Catholic) schools. According to Tyack and Hansot (1990) and Hawtrey (1896), economic factors were the major impetus for the rising "tide of coeducation." Simply put, it was cheaper to educate boys and girls together than to operate separate schools, which would have required duplicating expensive facilities, equipment, and personnel. Feminists of the day also valued coeducation as a necessary step in the women's rights movement and their influence contributed to the passage of Title IX of the Education Amendments of 1972, aimed at guaranteeing gender equity in federally financed schools, colleges, and universities. Finally, coeducation was considered "natural" in that it facilitated the development of positive relations with members of the opposite sex, allowed boys and girls the opportunity to learn to work together, and was conducive to happier marriages (Atherton, 1972; Hale, 1929).

In the second half of the 19th century, William Harris, superintendent of the St. Louis schools and later U.S. Commissioner of Education, argued that mixing the sexes improved instruction and discipline for boys and girls by merging their different abilities and allowing students of each gender to serve as a "countercheck" on the other (Harris, 1870). As we have seen with most educational reforms and innovations, the fanfare that welcomed coeducation very soon led to concerns and indictments. In his book, *Sex in Education,* Clarke (1873) purported that academic competition with boys overloaded girls' brains and interfered with the development of their reproductive organs.

Single-sex education (also less frequently called single gender and SS) garnered renewed interest in the 1990s from researchers, advocacy groups, and policymakers; and since 2003, there has been an extraordinary surge in interest in single-sex public education. The new regulations, issued by the U.S. Department of Education on October 25, 2006, fueled the fire of this renewed interest. Secretary Spellings, commenting on the "final rule," noted that

> Research shows that some students may learn better in single-sex education environments. The Department of Education is committed to giving

Anfara, V.A., & Mertens, S. B. (2008). Do Single-Sex Classes and Schools Make a Difference? *Middle School Journal,* 40(2), 52–59. Reprinted with permission from National Middle School Association.

communities more choice as to how they go about offering varied learning environments to their students. These final regulations permit communities to establish single-sex schools and classes as another means of
meeting the needs of students. (U.S. Department of Education, 2006)

Assessing the relative advantages and disadvantages of single-sex classes
and schools is difficult. As single-sex education gains interest and appeal, educators, policymakers, and advocates continue to search for research evidence
to legitimize this approach to improving student outcomes (e.g., academic,
behavioral, social, attendance, self-esteem). While this review of the research
will not be limited solely to middle grades schools, many of the studies that are
reviewed were conducted in middle grades schools. Considerable exploration
of single-sex education has occurred in the realm of legal and political issues,
but there has been comparatively little examination of student outcomes and
other educational implications. Salomone (2006), recognizing the problematic and inconclusive nature of this research literature, noted that most of
the research originates from private and denominational schools and from
abroad and tends to be anecdotal reports and scattered studies that lack scientific rigor. This installment of *What Research Says* will focus on what we currently know about single-sex education. Specifically, it will critically review in
relation to single-sex education (a) what proponents and critics claim, (b) what
researchers say about school culture and academic climate, (c) the attitudinal
effects, (d) academic issues, and (e) problems with the research.

The Proponents and Critics of Single-Sex Programs Speak

Proponents of single-sex education cite a variety of reasons such classes or
schools would be more appropriate than coeducational schools. These reasons are supported to some extent by experiential knowledge, ideological
beliefs, and data and include (a) the "boy crisis," (b) biological differences,
(c) achievement gaps, and (d) distractions. While concerns were expressed in
the late 1990s about short-changing girls, especially in regard to mathematics,
science, and technology classes, evidence began to surface that documented
a "boy crisis." This crisis was characterized by lower scores by males on the
National Assessment of Educational Progress (National Center for Educational
Statistics, 2005), higher dropout and suspension rates for boys (Mead, 2006), a
higher incidence of classification of learning disabilities, and lower test-taking
rates on assessments like the SAT and ACT. In the realm of biological research,
advances in brain-based research highlighted the fact that boys and girls are
"wired" differently which supported the contention that they should receive
differentiated educational experiences to meet their special needs. In support
of biological differences, Salomone (2006) stated,

> We know that girls, as a group, enter school with more advanced verbal
> and fine-motor skills, have longer attention spans, and greater impulse
> control. This . . . puts many young boys at a disadvantage in the lower

grades. At the same time, boys tend to have more advanced visual-spatial skills through much of schooling, which puts them at an advantage in math and science. (p. 787)

Another reason to consider single-sex education relates to the achievement gap that exists between the performance of boys and girls. Frequently, the focus of this achievement gap is on the educational needs of a targeted group of students like African American and Hispanic males. Finally, removing distractions by dividing the sexes has been offered as an argument in favor of single-sex education. Gurian and Henley (2001) asked teachers to discuss their experiences in single-sex classes and schools and were told that fewer discipline problems were evident. Ferrara and Ferrara (2004), studying a New York middle school, found that participation was more widespread and students were less self-conscious in single-sex classes. Bracey (2006) added some additional reasons for implementing single-sex educational programs, including: (a) improving girls self-esteem, confidence, and leadership skills; (b) increasing attention to pedagogically significant gender differences, particularly those found through brain research; and (c) controlling the behavior of boys.

Some critics of single-sex education note that separate is always "inherently unequal." They take this phrase from the famous *Brown v. Board of Education* decision. Greenberger, from the National Women's Law Center, characterized single-sex education as "an invitation to discriminate" (cited in Green, 2006, online). The National Coalition for Women and Girls in Education also expressed opposition to single-sex education and wrote,

> Single-sex education does not guarantee improved schools. Rather, the elements that enable children to succeed in single-sex education can be replicated in coeducational settings. These elements include a focus on core academics, small class size, qualified teachers, sufficient funding, and parental involvement. (2002, online)

Additional concerns deal with the limited opportunities for male and female students to work together and socialize, the potential for limited course offerings with honors and AP courses usually not being offered in single-sex schools, and the possibility for teasing to occur. Datnow, Hubbard, and Woody (2001) noted that students in their study reported "a significant amount of teasing . . . and being labeled as bad kids, or preppy, or . . . gay" (p. 7).

The Research

For most of the 20th century there has been little interest for researchers in the United States to study the effects of single-sex schooling in contrast to coeducational setting. Single-sex schooling was a perfectly legitimate option, but one that mainly existed within the context of private and denominational schools. Jill (1993) commented that the findings on single-sex education are a mix of "passionate conviction and rather ambiguous research results" (p. 90). While this certainly seems to be an accurate characterization, what is indisputable is that research about the merits of single-sex classrooms and schools has an international flavor. Researchers in England and Wales (Bell, 1989; Byrne, 1993; Dean, 1998; Gorard, 1998), South Africa (Lee & Lockheed, 1990; Mallam, 1993), the United States (Kumagai, 1995; Lee & Marks, 1992; LePore & Warren, 1997), New Zealand (Harker & Nash, 1997; Scott, 1991), and Australia (Smith, 1994; Willis & Kenway, 1986; Young & Fraser, 1992) have all added to the debate on the relative merit of single-sex education. Other countries, including Nigeria, Thailand, and Jamaica, have single-sex schools that have been researched.

Although most of the research has focused on the benefits for females, more recent attention has been given to the academic failure of males, particularly African American males. Research on single-sex education has sought to measure the effects of single-sex schooling on student outcomes like academic performance, self-esteem, attitudes toward academic subject matter, as well as students' preferences for single or coeducation schooling. Let us turn our attention to what we know about the relationship between single-sex schooling and these student outcomes.

Student Culture, Academic Climate, and Single-Sex Education

More than 40 years ago, sociologist James Coleman was one of the first researchers to question coeducational schools in the United States. In his book, *Adolescent Society,* he noted that "coeducation may be inimical to both academic achievement and social adjustment" for adolescents (1961, p. 51). After examining the value systems of adolescents in 10 secondary schools, he found that many more students would rather be good athletes or leaders in extracurricular activities than excellent students. He concluded that this "youth culture" (which he called a "cruel jungle of rating and dating," p. 51) exerted a negative influence on intellectual endeavors. From this conclusion it was determined that this coeducational environment was particularly harmful to girls, who were overly concerned about making themselves "desirable objects for boys" (p. 52). Twenty years later, John Goodlad, in *A Place Called School* (1984), agreed with Coleman's earlier assessment. While it must be acknowledged that much has changed in light of Title IX, researchers like Salomone (2003) claimed that most of what Coleman and Goodlad found is still true in high schools and middle schools today. What is important about this discussion is that these findings have resurfaced in recent years to support single-sex education, particularly for girls and minority boys. The argument is that, at least for some middle and high school students, coeducation fosters nonacademic values and heightens social pressures that distract students from the work of school. Studies conducted in New Zealand, Canada, and the United States (Jones, Shallcrass, & Dennis, 1972; Schneider & Counts, 1982) underscore the more academic orientation of single-sex schools and document more time spent on homework and a desire on the part of the students to be remembered for their academic abilities rather than their social popularity or involvement in extracurricular activities.

Attitudinal Effects and Single-Sex Schooling

A few published studies have investigated the hypothesis that girls in single-sex schools have higher self-esteem. Cairns (1990) investigated self-esteem for 2,295 students in 76 grammar and secondary schools in Northern Ireland. He concluded that single-sex schools provide benefits in terms of self-esteem. Supporting the opposite conclusion, Foon (1988) surveyed 1,675 secondary students in private coeducational and single-sex schools in Australia and found no significant differences in self-esteem between girls from coeducational and single-sex schools, although she reported higher self-esteem for boys attending single-sex schools. In Belgium, Brutsaert and Bracke (1994) found that girls do not seem to be influenced by the gender organization of the school and that boys were negatively affected because of the preponderance of female teachers, who unwittingly contribute to lowering the boys' overall sense of well-being.

There is something of a consensus among researchers that girls in single-sex schools tend to perceive math and science classes as less "masculine," and, therefore, have stronger preferences for them. Vockell and Lobonc (1981) administered a questionnaire to 476 single-sex and 280 coeducational students in U.S. high schools. They found that girls in single-sex schools rated physical sciences as less masculine than did females in coeducational settings. In contrast, Stables (1990) studied 2,300 students (ages 13–14) and found no differences in the perception of subject importance by sex or school type. He concluded that single-sex schools reduce the polarization of attitudes between the sexes.

In regard to sex stereotyping, no consistent relationship has been found between school type and degree of sex stereotyping. Lee and Marks (1994) found that sex stereotyping occurs with as much frequency in single-sex schools as in coeducational environments. Gill (1996), studying single-sex schools in New Zealand, also noted that "teacher awareness is of much more significance than school gender context in producing or overcoming stereotypical gender limitations on students" (p. 17).

Supporters of single-sex schools and classes maintain that they offer girls a "safe place" for learning. Similar arguments hold that single-sex schools allow teachers to challenge students' gendered perceptions and enhance their self-confidence in nontraditional subjects. The evidence generated in the United States in support of these claims is largely anecdotal, with much being reported in the popular press and conference presentations. Research from abroad (e.g., Parker & Rennie, 1997), though, reports girls having more positive attitudes toward math, science, and technology, along with a higher level of comfort, in classes that do not contain boys. According to Leslie (1999), girls describe their experiences in single-sex classes as "freedom to excel without social pressure" (online). More generally, the research suggests that girls show personal growth through improved confidence (Arbor, 1998), a positive self-image (Lee, 1986), and higher self-esteem (Mael, 1998). In the classroom, girls take more risks (Streitmatter, 1997) and ask more questions (Stutler, 1997). They also show a great interest in academics (Lee, 1986) and an increased educational ambition (Lee, 1986). Boys also benefit from improved self-esteem (Mael, 1998) and tend to ask more questions in class (Arbor, 1998).

Academic Issues and Single-Sex Schooling

While girls tend to perceive single-sex classes and schools to be superior, there are a number of studies that point to the fact that these perceptions have not translated into improved academic performance for girls in single-sex schools. Among the studies that have been conducted, Rowe (1988) examined 398 middle school students in Australia and found no significant differences in mathematics achievement. These findings have been supported by the research of Leder and Forgasz (1994), Workman (1990), Young and Fraser (1992), and Harker and Nash (1997).

Some studies, though, do show gains in academic achievement. These include the work of Lee and Bryk (1986), Marsh (1989), Lee and Marks (1990), Riordan (1985), and Lee and Lockheed (1990). Riordan tested for differences between Catholic single-sex schools and public coeducational schools in relation to reading and math. He found that while Catholic single-sex schools scored consistently higher than coeducational public schools, Catholic coeducational schools differed little from public coeducational schools.

Problems with the Research

This corpus of research is not without problems. Findings conflict, as exemplified by studies done by Kenway (1995) and Sukhnandan, Lee, and Kelleher (2000). While Kenway reported that boys in mathematics classes were noisier in the classroom, spent less time on task, and complained about missing girls who could help them with their work, Sukhnandan, Lee, and Kelleher found that boys viewed single-sex classes positively and reported being more interested and motivated in their work and that the absence of girls helped improve confidence and involvement levels.

There are numerous studies, but few high-quality ones that use comparison groups, control for confounding variables, or use national databases. As an example, in 1999 a California middle school (referred to as Single Sex Academy or SSA, see Herr & Arms, 2004) opened with single-sex classes and is considered the largest experiment in single-sex schooling in the United States. It serves a low-income, urban population of students of color. It was described as "an elaborate experiment to determine whether adolescent boys and girls learn better if separated from one another" (Haynes, 1999). SSA was a reconstituted school that was under extreme pressure to improve the low ranking on the Academic Performance Index, primarily determined by student scores on standardized tests. With no staff development related to single-sex education, teachers were left to do the best they could. Herr and Arms concluded that although SSA was deemed to be a success supporting single-sex schooling, there is no way of actually attributing the improvement to the gender composition of the school. More likely, this improvement was due to substantial changes in curriculum and instruction and other variables related to being reconstituted.

In 2005, the United States Department of Education, along with the American Institute for Research, tried to weigh in on the topic, publishing a meta-analysis comparing single-sex and coeducational schools (U.S. Department of Education, 2005). The authors started with 2,221 citations, which yielded 40 usable studies. Of these 40 studies, 41% favored single-sex schools, 45% found negative effects, and 6% had mixed findings.

Many of the studies from outside the United States (e.g., England) raise concerns about internal validity due to selection bias. Single-sex schools in these studies and contexts traditionally involve private schools with brighter students from more privileged backgrounds. The schools are populated with students who self-select, and the schools engage in a process referred to as "academic weeding-out" (Salomone, 2003, p. 190). Lee and Lockheed (1990) called this validity threat a "social phenomenon and a statistical nuisance" (p. 228).

Conclusion

The benefits of single-sex schooling remain unclear (Harker, 2000; Warrington, 2002). The research comparing the merits of single-sex education and coeducation has not yielded definitive answers. In spite of this conclusion, in 2002 and again in 2004, the Bush administration signaled its intent to promote single-sex schools through the easing of a "rigid" interpretation of Title IX (Davis, 2002). Simply put, when a single-sex school works, we are not exactly sure why it works. The research seems to point in the direction of benefits for poor and minority students and girls. But the presumption in favor of coeducation is found in both the law and in the minds of most Americans.

Salomone (2003) noted that single-sex education has been ideologically tied to racial segregation, which, in effect, causes us to be more critical of it and demand far more of it than we do of other "uncertain" educational innovations. As single-sex education gains more interest and appeal, policymakers, educators, and advocates must continue to search for empirical findings to legitimize this departure from what is considered the "norm." What seems to get lost in the search for definitive evidence is that the exact nature and benefits of single-sex education are highly contextual. School characteristics (e.g., class size, percentage of male and female teachers), teaching styles and instructional practices, and the curriculum, among other factors, all have significant effects on students' achievement. It depends on the students, their backgrounds, abilities, and needs, and it also depends on what we are looking for as the desired outcome of this initiative. Findings about single-sex education must be viewed and interpreted with a healthy dose of caution. As a number of researchers (Jackson & Smith, 2000; Marsh & Rowe, 1996) cautioned, the better performance of students in single-sex classes and schools is mainly attributable to a plethora of factors like student ability, socioeconomic status, type of school (private vs. public), school characteristics (e.g., size, organizational structures), selection bias, and effective teaching. When these factors are controlled for, the academic differences between students in single-sex education and coeducational schools are neither significant nor conclusive (Lingard et al., 2001).

References

Arbor, A. (1998). Single-gender public schools. *The Education Digest, 63*(7), 54–57.

Atherton, B. F. (1972). Co-educational and single sex schooling and happiness of marriage. *Educational Research, 15,* 221–226.

Bell, J. F. (1989). A comparison of science performance and uptake by fifteen-year-old boys and girls in co-educational and single-sex schools. *Educational Studies,* 15(2), 193–203.

Bracey, G. W. (2006). *Separate but superior? A review of issues and data bearing on single-sex education* (EPSL-0611-221-EPRU). Tempe, AZ; Arizona State University, Education Policy Research Unit.

Brutsaert, H., & Bracke, P. (1994). Gender context in elementary school. *Educational Studies,* 20(1), 3, 10.

Bureau of Education. (1883). *Co-education of the sexes in the public schools of the U.S.A.* Washington, DC: United States Government Printing Office.

Butler, N. M. (Ed.). (1910). *Education in the United States.* New York: American Book Company.

Byrne, E. (1993). *Women and science: The shark syndrome.* London: Falmer Press.

Cairns, E. (1990). The relationship between adolescent perceived self-competence and attendance at single-sex secondary school. *British Journal of Educational Psychology, 60,* 207–211.

Clarke, E. H. (1873). *Sex in education.* Boston: Rand, Avery, and Company.

Coleman, J. S. (1961). *The adolescent society.* New York: The Free Press.

Datnow, A., Hubbard, L., & Woody, E. (2001). *Is single gender schooling viable in the public sector? Lessons from California's pilot program.* Retrieved June 28, 2008, from . . .

Davis, M. (2002). Department aims to promote single-sex schools. *Education Weekly, 21*(36), 24–25.

Dean, C. (1998, 27 November). Failing boys, public burden number one. *Times Educational Supplement,* p. 1.

Ferrara, P.J., & Ferrara, M. M. (2004, Summer). Single-gender classrooms: Lessons from a New York middle school. *ERS Spectrum,* 26–32.

Foon, A. (1988). The relationship between school type and adolescent self-esteem, attribution styles, and affiliation needs: implications for educational outcome. *British Journal of Educational Psychology, 58,* 44–54.

Gill, J. (1996, April). *Different contexts, similar outcomes.* Paper presented at the annual meeting of the American Educational Research Association, New York.

Goodlad, J. I. (1984). *A place called school.* New York: McGraw-Hill.

Gorard, S. (1998). Four errors . . . and a conspiracy? The effectiveness of schools in Wales. *Oxford Review of Education, 24*(4), 459–472.

Green, E. (2006, October 27). Are single-sex classrooms legal? *U.S. News and World Report.* Retrieved June 27, 2008, from . . .

Gurian, M., & Henley, P. (with Trueman, T.). (2001). *Boys and girls learn differently! A guide for teachers and parents.* San Francisco: Jossey-Bass.

Hale, B. F. (1929). A debate on coeducation. *Minnesota Chats, 11,* 7–9.

Harker, R. (2000). Achievement, gender and the single-sex/coed debate. *British Journal of the Sociology of Education, 21*(2), 203–218.

Harker, R., & Nash, R. (1997, March). *School type and the education of girls: Co-ed or girls only?* Paper presented at the annual meeting of the American Educational Research Association, Chicago.

Harris, W. T. (1870). *Sixteenth annual report* (1869–1870). St. Louis, MO: St. Louis Board of Education.

Haynes, V. D. (1999). Boys and girls in a class apart. *Chicago Tribune Internet Edition*. Retrieved June 30, 2008, from . . .

Hawtrey, M. (1896). *The coeducation of the sexes.* London: Kegan Paul, Trench, Trubner & Co.

Herr, K., & Arms, E. (2004). Accountability and single-sex schooling; A collision of reform agendas. *American Educational Research Journal, 41,* 527–555.

Jackson, C., & Smith, D. (2000). Poles apart? An exploration of single-sex and mixed-sex educational environments in Australia and England. *Educational Studies, 26*(4), 409–422.

Jill, J. (1993). Re-phrasing the question about single sex schooling. In A. Reid & B. Johnson (Eds.), *Critical issues in Australian education in the 1990s* (pp. 90–99). Adelaide, Australia: Centre for Studies in Educational Leadership, University of South Australia.

Jones, J. C., Shallcrass, J., & Dennis, C. C. (1972). Coeducation and adolescent values. *Journal of Educational Psychology, 63*(4), 334–341.

Kenway, J. (1995). Masculinities in schools; Under siege, on the defensive and under reconstruction? *Discourse: Studies in the Cultural Politics of Education, 16,* 59–79.

Kolesnik, W. B. (1969). *Co-education: Sex differences and the schools.* New York: Vantage Press.

Kumagai, J. (1995). Do single-sex classes help girls achieve in physics? *Physics Today, 48,* 73–74.

Leder, G., & Forgasz, H. (1994, April). *Single-sex mathematics classes in a co-educational setting: A case study.* Paper presented at the annual meeting of the American Educational Research Association, New Orleans, LA.

Lee, V. E. (1986). Effects of single-sex secondary schools on student achievement and attitudes. *Journal of Educational Psychology, 78*(5), 381–395.

Lee, V. E., & Bryk, A. (1986). Effects of single-sex secondary schools on student achievement and attitudes. *Journal of Educational Psychology, 78*(5), 381–395.

Lee, V. E., & Lockheed, M. M. (1990). The effects of single-sex schooling on achievement and attitudes in Nigeria. *Comparative Educational Review, 4*(2), 209–231.

Lee, V. E., & Marks, H. M. (1990). Sustained effects of the single-sex secondary school experience on attitudes, behaviors and values in college. *Journal of Educational Psychology, 82*(3), 578–592.

Lee, V. E., & Marks, H. M. (1992). Who goes where? Choice of single-sex and co-educational independent secondary schools. *Sociology of Education, 65,* 226–231.

Lee, V. E., & Marks, H. M. (1994). Sexism in single-sex and coeducational independent secondary school classrooms. *Sociology of Education, 67*(2), 92–120.

LePore, P. C., & Warren, I. R. (1997). A comparison of single-sex and co-educational Catholic secondary schooling: Evidence from the National Educational Longitudinal Study of 1988. *American Educational Research Journal, 34*(3), 485–511.

Leslie, C. (1999). Separate and unequal? *Newsweek.* Retrieved June 28, 2008, from . . .

Lingard, B., Ladwig, J., Mills, M., Bahr, M., Chant, D., Warry, M., Ailwood, J., Capeness, R., Christie, P., Gore, J., Hayes, D., & Luke, A. (2001). The Queensland school reform longitudinal study. Vols. 1 & 2. Brisbane: Educational Queensland.

Mael, F. A. (1998). Single-sex and coeducational schooling: Relationships to socioemotional and academic development. *Review of Educational Research, 68*(2), 101–129.

Mallam, W. A. (1993). Impact of school type and sex of the teacher in female students' attitudes toward mathematics in Nigerian secondary schools. *Educational Studies in Mathematics, 24*(2), 223–229.

Marsh, H. (1989). Effects of attending single-sex and coeducational high schools on achievement, attitudes, behaviors, and sex differences. *Journal of Educational Psychology, 81*(1), 70–85.

Marsh, H., & Rowe, K. (1996). The effects of single-sex and mixed-sex mathematics classes within a coeducational school: A reanalysis and comment. *Australian Journal of Education, 40*(2), 147–162.

Mead, S. (2006). *The truth about boys and girls.* Washington, DC: Education Sector.

National Center for Educational Statistics. (2005). *The nation's report card: NAEP 2004 trends in academic progress.* Washington, DC: U.S. Department of Education. Retrieved June 27, 2008, from . . .

National Coalition for Women and Girls in Education. (2002). *Single-sex notice of intent comments.* Retrieved June 19, 2008, from . . .

Parker, L. H., & Rennie, L. J. (1997). Teachers' perceptions of the implementation of single-sex classes in coeducation schools. *Australian Journal of Education, 41*(2), 119–133.

Riordan, C. (1985). Public and Catholic schooling: The effects of gender context policy. *American Journal of Education, 93*(4), 518–540.

Rowe, K. J. (1988). Single sex and mixed sex classes: The effects of class type on student achievement, confidence and participation in mathematics. *Australian Journal of Education, 32*(2), 180–202.

Salomone, R. C. (2003). *Same, different, and equal: Rethinking single-sex schooling.* New Haven, CT: Yale University Press.

Salomone, R. C. (2006). Single-sex programs: Resolving the research conundrum. *Teachers College Record, 108,* 778–802.

Schneider, F. W., & Counts, L. M. (1982). The high school environment: A comparison of coeducational and single-sex schools, *Journal of Educational Psychology, 4*(6), 898–906.

Scott, A. C. (1991). *A girls-only science class in a co-educational secondary school.* Unpublished master's thesis, Victoria University of Wellington, New Zealand.

POSTSCRIPT

Are Single-Sex Schools and Classes Effective?

A myriad of questions remain regarding the value of single-sex education. The ACLU has raised a number of crucial questions on the topic. One of the main concerns is that sex segregation encourages teachers to oversimplify the issue of learning style differences and to ignore the more nuanced needs of both boys and girls. This and other important aspects are explored in the ACLU publication "Boys' Brains v. Girls' Brains: What Sex Segregation Teaches Students" (May 19, 2008).

In "Teaching Boys and Girls Separately," in *The New York Times* (March 2, 2008), Elizabeth Weil presents a critical exploration of the claims put forth by Leonard Sax and Michael Gurian. She states that "despite a lack of empirical evidence, a cottage industry has emerged working the 'boys and girls are essentially different, so we should educate them differently' angle." The Gurian Institute, for example, has been quite successful commercially by producing best-selling books on learning differences and providing training sessions for teachers across the country. Meanwhile, noted expert David Sadker contends that very little research actually exists on single-sex schools and their effectiveness is a big educational question mark.

Further exploration of the gender issue and the arguments over single-sex instruction may be found in "Same-Sex Schools," *American School Board Journal* (November 2002), by Kathleen Vail; "No Girls Allowed," *NEA Today* (April 2006), by Mary Ellen Flannery; "Closing the Gender Gap—Again!" *Principal* (March/April 2005), by David Sadker and Karen Zittleman; "Separating the Sexes: A New Direction for Public Education?" *The Christian Science Monitor* (May 24, 2004), by Teresa Mendez; and "Single-Sex Schooling: Is It Simply a 'Class Act'?" *Gender & Education* (March 2006), by Georgina Tsolidis and Ian R. Dobson.

A number of provocative books have been written on the topic, including Michael Ruhlman's *Boys Themselves: A Return to Single-Sex Education* (1996), Karen Stabiner's *All Girls: Single-Sex Education and Why It Matters* (2002), Leonard Sax's *Boys Adrift: The Five Factors Driving the Growing Epidemic of Unmotivated Boys and Underachieving Young Men* (2007), and Pedro A. Noguera's *The Trouble with Black Boys—and Other Reflections on Race, Equity, and the Future of Public Education* (2008). Finally, an interesting treatment of the issue is presented by E. Thomas Ewing in "The Repudiation of Single-Sex Education," *American Educational Research Journal* (Winter 2006).

ISSUE 18

Can Zero Tolerance Violate Students Rights?

YES: Hon. David Souter, from Majority Opinion in *Safford Unified School District #1 v. Redding* (June 25, 2009)

NO: Hon. Clarence Thomas, from Dissenting Opinion in *Safford Unified School District #1 v. Redding* (June 25, 2009)

ISSUE SUMMARY

YES: Supreme Court justice David Souter, delivering the opinion of the Court, hold that school officials, in carrying out a zero-tolerance policy on drug possession, violated a student's Fourth Amendment right against unreasonable search and seizure when they included a strip search of the girl.

NO: Justice Clarence Thomas, in dissent, states that the majority opinion imposes too vague a standard on school officials and that it grants judges sweeping authority to second-guess measures those officials take to maintain discipline and ensure safety.

Approximately a decade ago, after the tragedy at Columbine, school systems across the nation introduced zero-tolerance policies aimed at the curtailment of harmful student behaviors. The initial focus of these policies was on the elimination of weapons but soon spread to restrictions on any type of drugs or medication, legal or illegal, doctor-prescribed or readily available in stores. By 2006 about 95% of schools in the United States had zero-tolerance policies and nearly half of them reported taking serious action against students, including expulsion, suspension, and transfer to an alternative school.

While many of the practices involved in the enforcement of these policies have been welcomed by all members of the school community insofar as they promoted a safer environment for learning, questions have been raised in recent years about the appropriateness of some actions of school officials. Authors exploring this issue include Randall R. Beger, "Expansion of Police Power in Public Schools and the Vanishing Rights of Students," *Social Justice* (Spring/Summer 2002); Mary Ann Manos, *Knowing Where to Draw the Line: Ethical and Legal Standards for Best Classroom Practice* (2006); Kris Axtman, "Why

Tolerance Is Fading for Zero Tolerance in Schools," *The Christian Science Monitor* (March 31, 2005); Bob Herbert, "6-Year-Olds Under Arrest," *The New York Times* (April 9, 2007); and Elizabeth Frost, "Zero Privacy: Schools Are Violating Students' Fourteenth Amendment Right of Privacy Under the Guise of Enforcing Zero-Tolerance Policies," *Washington Law Review* (May 2006).

Media attention to this issue has stirred public concern and parents of students subjected to allegedly unfair treatment by school officials have initiated lawsuits. Lawyers pursuing such cases have often used a precedent established in the 1969 Supreme Court ruling in *Tinker v. Des Moines Independent School District* that students in school are still "persons" under the Constitution and are therefore possessed of fundamental rights that the state must respect. Subsequent Supreme Court cases involving First and Fourth Amendment rights are reviewed by Nelda Cambron-McCabe in "Balancing Students' Constitutional Rights," *Phi Delta Kappan* (June 2009). She concludes that while the courts have granted school officials considerable latitude in maintaining a school environment conducive to learning they must also honor students' rights in the process. An excellent source on this historical problem of appropriate balance is *From Schoolhouse to Courthouse: The Judiciary's Role in American Education* (2009), edited by Joshua M. Dunn and Martin R. West. The current period of security guards, metal detectors, surveillance cameras, locker raids, and book bag searches has captured the attention of the ACLU and other concerned groups.

The question of how far school authorities can go in fulfilling zero-tolerance policies came to a head in the Supreme Court's recent ruling in *Safford Unified School District #1 v. Redding*, argued April 21, 2009 and decided June 25, 2009. The case involved what is characterized as a strip search of a 13-year-old middle school student, Savana Redding, accused of hiding ibuprofen tablets in violation of the school's no-tolerance policy on drugs that banned the possession even of nonprescription pain relievers without explicit permission. School officials claimed that they were on high alert because a student had nearly died the year before after taking medication brought to the school by a friend and that they had good reasons to be suspicious of Savana despite her honor roll grades and spotless disciplinary record. After the event, Savana never returned to Safford Middle School. The Supreme Court ruled in her favor.

In the excerpts from the 8-1 ruling presented below, Justice Souter details the bases for the judgment, which included protection of the school officials from further suits, although Justices Stevens and Ginsburg dissented on that point. Justice Thomas, agreeing with the school official immunity point, was the lone dissenter on the central ruling regarding the violation of the student's rights.

YES ⤶

Hon. David Souter

Strip Search Violates 14th Amendment

J USTICE SOUTER delivered the opinion of the Court.

The issue here is whether a 13-year-old student's Fourth Amendment right was violated when she was subjected to a search of her bra and underpants by school officials acting on reasonable suspicion that she had brought forbidden prescription and over-the-counter drugs to school. Because there were no reasons to suspect the drugs presented a danger or were concealed in her underwear, we hold that the search did violate the Constitution, but because there is reason to question the clarity with which the right was established, the official who ordered the unconstitutional search is entitled to qualified immunity from liability.

. . .

The events immediately prior to the search in question began in 13-year-old Savana Redding's math class at Safford Middle School one October day in 2003. The assistant principal of the school, Kerry Wilson, came into the room and asked Savana to go to his office. There, he showed her a day planner, unzipped and open flat on his desk, in which there were several knives, lighters, a permanent marker, and a cigarette. Wilson asked Savana whether the planner was hers; she said it was, but that a few days before she had lent it to her friend, Marissa Glines. Savana stated that none of the items in the planner belonged to her.

Wilson then showed Savana four white prescription-strength ibuprofen 400-mg pills, and one over-the-counter blue naproxen 200-mg pill, all used for pain and inflammation but banned under school rules without advance permission. He asked Savana if she knew anything about the pills. Savana answered that she did not. Wilson then told Savana that he had received a report that she was giving these pills to fellow students; Savana denied it and agreed to let Wilson search her belongings. Helen Romero, an administrative assistant, came into the office, and together with Wilson they searched Savana's backpack, finding nothing.

At that point, Wilson instructed Romero to take Savana to the school nurse's office to search her clothes for pills. Romero and the nurse, Peggy Schwallier, asked Savana to remove her jacket, socks, and shoes, leaving her in stretch pants and a T-shirt (both without pockets), which she was then asked to remove. Finally, Savana was told to pull her bra out and to the side

From Supreme Court of the United States, June 25, 2009.

and shake it, and to pull out the elastic on her underpants, thus exposing her breasts and pelvic area to some degree. No pills were found.

Savana's mother filed suit against Safford Unified School District #1, Wilson, Romero, and Schwallier for conducting a strip search in violation of Savana's Fourth Amendment rights. The individuals (hereinafter petitioners) moved for summary judgment, raising a defense of qualified immunity. The District Court for the District of Arizona granted the motion on the ground that there was no Fourth Amendment violation, and a panel of the Ninth Circuit affirmed. . . .

A closely divided Circuit sitting en banc, however, reversed. Following the two-step protocol for evaluating claims of qualified immunity, . . . the Ninth Circuit held that the strip search was unjustified under the Fourth Amendment test for searches of children by school officials set out in *New Jersey* v. *T. L. O.*, . . . (1985). . . . The Circuit then applied the test for qualified immunity, and found that Savana's right was clearly established at the time of the search: " '[t]hese notions of personal privacy are "clearly established" in that they inhere in all of us, particularly middle school teenagers, and are inherent in the privacy component of the Fourth Amendment's proscription against unreasonable searches'" . . . . The upshot was reversal of summary judgment as to Wilson, while affirming the judgments in favor of Schwallier, the school nurse, and Romero, the administrative assistant, since they had not acted as independent decisionmakers. . . .

. . .

The Fourth Amendment "right of the people to be secure in their persons . . . against unreasonable searches and seizures" generally requires a law enforcement officer to have probable cause for conducting a search. "Probable cause exists where 'the facts and circumstances within [an officer's] knowledge and of which [he] had reasonably trustworthy information [are] sufficient in themselves to warrant a man of reasonable caution in the belief that' an offense has been or is being committed," . . . and that evidence bearing on that offense will be found in the place to be searched.

In *T. L. O.*, we recognized that the school setting "requires some modification of the level of suspicion of illicit activity needed to justify a search," . . . and held that for searches by school officials "a careful balancing of governmental and private interests suggests that the public interest is best served by a Fourth Amendment standard of reasonableness that stops short of probable cause" . . . . We have thus applied a standard of reasonable suspicion to determine the legality of a school administrator's search of a student, . . . and have held that a school search "will be permissible in its scope when the measures adopted are reasonably related to the objectives of the search and not excessively intrusive in light of the age and sex of the student and the nature of the infraction" . . . .

A number of our cases on probable cause have an implicit bearing on the reliable knowledge element of reasonable suspicion, as we have attempted to flesh out the knowledge component by looking to the degree to which known facts imply prohibited conduct, . . . the specificity of the information received, . . . and the reliability of its source. . . . At the end of the day, however, we have realized that these factors cannot rigidly control, . . . and we have come back to saying that the standards are "fluid concepts that take their substantive content from the particular contexts" in which they are being assessed. . . .

Perhaps the best that can be said generally about the required knowledge component of probable cause for a law enforcement officer's evidence search is that it raise a "fair probability" . . . or a "substantial chance" . . . of discovering evidence of criminal activity. The lesser standard for school searches could as readily be described as a moderate chance of finding evidence of wrongdoing.

. . .

In this case, the school's policies strictly prohibit the nonmedical use, possession, or sale of any drug on school grounds, including "'[a]ny prescription or over-the-counter drug, except those for which permission to use in school has been granted pursuant to Board policy.'" . . . A week before Savana was searched, another student, Jordan Romero (no relation of the school's administrative assistant), told the principal and Assistant Principal Wilson that "certain students were bringing drugs and weapons on campus," and that he had been sick after taking some pills that "he got from a classmate." . . . On the morning of October 8, the same boy handed Wilson a white pill that he said Marissa Glines had given him. He told Wilson that students were planning to take the pills at lunch.

Wilson learned from Peggy Schwallier, the school nurse, that the pill was Ibuprofen 400 mg, available only by prescription. Wilson then called Marissa out of class. Outside the classroom, Marissa's teacher handed Wilson the day planner, found within Marissa's reach, containing various contraband items. Wilson escorted Marissa back to his office.

In the presence of Helen Romero, Wilson requested Marissa to turn out her pockets and open her wallet. Marissa produced a blue pill, several white ones, and a razor blade. Wilson asked where the blue pill came from, and Marissa answered, "'I guess it slipped in when *she* gave me the IBU 400s.'" . . . When Wilson asked whom she meant, Marissa replied, "'Savana Redding.'" . . . Wilson then enquired about the day planner and its contents; Marissa denied knowing anything about them. Wilson did not ask Marissa any followup questions to determine whether there was any likelihood that Savana presently had pills: neither asking when Marissa received the pills from Savana nor where Savana might be hiding them.

Schwallier did not immediately recognize the blue pill, but information provided through a poison control hotline indicated that the pill was a 200-mg dose of an anti-inflammatory drug, generically called naproxen, available over the counter. At Wilson's direction, Marissa was then subjected to a search of her bra and underpants by Romero and Schwallier, as Savana was later on. The search revealed no additional pills.

It was at this juncture that Wilson called Savana into his office and showed her the day planner. Their conversation established that Savana and Marissa were on friendly terms: while she denied knowledge of the contraband, Savana admitted that the day planner was hers and that she had lent it to

Marissa. Wilson had other reports of their friendship from staff members, who had identified Savana and Marissa as part of an unusually rowdy group at the school's opening dance in August, during which alcohol and cigarettes were found in the girls' bathroom. Wilson had reason to connect the girls with this contraband, for Wilson knew that Jordan Romero had told the principal that before the dance, he had been at a party at Savana's house where alcohol was served. Marissa's statement that the pills came from Savana was thus sufficiently plausible to warrant suspicion that Savana was involved in pill distribution.

This suspicion of Wilson's was enough to justify a search of Savana's backpack and outer clothing. If a student is reasonably suspected of giving out contraband pills, she is reasonably suspected of carrying them on her person and in the carryall that has become an item of student uniform in most places today. If Wilson's reasonable suspicion of pill distribution were not understood to support searches of outer clothes and backpack, it would not justify any search worth making. And the look into Savana's bag, in her presence and in the relative privacy of Wilson's office, was not excessively intrusive, any more than Romero's subsequent search of her outer clothing.

. . .

Here it is that the parties part company, with Savana's claim that extending the search at Wilson's behest to the point of making her pull out her underwear was constitutionally unreasonable. The exact label for this final step in the intrusion is not important, though strip search is a fair way to speak of it. Romero and Schwallier directed Savana to remove her clothes down to her underwear, and then "pull out" her bra and the elastic band on her underpants. . . . Although Romero and Schwallier stated that they did not see anything when Savana followed their instructions, . . . we would not define strip search and its Fourth Amendment consequences in a way that would guarantee litigation about who was looking and how much was seen. The very fact of Savana's pulling her underwear away from her body in the presence of the two officials who were able to see her necessarily exposed her breasts and pelvic area to some degree, and both subjective and reasonable societal expectations of personal privacy support the treatment of such a search as categorically distinct, requiring distinct elements of justification on the part of school authorities for going beyond a search of outer clothing and belongings.

Savana's subjective expectation of privacy against such a search is inherent in her account of it as embarrassing, frightening, and humiliating. The reasonableness of her expectation (required by the Fourth Amendment standard) is indicated by the consistent experiences of other young people similarly searched, whose adolescent vulnerability intensifies the patent intrusiveness of the exposure. . . . The common reaction of these adolescents simply registers the obviously different meaning of a search exposing the body from the experience of nakedness or near undress in other school circumstances. Changing for gym is getting ready for play; exposing for a search is responding to an accusation reserved for suspected wrongdoers and fairly understood as so degrading that a number of communities have decided that strip searches in schools are never reasonable and have banned them no matter what the facts may be. . . .

The indignity of the search does not, of course, outlaw it, but it does implicate the rule of reasonableness as stated in *T. L. O.*, that "the search as actually conducted [be] reasonably related in scope to the circumstances which justified the interference in the first place." . . . The scope will be permissible, that is, when it is "not excessively intrusive in light of the age and sex of the student and the nature of the infraction." . . .

Here, the content of the suspicion failed to match the degree of intrusion. Wilson knew beforehand that the pills were prescription-strength ibuprofen and over-the-counter naproxen, common pain relievers equivalent to two Advil, or one Aleve. He must have been aware of the nature and limited threat of the specific drugs he was searching for, and while just about anything can be taken in quantities that will do real harm, Wilson had no reason to suspect that large amounts of the drugs were being passed around, or that individual students were receiving great numbers of pills.

Nor could Wilson have suspected that Savana was hiding common pain-killers in her underwear. Petitioners suggest, as a truth universally acknowledged, that "students . . . hid[e] contraband in or under their clothing," . . . and cite a smattering of cases of students with contraband in their underwear. . . . But when the categorically extreme intrusiveness of a search down to the body of an adolescent requires some justification in suspected facts, general background possibilities fall short; a reasonable search that extensive calls for suspicion that it will pay off. But nondangerous school contraband does not raise the specter of stashes in intimate places, and there is no evidence in the record of any general practice among Safford Middle School students of hiding that sort of thing in underwear; neither Jordan nor Marissa suggested to Wilson that Savana was doing that, and the preceding search of Marissa that Wilson ordered yielded nothing. Wilson never even determined when Marissa had received the pills from Savana; if it had been a few days before, that would weigh heavily against any reasonable conclusion that Savana presently had the pills on her person, much less in her underwear.

In sum, what was missing from the suspected facts that pointed to Savana was any indication of danger to the students from the power of the drugs or their quantity, and any reason to suppose that Savana was carrying pills in her underwear. We think that the combination of these deficiencies was fatal to finding the search reasonable.

In so holding, we mean to cast no ill reflection on the assistant principal, for the record raises no doubt that his motive throughout was to eliminate drugs from his school and protect students from what Jordan Romero had gone through. Parents are known to overreact to protect their children from danger, and a school official with responsibility for safety may tend to do the same. The difference is that the Fourth Amendment places limits on the official, even with the high degree of deference that courts must pay to the educator's professional judgment.

We do mean, though, to make it clear that the *T. L. O.* concern to limit a school search to reasonable scope requires the support of reasonable suspicion of danger or of resort to underwear for hiding evidence of wrongdoing before a search can reasonably make the quantum leap from outer clothes and backpacks to exposure of intimate parts. The meaning of such a search, and the degradation its subject may reasonably feel, place a search that intrusive in a category of its own demanding its own specific suspicions.

. . .

⚜

The strip search of Savana Redding was unreasonable and a violation of the Fourth Amendment, but petitioners Wilson, Romero, and Schwallier are nevertheless protected from liability through qualified immunity. . . .

➡ **NO**

School Officials Deserve Leeway

J USTICE THOMAS, concurring in the judgment in part and dissenting in part.

I agree with the Court that the judgment against the school officials with respect to qualified immunity should be reversed. . . . Unlike the majority, however, I would hold that the search of Savana Redding did not violate the Fourth Amendment. The majority imposes a vague and amorphous standard on school administrators. It also grants judges sweeping authority to second-guess the measures that these officials take to maintain discipline in their schools and ensure the health and safety of the students in their charge. This deep intrusion into the administration of public schools exemplifies why the Court should return to the common-law doctrine of *in loco parentis* under which "the judiciary was reluctant to interfere in the routine business of school administration, allowing schools and teachers to set and enforce rules and to maintain order." . . . But even under the prevailing Fourth Amendment test established by *New Jersey* v. *T. L. O.,* . . . all petitioners, including the school district, are entitled to judgment as a matter of law in their favor.

. . .

"Although the underlying command of the Fourth Amendment is always that searches and seizures be reasonable, what is reasonable depends on the context within which a search takes place." . . . Thus, although public school students retain Fourth Amendment rights under this Court's precedent, . . . those rights "are different . . . than elsewhere; the 'reasonableness' inquiry cannot disregard the schools' custodial and tutelary responsibility for children." . . . For nearly 25 years this Court has understood that "[m]aintaining order in the classroom has never been easy, but in more recent years, school disorder has often taken particularly ugly forms: drug use and violent crime in the schools have become major social problems." . . . In schools, "[e]vents calling for discipline are frequent occurrences and sometimes require immediate, effective action." . . .

For this reason, school officials retain broad authority to protect students and preserve "order and a proper educational environment" under the Fourth Amendment. . . . This authority requires that school officials be able to engage in the "close supervision of schoolchildren, as well as . . . enforc[e] rules against conduct that would be perfectly permissible if undertaken by an adult." . . . Seeking to reconcile the Fourth Amendment with this unique public school setting, the Court in *T. L. O.* held that a school search is "reasonable" if it is "'justified at its inception'" and "'reasonably related in scope to

From Supreme Court of the United States, June 25, 2009.

the circumstances which justified the interference in the first place.'" . . . The search under review easily meets this standard.

. . .

A "search of a student by a teacher or other school official will be 'justified at its inception' when there are reasonable grounds for suspecting that the search will turn up evidence that the student has violated or is violating either the law or the rules of the school." . . . As the majority rightly concedes, this search was justified at its inception because there were reasonable grounds to suspect that Redding possessed medication that violated school rules. . . . A finding of reasonable suspicion "does not deal with hard certainties, but with probabilities." . . . To satisfy this standard, more than a mere "hunch" of wrongdoing is required, but "considerably" less suspicion is needed than would be required to "satisf[y] a preponderance of the evidence standard." . . .

Furthermore, in evaluating whether there is a reasonable "particularized and objective" basis for conducting a search based on suspected wrongdoing, government officials must consider the "totality of the circumstances." . . . School officials have a specialized understanding of the school environment, the habits of the students, and the concerns of the community, which enables them to "'formulat[e] certain common-sense conclusions about human behavior.'" . . . And like police officers, school officials are "entitled to make an assessment of the situation in light of [this] specialized training and familiarity with the customs of the [school]." . . .

Here, petitioners had reasonable grounds to suspect that Redding was in possession of prescription and nonprescription drugs in violation of the school's prohibition of the "non-medical use, possession, or sale of a drug" on school property or at school events. . . . As an initial matter, school officials were aware that a few years earlier, a student had become "seriously ill" and "spent several days in intensive care" after ingesting prescription medication obtained from a classmate. . . . Fourth Amendment searches do not occur in a vacuum; rather, context must inform the judicial inquiry. . . . In this instance, the suspicion of drug possession arose at a middle school that had "a history of problems with students using and distributing prohibited and illegal substances on campus." . . .

The school's substance-abuse problems had not abated by the 2003–2004 school year, which is when the challenged search of Redding took place. School officials had found alcohol and cigarettes in the girls' bathroom during the first school dance of the year and noticed that a group of students including Redding and Marissa Glines smelled of alcohol. . . . Several weeks later, another student, Jordan Romero, reported that Redding had hosted a party before the dance where she served whiskey, vodka, and tequila. . . . Romero had provided this report to school officials as a result of a meeting his mother scheduled with the officials after Romero "bec[a]me violent" and "sick to his stomach" one night and admitted that "he had taken some pills that he had got[ten] from a classmate." . . . At that meeting, Romero admitted that "certain students were bringing drugs and weapons on campus." . . . One week later, Romero handed the assistant principal a white pill that he said he had

received from Glines. . . . He reported "that a group of students [were] planning on taking the pills at lunch." . . .

School officials justifiably took quick action in light of the lunchtime deadline. The assistant principal took the pill to the school nurse who identified it
as prescription-strength 400-mg Ibuprofen. . . . A subsequent search of Glines
and her belongings produced a razor blade, a Naproxen 200-mg pill, and several
Ibuprofen 400-mg pills. . . . When asked, Glines claimed that she had received
the pills from Redding. . . . A search of Redding's planner, which Glines had
borrowed, then uncovered "several knives, several lighters, a cigarette, and a
permanent marker." . . . Thus, as the majority acknowledges, . . . the totality
of relevant circumstances justified a search of Redding for pills.

. . .

The remaining question is whether the search was reasonable in scope.
Under *T. L. O.,* "a search will be permissible in its scope when the measures
adopted are reasonably related to the objectives of the search and not excessively intrusive in light of the age and sex of the student and the nature of
the infraction." . . . The majority concludes that the school officials' search of
Redding's underwear was not "'reasonably related in scope to the circumstances
which justified the interference in the first place,'" . . . notwithstanding the officials' reasonable suspicion that Redding "was involved in pill distribution," . . . .
According to the majority, to be reasonable, this school search required a showing of "danger to the students from the power of the drugs or their quantity" or a
"reason to suppose that [Redding] was carrying pills in her underwear." . . . Each
of these additional requirements is an unjustifiable departure from bedrock
Fourth Amendment law in the school setting, where this Court has heretofore
read the Fourth Amendment to grant considerable leeway to school officials.
Because the school officials searched in a location where the pills could have
been hidden, the search was reasonable in scope under *T. L. O.*

. . .

The majority finds that "subjective and reasonable societal expectations
of personal privacy support . . . treat[ing]" this type of search, which it labels a
"strip search," as "categorically distinct, requiring distinct elements of justification on the part of school authorities for going beyond a search of clothing
and belongings." . . . Thus, in the majority's view, although the school officials had reasonable suspicion to believe that Redding had the pills on her
person, . . . they needed some greater level of particularized suspicion to conduct this "strip search." There is no support for this contortion of the Fourth
Amendment.

. . .

۔(ۉ)۔

The analysis of whether the scope of the search here was permissible
under that standard is straightforward. Indeed, the majority does not dispute

that "general background possibilities" establish that students conceal "contraband in their underwear." . . . It acknowledges that school officials had reasonable suspicion to look in Redding's backpack and outer clothing because if "Wilson's reasonable suspicion of pill distribution were not understood to support searches of outer clothes and backpack, it would not justify any search worth making." . . . The majority nevertheless concludes that proceeding any further with the search was unreasonable. . . . But there is no support for this conclusion. The reasonable suspicion that Redding possessed the pills for distribution purposes did not dissipate simply because the search of her backpack turned up nothing. It was eminently reasonable to conclude that the backpack was empty because Redding was secreting the pills in a place she thought no one would look. . . .

Redding would not have been the first person to conceal pills in her undergarments. . . . Nor will she be the last after today's decision, which announces the safest place to secrete contraband in school.

. . .

The majority compounds its error by reading the "nature of the infraction" aspect of the *T. L. O.* test as a license to limit searches based on a judge's assessment of a particular school policy. According to the majority, the scope of the search was impermissible because the school official "must have been aware of the nature and limited threat of the specific drugs he was searching for" and because he "had no reason to suspect that large amounts of the drugs were being passed around, or that individual students were receiving great numbers of pills." . . . Thus, in order to locate a rationale for finding a Fourth Amendment violation in this case, the majority retreats from its observation that the school's firm no-drug policy "makes sense, and there is no basis to claim that the search was unreasonable owing to some defect or shortcoming of the rule it was aimed at enforcing." . . .

Even accepting the majority's assurances that it is not attacking the rule's reasonableness, it certainly is attacking the rule's importance. This approach directly conflicts with *T. L. O.* in which the Court was "unwilling to adopt a standard under which the legality of a search is dependent upon a judge's evaluation of the relative importance of school rules." . . . Indeed, the Court in *T. L. O.* expressly rejected the proposition that the majority seemingly endorses—that "some rules regarding student conduct are by nature too 'trivial' to justify a search based upon reasonable suspicion." . . .

The majority's decision in this regard also departs from another basic principle of the Fourth Amendment: that law enforcement officials can enforce with the same vigor all rules and regulations irrespective of the perceived importance of any of those rules. "In a long line of cases, we have said that when an officer has probable cause to believe a person committed even a minor crime in his presence, the balancing of private and public interests is not in doubt. The arrest is constitutionally reasonable." . . . The Fourth Amendment rule for searches is the same: Police officers are entitled to search regardless of the perceived triviality of the underlying law. As we have explained, requiring police to make "sensitive, case-by-case determinations of government need," . . . for a particular prohibition before conducting a search would "place police in an almost impossible spot" . . . .

The majority has placed school officials in this "impossible spot" by questioning whether possession of Ibuprofen and Naproxen causes a severe enough threat to warrant investigation. Had the suspected infraction involved a street drug, the majority implies that it would have approved the scope of the search. . . . In effect, then, the majority has replaced a school rule that draws no distinction among drugs with a new one that does. As a result, a full search of a student's person for prohibited drugs will be permitted only if the Court agrees that the drug in question was sufficiently dangerous. Such a test is unworkable and unsound. School officials cannot be expected to halt searches based on the possibility that a court might later find that the particular infraction at issue is not severe enough to warrant an intrusive investigation. . . .

In determining whether the search's scope was reasonable under the Fourth Amendment, it is therefore irrelevant whether officials suspected Redding of possessing prescription-strength Ibuprofen, nonprescription-strength Naproxen, or some harder street drug. Safford prohibited its possession on school property. Reasonable suspicion that Redding was in possession of drugs in violation of these policies, therefore, justified a search extending to any area where small pills could be concealed. The search did not violate the Fourth Amendment.

. . .

POSTSCRIPT

Can Zero Tolerance Violate Student Rights?

While public sentiment and media commentary tended to side with the final ruling in *Safford Unified School District #1 v. Redding*, the conduct of school officials charged with the responsibility of carrying out zero-tolerance policies will most likely come under further legal scrutiny. Does the Fourth Amendment require a stricter standard than "reasonableness" for justifying actions such as student strip searches? Is the zero-tolerance basis for school discipline itself faulty and in need of modification? Does the principle enunciated by Justice Stephen Breyer in an earlier case continue to guide legal opinions, namely that "school officials need a degree of flexible authority to respond to disciplinary challenges and the law has always considered the relationship between teachers and students special"?

These and related questions are explored in depth in "Law and Order in the Classroom" by Richard Arum and Doreet Preiss in *Education Next* (Fall 2009); *Zero-Tolerance Policies in Schools* (2009), edited by Peggy Daniels; and Bryan R. Warnick's "Surveillance Cameras in Schools: An Ethical Analysis," *Harvard Educational Review* (Fall 2007).

Additional perspectives on the privacy issue at hand and important subtopics can be found in these sources: Ross W. Greene, *Lost at School* (2008), which explores the need for changing the culture and practice of discipline in the schools; Joseph A. Lieberman, *School Shootings: What Every Parent and Educator Needs to Know to Protect Our Children* (2008), which identifies characteristics of the antisocial personality; Justin M. Bathon and Martha M. McCarthy, "Student Expression: The Uncertain Future," *Educational Horizons* (Winter 2008); Alfie Kohn, "Safety from the Inside Out: Rethinking Traditional Approaches," *Educational Horizons* (Fall 2004); Pedro A. Noguera, "Rethinking Disciplinary Practices," *Theory Into Practice* (Autumn 2003); Alfie Kohn, *Beyond Discipline: From Compliance to Community* (2006); and Anne Gregory and Dewey Cornell, "'Tolerating' Adolescent Needs: Moving Beyond Zero-Tolerance Policies in High School," *Theory Into Practice* (Spring 2009).

Discipline and classroom management are among the primary concerns of beginning teachers. No foolproof theories of discipline exist, but a wide-ranging exploration of ideas such as those in the sources cited above and those in first-hand anecdotal accounts by first-year teachers can help in the construction of a reasonable approach when coupled with the sage advice of veteran educators.

ISSUE 19

Do American Students Need More Time in School?

YES: Chris Gabrieli, from "More Time, More Learning," *Educational Leadership* (April 2010)

NO: Larry Cuban, from "The Perennial Reform: Fixing School Time," *Phi Delta Kappan* (December 2008)

ISSUE SUMMARY

YES: National Center on Time and Learning chairman Chris Gabrieli claims that current school time schedules are outmoded and calls for expansion of the instructional day and year to close the achievement gap and provide enrichment opportunities.

NO: Stanford University professor emeritus Larry Cuban reviews the history of school time expansion and finds scant research to support such demands.

Although wrangling about the quantity and quality of time spent in school has enlivened the discourse of professional educators for decades, the recent performance pressures brought about by the No Child Left Behind legislation and the increase in foreign competition have brought new urgency to addressing the issue. As Naomi Dillon points out, in "More Time for Learning," *American School Board Journal* (March 2010), expectations of student achievement have vastly increased while institutional time has remained stagnant. The efforts to alter the school day and the school year have been curtailed by politics and tradition, she claims. Most school districts adhere to a 6½-hour, 180-day academic calendar. However, on the present scene, the Obama administration clearly has the time-expansion goal on its education agenda and advocacy groups such as the National Center on Time and Learning have gained momentum, particularly as charter schools have multiplied nationwide.

The state of Massachusetts, in the forefront of the extended-time movement, has been joined by many states and local school systems across the nation. The superintendent of schools in Pittsburgh has been quoted as saying, "In 15 years I'd be surprised if the old school calendar still dominated in urban settings." In their book *Time To Learn* (2008), Chris Gabrieli and Warren Goldstein state that we have been mired in a mix of complacency and resignation regarding the expectations we hold for our public school system and our ability to narrow the achievement gap among racial and ethnic groups. The growing acceptance of longer school hours, however, is providing more time on task for students, more opportunities for experiential learning and enrichment activities, and more latitude for teachers to work with diverse skill levels at the same time. Gabrieli and Goldstein see a moral imperative to bring a lengthened school day and year particularly to students in low-income neighborhoods.

Public charter schools, freed from the restraints of the usual calendar, have been quick to embrace the "more time" approach. For example, the Knowledge Is Power Program (KIPP) schools run from 7:30 a.m. to 5 p.m., hold sessions on some Saturdays, and reduce summer vacation to about 7 weeks, thus adding some 600 hours to the school year. Jennifer Davis, president of the National Center on Time and Learning (NCTL), in "A Matter of Time," *Education Next* (Fall 2008), points to research on charter schools in New York City showing that more school time correlates with improved learning outcomes. David A. Farbman, a senior researcher at NCTL, in a December 2009 report, outlines progress at 655 schools in the organization's database in "Tracking an Emerging Movement," *Education Digest* (February 2010). Another report, *Extended School Year Fast Facts* (March 2009) by the Center for Education Policy, Applied Research and Evaluation at the University of Southern Maine, offers detailed international comparisons on school time showing American students receiving, on average, about 10 percent fewer instructional hours per year than their foreign counterparts. The report cites some cases, notably Sweden and Finland, where students spend *fewer* hours in school and yet consistently outperform American students on international achievement tests. This raises the question of quantity versus quality, mere allocated time versus academically engaged time. Other research on American public schools has shown large disparities in time allocation among urban areas, with New York City students getting about 8 weeks more than those in Chicago and Houston students getting five more weeks than those in Memphis, for example.

Questions have been raised about the wisdom of the current push for extended time, citing budget realities, restrictive state laws, and local regulations, and in some cases parental objections. Michael Jonas, in "Mixed Messages on Longer School Day?" *CommonWealth Magazine* (May 21, 2010), cites a study of the Massachusetts Expanded Learning Time program showing that an extended day is not making much of a difference—at a cost of an extra $1300 per student. Cristina Corbin, in "Extended School Year Would Have Dire Economic Effects, Critics Say," FOXNews.com (September 29, 2009), cites increased costs to school systems for overtime pay and summer air-conditioning, major cuts in hotel and tourism profits, and serious blows to summer camp operators when the school year is expanded or year-round schedules are adopted.

In the following articles Chris Gabrieli details the justification for the urgent expansion of school time, while Larry Cuban enumerates the many serious barriers to fulfillment of the movement's goals.

YES

Chris Gabrieli

More Time, More Learning

Just a few years ago, Clarence Edwards Middle School in the Boston neighborhood of Charlestown, Massachusetts, typified the achievement gap challenge we face across the United States. The middle school, which serves students in grades 6–8, had low scores on standardized achievement tests, an alarming level of bad behavior, and dwindling enrollment. Now, three years later, the school could be a national poster child for school improvement.

What changed? The school redesigned its education approach around expanded learning time.

Much remains the same there. The students still have the sort of demographics that generally overwhelm schools and tend to be concentrated in the lowest-performing schools—about 90 percent of the students qualify for free or reduced-price lunch, about 90 percent are minority, nearly one-quarter have limited English proficiency, and almost one-third are classified as having special needs. The school is still characterized by a high degree of student mobility.

Yet substantial improvements have taken place. In the past, Edwards students lagged far behind the state averages in their scores on Massachusetts's standardized tests. Bear in mind that Massachusetts is a predominantly suburban state with the highest National Assessment of Educational Progress (NAEP) scores in the United States. Eighth graders at Edwards have now narrowed that gap by two-thirds in science and by more than 80 percent in English language arts; they now score substantially higher than the state averages in math.

Failure rates have plummeted across the board, and the percentage of learners scoring in the highest band of success in math, advanced, has gone from about zero to level with the state average—19 percent. Every traditionally challenged subgroup has shown improvement. Just four years ago, only 15 percent of limited English proficient 8th graders reached proficiency in math; last year, 71 percent of this subgroup reached proficiency, compared with the state average of 12 percent.

The greatest opportunity that expanded learning time offers for improving academic achievement comes from being able to better individualize instruction—putting the right teachers with the right students and focusing on the right skills. The single biggest change in the academic program at

From *Educational Leadership*, April 2010, pp. 39–44. Copyright © 2010 by ASCD. Reprinted by permission. The Association for Supervision and Curriculum Development is a worldwide community of educators advocating sound policies and sharing best practices to achieve the success of each learner. To learn more, visit ASCD at www.ascd.org.

Edwards was adding an hour each day during which students receive small-group instruction and tutoring in the subject in which they lag most. Students receive either English or math support in the afternoon, with the students who are strong in both subjects focusing on science during that slot. In addition, more time has enabled the school to offer both science and social studies four days each week—twice the previous level.

The academic gains are matched by growth in opportunities for students to participate in enrichment activities. The school has a performing arts program that sends many students to Boston's audition-based performing arts high school—the Boston Arts Academy, also an expanded learning time school. Edwards is the only Boston middle school fielding teams in a variety of sports, including a football team that plays nearby suburban schools. And every 6th grader participates in the Citizen Schools program, which features elective apprenticeships with such professionals as corporate attorneys and software engineers from Google.

There's now a sense of positive energy, enthusiasm, and optimism in the building. Students have learned that through hard work, they can excel against the odds. But this requires time: Monday through Thursday, students at Edwards start school at 7:20 a.m. and finish at 4:00 p.m.—that's close to a nine-hour day. On Friday, their day finishes at 11:40 a.m.

Given the positive results, every middle school in Boston has now petitioned to become an expanded learning time school. And families are interested, too. Just three years ago, only 17 students picked Edwards as their first choice during Boston's middle school selection process. Last year, 250 chose Edwards—there's now a waiting list to get in.

With President Obama and U.S. Secretary of Education Duncan now challenging educators to move beyond a school schedule and calendar developed for a farm and factory era, expanded learning time is moving to center stage. At a time of diminishing resources, American Recovery and Reinvestment Act (ARRA) stimulus dollars are boosting the model because the Department of Education's regulations identify "increased learning time" as a core innovation that schools should promote. But simply expanding time willy-nilly at schools is not a silver bullet for success. We need to follow the example of Edwards—and use the time well.

The Emerging Field

For a long time, expanding learning time was more a vision than a reality. In 1994, the National Commission on Time and Learning issued a report titled *Prisoners of Time,* which referred to our current schedule as a fundamental "design flaw." The report argued that we needed to go from a system where seat time chiefly determined advancement (that is, time was fixed) regardless of achievement (that is, outcomes varied widely) to one in which we require that all students meet defined learning levels. Struggling students would need more time; advanced students would require additional challenges.

Charter school laws that emerged in the early 1990s gave some education pioneers the chance to create innovative schools. One celebrated example is the KIPP schools. Graduates of KIPP middle schools not only show large academic test score gains, but also carry that momentum forward into higher rates of college completion. One of the program's five core design pillars is an increase in the school schedule by 60 percent: Students attend school Monday through Friday from 7:30 a.m. to 5:00 p.m., a month longer into the summer, and about 18 Saturday mornings each year.

Two other leading charter management organizations—Achievement First (www.achievementfirst.org) and Uncommon Schools (www.uncommonschools .org)—also expand time with good results. Harvard professor Roland Fryer (Dobbie & Fryer, 2009) has recently shown that New York City's Harlem Promise Academies, part of Geoffrey Canada's Harlem Children's Zone, drive large gains for participants. By extending the school day and offering tutoring on Saturdays and in the summer, the academies provide 50 percent more time for all students and 100 percent more time for those who struggle the most.

The most persuasive evidence of the importance of expanding learning time to drive academic gains comes from Caroline Hoxby's major ongoing study of all New York City charter schools. She recently analyzed 30 different design variables at these 42 schools—such as curriculum, approach to discipline, teacher pay structures, and schedules—and found that the feature most convincingly correlated with academic success was increased learning time (Hoxby, Murarka, & Kang, 2009).

Our organization, the National Center on Time and Learning, has just published the first national census of expanded time schools (Farbman, 2009). We identified 655 such schools in 36 U.S. states and the District of Columbia. These schools add, on average, about 25 percent more time each year—or the equivalent of *three extra years of school* for students who attend such schools for their entire school career. Longer days account for most of the time expansion, but 20 percent of the schools have lengthened the school year as well.

These schools serve the neediest students in the United States. Students in expanded time schools are twice as likely to be minorities, and two-thirds are poor. Three-quarters of the schools are charters, but the most rapidly growing group is in-district conversions. We were heartened to see that these expanded time schools show higher academic achievement than the average for their host districts (Farbman, 2009).

For Whom Should the Expanded Day Bell Toll?

The most compelling initial target for expanding learning time [are] middle-grade students in high-poverty schools. The notable success of many expanded learning time schools at this level provides strong encouragement that this approach can succeed.

Children in our highest-poverty middle schools rarely participate in many programs so familiar to their more affluent peers—tutoring, summer institutes, martial arts courses, science camps, sports leagues, and the like—and rarely have strong homework support at home. For these students, schools must be muscular enough to get most of the job done.

Middle school is well documented to be the level at which students seem to diverge into two groups. One group tends to be well socialized to school, proficient academically, and on a strong path to high school graduation; the other group tends to show alienation from school and become at high risk of dropping out.

Through strong core instruction combined with individualized support, expanding learning time can ensure that at-risk students keep up academically; develop attachments to school through such activities as sports, arts, and drama; and develop the beliefs and behaviors consistent with success.

Many elementary schools have benefited from expanding learning time by both raising academic achievement and providing a well-rounded day. More learning time could benefit high schools as well, but to lesser effect in the context of the traditional high school structure. There are a number of impressive high schools across the United States that use expanded learning time, but expanded time did not drive their conversion. Rather, these schools have radically redesigned how they operate, and they happen to need and use more time to get the job done.

A Good Fit

To succeed, expanded learning time has to work for teachers, students, parents, and the education system. In general, teachers agree that they don't have enough time to help all students reach their academic goals, especially when students are already lagging. Teachers usually welcome the improved pace that expanded learning time provides as well as the opportunity to engage students in a wider variety of instructional approaches, including more project-based learning. Teachers' unions want to ensure that established teachers are offered choice and that they receive adequate compensation for more time. Charter schools usually recruit with the longer schedule as part of the plan and sometimes with moderately higher overall pay.

Students are often initially skeptical when they hear about expanded learning time, especially older students. But once they experience it, they typically accommodate to it quickly as their standard schedule. Many students are pleased with the far greater opportunities for enrichment and engagement through art, music, drama, robotics, sports, and the like. They also notice that their teachers have more time to support them and that their achievement typically improves.

Parents often flock to expanded learning time schools when they are available. They usually believe that with more time, schools can help their children do better academically; they also appreciate the better match between their work schedules and their children's school schedules. Affluent parents are more divided in their reaction to potential expansions of school schedules because they have often already invested time and money in placing their children in structured, supervised out-of-school activities to complement the content and schedule of school.

School districts are often eager to identify new levers to drive achievement gains in their lowest-performing schools. Their greatest challenges are finding the necessary funding and accommodating schools working on a different schedule. Charter schools, which have blazed the path, face fewer such challenges, although many raise private funding to help meet the greater costs.

With a Little Help from Uncle Sam

It takes resources and incentives to turn will into reality. In the final Race to the Top guidelines issue in November 2009, the U.S. Department of Education calls for time to be "significantly increased" and points to our research—that a minimum of 300 hours per year is necessary to effect real change. The department indicates that for schools to see the greatest improvements, they need to fully integrate expanded learning time and implement a balanced approach that provides more time for core academics, for enrichment subjects, and for teachers to collaborate and improve their craft. This high-bar definition rules out the possibility of schools adding only modest amounts of time for some students and calling it sufficient.

The Department of Education has laid out the acceptable approaches for state, district, and school use of American Recovery and Reinvestment Act (ARRA) funding to turn around the lowest-performing schools. Of the four alternatives defined, two models, *turnaround* and *transformation,* require the use of increased learning time. These regulations bind the new competitive programs—Race to the Top and Investment in Innovation (i3)—but also cover the longer-term School Improvement Fund. The latter has attracted less fanfare but deserves more attention: ARRA boosts this fund to $3.5 billion, which will flow to all 50 U.S. states, and as an element of Title I it will likely endure well beyond the life of the stimulus package.

Ten Keys to Success

In view of these developments, the increased learning time movement is likely to spread. The following keys are crucial to a successful implementation of expanded learning time for disadvantaged students.

Key 1: Schools must allot a sufficiently large amount of expanded time.
Modest amounts of increased time will not help schools reach their goals. In our experience, schools need a minimum of 300 hours each year—or an additional one hour and 45 minutes each day—to establish a balanced program and drive deep change. Successful expanded learning time schools range from those that offer about 25 percent more time to those that offer as much as 60 percent more time (for example, KIPP schools).

Key 2: Schools must fully integrate expanded time into a redesigned overall schedule.
Visitors to expanded learning time schools often ask, "At what time should I come to see the expanded time?" The additional time, however, is not tacked on to the end of the traditional schedule but rather is deeply integrated into a wholly reenvisioned day. A school could extend a math or English language

arts block from 45 minutes to 60 or 90 minutes; add time every day for social studies, science, or physical education; add an elective enrichment class in the middle of the day while core teachers are freed to collaborate in work groups; or expand time for lunch and recess.

Key 3: Schools should allocate expanded time to a balanced program.

Although most schools adopting expanded learning time want to drive academic achievement gains, there should be a healthy balance between the added depth allotted to core academics and the added breadth allotted to restore a well-rounded education. Schools should also strike a balance between expanded time for students to learn and for teachers to collaborate and improve.

Key 4: Schools must prioritize and focus expanded time.

Although expanded learning time is a welcome opportunity for principals and teachers because it holds the promise of benefiting all students, the most common mistake we have seen has been the failure to prioritize and focus. Some schools set out to do too many things and end up doing none of them very well. Including too many electives and enrichment opportunities can take away from the core mission of improving student achievement. It is important not to substitute a shallow exposure to many fields for a deeper mastery of one or two areas.

Key 5: Schools should change the schedule for all students.

This does not mean that all students have the identical schedule. On the contrary, expanded learning time allows for greater personalization, with students getting the level of intensive support or added challenge their skill levels dictate as well as the variety of education experiences that all children deserve.

Students accept the schedule as a fact of life, a crucial feature for middle and high school students who are unlikely to volunteer to stay longer after school. When all students stay, there is no sense of academic detention for some. The school can redesign the whole schedule; some students will be in music at noon whereas others will be in math at 3:30 [p.m.] Changing the schedule for all students commits the whole school to lasting institutional change.

Key 6: Schools should engage in a schoolwide planning process.

Drawing the faculty and community into the process of considering whether and how to expand learning time is an important opportunity to reinvigorate a school and gain buy-in from the people who will have to make it work. When done well, the process also forces a school to self-examine and use data to define strengths and weaknesses. A good planning process enables a shift to a data-driven, continuous-improvement culture, which is essential to long-term success.

Key 7: Schools should focus on strengthening core instruction and personalizing learning.

Successful expanded learning time schools are deeply committed to raising the quality of core instruction in every classroom through the use of data and collaborative improvement. In addition, these schools use frequent, well-aligned formative assessments to properly assess individual students' strengths and needs and to place students into well-designed interventions aimed at helping them catch up. Many successful expanded learning time schools offer students an extra class each day in the subject in which they struggle the most, with classmates at a similar level and a teacher who has expertise in this area. Some offer small or one-on-one tutoring sessions.

Key 8: Schools should offer engaging enrichment and opportunities for both exposure and mastery.

Enrichment opportunities that are structured as electives, taught by both teachers and outside partners, and interspersed throughout the day and year can engage students who are becoming increasingly alienated from school and who are at risk of dropping out. Students should have the opportunity to experience a wide variety of activities and achieve mastery in at least one of them.

Key 9: Schools should promote effective teacher collaboration and professional development.

Expanded learning time offers the opportunity to embed considerably more time for teachers to work together by grade or department and focus on specific instructional strategies that they can immediately put to use. However, it is easy to squander this time on low-intensity or administrative efforts and miss the chance to improve instructional effectiveness.

Key 10: Schools must change student and teacher beliefs and behaviors.

A growing body of evidence suggests that an optimistic belief that hard work will pay off is crucial to turning around our lowest-performing students and schools (see Blackwell, Trzesniewski, & Dweck, 2007). Struggling students from disadvantaged backgrounds often need help seeing that hard work will be rewarded with success and that delaying gratification and pursuing long-term goals are necessary.

Many teachers believe that with more time, they could succeed with far more struggling students. Expanded learning time enables students to do more of that hard work together and with teacher supervision—as opposed to the solo nature of homework—and allows more intentional efforts to build school community culture and values.

Not Solely Sufficient

If adding time alone were sufficient, every expanded learning time school would be a great success. But not every expanded school succeeds. Experience shows that a cluster of related school reforms needs to happen to enable the sort of performance one sees at Edwards Middle School or a high-performing KIPP school. At least three other drivers are key to success.

First, schools need *high levels of human capital* or, in plainer language, a strong principal and highly effective teachers. The process of planning for and implementing a redesign around more time is an extraordinary leadership opportunity for a principal who is a true instructional leader. Well-led schools can recruit and train excellent teachers and hone the skills of all incumbent teachers by using fair evaluation systems to ensure high standards.

Second, schools need to use *data-driven instructional approaches*. Although most schools in the United States might claim they use such approaches, this has not been our experience. Managing individual students' instruction on the basis of objective measures of their progress while using broader data to drive the discussion of how to improve enables school faculty to use added time most effectively.

Edwards initially used homegrown data to assess students and match instructional supports to their needs. More recently, the school has partnered with the Achievement Network (www.achievementnetwork.org) to implement six interim assessments each year; the resulting data drive professional development. The school credits this practice with a major surge in its third year in instructional effectiveness in English language arts.

Third, schools need to focus on building *high-performance cultures* in which teachers and students expect to succeed. Planning for expanded learning time leads naturally to a healthy discussion about the performance goals a school should pursue. We also encourage policies that require an agreement on goals between the school and the district or state. We favor focusing on exit-year proficiency—shouldn't the school's overall goal be to prepare its graduates for the next level of education?—and on including, in addition to academic goals, measures of student engagement and commitment.

Where We Go from Here

The movement to match learning time to student needs is still in the early stages of development. We need to dig down into the specific classroom practices that expanded time enables and figure out which ones are the most effective and which ones we can most readily scale up. We need to learn how to better use the resources of people, time, and money. For example, to what extent can we use staggered start times for teachers and community-based organizations? Although many of the most successful schools have all teachers at work for all of the expanded schedule, it may be more cost effective and broadly applicable to find ways to vary the approach.

The challenge will be to use the wave of resources from federal ARRA funding to launch thoughtful, well-targeted expanded learning time efforts. We need to understand how to use more learning time well to ensure that the U.S. ideal of equal opportunity for all through excellent public education becomes the norm—and not the celebrated exception.

References

Blackwell, L., Trzesniewski, K., & Dweck, C. S. (2007). Implicit theories of intelligence predict achievement across an adolescent transition: A longitudinal study and an intervention. *Child Development, 78*(1), 246–263.

Dobbie, W., & Fryer, R. G. (2009). *Are high-quality schools enough to close the achievement gap? Evidence from a bold social experiment in Harlem* (Working Paper No. 15473). Cambridge, MA: National Bureau of Economic Research.

Farbman, D. A. (2009). *Tracking an emerging movement: A report on expanded time schools in America.* Boston: National Center on Time and Learning. Available: www.timeandlearning.org/images/12.7.09FinalDatabaseReport.pdf

Hoxby, C. M., Murarka, S., & Kang, J. (2009). *How New York City's charter schools affect achievement.* Cambridge, MA: New York City Charter Schools Evaluation Project.

Larry Cuban

→ **NO**

The Perennial Reform: Fixing School Time

In the past quarter century, reformers have repeatedly urged schools to fix their use of time, even though it is a solution that is least connected to what happens in classrooms or what Americans want from public schools. Since *A Nation at Risk* in 1983, *Prisoners of Time* in 1994, and the latest blue-ribbon recommendations in *Tough Choices, Tough Times* in 2007, both how much time and how well students spend it in school have been criticized to no end.

Business and civil leaders have been critical because they see U.S. students stuck in the middle ranks on international tests. These leaders believe that the longer school year in Asia and Europe is linked to those foreign students scoring far higher than U.S. students on those tests.

Employers criticize the amount of time students spend in school because they wonder whether the limited days and hours spent in classes are sufficient to produce the skills that employees need to work in a globally competitive economy. Employers also wonder whether our comparatively short school year will teach the essential workplace behaviors of punctuality, regular attendance, meeting deadlines, and following rules.

Parents criticize school schedules because they want schools to be open when they go to work in the morning and to remain open until they pick up their children before dinner.

Professors criticize policy makers for allotting so little time for teachers to gain new knowledge and skills during the school day. Other researchers want both policy makers and practitioners to distinguish between requiring more time in school and *academic learning time,* academic jargon for those hours and minutes where teachers engage students in learning content and skills or, in more jargon, time on task.

Finally, cyberschool champions criticize school schedules because they think it's quaint to have students sitting at desks in a building with hundreds of other students for 180 days when a revolution in communication devices allows children to learn the formal curriculum in many places, not just in school buildings. Distance learning advocates, joined by those who see cyber-schools as the future, want children and youths to spend hardly any time in K-12 schools.

From *Phi Delta Kappan,* December 2008, pp. 240–250. Copyright © 2008 by Phi Delta Kappan. Reprinted by permission of Phi Delta Kappan and Larry Cuban.

Time Options

Presidential commissions, parents, academics, and employers have proposed the same solutions, again and again, for fixing the time students spend in school: Add more days to the annual school calendar. Change to year-round schools. Add instructional time to the daily schedule. Extend the school day.

What has happened to each proposal in the past quarter century?

Longer School Year

Recommendations for a longer school year (from 180 to 220 days) came from *A Nation at Risk* (1983) and *Prisoners of Time* (1994) plus scores of other commissions and experts. In 2008, a foundation-funded report, *A Stagnant Nation: Why American Students Are Still at Risk,* found that the 180-day school year was intact across the nation and only Massachusetts had started a pilot program to help districts lengthen the school year. The same report gave a grade of F to states for failing to significantly expand student learning time.

Year-Round Schools

Ending the summer break is another way to maximize student time in school. There is a homespun myth, treated as fact, that the annual school calendar, with three months off for both teachers and students, is based on the rhythm of 19th-century farm life, which dictated when school was in session. Thus, planting and harvesting chores accounted for long summer breaks, an artifact of agrarian America. Not so.

Actually, summer vacations grew out of early 20th-century urban middle-class parents (and later lobbyists for camps and the tourist industry) pressing school boards to release children to be with their families for four to eight weeks or more. By the 1960s, however, policy maker and parent concerns about students losing ground academically during the vacation months—in academic language, "summer loss"—gained support for year-round schooling. Cost savings also attracted those who saw facilities being used 12 months a year rather than being shuttered during the summer.

Nonetheless, although year-round schools were established as early as 1906 in Gary, Indiana, calendar innovations have had a hard time entering most schools. Districts with year-round schools still work within the 180-day year but distribute the time more evenly (e.g., 45 days in session, 15 days off) rather than having a long break between June and September. As of 2006, nearly 3,000 of the nation's 90,000 public schools enrolled more than 2.1 million students on a year-round calendar. That's less than 5% of all students attending public schools, and almost half of the year-round schools are in California. In most cases, school boards adopted year-round schools because increased enrollments led to crowded facilities, most often in minority and poor communities—not concerns over "summer loss."

Adding Instructional Time to the School Day

Many researchers and reformers have pointed out that the 6½-hour school day has so many interruptions, so many distractions that teachers have less than five hours of genuine instruction time. Advocates for more instructional time have tried to stretch the actual amount of instructional time available to teachers to a seven-hour day (or 5½ hours of time for time-on-task learning) or have tried to redistribute the existing secondary school schedule into 90-minute blocks rather than the traditional 50-minute periods. Since *A Nation at Risk,* this recommendation for more instructional time has resulted only in an anemic 10 more minutes per day when elementary school students study core academic subjects.

Block scheduling in public secondary schools (60- to 90-minute periods for a subject that meets different days of the week) was started in the 1960s to promote instructional innovations. Various modified schedules have spread slowly, except in a few states where block schedules multiplied rapidly. In the past decade, an explosion of interest in small high schools has led many traditional urban comprehensive high schools of 1,500 or more students to convert to smaller high schools of 300 to 400 students, sometimes with all of those smaller schools housed within the original large building, sometimes as separate schools located elsewhere in the district. In many of these small high schools, modified schedules with instructional periods of an hour or more have found a friendly home. Block schedules rearrange existing allotted time for instruction; they do not add instructional time to the school day.

Extended School Day

In the past half century, as the economy has changed and families increasingly have both (or single) parents working, schools have been pressed to take on child-care responsibilities, such as tutoring and homework supervision before and after school. Many elementary schools open at 7 a.m. for parents to drop off children and have after-school programs that close at 6 p.m. PDK/Gallup polls since the early 1980s show increased support for these before- and after-school programs. Instead of the familiar half-day program for 5-year-olds, all-day kindergartens (and prekindergartens for 4-year-olds) have spread swiftly in the past two decades, especially in low-income neighborhoods. Innovative urban schools, such as the for-profit Edison Inc. and KIPP (Knowledge Is Power Program), run longer school days. The latter routinely opens at 7:30 a.m. and closes at 5 p.m. and also schedules biweekly Saturday classes and three weeks of school during the summer.

If reformers want a success story in fixing school time, they can look to extending the school day, although it's arguable how many of those changes occurred because of reformers' arguments and actions and how many from economic and social changes in family structure and the desire to chase a higher standard of living.

Cybereducation

And what about those public school haters and cheerleading technological enthusiasts who see fixing time in school as a wasted effort when online schooling and distance learning can replace formal schooling? In the 1960s and 1970s, Ivan Illich and other school critics called for dismantling public schools and ending formal schooling. They argued that schools squelched natural learning, confused school-based education with learning, and turned children into obedient students and adults rather than curious and independent lifelong learners. Communication and instructional technologies were in their infancy then, and thinkers such as Illich had few alternatives to offer families who opted out.

Much of that ire directed at formal public schooling still exists, but now technology has made it possible for students to learn outside school buildings. Sharing common ground in this debate are deeply religious families who want to avoid secular influences in schools, highly educated parents who fear the stifling effects of school rules and text-bound instruction, and rural parents who simply want their children to have access to knowledge unavailable in their local schools. These advocates seek home schooling, distance learning, and cyber schools.

Slight increases in home schooling may occur—say from 1.1 million in 2003 to 2 to 3 million by the end of the decade, with the slight uptick in numbers due to both the availability of technology and a broader menu of choices for parents. Still, this represents less than 3% of public school students. Even though cheerleaders for distance learning have predicted wholesale changes in conventional site-based schools for decades, such changes will occur at the periphery, not the center, because most parents will continue to send their children to public schools.

Even the most enthusiastic advocates for cyberschools and distance education recognize that replacing public schools is, at best, unlikely. The foreseeable future will still have 50 million children and youths crossing the schoolhouse door each weekday morning.

3 Reasons

Reformers have spent decades trotting out the same recipes for fixing the time problem in school. For all the hoopla and all of the endorsements from highly influential business and political elites, their mighty efforts have produced minuscule results. Why is that?

Cost is the usual suspect. Covering additional teacher salaries and other expenses runs high. Minnesota provides one example: shifting from 175 to 200 days of instruction cost districts an estimated $750 million a year, a large but not insurmountable price to pay. But costs for extending the school day for instruction and childcare are far less onerous.

Even more attractive than adding days to the calendar, however, is the claim that switching to a year-round school will *save* dollars. So, while there are costs involved in lengthening the school calendar, cost is not the tipping point in explaining why so few proposals to fix school time are successful.

I offer two other reasons why fixing school time is so hard.

Research showing achievement gains due to more time in school are sparse; the few studies most often displayed are contested.

Late 20th-century policy makers seriously underestimated the powerful tug that conservative, noneconomic goals (e.g., citizenship, character formation) have on parents, taxpayers, and voters. When they argued that America needed to add time to the school calendar in order to better prepare workers for global competition, they were out of step with the American public's desires for schools.

Skimpy Research

In the past quarter century of tinkering with the school calendar, cultural changes, political decisions, or strong parental concerns trumped research every time. Moreover, the longitudinal and rigorous research on time in school was—and is—skimpy. The studies that exist are challenged repeatedly for being weakly designed. For example, analysts examining research on year-round schools have reported that most of the studies have serious design flaws and, at best, show slight positive gains in student achievement—except for students from low-income families, for whom gains were sturdier. As one report concluded: "[N]o truly trustworthy studies have been done on modified school calendars that can serve as the basis for sound policy decisions." Policy talk about year-round schools has easily outstripped results.

Proving that time in school is the crucial variable in raising academic achievement is difficult because so many other variables must be considered—the local context itself, available resources, teacher quality, administrative leadership, socioeconomic and cultural background of students and their families, and what is taught. But the lack of careful research has seldom stopped reform-driven decision makers from pursuing their agendas.

Conflicting School Goals

If the evidence suggests that, at best, a longer school year or day or restructured schedules do not seem to make the key difference in student achievement, then I need to ask: What problem are reformers trying to solve by adding more school time?

The short answer is that for the past quarter century—*A Nation at Risk* (1983) is a suitable marker—policy elites have redefined a national economic problem into an educational problem. Since the late 1970s, influential civic, business, and media leaders have sold Americans the story that lousy schools are the reason why inflation surged, unemployment remained high, incomes seldom rose, and cheaper and better foreign products flooded U.S. stores. Public schools have failed to produce a strong, post-industrial labor force, thus leading to a weaker, less competitive U.S. economy. U.S. policy elites have used lagging scores on international tests as telling evidence that schools graduate less knowledgeable, less skilled high school graduates—especially those from minority and poor schools who will be heavily represented in the mid-21st century workforce—than competitor nations with lower-paid workforces who produce high-quality products.

Microsoft founder Bill Gates made the same point about U.S. high schools.

> In district after district across the country, wealthy white kids are taught Algebra II, while low-income minority kids are taught how to balance a checkbook. This is an economic disaster. In the international competition to have the best supply of workers who can communicate clearly, analyze information, and solve complex problems, the United States is falling behind. We have one of the highest high school dropout rates in the industrialized world.

And here, in a nutshell, is the second reason why those highly touted reforms aimed at lengthening the school year and instructional day have disappointed policy makers. By blaming schools, contemporary civic and business elites have reduced the multiple goals Americans expect of their public schools to a single one: prepare youths to work in a globally competitive economy. This has been a mistake because Americans historically have expected more from their public schools. Let me explore the geography of this error.

For nearly three decades, influential groups have called for higher academic standards, accountability for student outcomes, more homework, more testing, and, of course, more time in school. Many of their recommendations have been adopted. By 2008, U.S. schools had a federally driven system of state-designed standards anchored in increased testing, results-driven accountability, and demands for students to spend more time in school. After all, reformers reasoned, the students of foreign competitors were attending school more days in the year and longer hours each day, even on weekends, and their test scores ranked them higher than [their] U.S. [counterparts].

Even though this simplistic causal reasoning has been questioned many times by researchers who examined education and work performance in Japan, Korea, Singapore, Germany, and other nations, "common sense" observations by powerful elites swept away such questions. So the U.S.'s declining global economic competitiveness had been spun into a time-in-school problem.

But convincing evidence drawn from research that more time in school would lead to a stronger economy, less inequalities in family income, and that elusive edge in global competitiveness—much less a higher rank in international tests—remains missing in action.

The Public's Goal for Education

Business and civic elites have succeeded at least twice in the past century in making the growth of a strong economy the primary aim of U.S. schools, but other goals have had an enormous and enduring impact on schooling, both in the past and now. These goals embrace core American values that have been like second-hand Roses, shabby and discarded clothes hidden in the back of the closet and occasionally trotted out for show during graduation. Yet since the origins of tax-supported public schools in the early 19th century, these goals have been built into the very structures of schools so much so that, looking back from 2008, we hardly notice them.

Time-based reforms have had trouble entering schools because other goals have had—and continue to have—clout with parents and taxpayers. Opinion polls, for example, display again and again what parents, voters, and taxpayers want schools to achieve. One recent poll identified the public's goals for public schools. The top five were to

- Prepare people to become responsible citizens;
- Help people become economically sufficient;
- Ensure a basic level of quality among schools;
- Promote cultural unity among all Americans; [and]
- Improve social conditions for people.

Tied for sixth and seventh were goals to

- Enhance people's happiness and enrich their lives; and
- Dispel inequities in education among certain schools and certain groups.

To reach those goals, a democratic society expects schools to produce adults who are engaged in their communities, enlightened employers, and hard-working employees who have acquired and practiced particular values that sustain its way of life. Dominant American social, political, and economic values pervade family, school, workplace, and community: Act independently, accept personal responsibility for actions, work hard and complete a job well, and be fair, that is, willing to be judged by standards applied to others as long as the standards are applied equitably.

These norms show up in school rules and classroom practices in every school. School is the one institutional agent between the family, the workplace, and voting booth or jury room responsible for instilling those norms in children's behavior. School is the agent for turning 4-year-olds into respectful students engaged in their communities, a goal that the public perceives as more significant than preparing children and youths for college and the labor market. In elite decision makers' eagerness to link schools to a growing economy, they either overlooked the powerful daily practices of schooling or neglected to consider seriously these other goals. In doing so, they erred. The consequences of that error in judgment can be seen in the fleeting attention that policy recommendations for adding more time in school received before being shelved.

Teaching in a Democracy

Public schools were established before industrialization, and they expanded rapidly as factories and mills spread.

Those times appear foreign to readers today. For example, in the late 19th century, calling public schools "factory-like" was not an epithet hurled at educators or supporters of public schools as it has been in the U.S. since the 1960s. In fact, describing a public school as an assembly-line factory or a productive cotton mill was considered a compliment to forward-looking educators who sought to make schools modern through greater efficiency in teaching and learning by copying the successes of wealthy industrialists. Progressive reformers praised schools for being like industrial plants in creating large, efficient, age-graded schools that standardized curriculum while absorbing millions of urban migrants and foreign immigrants. As a leading progressive put it:

> Our schools are, in a sense, factories in which the raw products (children) are to be shaped and fashioned into products to meet the various demands of life. . . . It is the business of the school to build its pupils to the specifications [of manufacturers].

Progressive reformers saw mills, factories, and corporations as models for transforming the inefficient one-room schoolhouse in which students of different ages received fitful, incomplete instruction from one teacher into the far more efficient graded school where each teacher taught students a standardized curriculum each year. First established in Boston in 1848 and spreading swiftly in urban districts, the graded school became the dominant way of organizing a school by 1900. By the 1920s, schools exemplified the height of industrial efficiency because each building had separate classrooms with their own teachers. The principal and teachers expected children of the same age to cover the same content and learn skills by the end of the school year and perform satisfactorily on tests in order to be promoted to the next grade.

Superintendents saw the age-graded school as a modern version of schooling well adapted to an emerging corporate-dominated industrial society where punctuality, dependability, and obedience were prized behaviors. As a St. Louis superintendent said in 1871:

> The first requisite of the school is Order: each pupil must be taught first and foremost to conform his behavior to a general standard. . . . The pupil must have his lessons ready at the appointed time, must rise at the tap of the bell, move to the line, return; in short, go through all of the evolutions with equal precision.

Recognition and fame went to educators who achieved such order in their schools.

But the farm-driven seasonal nature of rural one-room schoolhouses was incompatible with the explosive growth of cities and an emerging industrial society. In the early 20th century, progressive reformers championed compulsory attendance laws while extending the abbreviated rural-driven short hours and days into a longer school day and year. Reformers wanted to increase the school's influence over children's attitudes and behavior, especially in cities where wave after wave of European immigrants settled. Seeking higher productivity in organization, teaching, and learning at the least cost, reformers broadened the school's mission by providing medical, social, recreational, and psychological services at schools. These progressive reformers believed schools should teach society's norms to both children and their families and also educate the whole child so that the entire government, economy, and society would change for the better. So, when reformers spoke about "factory-like schools" a century ago, they wanted educators to copy models of success; they were not scolding them. That changed, however, by the late 20th century.

As the U.S. shifted from a manufacturing-based economy to a post-industrial information-based economy, few policy makers reckoned with this history of schooling. Few influential decision makers view schools as agents of *both* stability and change. Few educational opinion makers recognize that the conservative public still expects schools to instill in children dominant American norms of being independent and being held accountable for one's actions, doing work well and efficiently, and treating others equitably to ensure that when students graduate they will practice these values as adults. And, yes, the public still expects schools to strengthen the economy by ensuring that graduates have the necessary skills to be productive employees in an ever-changing, highly competitive, and increasingly global workplace. But that is just one of many competing expectations for schools.

Thus far, I have focused mostly on how policy makers and reform-minded civic and business elites have not only defined economic problems as educational ones that can be fixed by more time spent in schools but also neglected the powerful hold that socialization goals have on parents' and taxpayers' expectations. Now, I want to switch from the world of reform-driven policy makers and elites to teachers and students because each group views school time differently from their respective perch. Teacher and student perspectives on time in school have little influence in policy makers' decision making. Although the daily actions of teachers and students don't influence policy makers, they do matter in explaining why reformers have had such paltry results in trying to fix school time.

Differing Views of Time in School

For civic and business leaders, media executives, school boards, superintendents, mayors, state legislators, governors, U.S. representatives, and the President (what I call "policy elites"), electoral and budget cycles become the timeframe within which they think and act. Every year, budgets must be prepared and, every two or four years, officials run for office and voters decide who should represent them and whether they should support bond referenda and tax levies. Because appointed and elected policy makers are influential with the media, they need to assure the public during campaigns that slogans and stump speeches were more than talk. Sometimes, words do become action when elected decision makers, for example, convert a comprehensive high school into a cluster of small high schools, initiate 1:1 laptop programs, and extend the school day. This is the world of policy makers.

The primary tools policy makers use to adopt and implement decisions, however, are limited and blunt—closer to a hammer than a scalpel. They use exhortation, press conferences, political bargaining, incentives, and sanctions to formulate and adopt decisions. (Note, however, that policy makers rarely implement decisions; administrators and practitioners put policies into practice.) Policy makers want broad social, political, economic, and organizational goals adopted as policies, and then they want to move educators, through encouragement, incentives, and penalties, to implement those policies in schools and classrooms that they seldom, if ever, enter.

The world of teachers differs from that of policy makers. For teachers, the time-driven budget and electoral cycles that shape policy matter little for their classrooms, except when such policies carry consequences for how and what teachers should teach, such as accountability measures that assume teachers and students are slackers and need to work harder. In these instances, teachers become classroom gatekeepers in deciding how much of a policy they will put into practice and under what conditions.

What matters most to teachers are student responses to daily lessons, weekly tests, monthly units, and the connections they build over time in classrooms, corridors, during lunch, and before and after school. Those personal connections become the compost of learning. Those connections account for former students pointing to particular teachers who made a difference in their lives. Teacher tools, unlike policy maker tools, are unconnected to organizational power or media influence. Teachers use their personalities, knowledge, experience, and skills in building relationships with groups of students and providing individual help. Teachers believe there is never enough time in the daily schedule to finish a lesson, explain a point, or listen to a student. Administrative intrusions gobble up valuable instructional time that could go to students. In class, then, both teachers and students are clock watchers, albeit for different reasons.

Students view time differently as well. For a fraction of students from middle- and low-income families turned off by school requirements and expectations, spending time in classrooms listening to teachers, answering questions, and doing homework is torture; the hands of the clock seldom move fast enough for them. The notion of extending the school day and school year for them— or continuing on to college and four more years of reading texts and sitting in classrooms—is not a reform to be implemented but a punishment to be endured. Such students look for creative shortcuts to skip classes, exit the school as early as they can, and find jobs or enter the military once they graduate.

Most students, however, march from class to class until they hear "Pomp and Circumstance." But a high school diploma, graduates have come to realize, is not enough in the 21st-century labor market.

College for Everyone

In the name of equity and being responsive to employers' needs, most urban districts have converted particular comprehensive high schools into clusters of small college-prep academies where low-income minority students take Advanced Placement courses, write research papers, and compete to get into colleges and universities. Here, then, is the quiet, unheralded, and unforeseen victory of reformers bent on fixing time in school. They have succeeded unintentionally in stretching K-12 into preK-16 public schooling, not just for middle-and upper-middle class students, but for everyone.

As it has been for decades for most suburban middle-and upper-middle class white and minority families, now it has become a fact, an indisputable truth converted into a sacred mission for upwardly mobile poor families: A high school diploma and a bachelor's degree are passports to high-paying jobs and the American Dream.

For families who already expect their sons and daughters to attend competitive colleges, stress begins early. Getting into the best preschools and elementary and secondary schools and investing in an array of activities to build attractive résumés for college admission officers to evaluate become primary tasks. For such families and children, there is never enough time for homework, Advanced Placement courses, music, soccer, drama, dance, and assorted after-school activities. For high-achieving, stressed-out students already expecting at least four more years of school after high school graduation, reform proposals urging a longer school year and an extended day often strike an unpleasant note. Angst and fretfulness become familiar clothes to don every morning as students grind out 4s and 5s on Advanced Placement exams, play sports, and compile just the right record that will get them into just the right school.

For decades, pressure on students to use every minute of school to prepare for college has been strongest in middle-and upper-middle-class suburbs. What has changed in the past few decades is the spread of the belief that everyone, including low-income minority students, should go to college.

To summarize, for decades, policy elites have disregarded teacher and student perspectives on time in school. Especially now when all students are expected to enter college, children, youths, and teachers experience time in school differently than policy makers who seek a longer school day and school year. Such varied perceptions about time are heavily influenced by the socialization goals of schooling, age-graded structures, socioeconomic status of families, and historical experience. And policy makers often ignore these perceptions and reveal their tone-deafness and myopia in persistently trying to fix time in schools.

Policy elites need to parse fully this variation in perceptions because extended time in school remains a high priority to reform-driven policy makers and civic and business leaders anxious about U.S. performance on international tests and fearful of falling behind in global economic competitiveness. The crude policy solutions of more days in the year and longer school days do not even begin to touch the deeper truth that what has to improve is the quality of "academic learning time." If policy makers could open their ears and eyes to student and teacher perceptions of time, they would learn that the secular Holy Grail is decreasing interruption of instruction, encouraging richer intellectual and personal connections between teachers and students, and increasing classroom time for ambitious teaching and active, engaged learning. So far, no such luck.

Conclusion

These three reasons—cost, lackluster research, and the importance of conservative social goals to U.S. taxpayers and voters—explain why proposals to fix time in U.S. schools have failed to take hold.

Policy elites know research studies proving the worth of year-round schools or lengthened school days are in short supply. Even if an occasional study supported the change, the school year is unlikely to go much beyond 180 days. Policy elites know school goals go far beyond simply preparing graduates for college and for employability in a knowledge-based economy. And policy elites know they must show courage in their pursuit of improving failing U.S. schools by forcing students to go to school just as long as their peers in India, China, Japan, and Korea. That courage shows up symbolically, playing well in the media and in proposals to fix time in schools, but it seldom alters calendars.

While cost is a factor, it is the stability of schooling structures and the importance of socializing the young into the values of the immediate community and larger society that have defeated policy-driven efforts to alter time in school over the past quarter century. Like the larger public, I am unconvinced that requiring students and teachers to spend more time in school each day and every year will be better for them. How that time is spent in learning before, during, and after school is far more important than decision makers counting the minutes, hours, and days students spend each year getting schooled. That being said, I have little doubt that state and federal blue-ribbon commissions will continue to make proposals about lengthening time in school. Those proposals will make headlines, but they will not result in serious, sustained attention to what really matters—improving the quality of the time that teachers and students spend with one another in and out of classrooms.

POSTSCRIPT

Do American Students Need More Time in School?

One central aspect of the debate over time expansion in schools is this: to significantly improve student achievement the ways in which time is utilized must change. This is the main point of Douglas Fisher's article "The Use of Instructional Time in the Typical High School Classroom," *The Educational Forum* (Spring 2009). Although Fisher's focus is on secondary schools, his observations are relevant for elementary and middle schools as well. Too much "schooling" involves listening and waiting and too little time is spent closing the gap between what students know and what they need to know, Fisher contends. Similarly, Erika A. Patall, Harris Cooper, and Ashley Batts Allen, in "Extending the School Day or School Year: A Systematic Review of Research," *Review of Educational Research* (September 2010), conclude that extending school time can be an effective way to support student learning, particularly (a) for students most at risk of failure and (b) when considerations are made for how time is used. One important qualitative point is made in a Center for American Progress blog titled "Expanded Learning Time by the Numbers," (April 22, 2010) that explores the extent to which community-based organizations such as arts and cultural institutions take on more collaborative roles within extended-time schools.

Another crucial topic for consideration is the contribution of "summer loss" to the performance gaps among various identifiable groups. In "The Case Against Summer Vacation," *Time* (July 22, 2010), David Von Drehle contends that "larking through is a luxury we can't afford." Especially for children of low-income families "summer is a season of boredom, inactivity, and isolation" and this takes a steep toll on them. "It is among the most pernicious—if least acknowledged—causes of the achievement gap," he claims. By the end of elementary school low-income students have fallen nearly three grade levels behind, and summer is the biggest culprit. The topic is further explored by Donna Celano and Susan B. Neuman in "When Schools Close, the Knowledge Gap Grows," *Phi Delta Kappan* (December 2008).

Other aspects of the time allocation and use problem are treated in these sources: Karin Chenoweth, *How It's Being Done: Urgent Lessons from Unexpected Schools* (2009); *Choosing More Time for Students: The What, Why, and How of Expanded Learning* (2007), a Center for American Progress report by Elena Roche; Marilyn Crawford, "Think Inside the Clock," *Phi Delta Kappan* (December 2008); and Michael B. Horn, who, in "Innovative Approaches to School Time," a presentation to a U.S. Senate committee hearing on August 24, 2010, proposes a cost-effective solution: online learning.

ISSUE 20

Do Computers Negatively Affect Student Growth?

YES: Lowell Monke, from "The Human Touch," *Education Next* (Fall 2004)

NO: Frederick M. Hess, from "Technical Difficulties," *Education Next* (Fall 2004)

ISSUE SUMMARY

YES: Lowell Monke, an assistant professor of education, expresses deep concerns that the uncritical faith in computer technology in schools has led to sacrifices in intellectual growth and creativity.

NO: Frederick M. Hess, while sharing some of Monke's observations, believes that the tools of technology, used appropriately, can support innovation and reinvention in education.

The schools have not always used or responded to new media constructively, so it is crucial that media experts help teachers, administrators, and curriculum designers carve out appropriate strategies for dealing with new technologies. Some experts—while seeing many exciting possibilities in computer-based instruction, particularly in the realm of individualization and self-pacing—caution that we need far more sophisticated understanding of the processes of learning, human motivation, and factors involved in concentration. Others fear the controlling force of computer programs because it could lead to the diminution of the spontaneity and instinctive responses of the learner. The ultimate effect of the new technology could be a complete transformation of learning and the conception of organized education—but similar predictions were made with the advent of television and even radio.

In 1984 MIT professor Seymour Papert predicted, "There won't be schools in the future; I think that the computer will blow up the school." But Larry Cuban, in "Revolutions That Fizzled," *The Washington Post* (October 27, 1996), warns that the persistent urge to reengineer the schools has continually failed to transform teaching practices. Papert, writing in the same issue, counters that the computer makes possible John Dewey's depiction of learning through experimentation and exposure to the real world of social experience. Computer enthusiasts Jim Cummins of New York University and Dennis Sayers of the Ontario Institute for Studies in Education, in their 1996 book *Brave New Schools*, urge heavy investment in an Internet-wired nationwide school system.

On the negative side, Richard P. Lookatch, in "The Ill-Considered Dash to Technology," *The School Administrator* (April 1996), warns that "hardware hucksters have found K–12 schools to be open landfills for outdated central processing units, while software pushers find technology-zealous media specialists ideal targets for software, much of which ultimately ends up in a storage cabinet because it is either too frustrating, too complicated, or too poorly correlated to the curriculum." His position is that educational media offer no unique benefits and may well lead to inequity, lower standards, and wasted financial resources.

In "The Emperor's New Computer: A Critical Look at Our Appetite for Computer Technology," *Journal of Teacher Education* (May–June 1996), David Pepi and Geoffrey Schuerman pose several crucial questions, including the following:

- Is technology an effective catalyst for educational reform?
- Are past, current, and anticipated uses of technology consistent with contemporary theories of learning?
- Is using computers synonymous with good teaching?
- Does technology promote critical thinking?
- Does technology build cooperation?
- How much information can we tolerate?

In considering responses to such questions, the authors draw on Neil Postman's 1993 book *Technopoly*, in which "technopoly" is defined as a culture in which all aspects of human life must find meaning in terms of the current technology and in which there is no tolerance of alternative worldviews. It is Postman's opinion that we are moving toward that culture.

Books addressing the issue include Jane M. Healy's *Failure to Connect* (1998); Frederick Bennett's *Computers as Tutors: Solving the Crisis in Education* (1999); Clifford Stoll's *High Tech Heretic* (1999); Andrea A. DiSessa's *Changing Minds: Computers, Learning, and Literacy* (2000); Larry Cuban's *Oversold and Underused* (2001); and Seymour Papert's *The Connected Family* (1996). In his book, Papert states, "Despite frequent predictions that a technological revolution in education is imminent, school remains in essential respects very much what it has always been, and what changes have occurred (for better or for worse) cannot be attributed to technology."

The opinions that follow pit Lowell Monke, who feels that the computer's emphasis on information acquisition reconstitutes learning and shifts our values, against Frederick Hess, who holds out hope that the efficiencies of computer technology can free students and teachers for more creative exploration.

YES ↵

Lowell Monke

The Human Touch

In 1922 Thomas Edison proclaimed, "I believe the motion picture is destined to revolutionize our educational system and that in a few years it will supplant largely, if not entirely, the use of textbooks." Thus began a long string of spectacularly wrong predictions regarding the capacity of various technologies to revolutionize education.

What betrayed Edison and his successors was an uncritical faith in technology itself. This faith has become a sort of ideology increasingly dominating K–12 education. In the past two decades, school systems, with generous financial and moral support from foundations and all levels of government, have made massive investments in computer technology and in creating "wired" schools. The goal is twofold: to provide children with the computer skills necessary to flourish in a high-tech world and to give them access to tools and information that will enhance their learning in subjects like mathematics and history.

However, in recent years a number of scholars have questioned the vast sums being devoted to educational technology. They rarely quibble with the need for children to learn how to use computers, but find little evidence that making technology more available leads to higher student achievement in core subjects. As Stanford University professor Larry Cuban writes in *Oversold and Underused,* "There have been no advances (measured by higher academic achievement of urban, suburban, or rural students) over the past decade that can be confidently attributed to broader access to computers. . . . The link between test-score improvements and computer availability and use is even more contested."

While it is important to examine the relationship between technology and learning, that debate often devolves into a tit-for-tat of dueling studies and anecdotes. The problem with framing the issue merely as a question of whether technology boosts test scores is that it fails to address the interaction between technology and the values learned in school. In short, we need to ask what kind of learning tends to take place with the computer and what kind gets left out.

The Need for Firsthand Experience

A computer can inundate a child with mountains of information. However, all of this learning takes place the same way: through abstract symbols,

From *Education Next,* vol. 4, no. 4, Fall 2004, pp. 10–14. Copyright © 2004 by Education Next. Reprinted by permission of Hoover Institution, Stanford University.

decontextualized and cast on a two-dimensional screen. Contrast that with the way children come to know a tree—by peeling its bark, climbing its branches, sitting under its shade, jumping into its piled-up leaves. Just as important, these firsthand experiences are enveloped by feelings and associations—muscles being used, sun warming the skin, blossoms scenting the air. The computer cannot even approximate any of this.

There is a huge qualitative difference between learning about something, which requires only information, and learning from something, which requires that the learner enter into a rich and complex relationship with the subject at hand. For smaller children especially, that relationship is as physical as it is mental. Rousseau pointed out long ago that the child's first and most important teacher is his hands. Every time I walk through a store with my sons and grow tired of saying, "Don't touch that!" I am reminded of Rousseau's wisdom.

What "Information Age" values tempt us to forget is that all of the information gushing through our electronic networks is abstract; that is, it is all representations, one or more symbolic steps removed from any concrete object or personal experience. Abstract information must somehow connect to a child's concrete experiences if it is to be meaningful. If there is little personal, concrete experience with which to connect, those abstractions become inert bits of data, unlikely to mobilize genuine interest or to generate comprehension of the objects and ideas they represent. Furthermore, making meaning of new experiences—and the ideas that grow out of them—requires quiet contemplation. By pumping information at children at phenomenal speed, the computer short-circuits that process. As social critic Theodore Roszak states in *The Cult of Information*, "An excess of information may actually crowd out ideas, leaving the mind (young minds especially) distracted by sterile, disconnected facts, lost among the shapeless heaps of data."

This deluge of shapeless heaps of data caused the late social critic Marshall McLuhan to conclude that schools would have to become "recognized as civil defense against media fallout." McLuhan understood that the consumption and manipulation of symbolic, abstract information is not an adequate substitute for concrete, firsthand involvement with objects, people, nature, and community, for it ignores the child's primary educational need—to make meaning out of experience.

Simulation's Limits

Of course, computers can simulate experience. However, one of the by-products of these simulations is the replacement of values inherent in real experience with a different set of abstract values that are compatible with the technological ideology. For example, "Oregon Trail," a computer game that helps children simulate the exploration of the American frontier, teaches students that the pioneers' success in crossing the Great Plains depended most decisively on managing their resources. This is the message implicit in the game's structure, which asks students, in order to survive, to make a series of rational, calculated decisions based on precise measurements of their resources. In other words, good pioneers were good accountants.

But this completely misses the deeper significance of this great American migration, which lies not in the computational capabilities of the pioneers but in their determination, courage, ingenuity, and faith as they overcame extreme conditions and their almost constant miscalculations. Because the computer cannot traffic in these deeply human qualities, the resilient souls of the pioneers are absent from the simulation.

Here we encounter the ambiguity of technology: its propensity to promote certain qualities while sidelining others. McLuhan called this process amplification and amputation. He used the microphone as an example. The microphone can literally amplify one's voice, but in doing so it reduces the speaker's need to exercise his own lung power. Thus one's inner capacities may atrophy.

This phenomenon is of particular concern with children, who are in the process of developing all kinds of inner capacities. Examples abound of technology's circumventing the developmental process: the student who uses a spell checker instead of learning to spell, the student who uses a calculator instead of learning to add—young people sacrificing internal growth for external power.

Often, however, this process is not so easily identified. An example is the widespread use of computers in preschools and elementary schools to improve sagging literacy skills. What could be wrong with that? Quite a bit, if we consider the prerequisites to reading and writing. We know that face-to-face conversation is a crucial element in the development of both oral and written communication skills. On the one hand, conversation forces children to generate their own images, which provide connections to the language they hear and eventually will read. This is one reason why reading to children and telling them stories is so important. Television and computers, on the other hand, generally require nothing more than the passive acceptance of prefabricated images.

Now consider that a study reported in *U.S. News & World Report* estimated that the current generation of children, with its legions of struggling readers, would experience one-third fewer face-to-face conversations during their school years than the generation of 30 years ago. It may well be that educators are trying to solve the problem of illiteracy by turning to the very technology that has diminished the experiences children need to become literate.

Obsolete Lessons

But students need to start using computers early in order to prepare for the high-tech future, don't they? Consider that the vast majority of students graduating from college this past spring started kindergarten in 1986, two years after the Macintosh was invented. If they used computers at all in elementary school, they were probably command-line machines with no mouse, no hard drive, and only rudimentary graphics. By the time these students graduated from college, whatever computer skills they picked up in primary school had long been rendered obsolete by the frenetic pace of technological innovation.

The general computer skills a youth needs to enter the workplace or college can easily be learned in one year of instruction during high school. During the nine years that I taught Advanced Computer Technology for the Des Moines public schools, I discovered that the level of computer skills students brought to the class had little bearing on their success. Teaching them the computer skills was the easy part. What I was not able to provide were the rich and varied firsthand experiences students needed in order to connect the abstract symbols they had to manipulate on the screen to the world around them. Students with scant computer experience but rich ideas and life experiences were, by the end of the year, generating sophisticated relational databases, designing marketable websites, and creating music videos. Ironically, it was the students who had curtailed their time climbing the trees, rolling the dough, and conversing with friends and adults in order to become computer "wizards" who typically had the most trouble finding creative things to do with the computer.

Certainly, many of these highly skilled young people (almost exclusively young men) find opportunities to work on computer and software design at prestigious universities and corporations. But such jobs represent a minuscule percentage of the occupations in this nation. And in any case, the task of early education is not merely to prepare students for making a living; it is to help them learn how to make a life. For that purpose, the computer wizards in my class seemed particularly ill prepared.

So why is it that schools persist in believing they must expose children to computers early? I think it is for the same reason that we take our children to church, to Fourth of July parades, and indeed to rituals of all types: to initiate them into a culture—in this case, the culture of high technology. The purpose is to infuse them with a set of values that supports the high-tech culture that has spread so rapidly across our society. And this, as we shall see, is perhaps the most disturbing trend of all.

The Ecological Impact of Technology

As the promise of a computer revolution in education fades, I often hear promoters fall back on what I'll term the neutrality argument: "Computers are just tools; it's what you do with them that matters." In some sense this is no more than a tautology: Of course it matters *how* we use computers in schools. What matters more, however, is that we use them *at all*. Every tool demands that we somehow change our environment or values in order to accommodate its use. For instance, the building of highways to accommodate the automobile hastened the flight to the suburbs and the decline of inner cities. And over the past 50 years we have radically altered our social landscape to accommodate the television set. In his seminal book *Autonomous Technology,* Langdon Winner dubbed this characteristic "reverse adaptation."

Consider the school personnel who already understand, intuitively, how this principle works: the music teacher whose program has been cut in order to fund computer labs; the principal who has had to beef up security in order to protect high-priced technology; the superintendent who has had to craft an "acceptable use" agreement that governs children's use of the Internet (and for the first time in our history renounces the school's responsibility for the material children are exposed to while in school). What the computers-are-just-tools argument ignores is the ecological nature of powerful technologies—that is, their introduction into an environment reconstitutes all of the relationships in that environment, some for better and some for worse. Clinging to the belief that computers have no effect on us allows us to turn a blind eye to the sacrifices that schools have made to accommodate them.

Not only do computers send structural ripples throughout a school system, but they also subtly alter the way we think about education. The old saw, "To a man with a hammer everything looks like a nail," has many corollaries (the walls of my home once testified to one of my favorites: to a four-year-old with a crayon, everything looks like drawing paper). One that fits here is, "To an educator with a computer, everything looks like information." And the more prominent we make computers in schools (and in our own lives), the more we see the rapid accumulation, manipulation, and sharing of information as central to the learning process—edging out the contemplation and expression of ideas and the gradual development of meaningful connections to the world.

In reconstituting learning as the acquisition of information, the computer also shifts our values. The computer embodies a particular value system, a technological thought world first articulated by Francis Bacon and Rene Descartes four hundred years ago, that turns our attention outward toward asserting control over our environment (that is essentially what technologies do—extend our power to control from a distance). As it has gradually come to dominate Western thinking, this ideology has entered our educational institutions. Its growing dominance is witnessed in the language that abounds in education: talk of empowerment, student control of learning, standards, assessment tools, and productivity. Almost gone from the conversation are those inner concerns—wisdom, truth, character, imagination, creativity, and meaning—that once formed the core values of education. Outcomes have replaced insights as the yardstick of learning, while standardized tests are replacing human judgment as the means of assessment. No tool supports this technological shift more than computers.

In the Wrong Hands

There are some grave consequences in pushing technological values too far and too soon. Soon after my high-school computer lab was hooked up to the Internet, I realized that my students suddenly had more power to do more damage to more people than any teenagers in history. Had they been carefully prepared to assume responsibility for that power through the arduous process of developing self-discipline, ethical and moral strength, compassion, and connection with the community around them? Hardly. They and their teachers had been too busy putting that power to use.

We must help our young people develop the considerable moral and ethical strength needed to resist abusing the enormous power these machines give them. Those qualities take a great deal of time and effort to develop in a child, but they ought to be as much a prerequisite to using powerful computer tools as is learning how to type. Trying to teach a student to use the power of computer technology appropriately without those moral and ethical traits is like trying to grow a tree without roots.

Rather than nurture those roots, we hand our smallest children machines and then gush about the power and control they display over that rarefied environment. From the earliest years we teach our children that if they have a problem, we have an external tool that will fix it (computers are not the only tools; Ritalin, for example, is a powerful technology that has been scandalously overprescribed to "fix" behavior problems). After years of this training, when our teenagers find themselves confused, angry, depressed, or overwhelmed, we wonder why so many of them don't reach out to the community for help or dig deep within themselves to find the internal strength to persevere, but rather reach for the most powerful (and often deadly) tool they can find to "fix" their problems. Our attempts to use powerful machines to accelerate or remediate learning are part of a pattern that sacrifices the growth of our children's inner resources and deep connectedness to community for the ability to extend their power outward into the world. The world pays a high price for the trade-off.

The response that I often hear to this criticism—that we just need to balance computer use in school with more "hands-on" activities (and maybe a little character education)—sounds reasonable. Certainly schools should help young people develop balanced lives. But the call for balance within schools ignores the massive commitment of resources required to make computers work at all and the resultant need to keep them constantly in use to justify that expense. Furthermore, that view of balance completely discounts the enormous imbalance of children's lives outside of school. Children typically spend nearly half their waking life outside of school sitting in front of screens. Their world is saturated with the artificial, the abstract, the mechanical. Whereas the intellectual focus of schools in the rural society of the 19th century compensated for a childhood steeped in nature and concrete activity, balance today requires a reversal of roles, with schools compensating for the overly abstract, symbolic, and artificial environment that children experience outside of school.

Technology with a Human Purpose

None of this is to say that we should banish computers from all levels of K–12 education. As young people move into subject areas like advanced mathematics and chemistry that rely on highly abstract concepts, computers have much to offer. Young people will also need computer skills when they graduate. But computer-based learning needs to grow out of years of concrete experience and a fundamental appreciation for the world apart from the machine, a world in which nature and human beings are able to speak for and through themselves to the child. Experiences with the computer need to grow out of early reliance on simple tools that depend on and develop the skills of the child rather than complex tools, which have so many skills already built in. By concentrating high technology in the upper grades, we honor the natural developmental stages of childhood. And there is a bonus: the release of massive amounts of resources currently tied up in expensive machinery that can be redirected toward helping young children develop the inner resources needed to put that machinery to good use when they become adults.

There remains a problem, however. When Bacon began pushing the technological ideology, Western civilization was full of meaning and wretchedly short on the material means of survival. Today we face the reverse situation: a society saturated in material comforts but almost devoid of meaning. Schools that see their job as preparing young people to meet the demands of a technology-driven world merely embrace and advance the idea that human needs are no longer our highest priority, that we must adapt to meet the demands of our machines. We may deliver our children into the world with tremendous technical power, but it is rarely with a well-developed sense of human purpose to guide its use.

If we are to alter that relationship, we will have to think of technological literacy in a new way. Perhaps we could call it technology awareness. Whatever its name, that kind of study, rather than technology training, is what needs to be integrated into the school curriculum. I am currently working with the Alliance for Childhood on a set of developmental guidelines to help educators create technology-awareness programs that help young people think about, not just with, technology. This is not the place to go into the details of those guidelines. What I want to emphasize here is that they share one fundamental feature: They situate technology within a set of human values rather than out in front of those values. They do not start by asking what children need to do to adapt to a machine world, but rather, which technologies can best serve human purposes at every educational level and how we can prepare children to make wise decisions about their use in the future.

The most daunting problems facing our society—drugs, violence, racism, poverty, the dissolution of family and community, and certainly war—are all matters of human purpose and meaning. Filling schools with computers will not help find the answers to why the freest nation in the world has the highest percentage of citizens behind bars or why the wealthiest nation in history condemns a sixth of its children to poverty.

So it seems that we are faced with a remarkable irony: that in an age of increasing artificiality, children first need to sink their hands deeply into what is real; that in an age of light-speed communication, it is crucial that children take the time to develop their own inner voice; that in an age of incredibly powerful machines we must first teach our children how to use the incredible powers that lie deep within themselves.

Frederick M. Hess NO

Technical Difficulties

In 2000, at the height of the technology boom, Maine governor Angus King made a splash by proposing to give laptops to all of the state's 7th graders. His stated purpose was to "do something different from what everybody else is doing." Missing from the $50 million proposal, however, was any rationale related to school performance. No evident thought had been put into how this major investment in new technology would make schools more efficient, produce future savings, or enhance the learning process.

King's proposal was typical of the way in which technologies like the personal computer and the Internet have been used in public education. The tendency has been to sprinkle computers and Internet connections across classrooms in the pleasant hope that teachers will integrate them into their lessons. The purpose is seldom to make teachers more productive or to rethink the way in which lessons are delivered. Indeed, PCs often serve as little more than high-priced typewriters, sitting in the back of classrooms unused for most of the school day.

This state of affairs stands in sharp contrast to how technology is used by business and government enterprises that engage in competition with other manufacturers and service providers. To them, technology is not an end in itself, something to be adopted merely because it exists, but a tool for self-improvement. A competitive enterprise adopts new technologies when these enable workers to tackle new problems or to do the *same thing* as before, but in a *cheaper and more efficient* fashion. For example, technology investments enabled the U.S. Postal Service, under heavy competitive pressure from United Parcel Service and Federal Express, to trim its workforce by 16,000 in 2003. These cuts followed layoffs of 23,000 employees over the preceding two years. The cuts were made possible not by reducing service, but by substituting technology in areas where people were performing either routine tasks or roles that automated machines could handle more efficiently.

At a broader level, in recent years the nation's 100 largest companies improved productivity so rapidly that in 2003 it took only nine workers to do what ten workers had done in 2001. Economists have long recognized that the potential for growth in productivity is more limited in service sectors like education than in manufacturing or retail. Nonetheless, even the service sector has witnessed productivity gains of about 1 percent a year during the past three decades.

From *Education Next,* vol. 4, no. 4, Fall 2004, pp. 15–19. Copyright © 2004 by Education Next. Reprinted by permission of Hoover Institution, Stanford University.

Public schools, by contrast, have steadily *added* to the ranks of teachers and reduced class sizes even as they make ever-larger investments in new technologies. Spending on technology in public schools increased from essentially zero in 1970 to $118 per student in 2002 and $89 per student in 2003, according to *Education Week*. In 1998 there were 12.1 students for every computer connected to the Internet; by 2002, the ratio had dropped to 4.8 students per computer, according to the Department of Education. In the past five years alone, the nation has spent more than $20 billion linking schools and classrooms to the Internet through the federal E-rate program with little to show for it in the way of instructional changes or improved outcomes. Meanwhile, despite these huge new investments in technology, massive increases in the workforce of teachers drove the student-teacher ratio from 22 students per teacher to 16 students per teacher between 1970 and 2001.

Cultural Bias

Why have public schools failed so far to put all this fancy new technology to good use? One clear reason is that they face no pressure to do so. Organizations like the Postal Service make effective use of technology because they must keep up with FedEx, UPS, and other delivery services. Competitive enterprises are on a constant search for ways of boosting their productivity, holding down their costs, and developing innovative products—because they know that their competitors are always on the lookout for similar advantages. No executive wants to adopt a painful course like downsizing the workforce or imposing wrenching change. They take these steps only when compelled.

Public schools, however, are insulated from the pressures of competition. They thus have no reason to regard technology as a tool to trim their workforce or to rethink the ways in which they deliver education. This problem is compounded by the fact that collective-bargaining agreements between school districts and employee unions have made using technology to displace workers or reinvent processes extraordinarily difficult.

There is also a bias within the culture of education against ideas that seem too "businesslike." Indeed, the very words "efficiency" and "cost-effectiveness" can set the teeth of parents and educators on edge. Proposals to use technology to downsize the workforce, alter instructional delivery, or improve managerial efficiency are inevitably attacked by education authorities as part of an effort to, in the words of Henry Giroux, "Transform public education . . . [in order] to expand the profits of investors, educate students as consumers, and train young people for the low-paying jobs of the new global marketplace." The notion that the responsible use of public money is the work of some shadowy global conspiracy evinces a fundamental lack of seriousness about educating children.

Traditionalists insist that it is impossible to educate children more efficiently, that there is no way technology can be substituted for anything that educators do. They frequently compare the act of teaching to the arts: where the act of creation itself is the end product, it can be difficult or impossible to use technology to improve performance. As the late Daniel Patrick Moynihan, the legendary U.S. senator, was fond of saying, producing a Mozart quartet two centuries ago required four musicians, four stringed instruments, and, say, 35 minutes. Producing the same Mozart quartet today requires the same resources. Despite breathtaking technological advances, productivity has not changed.

In the case of schooling, however, this analogy is incomplete and ultimately misleading. In the arts, what has changed over two centuries is that, through radio, CDs, television, and digital media, the number of people able to *hear and appreciate* a given performance has increased dramatically, at an ever-decreasing cost. Improved technology has now made available to the general public what was once the preserve of the elite.

The spread of the Internet and other technological advances has created similar opportunities in education. For instance, during the 2002–03 school year, the Florida Virtual School enrolled more than 6,800 students in its 75 course offerings. Florida Virtual is a public entity that provides instruction to students in schools and districts throughout the state. The school provides web-based classes, instruction, and assessments to students in a variety of academic subjects and electives. Like virtual schools operating in 15 other states, Florida Virtual allows faculty to provide courses to a scattered student population. Programs like Florida Virtual may make it possible to provide some academic instruction more cheaply and more effectively, freeing up resources for other needs.

At the university level, nearly 2 million students took at least one course online in the fall of 2003. In a national survey of nearly 1,000 college administrators conducted by the Sloan Consortium, 57 percent of the administrators reported that Internet-based courses were already at least equivalent to traditional courses in quality. And a third of the administrators thought that the web-based courses would be superior to in-class instruction within three years. Such improvements are to be expected among the many colleges and universities now competing for students' distance-learning dollars. However, efforts to use the Internet in an effective manner are few and far between among K–12 public schools.

Technology and Data Management

Used wisely, information technology does have the capacity to help schools become dramatically more effective. Data systems that track information on individual students permit teachers to quickly check the performance of individual students on specific tasks. Information technology can also give school-site personnel unprecedented control over budgets and hiring and can increase their flexibility regarding resource allocation. The Learning First Alliance, a consortium that includes the National Education Association and the American Federation of Teachers, has highlighted how this has worked in districts like Long Beach and Chula Vista, California, and Aldine, Texas.

Outside of schooling, a compelling illustration of how accountability and technology can together improve public services comes from the remarkable success that New York City and other cities enjoyed using new tools to combat crime in the 1990s. The New York City Police Department introduced a system called CompStat, short for "comparative statistics." CompStat compiled data from police reports, crime complaints, arrests, and crime patterns. Over time, the system was broadened to include 734 categories of concern, measuring even the incidence of loud parties and of police overtime.

In the first five years after the 1993 introduction of CompStat, the number of homicides in New York City fell from 1,946 to 629—a rate of decrease three times that of the nation as a whole. Similar results were experienced in other cities that implemented the system, from Philadelphia to Los Angeles. Why did the system work? It helped to hold officers accountable, to pinpoint areas of concern, and to provide the information that can help all police focus on using their skills. In New York City, precincts were required to update their crime statistics on a weekly or daily basis, rather than on the monthly or quarterly basis that had traditionally been the norm. New software allowed department officials to precisely map clusters of crimes, correlating them with drug sale sites, areas of gang activity, schools, public housing, and other relevant locations, and to share the information department-wide within seconds.

In K–12 education, by contrast, we generally manage most information the same way stores managed inventory in the 1960s. Almost unbelievably in this day and age, the typical district spends 40 or more minutes a year per student collecting, processing, and reporting the data required by the U.S. Department of Education under the No Child Left Behind Act. That equates to more than 6,000 hours of employee time in a district with 10,000 students. The tremendous delays in processing data and the staff time consumed are the consequence of districts' having personnel fill out written forms and retyping data from one software package to another. Simply equipping districts to report data electronically and acquire data from existing databases is a daunting challenge.

When principals or teachers are asked for this information, those that have it available almost inevitably turn to large binders rather than more nimble electronic interfaces. When asked if he could pull some data on teacher absenteeism or staff training costs, one veteran principal in a well-regarded district spluttered, "Do you know what I do if I want substitute teacher data? I have [my secretary] go through the files and tally it up. She keeps a running total on a piece of graph paper for me. . . . If I want to check on a supply order, I call the deputy [superintendent] for services because we're old friends, and I know he'll actually have someone pull it for me."

Modern information technology offers a wealth of straight-forward, time-tested ways to make the necessary data widely and instantly available. There is an array of systems, produced by firms like Scantron and IntelliTools, that allow teachers to call up simple graphs detailing the performance of individual students at the push of a button. However, using these systems requires the consistent collection of information on student learning. Assigning paper-based quizzes ensures that almost all of the information on student mastery will be lost, while the software produced by a dozen or more firms is able to quickly read the results from electronically administered tests into an evolving portfolio of data that tracks student learning.

Ultimately, to be useful, this information has to be at people's fingertips. This is an eminently solvable technical challenge. Huge, complicated organizations, from Wal-Mart to the Internal Revenue Service, routinely track productivity figures, costs, and evaluative measures.

A New Role for Teachers

How else can technology support innovation and reinvention in education? Consider that, historically, teachers have been expected to perform a wide range of responsibilities. Each teacher is expected to design lesson plans, lecture, run class discussions, grade essays and exams, mentor colleagues, supervise homeroom, and patrol the cafeteria. Every year our high schools have tens of thousands of teachers giving variations of the same lectures on the Civil War, the digestive system, and the properties of quadratic equations. In fact, the job description of a teacher today is pretty similar to that of a teacher in 1950.

In medicine, by contrast, progress has been marked by specialization. Doctors with different types of training have taken on more precisely defined roles while less expensive professionals like registered nurses and physical therapists are now performing tasks that don't require a doctor's training. Similarly, 16-year-old volunteers using handheld scanners are able to track medical supplies and hospital inventory with a precision that would have been unimaginable even in the best-managed enterprise just two decades ago.

Imagine a hospital with no nurses or physicians' assistants or physical therapists, where doctors performed every task. We would need a slew of additional doctors, each would have less time to devote to any particular specialty, and costs would skyrocket.

How can technology enable teachers to specialize in the same manner as, say, doctors? Let's consider one classroom example in order to understand how technology can help teachers use their time more productively. Teachers know it is useful to have students write on a regular basis. When I taught high-school social studies, like so many of my colleagues, I required students to write at least three pages a week commenting on what we had read and discussed in class.

The problem is that, at a minimum, this meant my 150 students would turn in 450 pages a week of writing. A teacher who reads, marks, and comments on each student's weekly work in just five minutes will spend more than 12 hours a week simply providing feedback on such writing assignments. Most of this time isn't spent providing particularly cerebral feedback, but instead flagging obvious grammatical and structural problems and reminding students to write in complete sentences. Meanwhile, teachers also need to prepare for teaching, assess other assignments, assist and advise students, and lead a personal life. The result is often that teachers provide limited feedback, read student work sporadically, or (most commonly) assign less writing than might be ideal.

Once, such compromises were unavoidable. That is no longer the case. Today, for instance, there is essay-grading software, commercially available from companies like Vantage Learning or the Educational Testing Service, that can quickly and efficiently analyze pieces of writing on dimensions such as sentence construction, language, and mechanics. Several of these programs match the scores given by expert human raters more than 90 percent of the time, which is actually *higher* in some cases than the rate of agreement among multiple human readers. How can this be? In most cases, we're not talking about evaluating Proustian prose; we're talking about helping the typical 4th grader learn to write clearly and effectively. Most of the mistakes that students make and most of the feedback they need are pretty predictable.

Clearly technological tools cannot imitate the full range of skills that a teacher brings when reading a student's essay. Technology cannot gauge a student's growth, analytic prowess, possible interests, or unexpected developments. However, assessment software can replicate the routine elements of evaluation, providing more complete feedback on the essentials while freeing up teachers to make fuller use of their expertise. The result is that teachers spend less time on trivia while adding more value. Rather than requiring hundreds of thousands of teachers to spend hundreds of hours a year circling dangling participles or errant commas, the sensible substitution of technology can help ensure quality feedback while allowing teachers more time for preparation, instruction, and tutoring.

Human ingenuity is the most expensive commodity in the developed world. People are costly to employ; no well-run organization hires reams of bodies when it is possible to hire more selectively and use employees more thoughtfully. This is why efforts to reduce class size are a static, unimaginative, and inefficient way to improve schooling. These efforts presume that teachers need to perform all the duties and tasks now in place; helping them accomplish these tasks more effectively thus requires shrinking the number of students they must teach. However, if we were to retool the teacher's role in a way that used scarce resources like teachers' time and expertise more carefully, teachers could spend more time on the areas where they add value even while working with larger classes of students. If grading essays or examining student performance on weekly quizzes took only half as much time as it currently does, a teacher could work with more students and still have *more* instructional time for each student in that class.

A Tool, Not a Miracle Cure

The nation continues to blithely operate schools in a fashion that was dated in the 1970s and that today would be deemed irresponsible in a toothpaste factory. Rather than demand that education dollars be invested with particular care, we pour money into technology with little thought to how these tools might be used most sensibly.

The ability to instantly share full information on student performance, school performance, and costs across vast distances permits a focus on results that was simply not feasible until the most recent decade. The information technology that makes the easy sharing of information possible is the engine that makes tough-minded accountability, school choice, and visionary leadership a possibility.

Using new technological tools to relieve educators of routine functions will help them focus on those roles that add substantial value—enhancing their contribution, making the organization more productive, and thereby increasing both the benefit to the customer and the resources available to reward employees. Reducing rote demands allows people to focus on what they do best and reduces the number of talented workers who need to be hired—which, in turn, allows us to pay employees more.

Ultimately, if leaders lack the tools to increase efficiency, streamline their workforce, or sensibly reallocate resources, they won't. Technology is not a miracle cure. It is a tool. Used wisely, it can help professionals to take full advantage of their skills, slash the time spent on rote tasks, and concentrate resources and effort where they are needed most.

POSTSCRIPT

Do Computers Negatively Affect Student Growth?

A few years ago educational reformer John I. Goodlad declared that "school" should be considered a concept rather than a place and that this formulation would seem to be an appropriate keynote for education in the twenty-first century. Certainly, advocates of computerization and global networking would be comfortable with the idea. But today, as more school systems are being "wired," questions of initial cost, hardware obsolescence, variable availability, software quality and appropriateness, teacher reluctance, and productive utilization remain to be discussed and resolved.

Help in exploring these and related questions may be found in Gary Kidd's "Using the Internet as a School," *The Educational Forum* (Spring 1996); "Unfilled Promises," by Jane McDonald, William Lynch, and Greg Kearsley, *The American School Board Journal* (July 1996); Frederick Bennett's *Computers as Tutors* (1999); Leon Botstein's "A Brave New World?" *The School Administrator* (March 2001); Craig A. Cunningham's "Improving Our Nation's Schools Through Computers and Connectivity," *Brookings Review* (Winter 2001); R. W. Burniske's "When Computer Literacy Goes Too Far," *Phi Delta Kappan* (March 2001); and Frederick Bennett's "The Future of Computer Technology in K–12 Education," *Phi Delta Kappan* (April 2002). The April 1996 issue of *The School Administrator* contains a number of articles on such topics as Internet access and technology's usefulness in the inclusion of disabled students. Other journal issues devoted to the controversy include *Educational Leadership* (November 1997), *Contemporary Education* (Winter 1997), *NASSP Bulletin* (November 1997), *Theory Into Practice* (Winter 1998), *The School Administrator* (April 1999), *NASSP Bulletin* (May 1999 and September 1999), *Principal* (January 2000), *The Futurist* (March–April 2000), *Educational Leadership* (October 2000), *Kappa Delta Pi Record* (Fall 2000), *American Educator* (Fall 2001), *The School Administrator* (October 2001), *NASSP Bulletin* (November 2001) and *The School Administrator* (August 2005). Recent sources of special interest include Todd Oppenheimer's *The Flickering Mind: The False Promise of Technology in the Classroom and How Learning Can Be Saved* (2003), Gene I. Maeroff's *A Classroom of One: How Online Learning Is Changing Our Schools and Colleges* (2002), Jane M. Healy's "Young Children Don't Need Computers," *Principal* (May–June 2003) and Mark Bauerlein's book, *The Dumbest Generation: How the Digital Age Stupifies Young Americans and Jeopardizes Our Future* (2008).

Finally, educational psychologist Richard P. Lookatch has argued that multimedia use in school offers students the opportunity to interact with the images behind a glass screen, but the looming danger is that it replaces students' interaction with each other and their environment.

ISSUE 21

Is the "21st Century Skills" Movement Viable?

YES: Andrew J. Rotherham and Daniel T. Willingham, from "21st Century Skills: The Challenges Ahead," *Educational Leadership* (September 2009)

NO: Diana Senechal, from "The Most Daring Education Reform of All," *American Educator* (Spring 2010)

ISSUE SUMMARY

YES: Education policy expert Rotherham and psychology professor Willingham see great promise in the movement to bring needed skills to all students if the delivery system works satisfactorily.

NO: Education writer and former teacher Diana Senechal expresses deep concern about the movement's focus on current societal needs to the detriment of core academic studies.

Calls for adoption of national standards, national tests, and even a national curriculum are on the increase. As Walter Isaacson of the Aspen Institute states, in "How to Raise the Standard in America's Schools," *Time* (April 15, 2009), "Without national standards for what our students should learn, it will be hard for the U.S. to succeed in the 21st century economy." But the prospect of such a development is politically explosive. Isaacson characterizes it this way: "The right chokes on the word *national,* with its implication that the feds will trample on the states' traditional authority over public schools, and the left chokes on the word *standards,* with the intimations of assessments and testing that accompany it." The present-day reality is that two-thirds of American students attend school in states with mediocre standards or worse, according to research by the Thomas B. Fordham Institute.

A number of movements are afoot to define what is most needed in the realm of school improvement. The National Governors Association and the Council of Chief State School Officers, with financial support from private foundations and federal support from the "Race to the Top" fund, have begun to develop a Common Core State Standards Initiative (CCSSI) to cover tests, curriculum, and teacher training. To date 40 states and the District of Columbia have joined the effort. The Thomas B. Fordham Institute recently produced a document compiled by Chester E. Finn, Jr. and Michael J. Petrilli titled *Now What? Imperatives & Options for "Common Core" Implementation & Governance* (October 2010). The report calls for a Common Core Coordinating Council as a starting point, with the purpose of preserving independence from Washington. The Center for Public Education in Alexandria, Virginia has issued a report, *Defining a 21st Century Education* (July 2009) by Craig D. Jerald, that analyzes the major forces reshaping skill demands (automation, globalization, corporate changes, demographics, and personal risk and responsibility).

Perhaps most visible is the Partnership for 21st Century Skills in Tucson, Arizona, which has broad support from the business and technology communities and the Association for Career and Technical Education. In its *Framework for 21st Century Learning,* the Partnership has identified the skills essential for success in today's world, such as creativity, critical thinking, problem solving, communication, and collaboration. The Framework delineates core subjects and twenty-first-century themes (such as global awareness) and life and career skills (such as adaptability, self-direction, productivity, and cross-cultural understanding). Paige Johnson, in "The 21st Century Skills Movement," *Educational Leadership* (September 2009), states that "to successfully face rigorous higher-education courses and a globally competitive work environment, schools must align classroom environments and core subjects with 21st century skills." Or, as Richard H. Hersh, in "A Well-Rounded Education for a Flat World," *Educational Leadership* (September 2009) puts it, we need "a pervasive school culture that refuses to define education as the passive reception of knowledge and instead celebrates demanding, profoundly engaging, and authentic educational experiences." More specifically, Bernie Trilling, global director of the Oracle Education Foundation, in "Leading Learning in Our Time," *Principal* (January/February 2010), espouses "inquiry- and design-based projects rooted in driving questions and real-world problems" that would engage students in a deeper understanding and effective use of knowledge.

Those who have reservations about the 21st Century Skills model are concerned that it may just become another pedagogical fad, that it demands too much change too fast, that it is too oriented to economic forces, that the skills emphasis downplays subject matter content, and that the recommended skills are in need of more specific definition. Education columnist Jay Mathews, initially very doubtful about the model for some of the reasons cited above, was moved toward a level of acceptance by the Craig Jerald report (see above) and educator Tony Wagner's *The Global Achievement Gap* (2008). In his article "Class Struggle," *The Washington Post* (December 4, 2009), Mathews finds that Jerald is especially clear about what the skills movement really means for schools, namely the artful blending of factual knowledge and the types of thinking required to apply that knowledge in meaningful and useful ways.

In the first of the following articles, Andrew J. Rotherham and Daniel T. Willingham offer their version of the "21st Century Skills" approach to the improvement of American schooling. In the second article, Diana Senechal details her specific objections and calls for maintenance of the true purposes of education.

YES ↵

**Andrew J. Rotherham and
Daniel T. Willingham**

21st Century Skills:
The Challenges Ahead

A growing number of business leaders, politicians, and educators are united around the idea that students need "21st century skills" to be successful today. It's exciting to believe that we live in times that are so revolutionary that they demand new and different abilities. But in fact, the skills students need in the 21st century are not new.

Critical thinking and problem solving, for example, have been components of human progress throughout history, from the development of early tools, to agricultural advancements, to the invention of vaccines, to land and sea exploration. Such skills as information literacy and global awareness are not new, at least not among the elites in different societies. The need for mastery of different kinds of knowledge, ranging from facts to complex analysis? Not new either. In *The Republic,* Plato wrote about four distinct levels of intellect. Perhaps at the time, these were considered "3rd century BCE skills?"

What's actually new is the extent to which changes in our economy and the world mean that collective and individual success depends on having such skills. Many U.S. students are taught these skills—those who are fortunate enough to attend highly effective schools or at least encounter great teachers—but it's a matter of chance rather than the deliberate design of our school system. Today we cannot afford a system in which receiving a high-quality education is akin to a game of bingo. If we are to have a more equitable and effective public education system, skills that have been the province of the few must become universal.

This distinction between "skills that are novel" and "skills that must be taught more intentionally and effectively" ought to lead policymakers to different education reforms than those they are now considering. If these skills were indeed new, then perhaps we would need a radical overhaul of how we think about content and curriculum. But if the issue is, instead, that schools must be more deliberate about teaching critical thinking, collaboration, and problem solving to all students, then the remedies are more obvious, although still intensely challenging.

From *Educational Leadership,* September 2009, pp. 16, 18–21. Copyright © 2009 by ASCD. Reprinted by permission. The Association for Supervision and Curriculum Development is a worldwide community of educators advocating sound policies and sharing best practices to achieve the success of each learner. To learn more, visit ASCD at www.ascd.org.

What Will It Take?

The history of U.S. education reform should greatly concern everyone who wants schools to do a better job of teaching students to think. Many reform efforts, from reducing class size to improving reading instruction, have devolved into fads or been implemented with weak fidelity to their core intent. The 21st century skills movement faces the same risk.

To complicate the challenge, some of the rhetoric we have heard surrounding this movement suggests that with so much new knowledge being created, content no longer matters; that ways of knowing information are now much more important than information itself. Such notions contradict what we know about teaching and learning and raise concerns that the 21st century skills movement will end up being a weak intervention for the very students—low-income students and students of color—who most need powerful schools as a matter of social equity.

The debate is not about content versus skills. There is no responsible constituency arguing against ensuring that students learn how to think in school. Rather, the issue is how to meet the challenges of delivering content and skills in a rich way that genuinely improves outcomes for students.

What will it take to ensure that the idea of "21st century skills"—or more precisely, the effort to ensure that all students, rather than just a privileged few, have access to a rich education that intentionally helps them learn these skills—is successful in improving schools? That effort requires three primary components. First, educators and policymakers must ensure that the instructional program is complete and that content is not shortchanged for an ephemeral pursuit of skills. Second, states, school districts, and schools need to revamp how they think about human capital in education—in particular how teachers are trained. Finally, we need new assessments that can accurately measure richer learning and more complex tasks.

For the 21st century skills effort to be effective, these three elements must be implemented in concert. Otherwise, the reform will be superficial and counterproductive.

Better Curriculum

People on all sides of this debate often speak of skills and knowledge as separate. They describe skills as akin to a function on a calculator: If your calculator can compute square roots, it can do so for any number; similarly, if a student has developed the ability to "think scientifically," he or she can do so with any content. In this formulation, domain knowledge is mainly important as grist for the mill—you need something to think *about.*

Skills and knowledge are not separate, however, but intertwined. In some cases, knowledge helps us recognize the underlying structure of a problem. For example, even young children understand the logical implications of a rule like "If you finish your vegetables, you will get a cookie after dinner." They can draw the logical conclusion that a child who is denied a cookie after dinner must not have finished her vegetables. Without this familiar context, however, the same child will probably find it difficult to understand the logical form *modus tollens,* of which the cookie rule is an example. (*If P, then Q. Q is false. Therefore, P is false.*) Thus, it's inaccurate to conceive of logical thinking as a separate skill that can be applied across a variety of situations. Sometimes we fail to recognize that we have a particular thinking skill (such as applying *modus tollens*) unless it comes in the form of known content.

At other times, we know that we have a particular thinking skill, but domain knowledge is necessary if we are to use it. For example, a student might have learned that "thinking scientifically" requires understanding the importance of anomalous results in an experiment. If you're surprised by the results of an experiment, that suggests that your hypothesis was wrong and the data are telling you something interesting. But to be surprised, you must make a prediction in the first place—and you can only generate a prediction if you understand the domain in which you are working. Thus, without content knowledge we often cannot use thinking skills properly and effectively.

Why would misunderstanding the relationship of skills and knowledge lead to trouble? If you believe that skills and knowledge are separate, you are likely to draw two incorrect conclusions. First, because content is readily available in many locations but thinking skills reside in the learner's brain, it would seem clear that if we must choose between them, skills are essential, whereas content is merely desirable. Second, if skills are independent of content, we could reasonably conclude that we can develop these skills through the use of *any* content. For example, if students can learn how to think critically about science in the context of any scientific material, a teacher should select content that will engage students (for instance, the chemistry of candy), even if that content is not central to the field. But all content is not equally important to mathematics, or to science, or to literature. To think critically, students need the knowledge that is central to the domain.

The importance of content in the development of thinking creates several challenges for the 21st century skills movement. The first is the temptation to emphasize advanced, conceptual thinking too early in training—an approach that has proven ineffective in numerous past reforms, such as the "New Math" of the 1960s (Loveless, 2002). Learning tends to follow a predictable path. When students first encounter new ideas, their knowledge is shallow and their understanding is bound to specific examples. They need exposure to varied examples before their understanding of a concept becomes more abstract and they can successfully apply that understanding to novel situations.

Another curricular challenge is that we don't yet know how to teach self-direction, collaboration, creativity, and innovation the way we know how to teach long division. The plan of 21st century skills proponents seems to be to give students more experiences that will presumably develop these skills—for example, having them work in groups. But experience is not the same thing as practice. Experience means only that you use a skill; practice means that you try to improve by noticing what you are doing wrong and formulating strategies to do better. Practice also requires feedback, usually from someone more skilled than you are.

Because of these challenges, devising a 21st century skills curriculum requires more than paying lip service to content knowledge. Outlining the skills in detail and merely urging that content be taught, too, is a recipe for failure. We must plan to teach skills in the context of particular content knowledge and to treat both as equally important.

In addition, education leaders must be realistic about which skills are teachable. If we deem that such skills as collaboration and self-direction are essential, we should launch a concerted effort to study how they can be taught effectively rather than blithely assume that mandating their teaching will result in students learning them.

Better Teaching

Greater emphasis on skills also has important implications for teacher training. Our resolve to teach these skills to all students will not be enough. We must have a plan by which teachers can succeed where previous generations have failed.

Advocates of 21st century skills favor student-centered methods—for example, problem-based learning and project-based learning—that allow students to collaborate, work on authentic problems, and engage with the community. These approaches are widely acclaimed and can be found in any pedagogical methods textbook; teachers know about them and believe they're effective. And yet, teachers don't use them. Recent data show that most instructional time is composed of seatwork and whole-class instruction led by the teacher (National Institute of Child Health and Human Development Early Child Care Research Network, 2005). Even when class sizes are reduced, teachers do not change their teaching strategies or use these student-centered methods (Shapson, Wright, Eason, & Fitzgerald, 1980). Again, these are not new issues. John Goodlad (1984) reported the same finding in his landmark study published more than 20 years ago.

Why don't teachers use the methods that they believe are most effective? Even advocates of student-centered methods acknowledge that these methods pose classroom management problems for teachers. When students collaborate, one expects a certain amount of hubbub in the room, which could devolve into chaos in less-than-expert hands. These methods also demand that teachers be knowledgeable about a broad range of topics and are prepared to make in-the-moment decisions as the lesson plan progresses. Anyone who has watched a highly effective teacher lead a class by simultaneously engaging with content, classroom management, and the ongoing monitoring of student progress knows how intense and demanding this work is. It's a constant juggling act that involves keeping many balls in the air.

Part of the 21st century skills movement's plan is the call for greater collaboration among teachers. Indeed, this is one of the plan's greatest strengths; we waste a valuable resource when we don't give teachers time to share their expertise. But where will schools find the release time for such collaboration? Will they hire more teachers or increase class size? How will they provide the technology infrastructure that will enable teachers to collaborate with more than just the teacher down the hall? Who will build and maintain and edit the Web sites, wikis, and so forth? These challenges raise thorny questions about whether the design of today's schools is compatible with the goals of the 21st century skills movement.

For change to move beyond administrators' offices and penetrate classrooms, we must understand that professional development is a massive undertaking. Most teachers don't need to be persuaded that project-based learning is a good idea—they already believe that. What teachers need is much more robust training and support than they receive today, including specific lesson plans that deal with the high cognitive demands and potential classroom management problems of using student-centered methods.

Unfortunately, there is a widespread belief that teachers already know how to do this if only we could unleash them from today's stifling standards and accountability metrics. This notion romanticizes student-centered methods, underestimates the challenge of implementing such methods, and ignores the lack of capacity in the field today.

Instead, staff development planners would do well to engage the best teachers available in an iterative process of planning, execution, feedback, and continued planning. This process, along with additional teacher training, will require significant time. And of course none of this will be successful without broader reforms in how teachers are recruited, selected, and deselected in an effort to address the whole picture of education's human capital challenge.

Better Tests

There is little point in investing heavily in curriculum and human capital without also investing in assessments to evaluate what is or is not being accomplished in the classroom. Fortunately, as Elena Silva (2008) noted in a recent report for Education Sector, the potential exists today to produce assessments that measure thinking skills and are also reliable and comparable between students and schools—elements integral to efforts to ensure accountability and equity. But efforts to assess these skills are still in their infancy; education faces enormous challenges in developing the ability to deliver these assessments at scale.

The first challenge is the cost. Although higher-level skills like critical thinking and analysis can be assessed with well-designed multiple-choice tests, a truly rich assessment system would go beyond multiple-choice testing and include measures that encourage greater creativity, show how students arrived at answers, and even allow for collaboration. Such measures, however, cost more money than policymakers have traditionally been willing to commit to assessment. And, at a time when complaining about testing is a national pastime and cynicism about assessment, albeit often uninformed, is on the rise, getting policymakers to commit substantially more resources to it is a difficult political challenge.

Producing enough high-quality assessments to meet the needs of a system as large and diverse as U.S. public schools would stretch the capacity of the assessment industry and incentives do not exist today for many new entrants to become major players in that field. We would need a coordinated public, private, and philanthropic strategy—including an intensive research and development effort—to foster genuine change.

Substantial delivery challenges also remain. Delivering these assessments in a few settings, as is the case today, is hardly the same as delivering them at scale across a state—especially the larger states. Because most of these assessments will be technology-based, most schools' information technology systems will require a substantial upgrade.

None of these assessment challenges are insurmountable, but addressing them will require deliberate attention from policymakers and 21st century skills proponents, as well as a deviation from the path that policymaking is on today. Such an effort is essential. Why mount a national effort to change education if you have no way of knowing whether the change has been effective?

A Better, But Harder, Way

The point of our argument is not to say that teaching students how to think, work together better, or use new information more rigorously is not a worthy and attainable goal. Rather, we seek to call attention to the magnitude of the challenge and to sound a note of caution amidst the sirens calling our political leaders once again to the rocky shoals of past education reform failures. Without better curriculum, better teaching, and better tests, the emphasis on "21st century skills" will be a superficial one that will sacrifice long-term gains for the appearance of short-term progress.

Curriculum, teacher expertise, and assessment have all been weak links in past education reform efforts—a fact that should sober today's skills proponents as they survey the task of dramatically improving all three. Efforts to create more formalized common standards would help address some of the challenges by focusing efforts in a common direction. But common standards will not, by themselves, be enough.

The past few decades have seen great progress in education reform in the United States—progress that has especially benefited less-advantaged students. Today's reformers can build on that progress only if they pay keen attention to the challenges associated with genuinely improving teaching and learning. If we ignore these challenges, the 21st century skills movement risks becoming another fad that ultimately changes little—or even worse, sets back the cause of creating dramatically more powerful schools for U.S. students, especially those who are underserved today.

References

Goodlad, J. I. (1984). *A place called school*. New York: McGraw-Hill.

Loveless, T. (2002). A tale of two math reforms: The politics of the new math and NCTM standards. In T. Loveless (Ed.), *The great curriculum debate* pp. 184–209). Washington, DC: Brookings.

National Institute of Child Health and Human Development Early Child Care Research Network. (2005). A day in the third grade: A large-scale study of classroom   quality and teacher and student behavior. *Elementary School Journal, 105,* 305–323.

Shapson, S. M., Wright, E. N., Eason, G., & Fitzgerald, J. (1980). An experimental study of the effects of class size. *American Educational Research Journal, 17,* 141–152.

Silva, E. (2008). *Measuring skills for the 21st century.* Washington, DC: Education Sector. Available: www.educationsector.org/usr_doc/MeasuringSkills.pdf

Diana Senechal   ➜ **NO**

The Most Daring Education Reform of All

It is an old story, a worn deck of words: reformers insist that traditional schooling has failed and that only a new approach can save us. John Dewey wrote in 1899 that "it is radical conditions which have changed, and only an equally radical change in education suffices." He characterized the traditional classroom as "rows of ugly desks placed in geometrical order," all made for listening, which meant "the dependency of one mind upon another," or "passivity, absorption." Over the past century, many reformers have disparaged whatever preceded their proposals, be it the public school system as a whole, a literature curriculum, the teacher standing at the front of the room, or the use of the blackboard. The old ways have to go, they say; to keep them is to cling to failure. In demanding an overhaul, these reformers echo an old American theme: a longing for a new country, a new life, a new structure, a new faith, a new solution, a new invention, a new technology, a new self. They partake in an American tradition without heeding history or tradition; they glorify the new because it is new, while disparaging the old because it is old. Often their "new" reform is not new at all, nor are the "old" practices obsolete. Nonetheless, they brandish jargon, break apart schools, toss out curricula, and proclaim the superiority of their plans, chaining education to passing fashions without considering what should endure.

In recent years, some particularly vocal reformers have demanded that we infuse all learning with "21st-century" skills; like their predecessors, they clamor for newness. The 21st-century-skills movement consists of a loose association of educators, policymakers, government leaders, business and technology firms, and others. Citing changes in the global economy and national job market, they call for an emphasis on 21st-century skills in all of education, from elementary school through college. These skills (all of which existed long before the 21st century) include broad concepts such as creativity, innovation, problem solving, communication, collaboration, teamwork, and critical thinking, as well as media and technology literacy, financial literacy, health literacy, and global literacy. Leading the charge has been a coalition called the Partnership for 21st Century Skills (P21), whose membership organizations include Adobe Systems, Apple, Dell, Hewlett-Packard, Microsoft, and Verizon. P21 argues that "every aspect of our education system . . . must be aligned to prepare citizens with the 21st century skills they need to compete." Accordingly, it offers schools, districts, and states "tools and resources to help facilitate and drive change."

Technology figures large in the 21st-century-skills movement, but technology itself is not the problem. It is a reality of life, and in one form or another it has always surrounded us. Having worked as a computer programmer and electronic publisher, having developed an interactive database for my former school, having recorded and mixed songs on my computer, having stayed up many a night to get a program right, I know how intriguing and promising technology can be. But having wasted many hours on the Internet, I also know how it can distract. Technology should be a tool at our disposal; it should serve rather than hinder us. When states and districts heed reformers' calls for technology in all grades and subjects, this leads to situations where teachers must use technology in class, whether or not it serves the lesson well. The problem lies in the reformers' haste and dogmatism.

Far too often, the 21st-century-skills argument carries a tone of urgency, even emergency: We no longer live in a world of books, paper, and pen. Children grow up surrounded by digital media. They can communicate with peers around the world; they can find obscure information in seconds. Yet they are unprepared for the jobs of today. We still treat them as passive recipients of knowledge; we still drill them on facts that they could just as easily Google. If we do not act now, we will lose our global competitiveness—so everyone who cares about our future should jump on board. Employers need people who can create, solve problems, work together, use technology, and think critically. We must make our students critics, innovators, and team players; we should teach them to communicate in the broad sense of the word by infusing their coursework with blogging, recording, filming, texting, collaborating, and tweeting.

Proponents of 21st-century skills often assume that the schools' primary objective is to meet the demands of the day—including the demands of the workplace and transient fashions. Even the movement's most reasonable and thoughtful proponents sometimes share this assumption. In his report *Defining a 21st Century Education,* Craig D. Jerald acknowledges the importance of a traditional core curriculum yet places overwhelming emphasis on employers' demands. In *The Global Achievement Gap,* Tony Wagner seems at times oblivious to the deficiencies of the schools he praises (and their notable similarities at times to the very schools he chides). Yet both authors deserve credit for steering clear of the movement's excesses. Too often, the champions of the movement laud the liberal arts in the abstract, but make practical suggestions that trivialize subject matter. P21 suggests that students engage in projects such as making an audio commercial for a favorite short story, devising a business plan for selling snacks, or creating an online game to expand younger students' global awareness. P21 claims to support "mastery of core academic subjects" but disregards the structured study, discipline, and concentration that such mastery entails.

As Diane Ravitch has shown, there is nothing new about the proposals of the 21st-century-skills movement. They echo progressive ideas of the past 100 years. Since the late 19th century, progressives have demanded that education be more immediate, useful, and relevant, with more attention to hands-on activities and less emphasis on formal academic study and explicit instruction. While some of these ideas, taken in moderation, have the potential to enhance a curriculum, reformers have often carried them to extremes, forsaking intellectual study in the name of "real life." In 1898, Dewey wrote that systematic reading and writing instruction was rendered unnecessary by "the advent of quick and cheap mails, of easy and continuous travel and transportation, of the telegraph and telephone, the establishment of libraries," and other changes. The schools' "fetich" *[sic]* for reading and writing instruction was a hindrance, he said; "the claims of the present should be controlling." The mantra of the "claims of the present" has been repeated so often that we must ask: Is it perhaps in the nature of a good education to be slightly out of step with the present? Could it be that in order to endure, an education must be unfettered by the times? Is it possible that the claims of the present—which we often cannot accurately identify—should *not* be controlling?

Perhaps so. Efforts over the decades to bring schools up-to-date have not worked as intended. They have met with resistance or obstacles; they have caused losses; they have missed the mark. Of course schools should teach critical thinking, problem solving, and other skills; they should help students master new technologies that can further their intellectual development. But they cannot do any of this without a foundation. When hyperbole goes unchecked, the reform loses sight of the complements it needs. Reformers forget, for instance, that knowledge enhances the very learning process in a number of ways, as Daniel T. Willingham and other cognitive scientists have found. They forget that fluency in the fundamentals allows students to engage in inquiry. They forget that content is not simply dry matter; it has shape and meaning; it is the result of centuries of critical thought and the basis for future critical thought. To neglect to teach our intellectual and cultural traditions is to limit the kind of thinking that students will be able to do throughout their lives.

What would our schools gain by embracing 21st-century skills, and what would they lose? It is the loss that deserves special attention, as the 21st-century reformers, in their euphoria, have seen only gain in their plans. The gain is possible, but only if we put the skills in proper perspective, recognizing their long legacy and their dependence on subject matter knowledge.

The classroom that 21st-century-skills proponents envision—a place where students are collaborating, creating, and critiquing—may not be as promising as it seems. A video by the George Lucas Educational Foundation shows middle school students comparing two magazine photos in light of gender roles; other students filming a poetry project; third-graders watching a nature film and learning how the film was made; fourth-graders making animated short videos; seventh-graders analyzing newspaper photos of the war in Iraq; and other lessons and activities. These examples are supposed to show what students *should* be doing in class: discussing important issues, analyzing the information around them, and creating things. Near the end of the video, the narrator comments: "As courses and projects featuring elements of media literacy find their way into more and more classrooms, writing English might become just one of several forms of expression, along with graphics, cinema, and music, to be taught in a basic course called communication." This is where the losses begin.

First of all, with such a diffuse curriculum, students lose the opportunity to master the fundamentals of any subject. Students are supposed to jump into "big issues" (for which they may have no preparation) and to express themselves through numerous media before they are fluent in any. How can students learn the basics, not to mention the more complex ideas, when they are spread so thin? There have been similar efforts over the past century to generalize and expand subjects beyond their disciplinary base—for instance, by replacing history with social studies—and the drawbacks have been similar: students end up writing about their own communities, reading charts and graphs in a superficial way, learning disconnected tidbits about cultures around the world, and knowing little history. To learn something well, we need focused study and practice. Survey courses are essential, but their topics should not be as broad and vague as "communication." Filming a poetry project and analyzing war photos may be fruitful activities, but a communications course consisting of disjointed projects is unlikely to teach students how to communicate well. Such a course may offer, in the words of Robert Frost, "A little bit of every-thing, / A great deal of none."

Second, in their efforts to make schools current, reformers neglect to offer the very stability that students need in order to make sense of the choices, clamor, and confusion of the present—that is, to exercise critical thinking. If teachers must ceaselessly change their curriculum to match what is happening in society (or, more narrowly, the workplace), neither they nor their students will have the opportunity to step back and reflect. It is difficult to think about the workings of a roller coaster while on a roller coaster ride; it is difficult to analyze weather pat-terns while driving through a blizzard. Critical thinking requires perspective and a certain distance from one's personal experiences. Schools need to offer a degree of stability and quiet—precisely so that students may grapple with important questions and teachers may carry out their responsibilities with integrity.

If we always must be up-to-date, then we are continually distracted and diverted. As soon as a school has caught up with the newest pedagogy and the technology that supports it, something newer comes along, making the newly acquired methods and machines seem dated once again. In the scramble to keep up, schools reflect the incoherence of the larger culture. They become susceptible to suggestions that what they are doing is not good enough, not current enough, not cutting-edge enough. Once, at a school where I taught, I heard a visiting administrator speak to science teachers about ways to boost student performance at the science fair. He told them never to have students use PowerPoint for the presentations. "PowerPoint sends up a red flag," he said. "It's telling everyone that your school is still in the '90s." He recommended using Flash instead. He wasn't concerned with the deficiencies (or strengths) of PowerPoint per se, but rather with its appearance and connotations. It would be unthinkable, presumably, for a student to submit a brilliant science report on paper. Substance defers to fashion in such a world view.

If we keep on chasing the newest thing, we will not only distract our-selves but repeat old mistakes. Educator, historian, and philosopher Isaac Leon Kandel criticized this tendency in 1943, noting in *The Cult of Uncertainty* that too many educators and education reformers "seek novelty rather than perfec-tion and call this process 'adapting education to changing needs.'" Reformers often chastise those who resist change, as though change were always correct. Thus reformers have ignored a great resource; the resisters may have some-thing important to say. By no means should we be complacent—we have a lot of work to do—but we should never sacrifice our best judgment. That would be the worst form of complacency and of change. If we jump on the 21st-century-skills bandwagon (or any bandwagon) just because others say we should, we give up critical thought.

The 21st-century-skills movement brings a third loss, greater than all the rest. When schools rush to adopt whatever is supposedly modern, they lose sight of the true purposes of education. According to E. D. Hirsch, Jr., the central purpose used to be to create virtuous citizens with enough shared knowledge for all to participate in the public sphere. A complementary purpose of education is to prepare us for solitude, which is part of every life; if we know how to be alone, then we may be less prone to distraction, escapism, and boredom. Education also exists for its own sake: an endless adventure, a struggle, a delight. At its fullest and best, education prepares us to be with others and apart, to enjoy the life of the mind, to survive and prosper, to bring up new generations, to act with integrity and conscience, to pursue useful and interesting work, and to participate in civic and cultural action and thought. If schools try to be up to date all the time, then they are reduced to chasing fads and obeying the whims of the market. Part of the schools' work is to help prepare students for their future occupations, but they do not achieve this by scurrying to meet employers' demands.

Employers may know what kinds of skills they need, but they do not nec-essarily know how this translates into instruction. Their perceptions are bound to the workplace and should not control curricula. The Conference Board, an organization that disseminates business and economics information, prepared a survey in collaboration with three organizations: P21, Corporate Voices for Working Families, and the Society for Human Resource Management. They asked employers to rank various subjects and skills according to their impor-tance. Only a small percentage of employers assigned a high rank to humani-ties, arts, history, and geography, while the vast majority assigned a high rank to teamwork, collaboration, professionalism, and work ethic. But does this mean that students do not need humanities, arts, history, and geography? Certainly not—it is hard to imagine how one could be a good journalist or global busi-ness analyst without a background in history and geography, a good trade publisher or human rights advocate without a background in humanities, or a good architect or graphic designer without a background in arts. As citizens, all employees need a strong foundation in the arts and sciences. Such education contributes to our quality of life in myriad ways—by enhancing our reason-ing, vocabulary, and perspective, by creating common understandings, and by allowing for a varied life outside of work. If schools were to take employers' priorities literally, they would emphasize group projects no matter what they contained. This would not be good academic *or* vocational education.

It is time to stop the waste. Instead of rushing to incorporate 21st-century skills in all aspects of school, instead of embracing any change for its own sake, we should pursue perfection in curriculum and pedagogy. Pursuing perfection is not the same as attaining it; it is unlikely that we will ever have anything close to perfect schools or a perfect society. Yet that is the generosity of perfection. It is unattainable, yet to strive for it is within our reach, and it always gives us more to strive for. It is striving that has led to great accomplishments in letters, sciences, arts, athletics, and manual trades; it is striving that has enabled humans to live and treat each other with dignity; it is striving that has sharpened our senses and our wits. It involves soul searching, as we must examine our performance daily, not in relation to test scores alone, but in relation to our ideals. Today the word "idealist" seems to connote fanciful or wishful thinking, but idealism need not be naive or flimsy. Musicians must be able to imagine how a piece should sound, and they must know how to come closer to that imagined version. The discrepancy does not break them, nor does it break a school. Perhaps that is a form of happiness: having something worth laboring for and having an inkling of how to go about it.

To pursue perfection, we must first establish the meaning and purposes of education, then refine the methods for fulfilling those purposes. We should dare to specify what we will teach: the disciplines, works, ideas, and historical periods; the things to be mastered, grasped, and pondered. Once we have established our core—our understanding of education's meaning, purpose, and content—and once we have a curriculum rich in literature, history, science, mathematics, and arts, we can consider how to make necessary changes to our schools without falling prey to fads, without losing our equilibrium, without letting anyone convince us that things of lasting beauty are passé. In an interview with John Merrow of Learning Matters, Diane Ravitch summed up the problem: "American education doesn't need innovation. American education needs purpose; it needs definition; it needs a vision of what good education is; and it needs to focus on what's important, which is good teachers, involved parents, willing students, adequate community resources, community support for education, and a solid, rigorous, coherent curriculum. Lacking all of those things, . . . innovation is just another distraction, and it has been for many years."

In seeking perfection, we must cherish and strengthen what has worked. Forms of instruction deemed "traditional" have much to offer us still. Moreover, most practices require a union of opposing principles. For students to engage in inquiry, they must have a strong foundation of knowledge. To participate well in class or group discussions, students need to learn to listen. Student collaboration is important, but it requires that students also work alone, so that they may bring something to each other. And students become active learners not only by talking and doing, but by sitting still with their thoughts. Conversely, the student who cannot listen to others is trapped in his or her own limited perspective.

Reformers of different stripes often malign the "traditional" style of teaching, claiming that it has failed our children. Perhaps it worked in the past, they say, but it no longer works; perhaps it worked for an elite but not for the poor; perhaps it never worked to begin with. But what is this traditional teaching? Critics often say that in the old days, the teacher stood at the front of the room and lectured, and students took notes silently. Children, they say, were treated as "empty vessels" to be filled, not as thinking human beings. But this description fails to account for the variety in our tradition, which has included discussions, debates, projects, participatory lectures, seminars, laboratories, tutorials, and different ways of handling all of these. Moreover, it is not true that students who listen to the teacher are empty vessels. To the contrary, listening requires the exercise of knowledge and reasoning. William Torrey Harris wrote in 1897 that the recitation was an excellent way for students to learn from each other: "The pupil can, through the properly conducted recitation, seize the subject of his lesson through many minds. He learns to add to his power of insight the various insights of his fellow pupils." Listening is by no means passive: a student who can silently ponder another person's words will be able to enjoy lectures, plays, speeches, readings, and thoughtful conversations.

Those calling for 21st-century skills often point to the need for greater student engagement. But true engagement is not entertainment; it is involvement, which may be invisible at times. The traditional classroom encourages such involvement when the teachers teach subjects they know and love, the school has a true curriculum, and the students live up to the demands of the course. In these cases, the teachers give stimulating and substantial lessons; students absorb the material, think about it on their own, bring their questions and observations to class discussion, and strive for precision and thoughtfulness in their work. In contrast, when teacher preparation programs emphasize process over subject matter, when schools have weak curricula, and when many students fail to do homework, or are distracted and disruptive during class, the best aspects of this kind of classroom fall apart. The teacher's effort goes into maintaining discipline, and students learn little.

Far too many reformers perceive a lack of student "engagement" but misdiagnose it. They assume that if only the students were more visibly active, the learning would flow from there. Everything, then, is directed toward keeping students busy and stimulated: visuals, group work, individualized instruction, use of social networking tools such as Facebook, the building of self-esteem, and so forth. But this emphasis on activity and good feeling comes at a great cost and leads to complications. Students do not develop the ability to listen, to absorb material, or to think on their own. They become accustomed to rapid chatter, constant visual displays, and frequent celebrations of their accomplishments, which may not be substantial. Students reach the point where they cannot tolerate stillness, where they need to be facing their peers, doing something with their hands, and talking. Or they reach a point where they cannot take their peers any more and break into fights. For teachers, the main challenge in these settings is to make everyone "accountable"—that is, responsible for a concrete task that they must do to complete the group activity. Deeper engagement is sacrificed for a more trivial kind, and quiet, independent thought has little place.

At my former school, I led lunchtime literature clubs for fourth- and fifth-graders. The fifth-grade group read *The Adventures of Huckleberry Finn*. One day, close to the end of the school year, we read the passage where Huck decides not to betray Jim. We discussed Huck's confusion, which was still present even as he made the decision he knew was right. The discussion was slow, with pauses. At one point, the room fell into a long silence. One student said, "Ms. Senechal, you're quiet today!" Another student responded, "She's thinking. There's a lot to think about here." I see her comment as a tribute to the book, not to my teaching, but I am proud that the students were able to appreciate the quiet in the room.

Teachers should not have to give up intellectual authority in the classroom; they should bring their knowledge, insight, and expertise to students. Socrates, lauded by 21st-century-skills proponents for teaching through inquiry, led such inquiry every step of the way. Peter W. Cookson, Jr., speculates that were Socrates alive today, he "would embrace the new learning era with all the energy he had"; yet it seems more likely that he would regard it with deep skepticism. In Plato's *Crito,* Socrates asks, "Should a man professionally engaged in physical training pay attention to the praise and blame and opinion of any man, or to those of one man only, namely a doctor or trainer?" To Socrates, not all opinions were equal, and they should not all be equal in the classroom today. The teacher should encourage students to think for themselves but should also prepare them to do so—through instruction, challenge, and correction. Students should have opportunities to discuss and test their ideas, but they should not be called experts before they actually are. They should be regarded as apprentices. One of the benefits of apprenticeship is that it allows for a long period of learning.

As an undergraduate at Yale, I had the good fortune of taking John Hollander's advanced poetry writing seminar. On the first day of the seminar, he established the guidelines for the course: First, this was not a free-for-all workshop where we would be commenting on each other's work. Second, he was not going to tell any of us whether we had the makings of a poet; it was far too soon to know. Third, class would revolve around the discussion of specific problems, dilemmas, or principles in poetry. I remember how happy I was to hear all of this, to know that I was there to learn from him, not to impress. His lectures were great intellectual romps; I wish I could be in that classroom again. When asked to describe a favorite teacher, I often describe Hollander. He had a gift for going on seeming tangents, then bringing them back to his original point by surprise. As a student listening to him lecture, I was anything but passive. I was enthralled, full of thoughts and questions, and I would stay that way for days as I turned his words over in my mind.

Just as we should preserve the best of traditional teaching, we should preserve the best of traditional content. We may argue about what should be included in a curriculum, but we should not avoid curriculum. We should make sure that young people leave school informed of the past so that they do not get swept up in the rages of the present. We should keep our lives and culture resonant by studying excellent literature, philosophy, historical thought, science, mathematics, and art—by reading poetry aloud, singing, and returning to books we read long ago. We should expect students to memorize poems, monologues, and parts of speeches; to read classic novels and essays; to discuss and analyze what they have read; and to write with clarity and verve. Much of this activity is solitary and requires quiet. In mathematics, they should learn to calculate nimbly so that the more advanced topics do not daunt them, and each topic should be taught in as much depth and with as much precision as possible. Students should read primary and secondary texts in history; they should learn enough facts to describe and explain historical events, discuss historical questions, and conduct research fruitfully. And there should be electives, including rigorous vocational training, in addition to the core studies.

But how are we to accomplish this? The first step is to combat the excessive careerism and pragmatism in educational discussion—to remind ourselves and each other that schools are here not only to serve immediate practical purposes, but to teach things that last a lifetime and merit passing on to future generations. The second is to insist on a superb curriculum, with the best of the old and the best of the new, from the earliest grades on up. The curriculum should be the soul of a school; it should abound with works and topics that fill the mind and deepen one's outlook on life. It should be both fixed and changing: stable enough that teachers need not rewrite it from scratch every year, yet flexible enough that they may supplement it daily, revise it over time, and teach it in the way that they judge best. We must also call for greater emphasis on liberal arts in teacher preparation, so that teachers entering the classroom are fully prepared to teach their subject, and so that the field of education may be enriched by intellectual knowledge and traditions. Many questions remain unresolved, and new ones will arise, but this is a strong beginning.

Certainly, schools should use some projects (as most already do) and some technology (as most already do). When they do, it should suit the situation, and teachers should use their discretion. A Shakespeare course, for instance, need not be infused with 21st-century anything whatsoever. Some teachers teach mesmerizing Shakespeare courses with nothing but the book. Others might supplement readings and discussions with pictures and recordings; circumstances permitting, they might take students to see a Shakespeare play or have them act out selected scenes in the classroom. But whatever they decide to add, it must further students' understanding of Shakespeare. Twitter, Facebook, and texting add nothing to Shakespeare; they are only distractions. On the other hand, technology as a subject is not a distraction; some high schools have developed terrific computer programming, robotics, and sound engineering courses and afterschool clubs. In such cases, students learn how to make technology do what they want, and they learn the science and logic behind it. They learn much more about technology this way than they would by blogging and texting—activities they likely pursue on their own.

If teachers can focus on teaching their subjects, then they can go deeper. Creativity, problem solving, communication, and critical thinking make sense only in the context of specific studies.

Creativity and innovation, for example, require much knowledge and practice. When we take them too lightly, we encourage and even celebrate shoddiness. Mediocre creation abounds, as does false innovation, and it is not clear that this helps either the creator or the audience. Once, I attended a professional development session where we were told about the power of the Internet as a motivator for students. The speaker cited the example of a student who, as a result of a blogging project, had become excited about poetry and started posting her own poems on the school blog. I took a look at the poems that evening, Googled a few lines, and saw that all but one were plagiarized—not from first-rate poets, but from websites that featured sentimental and inspirational verse. Why was this not caught earlier? Anyone paying close attention to the poems themselves would likely have suspected that they weren't hers (the language was an adult's, and hackneyed at that). The presenters were genuinely excited that the Internet had motivated a student to write; perhaps they chose not to judge the poems lest they interfere with her creative process. This is the danger: when we value creativity (and technology) above the actual quality of the things created, we lose sight of what we are doing and why.

Proponents of 21st-century skills often treat innovation as though it can be taught on its own—yet our most celebrated innovators did not make discoveries in a void. Benjamin Franklin studied the writing of Joseph Addison in order to arrive at his own style. Albert Einstein read Euclid's *Elements* at age 12 and called it the "holy little geometry book." Aaron Copland praised his composition teacher, Rubin Goldmark, for bringing forth a generation of composers through rigorous traditional instruction. Even our democratic system of government was influenced by ancient democracies and by the British parliamentary system; its founders were well versed in history and philosophy. This is not to say that the study of the past guarantees innovation, only that innovation cannot do without it. To say we should teach innovation is really to say we need a strong liberal arts curriculum, which will supply the foundation for innovation.

Problem solving, when taken out of context, means just as little as creativity or innovation. To solve problems well, students must understand the problem to be solved, have the necessary information for solving it, and know solutions to similar problems. To translate a literary work, one needs not only knowledge of the source and target languages, but a keen sense of the nuances of words, the rhythms of phrases, the author's tone, and much more. In mathematics, one problem leads to the next; someone familiar with the Pythagorean theorem will grasp its corollaries with much more ease than one who has never seen it. Even listening to music is a kind of problem solving; we need musical knowledge in order to find our way through the sounds, to recognize allusions, and to grasp how the composer plays with forms.

Communication is likewise dependent on knowledge and practice. To communicate well, students must have something to say and models for saying it well. We do nothing to elevate the level of communication by having them read and write blogs, watch and make videos, and send text messages and tweets during English and history classes. Students know how to use the equipment, but their writing ability remains deplorably weak, forcing colleges to offer remedial writing courses and to assist students with basic writing throughout their undergraduate years. To write well, students must read excellent writing, and they must study subjects in depth and detail. Students learn much more about communication through the study of logic, philosophy, history, and literature than through immersion in social networks, online chatter, and other media already familiar to them. To learn the basics of argument and fallacy, students might read Corbett and Connors' *Classical Rhetoric for the Modern Student,* Strunk and White's *Elements of Style,* and George Orwell's "Politics and the English Language." As they read Shakespeare, they might consider how words can be twisted by listener and speaker alike—by Macbeth and the witches, by Lear and the Fool. In works with a political allegory, such as Orwell's *Animal Farm* and *1984,* they might look at how language is used to control people and distort the truth. They may also observe the nobler uses of language—for instance, to bring about good, preserve cultural memory, and promote understanding—as well as the playful, fantastical, and musical aspects of language. Any history or literature course should involve close study of the meanings, origins, pitfalls, power, and delight of words.

Through such study, students not only come to a deeper understanding of language, but begin to see their problems and needs in perspective. They learn that humans can communicate not only in "real time" but across cultures and centuries. If they read the *Iliad,* they will see Hector's tenderness toward his wife and son when he explains why he must go to war; they will see Achilles' ambivalence about entering battle, his knowledge of his "two fates"; they will see complex humans in a strange and brutal war. Students learn to appreciate both the familiar and unfamiliar; literature does much more than illuminate their lives, though it does this amply. Students learn that people throughout the ages have experienced joys, losses, jealousies, and triumphs. Young teens flummoxed by fleeting attractions may enjoy the vicissitudes of *A Midsummer Night's Dream* or Gogol's short stories. Those feeling sadness may find company in a Tennyson poem; those experiencing tumult may revel in Baudelaire; those critical of social trends may delight in the essays of Chesterton; those thirsting for justice may be inspired by the writings of Martin Luther King, Jr. But such literature does not stop at meeting our needs; it takes us beyond what we have felt and known. Education philosopher Michael John Demiashkevich wrote, "Now, would it not be good if instead of a whirl to the next town which may leave one as empty if not more so than he was before taking it, people developed liking for recreational excursion into literature which, in the words of Sir Walter Raleigh, 'is the record of man's adventures on the edge of things.'"

Perhaps critical thinking—thinking on the edge of things—is the trickiest of all the 21st-century skills. If we want to encourage and teach critical thinking, we should practice it ourselves. This means that we should beware of comprehensive solutions, sweeping reforms, catch phrases, and fads. Instead, we should closely study curricula and instructional approaches of the past, to find the best in them, learn from them, and build on them where possible. We could look at 19th-century textbooks (such as John S. Hart's grammar books or the McGuffey Readers) to see what insights they hold. We could seek ways to combine disciplined practice with inspiring lessons, projects, and discussions. We could seek out the best textbooks—not necessarily those that dominate the market—and supplement them with an array of primary and secondary sources, especially since so many important primary sources—many dating back centuries—are now online. We could hold professional development sessions on academic topics themselves. We could look at inspiring examples of other teachers and schools; we could take our own education to new levels, whether through formal coursework or independent study. The point is to act with full mind and conscience, to make the learning rich and thorough, and to keep an eye out for substance, beauty, and meaning.

When the frenzy over 21st-century skills passes—and it will—students will see that their opportunities depend largely on their knowledge. Many will graduate with blogging experience, but those who can write a strong essay on a Supreme Court case will be better prepared to enter the fields of history, law, or journalism. Many will have online science portfolios, but those who have studied calculus, have read parts of Newton's *Principia,* and can prove Kepler's second law (for example) will be much better prepared to study physics at an advanced level. Many will have written acrostic poems, but those who have studied sonnets closely will be familiar with a kind of poetic logic that they can carry into their life, work, and writing. Many will have communicated with peers around the world in English, but those who study a modern or ancient language will gain deeper insight into other cultures as well as their own. The ability to make a YouTube video or podcast will mean little in the long run if the other things are absent. Moreover, those technologies may be obsolete in another few years, but literature, science, languages, mathematics, history, music, art, and drama will stay.

Our schools are in need of repair—but we will not improve them by scorning tradition or succumbing to the "claims of the present." We will never reach perfection, but the more we strive for it, learning from history as well as experience, the closer we will come. We must be willing to seek out excellence, nurture it, defend it, and live up to it. We must be willing to lift the levels of the subjects we teach, the books we include, the assignments and corrections we give, and the way we conduct ourselves daily. Lifting the levels does not mean racing to catch up with a movement's demands; it means standing back from the race, focusing on what it means to educate in the full sense, and honoring this understanding in all of our work. To make changes thoughtfully—to keep the layers of past and present in everything we do—may be the most daring education reform of all.

POSTSCRIPT

Is the "21st Century Skills" Movement Viable?

The focus of this issue has been on the 21st Century Skills model for school improvement and the concerns about its appropriateness at this time and its potential effect on traditional elements of the curriculum. As indicated in the introduction, the larger context is the growing desire in many quarters for a nationwide consensus on what needs to be taught and how it should be taught. In many ways the arguments presented here are akin to the ideas put forth in Issue 1 of this book by John Dewey and Robert Hutchins. Dewey and his progressive education colleagues advocated experiential learning in which students were involved in collaborative activity to address real-life problems, while Hutchins championed cultural literacy and academic disciplines for mental development.

The larger context also has political ramifications. The locus of control has been shifting away from the American tradition of local financing and decision making as both Republican and Democratic administrations have fashioned national policy agendas. This trend is detailed in the Alliance for Excellent Education's 2009 policy brief titled *Reinventing the Federal Role in Education: Supporting the Goal of College and Career Readiness for All Students.* Some other commentary on the political dimension can be found in "E Pluribus Unum?" *Education Next* (Spring 2009), a forum by Chester E. Finn, Jr. and Deborah Meier; "National Education Standards: To Be or Not To Be?" *Educational Leadership* (April 2010) by Paul E. Barton; "The Race to Centralize Education," *The New American* (October 25, 2010) by William P. Hoar; "Standards, Teaching, and Learning," *Phi Delta Kappan* (December 2009/January 2010) by Mike Rose; "Why Public Schools Need Democratic Governance," *Phi Delta Kappan* (March 2010) by Diane Ravitch; "School Boards in America: Flawed But Still Significant," *Phi Delta Kappan* (March 2010) by Gene I. Maeroff; and "Debunking the Case for National Standards," *Education Week* (January 14, 2010) by Alfie Kohn.

The Winter 2010/2011 issue of *American Educator* features the theme "Common Core Curriculum: An Idea Whose Time Has Come," with provocative articles by Diana Senechal, Linda Darling-Hammond, and E. D. Hirsch, Jr. Of special interest are Diane Ravitch's "In Need of a Renaissance," *American Educator* (Summer 2010) and "In the Future, Diverse Approaches to Schooling," *Phi Delta Kappan* (November 2010) by Paul Hill and Mike Johnston who contend that schooling alternatives are now emerging and that new approaches to government funding and oversight are also likely to emerge.

Contributors to This Volume

EDITOR

JAMES WM. NOLL has retired from his professorial position in the College of Education at the University of Maryland in College Park, Maryland, where he taught philosophy of education and chaired the Social Foundations of Education unit. He has been affiliated with the American Educational Studies Association, the National Society for the Study of Education, the Association for Supervision and Curriculum Development, and the World Future Society. He received a B.A. in English and history from the University of Wisconsin-Milwaukee, an M.S. in educational administration from the University of Wisconsin, and a Ph.D. in philosophy of education from the University of Chicago. His articles have appeared in several education journals, and he is co-author, with Sam P. Kelly, of *Foundations of Education in America: An Anthology of Major Thought and Significant Actions* (Harper & Row, 1970). He also has served as editor and editorial board member for McGraw-Hill/Dushkin's *Annual Editions: Education Series.*

AUTHORS

MORTIMER J. ADLER (1902–2001) taught philosophy at the University of Chicago, served on the board of the Encyclopedia Britannica, founded the Aspen Institute, and co-edited *The Great Books of the Western World.*

VINCENT A. ANFARA, JR. is associate professor in the Department of Theory and Practice in Teacher Education, University of Tennessee, Knoxville, and is co-editor (with Steve Mertens and Kathleen Roney) of *An International Look at Educating Young Adolescents* (2009).

RAY BACCHETTI is former vice president for planning and management at Stanford University and is a scholar at the Carnegie Foundation for the Advancement of Teaching.

CARSON M. BENNETT (1924–2010) was professor of educational psychology at Ball State University in Muncie, Indiana.

DOUGLAS J. BESHAROV is professor at the University of Maryland's School of Public Policy and a scholar at the American Enterprise Institute for Public Policy Research.

WILLIAM J. BRENNAN, JR. (1906–1997) was an associate justice of the Supreme Court for 34 years during the administrations of eight presidents.

STUART BUCK is a doctoral fellow in education reform at the University of Arkansas and author of *Acting White: The Ironic Effect of Desegregation* (2010).

WARREN BURGER (1907–1995) was the chief justice of the United States from 1969 to 1986.

DOUGLAS M. CALL is a research associate at the University of Maryland's School of Public Policy.

WADE A. CARPENTER is associate professor of education at Berry College, Mount Berry, Georgia.

JAMIN CARSON is assistant professor at East Carolina University. His research interest is in the philosophical foundations of education.

KARIN CHENOWETH is senior writer at the Education Trust and former education columnist at *The Washington Post.* She is author of *How It's Being Done: Urgent Lessons in Unexpected Schools* (2009).

GARY K. CLABAUGH is professor of education at La Salle University in Philadelphia and co-founder (with Edward G. Rozycki) of *newfoundations .com* which explores reflective educational practice.

EVANS CLINCHY is senior consultant at the Institute for Responsive Education at Northeastern University in Boston and editor of *Transforming Public Education.*

ANDREW COULSON is director of Center for Educational Freedom at the Cato Institute. He is author of *Market Education: The Unknown History* (1999).

LARRY CUBAN is professor emeritus of education, Stanford University. He is the author of *As Good As It Gets: What School Reform Brought to Austin* (2010), *Hugging the Middle: How Teachers Teach in an Era of Testing and Accountability* (2008), and *The Blackboard and the Bottom Line: Why Schools Can't Be Businesses* (2007).

JOHN DEWEY (1859–1952) was a leading American philosopher who taught at the University of Michigan, the University of Chicago (where he founded a laboratory school to test his ideas), and Columbia University (where he spawned the progressive education movement). His most famous book is *Democracy and Education* (1916).

DAVID ELKIND is professor of child development at Tufts University where he conducts research in the cognitive, perceptual, and social growth of children based on the theories of Jean Piaget.

CHESTER E. FINN, JR. is president of the Thomas B. Fordham Foundation, senior fellow at Stanford's Hoover Institution, and senior editor of *Education Next*.

CHRIS GABRIELI is chairman of the National Center on Time & Learning and adjunct lecturer at the Harvard School of Education. He is the coauthor, with Warren Goldstein, of *Time to Learn* (2008).

CHARLES L. GLENN is professor of administration, training, and policy studies and fellow of the University Professors Program at Boston University.

JAY P. GREENE is professor of education reform at the University of Arkansas and a fellow at the George W. Bush Institute.

FREDERICK M. HESS is a resident scholar at the American Enterprise Institute in Washington, DC and author of *Common Sense School Reform*.

JOHN HOLT (1923–1985) was an educator and a critic of public schooling who authored several influential books on education and promoted home schooling.

DAVID L. KIRP is professor at the Goldman School of Public Policy at the University of California at Berkeley. Author of *The Sandbox Investment: The Preschool Movement and Kids-First Politics* (2007).

HENRY LEVIN is the William Heard Kilpatrick professor of economics and education at Teachers College, Columbia University, and director of the National Center for the Study of Privatization in Education.

STEVEN MALANGA is a contributing editor at *City Journal* and a senior fellow at the Manhattan Institute for Policy Research.

LOUIS MALFARO is vice president of the American Federation of Teachers and secretary-treasurer of the Texas AFT.

PETER MEYER, a former news editor of *Life* magazine, is a freelance writer and a contributing editor of *Education Next*.

LOWELL MONKE teaches at Wittenberg University in Ohio and is co-author of *Breaking Down the Digital Walls: Learning to Teach in the Post-Modern World* (2001).

KRISTAN A. MORRISON is associate professor in the School of Teacher Education and Leadership at Radford University. Author of *Free School Teaching: A Journey into Radical Progressive Education* (2007).

JOE NATHAN is director of the Center for School Change in the Hubert H. Humphrey Institute of Public Affairs at the University of Minnesota, Minneapolis.

LINDA NATHAN is headmaster of the Boston Arts Academy, a public high school for the visual and performing arts.

PAUL E. PETERSON is the Henry Lee Shattuck professor of government and director of the Program on Education, Policy, and Governance at Harvard University. He is a senior fellow at the Hoover Institution and editor-in-chief of Education Next.

DIANNE PICHÉ is a civil rights lawyer, teacher, and advocate who serves as executive director of the Citizens' Commission on Civil Rights in Washington, DC.

DIANE RAVITCH is research professor of education at New York University and a historian of education. Her most recent book is *The Death and Life of the Great American School System* (2010).

CARL R. ROGERS (1902–1987), a noted psychologist and educator, taught at the University of Chicago and the University of Wisconsin-Madison. He introduced the client-centered approach to psychotherapy in 1942, and he was the first psychologist to record and transcribe therapy sessions verbatim. He authored *On Becoming a Person* (1972), among many other influential works.

ANDREW J. ROTHERHAM is cofounder of Bellwether Education Partners, an organization working to improve outcomes for low-income students. He was also a founder of Education Sector, a reform group, and served in the Clinton White House advising on domestic policy.

MARA SAPON-SHEVIN is professor of inclusive education in the Teaching and Leadership Department in the School of Education at Syracuse University and author of *Widening the Circle: The Power of Inclusive Classrooms* (2007).

ROGER SCRUTON is a British philosopher who has taught at Boston University, the Institute for the Psychological Sciences, and Princeton University. He is author of *Culture Counts* (2007).

DIANA SENECHAL taught English and theater in the New York City public schools and has worked as an editor and counselor. Her recently released book is *Republic of Noise: The Loss of Solitude in Schools and Culture* (R&L Education 2011).

ANDY SMARICK is visiting fellow at the Thomas B. Fordham Institute and adjunct fellow at the American Enterprise Institute. He recently became Deputy Commissioner of the New Jersey Department of Education.

DAVID SOUTER served on the U.S. Supreme Court as associate justice from 1990, when he was nominated by then-president George H. W. Bush, until his retirement in 2009.

CLARENCE THOMAS is an associate justice on the U.S. Supreme Court, having been nominated in 1991 by then-president George H. W. Bush.

MARC TUCKER is president of the National Center on Education and the Economy and was vice-chair of the New Commission on the Skills of the American Workforce.

CHRIS WHITTLE is chairman of Whittle Communications, founder of Channel One, and CEO of Edison Schools, Inc. He is author of *Crash Course: Imagining a Better Future for Public Education* (2006).

DANIEL T. WILLINGHAM is professor of cognitive psychology at the University of Virginia. He is the author of *Why Don't Students Like School?* (2009).